Reproducing Empire

Race, Sex, Science, and
U.S. Imperialism in Puerto Rico

Laura Briggs

UNIVERSITY OF CALIFORNIA PRESS
Berkeley · Los Angeles · London

University of California Press
Berkeley and Los Angeles, California

University of California Press, Ltd.
London, England

© 2002 by the Regents of the University of California

Library of Congress Cataloging-in-Publication Data

Briggs, Laura, 1964–.
  Reproducing empire : race, sex, science, and U.S. imperialism in Puerto Rico / Laura Briggs.
       p.   cm. — (American crossroads ; 11)
  Includes bibliographical references and index.
  ISBN 0–520–22255–5 (cloth : alk. paper).—ISBN
0–520–23258–5 (pbk. : alk. paper)
  1. Birth control—Puerto Rico—History.   2. Sterilization (Birth control)—Puerto Rico—History.   3. Prostitution—Puerto Rico—History.   4. Prostitution—History.   5. Puerto Ricans—United States.   6. United
States—Relations—Puerto Rico.   7. Puerto Rico—Relations—United States.   I. Title.   II. Series.
HQ766.5.P8 B75   2002
363.9′6′097295—dc21   2002001851

Manufactured in the United States of America

10 09 08 07 06 05 04 03 02
10 9 8 7 6 5 4 3 2 1

para Ana

Contents

Acknowledgments

It's a lie that scholarly work takes place in splendid isolation, or maybe I just need more help than most. But this project was born of the inspiration of many people and places, and has been shaped by all those willing to help, listen, support, disagree, and make suggestions. Its earliest genesis was in the lively intellectual and activist community of Boston, where those involved with the Reproductive Rights Network, *Sojourner,* *Gay Community News,* and Fenway Community Health Center taught me how to ask questions about medicine, science, and health and how they shaped the politics of gender, race, and imperialism. In Santo Domingo, the feminists of the *Centro de Investigación para Acción Feminina* and the crumbling infrastructure of the city itself, pushed me to think about the supposed beneficence of "development" and its history.

This book began as a dissertation in Brown University's American Civilization Department, where it benefited immensely from that confluence of smart people. I particularly thank my dissertation director, Mari Jo Buhle, who provided this project with wise guidance, and readers Anne Fausto-Sterling and Nancy Armstrong. Others who contributed in invaluable ways include Sarah Leavitt, Sarah Purcell, Caroline Cortina, Marie Myers, Laura Prieto Chesterton, Jane Lancaster, Lisa Duggan, Len Tennenhouse, Paul Buhle, Neil Lazarus, Robert Lee, Jen Ting, Jessica Shubow, Melani McAlister, Gail Bederman, DeWitt Kilgore, Anna Pegler Gordon, Rich Meckel, Cynthia Tolentino, Nate Schellenbach, and Beth Kling.

The research phase of this book was aided by grants from the Rockefeller Archives Center, Johnson and Johnson, and the Woodrow Wilson Foundation. Archivists are crucial to the doing of history, and this project is no exception. I want to thank archivist Tom Rosenbaum of the Rockefeller Archive Center; Mitchell Yockelson, Military Reference Branch, National Archives and Records Administration; Richard and Elin Wolfe and the staff of the Rare Book Room, Countway Library of Medicine, Harvard University; and Aura Jiménez, of the Colección Puertorriqueña of the Biblioteca del Recinto de Ciencias Medicas. Numerous reference librarians helped me locate obscure information, including especially Ruth Dickstein, University of Arizona Library; the staff of the Boston Public Library; and in Puerto Rico, the staffs of the Colección Puertorriqueña of the Biblioteca Lazarre and of the Biblioteca Monserrate Santana de Palés de Trabajo Social.

Materials from the Rockefeller Archives and Countway and Schlesinger Libraries are used with permission.

In Puerto Rico, I was met with exceptional help. I want to thank Idalia Colón Rodón, former director of the Asociación Puertorriqueña Pro Bienestar de la Familia, for thoughtful conversation and her deep and sensitive knowledge of the birth control movement's history on the island; the staff of the Asociación's Centro de Planificación Familiar Celestina Zalduondo for allowing me to take over their conference room for several days; Dr. Rafael Quinquilla of that organization; Dr. Karlis Adamsons, head of ob/gyn at the University of Puerto Rico's Medical School; and Dr. Adalberto Fuertes de la Habra. Numerous scholars at the University of Puerto Rico helped me hone this project and offered research suggestions, including Judith Rodríguez, Ana Luisa Dávila, Lilliana Ramos Collado, and Alice Colón, who shared with me her extensive research notes from insular newspapers.

I received crucial research assistance from Yudith Arreguin and Tania and Gwen Lanphere, and administrative help from Lauren Johnson.

The writing of this book was facilitated by the financial and intellectual support of a fellowship at the Charles Warren Center for Studies in American History at Harvard University, and, at the University of Arizona, a junior sabbatical, a Social and Behavior Sciences Research Institute Small Grant, a grant from the Provost's office, and a Women's Studies Advisory Committee grant. I presented parts of this research to a number of audiences, all of whom helped it immeasurably, and some of whom kept me from embarrassing mistakes. I am particularly grateful to my colleagues at the University of Arizona in the History Department colloquium; in the Sex, Race, and Globalization seminar; and in the Comparative Cultural and Literary Studies colloquium; at the University of Michigan's Institute of Advanced Studies "Aftermath of Empire" seminar; and at Harvard's Charles Warren Center seminar, all of whom made intensive time and space to help me with this work. I also want to thank my students at the University of Arizona, who provided a thoughtful and critical audience for many of the ideas in this book, and who always asked challenging questions.

This project is immeasurably stronger for many people's generosity with that most scarce of academic commodities—time. I am indebted to many people who read parts of it: Karen Anderson, Warwick Anderson, Yamila Azize Vargas, Sanjoy Bhattacharya, Truman Clark, Mark Garrett Cooper, Susan Craddock, Sarah Deutsch, Myra Dinnerstein, Kate Dudley, Sharla Fett, Marlene Fried, Ramón Gutiérrez, Donna J. Guy, Evelynn Maxine Hammonds, Nancy Rose Hunt, Janet Jakobsen, Miranda Joseph, Elizabeth L. Kennedy, Kari McBride, Jan Monk, Mark Nichter, Ana Teresa Ortiz, James T. Patterson, Susan Phillips, Barbara Rosenkrantz, Johanna Schoen, Banu Subramaniam, and Carmen Whalen.

Many people at the University of California Press helped make this a better book, and I owe a debt of gratitude to them all. In particular, I want to thank Monica McCormick, whose sense of humor and understanding got this project through some rough patches. Peggy Pascoe and George Lipsitz each read the entire manuscript twice, and their generous readings and detailed, incisive critiques helped immeasurably.

Finally, I want to thank Liz Hill, Don Hernstrom, and Madeleine Hernstrom-Hill, who opened their home to me repeatedly so I could do work in Boston; Santiago and Francia Ortiz, who put me up while I was in Puerto Rico; and my parents, Karen Williams and Adam Briggs. My family, Ana Ortiz and Maribel Inzunza Briggs Ortiz, lived with this project and helped it along.

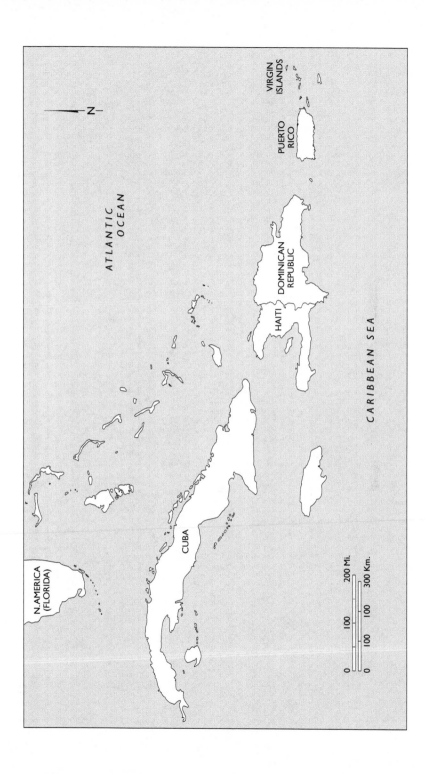

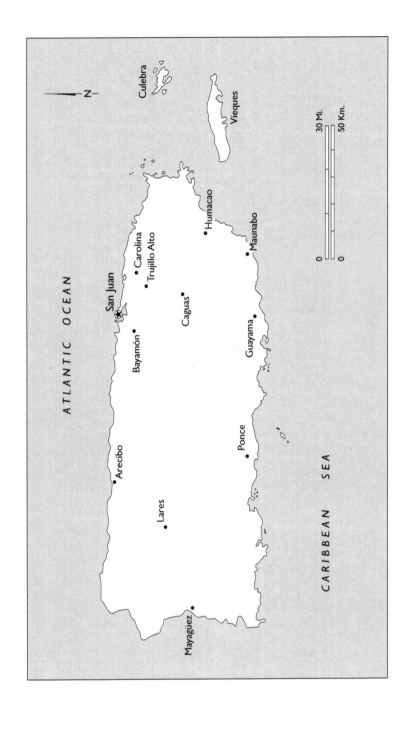

Colonialism

Familiar Territory

The term *globalization* is a placeholder, a word with no exact meaning that we use in our contested efforts to describe the successors to development and colonialism. Few would argue that the aggregate result of military interventions in the name of humanitarian concerns, free-trade agreements, and new forms of internationalization of labor and capital ought to be called colonialism, but many would insist that these things have something to do with exploitation, that some nations and territories benefit to the detriment of others. Others would insist that, on the whole, globalization is a good thing, that the "New World Order" redounds to the benefit of all. And there is, of course, a triumphalist version that holds that globalization is the ultimate victory of capitalism over communism. Historical studies can contribute to this conversation by offering a perspective on what came before globalization. *Reproducing Empire* seeks to do that. It looks at the ways that first colonialism and then development were elaborated in Puerto Rico, and at the systems in which they were imbricated in other empires and in the mainland United States. If we want to understand what is at stake in the forms in which globalization takes shape, we need to look to how these earlier models developed, especially at what some would call the good effects of colonialism: changes in family forms, women's rights, and science and medicine. This book explores with some skepticism the assurance with which these things were promoted as a social benefit and examines the politics beneath these issues—and sometimes quite explicitly on the sur-

face. It argues that a great many debates centered around family, reproduction, and sexuality also served as an opportunity to work out much
broader cultural questions about poverty, ideology, nationality, race,
and gender.

The book is centrally interested in Puerto Rico. Puerto Rico is a good
place to think about the meanings of colonialism and globalization
because it has for a century been where the U.S. has worked out its
attitudes toward its own expansionism. These attitudes have wavered
between celebration and denial, most often managing an unlikely combination of the two. In 1898 Puerto Rico was the "good" territorial possession (unlike Cuba and the Philippines), where people appreciated the
United States and the gifts it had to offer its less fortunate neighbors.
Political cartoons from the period depict Puerto Rico as a polite school-
child, sometimes female, in contrast to the ruffian boys Cuba and the
Philippines (who were rudely waging guerrilla wars against the U.S.).[1] In
the late 1940s and early 1950s, as the Third World became a Cold War
battleground, Puerto Rico became (largely through massive federal-
government subsidies) a political showcase for the prosperity and democracy promised by close alliance with the United States.[2] Puerto Rico was
a proof-text for assertions about the benevolent mission of the United
States overseas. Puerto Rico has also been the site of profound denial and
silence (the U.S.?—expansionist?). How many non–Puerto Ricans in the
United States could describe the island's status vis-à-vis the mainland?
Some would go so far as to insist that Puerto Rico is not part of the
United States.[3] That people get it wrong is not an accident. This ignorance is produced and maintained through silences in the media, in popular culture, and in the teaching of U.S. history, which exist alongside a
prominent public narrative in which the U.S. is a major anti-imperialist
force in the world, the nation that insists upon the integrity of national
boundaries and that is the protector of victimized populations within national boundaries (these latter two assertions, of course, are fundamentally at odds, but that is another story).

The more than three million Puerto Ricans living on the mainland
have also helped inaugurate another feature of globalization: a particular, late-twentieth-century form of the racialization of that part of an in-
ternationalized labor force that comes to the United States. In her work
on the multiple ways that elite Hong Kong-ers negotiate identity and establish citizenships, Aihwa Ong has shown that it is entirely possible,
and not even that unusual, for a person's business to have its home in one
nation, for his or her passport to belong to another nation, and for that

person's teenage children to live in a third nation. The work of trying to include such people, when they arrive in the United States, in the political or social identity of "Asian American" that was constituted in relation to a particular Chinese-American and Japanese-American history of race dating to the late nineteenth century, creates odd ironies and incongruities, to say the least.[4] While this kind of movement of an international business elite is considerably different from the migration of working-class laborers (as Ong well knows[5]), it also points up the essential constructedness of race and the ideological work required to define international migrants who come from internally heterogeneous nations as members of a small (though not fixed) number of "races" in the United States.

While this is not a process new to the twentieth century, the work of incorporating new nationalities into modern racial categories did change in the post–World War II period with the implementation of policies encouraging migration of Puerto Ricans to the mainland, and after 1965, with the lifting of some immigration restrictions. Two features distinguished this change. First, this ideological work was accomplished through social science (as well as the older sites of racialization, science and medicine). Second, public policy related to labor migrants has had to contend with the neoconservative narrative of race, which locates racialized minorities as not-very-successful immigrants in the pull-yourself-up-by-your-bootstraps mold. (The Hmong, for example, who were referred to as a "Stone Age tribe" when the CIA recruited them as allies during the U.S. war in Indochina, and who later became "refugees," were by the late 1990s construed as "failed wage workers" in the context of the U.S. welfare-reform debate[6]). The neoconservative position argues that the structural and systemic barriers to political and economic success in the United States are not very great, and its proponents cite the present-day success of those Irish, Italians, and Jews whose ancestors immigrated in the late nineteenth and early twentieth centuries. Neoconservatives further suggests that there is something about the members of racialized minority groups themselves—particularly how they form families and raise their children—that produces their lack of political and economic success as groups.

Two forms of this argument began to circulate in the 1950s and were fairly well codified by the late 1960s: the position associated with the Moynihan Report, the contemporary shorthand form of which is the "welfare queen," and the notion of a "culture of poverty." Though these ideas have now become so closely linked as to be inseparable, initially the former was about African Americans, the latter, about Puerto Ricans. These notions became entwined through a reciprocal, cyclical process: the racialization of Puerto Ricans as "Negroes" ("Hispanics" emerged later) and the inscription of both groups' principal characteristic as their "bad" families. This work of turning immigrants into racialized minorities in the United States assumed its characteristic, neoconservative-inflected form through this conflation of "culture-of-poverty" Puerto Ricans and "matriarchal" African Americans.

Reproducing Empire tracks the changes in the form and content of colonialism through the lens of reproduction and sexuality. From the exotic, tropical prostitute (seductive but brimming with disease), to the impoverished, overlarge family (produced by ignorance and brainwashing by the Catholic Church), to overpopulation, to the notion of the "culture of poverty," Puerto Rican sexuality has been defined by its deviance, and the island as a whole has been defined by its sexuality. Methodologically, this book contends that forms of sexuality are crucial to colonialism, from imperialism to development, from U.S. involvement overseas to the migration of the refugees of these processes to the mainland. Scholars have helped us see how reproduction has been central to the work of racialization on the mainland ("the welfare queen" and her antecedents participated in defining the meaning of "blackness" for generations in the United States, for example). Equally so, reproduction and sexuality have defined the difference that makes colonialism in Puerto Rico possible and necessary, what makes "them" need "our" regulation and governance.

"BAD" PUERTO RICAN FAMILIES
AND THE WORK OF COLONIALISM

Two examples from the late twentieth century suggest something of the importance of thinking of family as an axis of colonialism. In 1991 a book by the neoconservative, Linda Chavez, Out of the Barrio, suggested the ways Puerto Ricans mattered to the neoconservative argument. She argued that Mexican and Cuban Americans were following the trajectory of earlier immigrants toward assimilation and success in the United States (an argument that is easier to make for relatively well-off Cubans than for conspicuously undereducated and underemployed Mexican Americans, but so be it). The "Hispanic" group that was not making it she termed "the Puerto Rican exception." Why, she asked, were Puerto Ricans on the mainland doing so badly? She recounted the flight, in the 1950s and '60s, of garment industry and other manufacturing jobs that had been held by many Puerto Rican women from the major northeastern cities, where Puerto Ricans mostly settled. "But Puerto Rican families, by and large, chose to stay, and many ended up on welfare," she wrote. (Were they supposed to follow the garment industry to the free-trade zones of the Dominican Republic or Indonesia?) Chavez continued:

> The fact that so many were eligible for welfare reflected another aspect of their life in the United States: their growing propensity to form families without benefit of marriage—a tradition with roots on the island but which has transmogrified into welfare dependency in the United States. . . . By tradition, fathers of such children were expected to provide for their welfare. . . . The "adaptation process" [to the U.S.] saw many Puerto Rican fathers abandoning responsibility for their children to the state.[7]

There is a subtle slippage that is revealing here: Puerto Ricans have been made into immigrants in this passage, people whose lives were changed (for the worse) by leaving the "traditions" of the island and coming to the United States. Yet Puerto Rico is part of the United States, and there was (then) an AFDC program on the island. If AFDC (Aid to Families with Dependent Children, the federal program that Chavez is calling "welfare") made bad families, it ought to have done so just as much on the island as on the mainland. Chavez quotes L. H. Gann and Peter Duignan, who made this mistake explicitly: Puerto Ricans, they wrote, were "the first immigrant group who unwittingly moved into . . . a welfare economy." As U.S. citizens, Puerto Ricans were not immigrants, and it is at least as plausible to argue that it was the island, not New York, that was turned into a welfare economy in the fifties, through the deliberate work of development officials in destroying its agriculture in favor of wage-labor and government subsidies.[8] However, it is important to Chavez's argument, and the neoconservative position in general, to turn everybody into immigrants, whether they arrived in chains as slaves or had their land seized economically and militarily, like Puerto Ricans, Native Americans, and Mexicans. As Chavez continues, we learn that what makes Puerto Rican families fail to (re)produce Horatio Alger–style striving is a "surprisingly strong family attachment and traditional family values" and a reluctance to send their children to day care, and hence an inability of single mothers of young children to stay continuously in the paid labor force. This was a startling diagnosis in 1991, coming just a year before the Republican convention in which "family values" provided such an overwhelming trope of everything good that was endangered in the U.S. as to become almost a self-parody. It was also only a few years after what some have called a "moral panic" about day care, in which media coverage and prosecutors focused obsessively on questions of sexual-abuse and even satanic-ritual-abuse cults in day-care centers. In other words, at precisely the moment when family values and rejection of day care were being congealed into a fetish and symbol of white America, Chavez was condemning Puerto Ricans for embodying these ideals too strongly.

Yet, as peculiar as this seems on the face of it, the fact is that no matter where Puerto Ricans have lived or what form their families may have taken, the Puerto Rican family structure has been pathologized. Writers like Chavez, or even the more sympathetic ethnographer of Puerto Rican crack dealers, Philippe Bourgeois,[9] have assumed that the "problem" of disorganized Puerto Rican families only emerged after they arrived in New York. Yet North American, middle-class Puerto Rican, and even Spanish commentators on the lives of working-class people on the island have *always* argued that their families were a problem, back at least to the middle of the nineteenth century. Furthermore, the prescriptive literature on what the Puerto Rican family should look like has encompassed an endless series of double-binds. In the science of reproduction and the medicine of sexually transmitted diseases and birth control, in demography, history, and sociology, Puerto Rican families have been either too close or too fragmented, too big and cohesive or too limited and fractured. Puerto Rican sexuality and reproduction have been reputed to produce disease, literally and metaphorically. Early in the twentieth century, military officials and reformers diagnosed the island as suffering from an epidemic of venereal disease caused by prostitution, adultery, and the passing of the disease from immoral husbands to innocent wives and children. In this discourse, women have used birth control and sterilization excessively or not enough. In public policy, overpopulation was blamed for the poverty on the island during the Depression (with eugenics the cure). The excessive birth rate was blamed for the slowness and limitations of industrial "development" on the island, and for contemporary Puerto Rican poverty on the mainland. At the same time, in the symbolic economy of nationhood, woman has been the mother of the nation; woman's sexual deviance has been about the failure of nationhood. For U.S. colonialists, Puerto Rican nationalists, and reformers both on and off the island, these ways of thinking about the island as a nation or a failed nation (or as part of the United States or a failure as part of the United States) have been terribly productive. They have generated significant controversies at regular intervals, controversies that have realigned political power, public policy, meanings of gender and race, and the direction of economic initiatives.

Further, right-wing attacks on Puerto Rico and Puerto Ricans, even more virulent than those of the neoconservative Chavez, have been common, particularly in response to the growing pro-statehood movement. Conservative newspaper columnist Don Feder, for example, explained the reasons that he objected to statehood for the island.

> Current caps will come off federal welfare spending for the island. . . . We need more non-English speakers in this country like we need more welfare recipients, higher crime rates and an alien culture—all of which we'll get with Puerto Rican statehood. The issue is such a no-brainer that only a multiculturalist, a welfare-state Democrat or a pandering Republican could possibly support Puerto Rican statehood. English First . . . Executive Director Jim Boulet Jr. sardonically notes, "Puerto Rico is as proud of its language and culture as the United States used to be of ours."[10]

While Feder and Boulet seem to be under the mistaken impression that Puerto Rico is not part of the United States as a Commonwealth, their panic about what would happen should it become part of the U.S. under conditions of equality makes clear their investment in thinking of the island as permanently inferior to and essentially outside of the United States.

One of the key ways that this Puerto Rican "difference" has been produced is one that Feder implicitly alludes to with the reference to welfare: they are poor because they are (all?) women with children but no husbands. Feder's piece termed Puerto Rico a "Caribbean Dogpatch." Dogpatch was, of course, the home of comic-strip hillbilly L'il Abner and a band of poverty-stricken, congenitally stupid people with an agrammatical dialogue—including Mr. and Mrs. J. P. McFruitful and their forty children and Miss Ann Yewly Fruitful, head of the Militant Unwed Mothers (MUMS).[11] Chavez makes Feder's implicit point explicitly: the reason that Puerto Ricans are not succeeding politically and economically is their fatherless families. Yet, if welfare and single motherhood (which conservatives argue is *caused* by welfare) have emerged in recent years as the explanation for why Puerto Ricans are poor, other social-structural diagnoses have equally been hung on the family. On the island in the 1940s and 1950s, early efforts to turn a profit in state-sponsored industrialization failed. The industries were kept alive through significant federal subsidies, including AFDC and food stamps, which expanded the monetarized consumer economy. Meanwhile, policy experts tried to

explain what was wrong with the island's economy. In the context of the
Cold War, U.S. colonialism did not emerge as a politically popular answer, but "overpopulation" did. Women were having too many children
and there was not enough food to go around—this, in spite of the fact
that rises in per capita income were far outstripping increases in population and the birthrate was dropping. The policy response to this "problem"—the development of new birth control technologies and the widespread use of surgical sterilization—was pioneered in Puerto Rico. And
while overpopulation was a new discourse to the mainstream of public
policy and the "development" establishment in the postwar period (previously, it had been confined to politically marginal birth-controllers), it
was not new to Puerto Rico. The language of overpopulation had dominated the political and public health landscape in Puerto Rico in the
1920s and 1930s, pioneered by U.S. eugenic scientists like Raymond
Pearl and funders like Clarence Gamble in their research on the island,
where they had worked alongside an emergent class of Puerto Rican professionals, especially physicians and social workers. Even before the
1920s, moral reformers, the military, and colonial officials had located
what was wrong with the "natives" in sexuality, as they targeted venereal disease, prostitution, and immoral sexual relations as key arenas for
reform if Puerto Ricans were to become citizens.

Unlike some studies of colonialism, this book does not look to either
the economy or public policy as the a priori keystones to the story. These
kinds of analysis represent well-worn pathways and form the outlines of
work done by many brilliant scholars, including insightful Marxist histories of the economies of imperialism and countless histories of the public policy of diplomacy, international relations, and the relationship between individual nations or regions. These two approaches have more
often than not been at odds, with practitioners on both sides seeing the
others as ideologues or as missing the point. Postcolonial studies, however, has suggested that the economy and public policy are neither mutually exclusive nor the whole story. In a real sense, Edward Said inaugurated the field of postcolonial studies when he argued in *Orientalism*
that the way Europeans produced "the East" as inferior, lacking, and
hence in need of colonization was by making it into a subject of literature and scholarship—in science, linguistics, history, geography, and so
forth. In a passage that is iconic for his entire project, Said points out that
when Napoleon and his army arrived in Egypt, they immediately set up
a research institute. The ability to think and manipulate knowledge
about Egypt was necessary to either invade or rule it. Said's method-

ological innovation was to point out that the concept of *culture*—be it "high" culture, academic knowledge, or mass-media(ted) culture—is inseparably imbricated in both economy and policy; it is neither a weak echo of the economy (as its superstructure) nor an essentially trivial influence on the important work of public policy-making or diplomacy. It is in this sense of the term *culture* that we can locate the historical, political work done by scientific and social scientific ideas about family, reproduction, and sexuality in Puerto Rico.

In both Chavez and Feder, Puerto Rican "inferiority" is produced through knowledge about the bodies and behavior of Puerto Rican women. Puerto Rican "difference" is represented in popular culture and public-policy debate through women's sexuality and reproduction: through their inordinate attachment to family, lack of work ethic, and excessive use of welfare (Chavez), and in their promiscuous sexuality, in the island's overpopulation, and in the "culture of poverty."[12] In Edward Said's sense, the necessity for U.S. rule of Puerto Rico (a rule that precludes inclusion on egalitarian terms, but does not permit Puerto Ricans simply to go their own way, either) is produced through both a popular culture and an academic knowledge of Puerto Rican sexuality. The U.S. has established more than a few research institutes since its invasion, and in fact, U.S. academics have often referred to the entire island as a social-science laboratory, or a "test tube." The language is telling. It is precisely through science and social science that Puerto Rican difference has been produced and located in women's sexuality and reproduction. Because both are understood to be progressive (in both senses—as politically liberal and as crucial to progress), creating Puerto Rican difference within these kinds of idioms and activities makes it possible to conceive of these meaning-making activities as exclusively benevolent.

NONE OF THE ABOVE: THE STATUS QUESTION

In terms of the importance of the state (or lack thereof), Puerto Ricans have repeatedly made the case for the essential impotence of state forms in organizing their relationship with the United States. The political status of the island has long been one of the most important questions for Puerto Rican politicians: whether the island's relationship with the United States should be one of independence or statehood, or whether the island should maintain its current, Commonwealth status (also called "colony" status by its opponents). Yet, in a December 13, 1998, plebiscite, voters took a look at the available options and voted for "none of the above." Perhaps "none of the above" is the right answer to this multiple-choice question—that political rhetoric notwithstanding, very little has been resolved since 1898 in terms of the status question. There have been struggles over power, to be sure, but it is not so clear that they have been won or lost in relation to status. While most commentators took the plebiscite results to be an endorsement of Commonwealth, one can also take "none of the above" literally, or at least metaphorically. As the proliferation of plebiscites makes clear, Commonwealth is an unsatisfying compromise, a stopgap that makes no one truly happy. While it was manipulation and backroom dealing that kept the Commonwealth, or the Estado Libre Asociado (literally, Free Associated State) off the ballot, there was a time when no amount of maneuvering could have bested its defenders, the Partido Popular Democrático (PPD), which governed the island virtually unchallenged for decades. Its absence from the ballot suggests a real decline in the dominance of those who support the Commonwealth option. At the same time, on the mainland, the liberal architects of Commonwealth status have clearly lost sway as well. During his presidency, George H. W. Bush suggested that independence would be a good thing for the island, evidently with the intention of getting rid of U.S. responsibility for an impoverished island full of people who don't even speak English. President Bill Clinton went further, ending one of the foundations of the island's economy under Commonwealth status—the enabling legislation that had permitted corporations to avoid paying federal taxes. Clinton's move precipitated a significant de-industrialization of the island.

Another sense in which "none of the above" seems a poetically accurate expression of an appropriate refusal by Puerto Ricans to believe that anything important could be resolved in a status plebiscite was the fundamental uncertainty about whether a vote for a change in status would have any chance of being honored. Because of opposition in the U.S. Senate, the 1998 plebiscite legislation included no mechanism through which a Puerto Rican demand for statehood, had it won, could even have been considered. At the same time, independence activism has been so repressed that it would be difficult to argue that there has ever been open debate on independence on the island. In the 1930s, police opened fire on a nationalist march, killing seventeen and wounding hundreds more. At mid-century, independence leader Pedro Albizu Campos suffered long imprisonment. There was also documented disruption of nationalist activities in the 1960s by COINTELPRO, the FBI's counterintelligence program. In 1978 police in Puerto Rico ambushed and murdered two young independence activists on a hilltop at Cierro Maravilla (and a subsequently admitted Justice Department cover-up of the incident also lent credence to suspicion of FBI involvement).[13] Lest we think those days are past or that repression is confined to the island, Puerto Rican independence activists who participated in a bombing campaign in the 1970s and '80s were still in mainland jails in 1999, sentenced as "terrorists" to exceptionally long prison terms, despite the fact that all they were charged with was minor property damage. A Clinton pardon generated the charge that he was soft on terrorism, which elicited an incompetent to nonexistent white liberal defense. In Boston in August 1999, Steve Fernández, an activist with a group called Latinos United for Social Change, was arrested at that city's annual Puerto Rican festival for participating in a picket line where demonstrators carried signs naming Puerto Rico as a colony of the U.S. and for protesting the U.S. Navy's use of the island of Vieques as a weapons testing ground, including killing a resident and bombing with nuclear materials. Throughout the century, even to speak about independence has invited a high degree of scrutiny, harassment, and even physical violence from insular and mainland officials. That a plebiscite vote for independence—or statehood—would in itself result in change seems unlikely.

Even so, independence has been a distinctly unpopular option among Puerto Ricans on the island, to a degree that seems hard to understand strictly in terms of repression. In the 1998 plebiscite, independence drew just 2.5 percent of the vote. The extent of the opposition to independence on the island seems inexplicable to many U.S. Anglos, especially those on the left who are steeped in the mythology of Patrick Henry and Ché Guevara. This liberal "commonsense" about independence has generated a condescension toward Puerto Ricans that is in some ways no less withering than the open contempt exhibited by conservatives like Feder and Chavez. A *San Francisco Chronicle* editorial days after the plebiscite captures this attitude memorably:

Residents of Puerto Rico have a range of rights and limits. They are American citizens but pay no taxes and cannot vote in presidential elections. The island's 4 million residents have a great degree of self-government though their single representative to Congress is a non-voting observer. They may serve in the U.S. military and use the Postal Service, but can have their own Olympic teams and use Spanish and English as official languages. This crazy-quilt of special deals and subordinate status apparently suits many Puerto Ricans. It may puzzle many Americans who

feel ashamed that the territory lingers in the colonial existence, where it has
been since the Spanish-American War. But the outcome suggests there is no
groundswell for change.[14]

What seems to escape the editorial writer—though not, one suspects, most
Puerto Ricans—is the possibility that independence could bring an end to
the "special deals" without simultaneously ending the "subordinate status." It is not so much that the "subordinate status . . . suits many Puerto
Ricans" while shaming (mainland) Americans, but rather that most Puerto
Ricans believe in the inevitability of American domination, whereas (pur-
portedly ashamed) Anglos prefer to think that a century of domination can
be ended with the establishment of a separate government on the island.
There are many in Grenada, Panama, Nicaragua, El Salvador, and Colombia—to take some recent examples of U.S. military intervention in Latin
America and the Caribbean—who would take issue with that account.

Further, some argue that status per se—the form of the state—is a red
herring, that the question is, rather, the economy. This so-called post-
nationalist position in Puerto Rican politics, as exemplified by Ramón
Grosfoguel, suggests that the island's economy has been so thoroughly
integrated into the U.S. economy that it is best thought of as a regional
economy of the United States, not one that could be separated with the
advent of a new government—that is, it is more like Mississippi, say,
than like China, with all that that suggests about the value of independence. This is a process that to varying degrees describes all of Latin
America; there is no Latin American political or economic entity that exists completely "outside of" international capitalism or of the U.S. economy. If Grosfoguel is right, then the best strategy for Puerto Rico would
be to accept the inevitability of its subordinate status with respect to the
U.S. economy and cut the best deal it can with the United States.

> In the current Caribbean context there is no space external to U.S.
> hegemony. . . . Even the most "independent" republic cannot escape U.S.
> control. Any attempt to subvert this order is militarily or economically
> destroyed. . . . The Puerto Rican people's strategy has been pragmatic
> rather than utopian; that is, they are not struggling to be freed from
> imperialist oppression (which is highly improbable and perhaps even
> undesirable under the present circumstances) but are instead attempting
> to struggle for a milder version of this oppression. They would rather be
> exploited with some benefits than be exploited with no benefits.[15]

While Puerto Rico's $8,000 per capita annual income is only half that of
Mississippi, the poorest state in the union, it is about twice that of the

nearby Dominican Republic. The Dominican Republic shares a great deal of Puerto Rico's history with both Spanish and U.S. administrations, and many fear Puerto Rico would share a fate similar to the Dominican Republic's if independence from the United States were in its future. The $10 billion Puerto Rico receives in federal aid, while far less than the island would be entitled to were it a state, stands in striking contrast to the $190 million the Dominican Republic owed in 1998 just to service its more the $4 billion in foreign debt.[16]

An account of the economy cannot tell us very much about the content of the relationship between Puerto Rico and the mainland United States. One still needs to describe how most Puerto Ricans and North Americans think about this relationship, the content of conflict over it, and the crucial importance for the mainland U.S. of being able to identify the federal role on the island as one of performing good works. Questions of economy and status are not and have not been very productive arenas in which to debate the U.S. role. Instead, U.S. Anglos—and Puerto Ricans in response—have consistently discussed the relationship of the island and the mainland in terms of one of the two great modernist narratives, and often both: women's rights and scientific progress. The U.S. has understood itself as bringing public health, science, technology, and improvements in the status of women to the island. These stories have been especially powerful when the two could be said to be happening at the same time; for example, the United States in the 1950s and '60s (and again, recently) has promised that better birth control technology could free women from unwanted childbearing while ridding Puerto Rico of inadequate housing, crime, and poverty caused by overpopulation. The power of this narrative is suggested by the fact that the term *overpopulation* could drive rhetoric and policy among Puerto Ricans and North Americans without any empirical evidence at all that rising population caused—or was even historically correlated with—rising rates of poverty, unemployment, or any of these things. The force of the belief that the U.S. was "doing good," and that women, sex, and reproduction were a fulcrum of modernization made this story tremendously effective, a bulldozer that leveled all counterevidence in its path. At the same time, such narratives have provided resources for Puerto Rican thought across the political spectrum, from offering a model for how to improve life on the island to a symptom of how U.S. imperialism works by, for example, robbing Puerto Rican women of their reproductive ability. Sex, science, and reproduction have been tremendously important as the subjects of negotiation and controversy for the relationship between island and mainland.

SCIENCE, SEX, AND GENDER

In quite different ways, both the liberal author of the *San Francisco Chronicle* editorial and the conservative columnist Don Feder express a belief in Puerto Rican inferiority and a disavowal of North American responsibility for the situation on the island. Feder cannot imagine why the U.S. should be forced to include these Spanish-speaking, welfare-seeking, crime-ridden folks of alien culture (imagining them fundamentally as immigrants); the *Chronicle* writer thinks all Americans live in the mainland United States—not throughout the American hemisphere, or even throughout the United States, which would include Puerto Rico—and that they are shamed by the island's colonial status (imagining Puerto Ricans as people whose political traditions and desires are less democratic than those of people from the mainland, people who sorrowfully wish the U.S. could treat them better, but who recognize that that is not possible until they improve). Both writers take up the major themes of U.S. political discourse about Puerto Rico throughout the century. The "difference" of Puerto Ricans is expressed, in conservative terms, as horrifying, as utterly alien; in liberal terms, as assimilable but in need of "our" help. In both cases, the possibility of any U.S. role in creating the situation on the island is rejected out of hand.

This book is interested in these two questions. How has Puerto Rican difference been produced, and how has the U.S. role on the island been denied? These two impulses work together, as both cause and effect. Puerto Ricans' difference (inferiority, inadequacy) makes them not Americans. If Puerto Ricans are poor, it cannot have anything to do with the United States or colonialism. But if Puerto Rican poverty is caused by something about Puerto Ricans themselves, then they need the United States to help them. Together, these ideas re-inscribe Puerto Ricans as (inferior) Americans while at the same fundamentally rejecting them as alien. It is this kind of double bind that Homi Bhabha had in mind when he said of colonial authority that it "repeatedly turns from *mimicry*—a difference that is almost nothing but not quite—to *menace*—a difference that is almost total but not quite. The twin figures of narcissism and paranoia repeat furiously, uncontrollably."[17] It is exactly this back-and-forth movement among kinds or degrees of Puerto Rican difference that characterizes the U.S. story about and images of the island.

Science studies scholars, in books like *The Leopard's Spots* and *The Mismeasure of Man,* have helped us see that scientific ideas are one important way by which racial difference was produced, maintained, and made sense of, especially in the nineteenth century.[18] However, this scholarship has understood the production of racial difference to be something that science did primarily to male bodies, especially those of Africans, African Americans, and indigenous men. At the same time, scholars of women and gender in the United States and Great Britain have shown how extensively medicalized women's bodies have been, and through ideas about things like hysteria and premenstrual syndrome, how extensively the cultural meaning of gender has been influenced by scientific ideologies of the female body.[19] With respect to Puerto Rico, we need to bring these stories together, to discover how science, medicine, and social science have produced racial difference through descriptions of and interventions upon women's bodies, particularly through their sexuality and reproduction. Eileen Findlay has argued for nineteenth-century Puerto Rico that sexuality "becomes explicitly politicized at certain historical moments. This seems to be particularly true in times of change and transition."[20] One can extend that insight to say that sexuality and reproduction are used to *produce* change and transition. The "tropical" and "colonized" bodies of Puerto Rican women have been tremendously useful for an astonishingly broad array of players seeking political power, authority, and legitimacy in Puerto Rico. For feminists, nationalists, the U.S. military, the federal government, philanthropists, and academic scientists and social scientists, it has been important to "know" Puerto Rican women's bodies, and to rescue, condemn, or defend working-class women. This fact has been important to the U.S. imperial project on the island.

With respect to women's history and feminist work in general, this book responds to a tradition that regards women's complicity with colonial projects with disappointment and moral disapprobation. It seeks to show how this complicity was shaped, not by bad politics or moral failings exactly, but by specific political contexts and, more generally, by the uncritical approval of intellectual and political paradigms that centered particular understandings of "the people," and of working-class, Puerto Rican women's sexuality, as having been shaped by victimization and hence available for "rescue." This is an extended elaboration of Gayatri Spivak's insight about the problem of leftist and feminist intellectuals "speaking for" rather than "speaking to" colonized women.[21] It is also an opportunity to make the history of Puerto Rican feminist activism much more prominent than it has often been in the writing of U.S. women's history, where the extensive reliance on paradigms of Puerto Rican women's victimization (by machismo, the Catholic Church, and/or colonialism) has often rendered Puerto Rican feminism as either nonexistent or always already co-opted.

Some of the best resources for beginning to think about ideologies of family, sexuality, and reproduction as animating imperial and racial projects lie in the writings of scholars of Asia, Africa, and Latin America, who have begun to greatly expand our imagination of how "the colonial" works. Colonialism, in this account, is a modernist institution, fundamentally a practice—not of atavism in savage lands, as the *Heart of Darkness* narrative would have it—but of producing modern citizen-subjects in metropoles as well as colonies. *Reproducing Empire* begins with a specific narrative familiar to scholars of colonialism, but still strange in histories of the metropole. It provides a re-reading of the great international prostitution reform movements of the nineteenth and early twentieth centuries—movements that were organized against public-health measures, libertine men, and "white slavery," and that were designed to provide answers, not to a series of merely "domestic" problems in the U.S. or England, but to local issues that had extensive roots in imperial questions. The book explores how, at one moment in the quest for modernizing empire, armies, colonial officials, and reformers made prostitution reform and ways of organizing domesticity into technologies of empire. The first chapter disputes a number of commonplace, if not always fully articulated, assumptions about colonialism: that it primarily involved men, militarism, and economics; that it was an unfortunate thing that happened "over there," far from the quotidian concerns of the metropole; and that U.S. colonialism was either (for left commentators) among the worst in the history of the world or (for its mainstream minimizers) principally benevolent. *Reproducing Empire* argues that colonialism was powerfully about the marked-female questions of sex and domesticity; that imperial prostitution policy was as much about making England or the United States modern as it was about domesticating India or Puerto Rico; that colonialism was systemic and coordinated, not disjointed; and that the ways in which the United States was imbricated in it were unremarkable, neither better nor worse but simply another specific form of colonialism.

Studying sex and family opens up new windows on how colonialism works. As Ann Stoler suggests, one of the insights it provides is that the Manichaeanism of colonialism—the dividing of the world into colonizers and colonized that sees little heterogeneity within these groups—is itself an ideology of colonialism, a dualism imposed upon a far more complex world. Chapter 2 explores how, in Puerto Rico, making Americans and Puerto Ricans into two different, opposed groups required considerable work. Puerto Ricans and some North Americans insisted on seeing themselves as the same—common participants in New World political traditions based on "rights-of-man" liberalism, revolution from Europe, ethnic and racially mixed populations, labor-union-based socialism, and universal manhood suffrage. Prostitution policy shored up two North American strategies for differentiating Americans from "natives." One held that Puerto Ricans were, by definition, sick and needed to be kept at arm's length from our soldiers and sailors, who could be infected by them and thus endanger wives and children on the mainland. A second, more liberal view held that Puerto Rican prostitutes were vectors for disease that endangered innocent Puerto Rican women and children, and that Puerto Ricans were thus in need of assimilation into North American medical and public-health administration, which could save them from themselves. Both of these strategies relied on a constitution of the public sphere as male and the private as female; in both cases, it was the work of U.S. modernism and science to protect, not an explicit (public) colonialism, but (private) women and children. This public/private dichotomy, however, engendered two kinds of misappropriation— one anti-colonialist, the other feminist. Puerto Rican men offered to protect Puerto Rican women from the North Americans by opposing the incarceration of prostitutes, while elite North American and Puerto Rican women also tried to rescue prostitutes through reform work inside and outside prisons.

Chapter 3 explores how, in the decades of the twenties and thirties, other battles over reproduction and sexuality, specifically, battles over birth control and eugenics, became staging grounds for struggles over class and nationalism. In the 1920s, U.S. Republican administrations withdrew from giving the island much attention, and then, in the 1930s, New Deal liberals took a renewed U.S. interest in the island with a vengeance. Neither impulse was well received on the island, but the combination contributed to a vigorous nationalist movement that initiated a decades-long tendency to associate birth control and efforts to limit women's fertility with U.S. influence, even in the absence of U.S. mainland support for birth control. At the same time, other political alignments developed that were neither exactly opposed nor congruent: feminist nationalists who fought for birth control; North American feminists who supported Puerto Rican woman suffrage, the establishment of the female professions of nursing and social work, and ultimately birth control clinics through them; scientific modernizers, male and female, who found in eugenics a language to shift the terrain of debates about Puerto Rican unfitness from one of geography, in which Puerto Ricans were tropical, hence racially not-white and therefore unfit for independence, to one of class, in which poor Puerto Ricans required help from their (Puerto Rican) social betters and encouragement to have smaller, eugenic families. As Gladys Jiménez-Muñoz has observed in her study of the suffrage struggles of the 1920s, this was a period in which gender was the symbolic language of politics. One could also add that sexuality and reproduction provided a related terrain upon which scientific modernizers and nationalists contended with each other for authority (with feminists found on every possible side of the debate), and that the ability to produce the most compelling narrative about working-class-women's sexuality and reproduction was important to this battle.

The second half of the book takes up the period roughly from 1940 to the 1970s. In the 1940s, on the island, the importance of North American support for the scientific, modernizing elite—increasingly educated in the United States—became clear. In the context of Third World decolonization and the Cold War, development became an anti-Communist policy, and one of the first places it was tried was in the "laboratory" of Puerto Rico. It relied on four key components: population control and a centralized state, and export-substitution industrialization and a rising standard of living, the latter two predicated on U.S. aid and loans. In retrospect, it is clear how development policy fostered not only Cold War battlegrounds in places like Vietnam, Korea, Angola, Guatemala, and the Dominican Republic, but also how it gave rise to the Latin American debt crisis and ongoing civil wars throughout Africa, by making the capture of the colonial state the sine qua non of decolonization struggles and keeping in place the essentially arbitrary colonial map of Africa. The Puerto Rican policy innovation, of persuading U.S. firms to employ a (largely female) work force outside the mainland and away from U.S. consumers and the mainland's apparently reliable political and physical infrastructure, was deemed a success—and contributed to the current situation, whereby virtually all manufacturing for U.S. markets is done in the Third World. Yet, for all that this is the hard language of policy and economy, it is important to note the extent to which it was accomplished under the rubric of solving the problem of overpopulation. Explicitly, the poverty of the Third World was seen not so much as the legacy of colonialism—the former colonial powers composed a significant segment of NATO, after all, and could hardly be identified as the problem in U.S. development rhetoric—but rather as a problem of overpopulation, which would be solved through a combination of industrialization initiatives, techno-scientific solutions (from the birth control pill to the Green Revolution in agriculture), and modernization of the state.

Chapter 5 looks at the politics of sterilization. The charge of genocide was leveled at modernizers by nationalists, who contended that the modernizers wished to end Puerto Rican existence within a generation by limiting fertility. Although the charge was not literally true, it certainly captured memorably the extent to which reproduction and women's role was rendered the battleground of the Cold War in the Third World. One of the few places where one can find the rhetoric of women's rights in the United States in the 1950s is in the pronouncements of social scientists about what needed to change in Puerto Rico—namely, the culture of *machismo*—the only Spanish word that every North American knows. Chapter 6 takes up the massive postwar Puerto Rican migration to the U.S. mainland, significantly, to New York, and the specific ways that it re-staged debates about race, class, and anti-poverty policy in New York and nationally. The social science of Puerto Rican women and families— that women are oppressed, that families are too big, that fathers do not marry the mothers of their children—shaped the social science of Puerto Ricans on the mainland. This is unsurprising, given the dominance at the time of Robert Park's idea of a "race-relations cycle" that stresses stages of assimilation and the essential comparability of all immigrant groups. Puerto Ricans were thus compared to the other group of racialized migrants that came to New York in large numbers at about the same time: African Americans. The hostility that generally greeted Puerto Rican and black migrants took a familiar form: the charge that they were a drain on the city's welfare system. This, even before a significant number of Puerto Ricans or blacks were eligible for welfare. By 1966, the New York struggles over Puerto Ricans, African Americans, welfare policy, and family structure were taken up in the Moynihan Report as a problem for federal policy. At the same time that they damned Puerto Rican and black family structure, however, federal anti-poverty initiatives opened up new possibilities and new arenas for activism, both literally and symbolically, by giving War on Poverty funds to activists in and among urban working-class people and by making sex and reproduction, again, an explicit battleground. These groups included the Welfare Rights Organization, the Young Lords Party, and various short-lived New Left– and Black Panther–inspired groups like La Brecha. Unlike most nationalist groups dedicated to racial justice of the period, Puerto

Rican groups made feminism and reproductive rights foundational to their politics.

This argument, I hope, begins to point up some of the possibilities of thinking about gender, sex, and reproduction as a framework for understanding Puerto Rico. Puerto Rico was a key place in which U.S. colonialism was honed, a kind of colonialism and racialization we are now reaping as globalization.

Sexuality, Medicine, and Imperialism

*The International Traffic
in Prostitution Policy*

In order to tell the stories of Puerto Rico and its twentieth-century relationship to the United States, this book begins earlier and further afield. Puerto Rico has been alternately the subject of neglect and obsessive interest in academic scholarship, public policy, and popular culture, and it is not the intention here to reproduce what has sometimes verged on the prurient interest of some of this writing and policy, doubly so since the subject of this book is sex. This book will not follow in the footsteps of those who have tried to show what was unusual or peculiar about Puerto Rican sex, or make Puerto Rican sex "tell the truth," as Foucault says. Rather, the goal is to understand how knowledge about colonized sexuality works, what it accomplishes culturally and politically. The first move in such an analysis needs to be to refute any notion of the uniqueness of Puerto Rican sexuality, and to turn instead to an understanding of discourses of sexuality as a tool of empire, as anthropologist Ann Stoler, in particular, has been urging. This chapter is an effort, then, to place twentieth-century Puerto Rico in the context of an international imperialist system, and to make clear that it is nothing about Puerto Rico, per se, that makes sexuality such a central issue.

This chapter takes issue with three commonsense (and frequently academic) assumptions that have been influential in how we (mis)read the historical and political "question" of Puerto Rico and the significance of sexuality to it. First, colonialism was not a series of isolated incidents, in which larger powers opportunistically or strategically took advantage of smaller ones. This assumption, although rarely articulated in this way, is nevertheless key to the belief that the U.S. participation in colonial practices—first through continental expansion, later through the seizure of insular possessions—was lackadaisical, partial, and accidental. Rather, the United States was a full participant in what is recognizable as a colonial system—an international economic, political, and cultural system that shared common assumptions, strategies, and rules. A not insignificant example is the shared belief in the importance of, the funding of, and the circulation of information about an imperial science called tropical medicine. While we tend to think of the Cold War as a geopolitical system, we regard nineteenth- and early-twentieth-century colonialism as much more disjointed (perhaps because more multilateral). My argument is simply that we ought to think of the period before 1945 as just as organized as the period after (albeit with substantially different ground rules). Second, this chapter make the feminist argument that the "private" sphere is and was fundamentally political, that ways of organizing sexuality structured imperial armies, labor forces, public policy, and debate about reform. It explores the sense in which prostitution policy was a technology of empire that was reiterated, surprisingly intact, from one empire to another. Third, this chapter points to a specific instance of a larger dynamic: colonialism was not something that happened "over there," with little or no effect on the internal dynamics and culture of the imperial power itself. Although many have made this point before, it is nevertheless true that one of the things that allows and perpetuates the scholarly neglect of the history of Puerto Rico is the belief that it is important only to Puerto Ricans, or North Americans visiting the island. On the contrary, colonialism has had a profound effect on culture and policy on the mainland. Specifically, this chapter traces the nineteenth- and twentieth-century history of the belief in syphilis as a disease of "foreigners" or the impoverished classes, and suggests that this belief had everything to do with colonial prostitution policy and the origins of scientific research on syphilis in (imperial) tropical medicine.

In the middle of the nineteenth century, reformers, building on the legacy of an international antislavery movement, began to speak of an international traffic in prostitutes. Yet it is equally possible and probably more accurate to speak of an international traffic in prostitution policy, as empire after empire learned from the paradigmatic British how to run a modern empire. Methods of managing women, disease, and armies moved from place to place, and these policies were adopted by the United States as well in its overseas ventures. Despite our preference to locate imperialism elsewhere, any serious look at U.S. history—from the earliest days of the French, Spanish, and English presence on this continent to the most recent immigrant's decision to flee the economic or military upheavals in which U.S. interests are implicated—would have to conclude that colonialism and its related processes are an integral part of U.S. national formation. This chapter explores the context in which U.S. policy in Puerto Rico came to be so deeply entangled with questions of sexuality and reproduction by locating it within a larger international set of questions of imperialism, science, and sex.

Colonial prostitution and its regulation were the subject of considerable debate in the nineteenth century, centering particularly around the British Contagious Diseases (CD) Acts. From 1864 to 1886 the CD Acts required that prostitutes working in and near areas where soldiers were stationed in England be registered, "inspected" vaginally for signs of syphilis at regular intervals, and confined to a lock hospital if found to be ill.[1] That policy, or another like it, was also enacted in Britain's colonies, and generally for a longer period of time and often far more extensively. Indeed, a policy of required medical inspection and lock hospitals existed in some form in British India from the end of the eighteenth century, predating the enactment of the English policy by a half-century.[2] The registration and inspection policy did not begin with the British— its origin was Paris, and French colonies enacted it as well—but the relentless march of the British Empire assured that its international spread would be associated with the English legislation. The prostitution policy embodied in the CD Acts was regarded primarily as an India measure by reformers in the United States. A Rockefeller Foundation official, writing in 1916 of the history of opposition to the CD Acts, claimed that they "enforced a medical examination of prostitutes for the protection of the troops against venereal disease both at home and in India."[3] The enactment of the first of the English CD Acts in 1864 also followed the bloody 1857 Indian rebellion, which resulted in the influx of more than 55,000 troops to the Indian subcontinent to protect European life and property, where they remained for the rest of the century. The measures were legislated at a moment when British policy was particularly concerned that only the strength of its army secured its imperial holdings. Religious objections to the state's role in apparently sanctioning vice (through a process opponents considered the licensing of prostitution) could be overridden in the paranoia of the post-rebellion period; syphilis and other venereal diseases were simply another thing that "threatened the army from without," in historian David Arnold's phrase.[4]

The management of the relationship between Indian prostitutes and British soldiers was part of a broader British organization of domesticity in the colonies. The apparent taken-for-grantedness of soldiers' "need" for prostitutes need not have been so. No one ever suggested that the vast numbers of unmarried women missionaries that encircled the globe were in need of paid sexual service to maintain their health. Hydraulic models of spermatic pressure notwithstanding, the soldiers' requirement for prostitutes had to be produced and culturally managed as part of an ideology about working-class masculinity. Furthermore, it was not universally true that what was being sold was merely sexual; it could equally be domestic. The Indian Medical Board, in seeking ways to curtail venereal infection among the troops, recommended in 1810:

> Inducements might be held out to the men to attach themselves individually to individual Native women, [since] it [is] well known, how much more efficient those Corps are, which have Native women attached to them, than those are which have not been so provided. . . . The soldiers so attached, if they have been at all cautious in their choice, are not only kept free from the venereal infection, but have more attention paid to providing and dressing of their victuals and to other comforts conducive to health than can be given in this climate by European women, who in general are not equal to the exertions necessary.[5]

In other words, British officials were concerned not simply with soldiers' purported need for heterosexual outlets, but also with the improved efficiency of the Army when "native" women did the reproductive work of caring for the cleanliness, feeding, and comfort of soldiers.

After the rebellion, the British regarded the question of soldiers sharing domesticity with Indian women—though not commercial sex—quite differently. Concubinage was sharply condemned and suspect as disloyal. Indian prostitutes were no longer regarded as engaged in one along a continuum of potential practices with soldiers; rather, they were increasing described as belonging to a separate caste. Indeed, the Contagious Diseases and Cantonments Acts, passed in India after the rebellion, differed from the English CD Acts in one important respect: they required prostitutes to register with authorities, then volunteer for routine medical exams for signs of venereal disease. Under the English CD Acts, a police officer would have had to swear before a magistrate that a woman was a common prostitute in order for her to be subject to such measures. In other words, English women were treated as involved in a criminal act, whereas Indian women were understood as belonging to a class, of being (ontologically and essentially) prostitutes. Moreover, prostitutes for "English use" were not supposed to engage in sex with Indian men; in this sense, too, they were constituted as belonging to a particular kind of class, one that was monitored not only for disease, but for maintaining some peculiar kind of racial purity.[6]

Other measures, too, reconstituted the kinds of domesticity Englishmen could find, as Kenneth Ballhatchet has shown. Officers were urged to bring their (English) wives to India in order to prevent them taking up with local women. The prevalence of Burmese concubines and wives among English government officials there created something of a scandal in India, and the effort to keep the upper classes in line occupied considerable energy. In the military, the terms of enlisted men were also greatly reduced. With the introduction of the short-service system, working-class recruits were no longer expected to serve for life, but rather first for twenty-one years and then for just six years. Maintaining celibacy was no longer thought to be impossible, though recourse to prostitutes was more commonly anticipated; at any rate, the questions of marriage and concubinage were no longer expected to arise. For those of us trained to see questions of sexuality and domesticity as essentially trivial, it is worth noting that the entire imperial British military was reorganized around it.[7]

Each of these iterations of policy regarding domestic arrangements and prostitution represented a different configuration of class, race, and family. If the nineteenth century was the moment of multiple efforts to consolidate an English bourgeois domesticity organized around the nuclear family, these were articulations of it.[8] In the early part of the century, not everyone had to be in a nuclear family. Working-class enlisted soldiers were not expected to marry, but to devote their lives to the business of serving the empire, much as many of their counterparts in domestic service anticipated belonging lifelong to the family they served, not their own. In India, soldiers could be expected to take up with Indian prostitutes. Their relationships might or might not produce a kind of partial domesticity; if it did, it was presumed to be good for the empire. The haphazard and contested early life of registration represented an effort to make these liaisons safe, not so much for soldiers per se, as for the army as a whole; to the extent that prostitutes were ambivalently made imperial citizens through registration, they were also rendered safe. In the post-rebellion period, however, domesticity was policed differently. Upper-class officers were supposed to form white nuclear families. Meanwhile, working-class English enlisted men, too, were transformed into potential heads of nuclear families through the short-service system; after their soldiering years, they were expected to settle down and form families. Hence, the new, more extensive and more regularized CD Acts became less about sanctioning a kind of interracial domesticity and more about keeping soldiers safe for the day when they would become husbands and fathers of (white, English) women and children.

THE CD ACTS AS IMPERIAL SYSTEM

Struggles over reproduction and sexuality provide a powerful lens onto the ideologies and passions that animated the exercise of colonial power. Prostitution, in particular, is a multivalent and complex question. It is at once a tremendously flexible symbol, a revealing facet of social organization, and an often difficult way of life. Prostitution provides an excellent entrée into the ways colonialism reorganized social relations and culture "on the ground," at considerably closer range than can be found in the often abstract narratives of economics or diplomacy.[9] It is simultaneously a form of labor, and hence a strategy of economic accumulation and a site of repressive state intervention, and a question and symbol of sexual transgression, always fraught with danger, immorality, and contagion. As feminists have noted, prostitution is also an important site of cultural negotiation over power and the social organization of gender in the domestic, sexual, and reproductive spheres. Prostitution illuminates "a society's organization of class and gender: the power arrangements between men and women's economic and social status; the prevailing sexual ideology; . . . the ways in which female erotic and procreative sexuality are channeled into specific institutional arrangements; and the cross-class alliances and antagonisms between reformers and prostitutes."[10] Up to the present, prostitution remains one of the key questions for any army engaged in the garrisoning of troops outside of domestic borders, and one of the first and always extensive negotiations with the receiving society.[11] Confronted with similar problems, imperial nations in the late nineteenth and early twentieth centuries looked to England for strategies for solving them. It is this multivocality of prostitution—the fact of its being simultaneously the subject of a reform movement, the site of medical and public health research and state supervision, a military problem, a potent symbol, and a way of life and means of earning a living—that makes it so interesting to understand in the colonial context. Prostitution has been a rich source of metaphors about the situation of colonized nations, and as an actual (non-metaphoric) relationship, it has been a site of complex negotiation of forms of colonial labor and domesticity, as well as a good thing for political players of every stripe to take a position on.[12] Discourses of domesticity, family, and sexuality are neither minor nor simply ideological: they lie at the heart of colonialism.

Following Foucault, it has become commonplace to say that what characterizes a state (or colony) as modern is its bureaucracy, its systems for administering and organizing populations, citizens, punishments.[13] One of the features of modern colonial states was that their characteristic response to the problem of prostitution was bureaucratic—medical inspection, registration, and incarceration in lock hospitals. At home, colonial nations in the nineteenth century were building a public health bureaucracy through the development of statistics (the root of the word is *state*, as in, "numbers kept by the state"), with the establishment of departments of public health, and thereafter, with the enactment of regulatory measures governing things like clean water, spitting, defecating, animals, vaccination, food, and the movements of the sick and carriers of disease. Statistics were important because they enabled bureaucrats to turn individuals' birth, death, and health status into certain kinds of politically important aggregates, like class, race, occupation, neighborhood, or district. The arguments in favor of public health measures overwhelmed their opponents: the public health bureaucracy kept people alive who would have died, and healthy, those who would have been sick. Yet these registrative and regulatory measures also vastly increased the authority and reach of the state and its ability to intervene, sometimes drastically, in intimate areas of people's lives. If, on balance, this seemed a worthwhile tradeoff in metropolitan nations—and even this was controversial, as suggested by the public debate over whether New York's "Typhoid Mary" should be incarcerated—the question was even more charged in the colonies.[14] On the one hand, the argument for curing the ills of the "natives" seemed all the more compelling; on the other hand, the legitimacy of the state was far more disputed. For colonizing powers, science and medicine were an important means of extending their authority over the local population—in some sense, they even created the population as such (no more disparate tribes, clans, language groups, etc.) through public health and census statistics—while providing an anchoring argument about the legitimacy of their rule. The CD Acts and their analogues served to organize "disorderly" women, often limiting their mobility to segregated districts, enrolling them as imperial citizens through the essentially bureaucratic process of registration, and sometimes restricting their clients by race.

Another thing that made medical inspection and registration modern was that its way of understanding prostitution relied on a scientific vocabulary of disease control. Many historians have argued that the development of a specialized science of tropical medicine was a key technology of colonial rule.[15] Tropical medicine, prostitution regulation, and the science of venereal disease had entwined histories. The laboratory science of syphilis developed out of the colonial science of tropical medicine. Syphilis (only irregularly distinguished from gonorrhea) was no mere inconvenience, but a frightening disease that at some times seemed to go away of its own accord and at others caused horrifying disfigurement, madness, and death. Laboratory science, together with modern methods of registration, gynecological examination, public health, statistical recordkeeping, and organization and orchestration of populations could keep it at bay.

THE SPREAD OF THE ACTS

The CD Acts and other similar legislation spread throughout the British empire from India. Small-scale regulation of prostitution had already existed in Gibraltar, Malta, Hong Kong, and Victoria, Australia, even before passage of the first English Domestic Act in 1864.[16] Subsequently, registration spread rapidly through British Asia and North Africa, including Malaya (1864), Singapore (1870), and then Egypt and Sudan (1898).[17] CD Acts were also passed in Queensland (1868) and Tasmania (1879).[18] Registration spread more slowly in sub-Saharan Africa. According to Megan Vaughan, British officials were reticent about intervening in the sexual lives of African women. In Uganda and Southern Rhodesia, the British military preferred to devolve that responsibility onto local, tribal, power structures. Thus, there were no CD Acts as such in British East and Southern Africa, but rather a series of acts designed to strengthen local elite men's control over prostitution, adultery, and morality. There were at least two exceptions to this general rule. In the decade before the First World War, mandatory medical inspection was introduced in the Uganda protectorate in response to an apparent epidemic of syphilis (an epidemic that by the mid–1920s seemed not to have been syphilis at all, but yaws).[19] The more significant exception was the Cape Colony, where a CD Act was passed in 1868 under pressure from the War Office, which claimed that British troops were being "more than decimated" by venereal disease. The other source of pressure was military physicians, often recently arrived from India.[20] This legislation was, at first, short-lived:

a reform movement, led by Cape liberals and ministers opposed to the apparent state sanction of vice, got it repealed in 1872. A few years later, however, a movement began to reintroduce the legislation in order to protect the colonists, and a second Act was passed in 1885. Within a few more years, the first lock hospital was erected in Cape Town. Elsewhere, in the Belgian Congo, the Baptist Missionary Society, Belgian officials, and the Catholic Church were extensively involved in various eugenic and pronatalist efforts, including anti-syphilis and anti-yaws work.[21]

Registration spread quickly through other colonies and metropoles. In the three decades after the passage of the CD Acts in England, similar measures had been introduced in a multitude of places, including Java, Sumatra, Argentina, Cuba, Guatemala, Brazil, Japan, Russia, and German Africa.[22] Such legislation already existed in the French-colonized Caribbean and Africa. Thus, in the space of a handful of years in the nineteenth century, registration and medical inspection of prostitutes went from being an anomalous policy, existing only in places colonized by the French and in some localities in India, to being the rule throughout the areas of European governance and in imperial Japan. Hence, prostitution policy provides a good window into the ways that imperialism may be viewed, not as a series of isolated policies promulgated in diverse geographic entities, but as an international system developed by imperial powers in communication with one another and constituted in part by ideologies and policies associated with domesticity.

Of course, the registration of prostitutes intervened in divergent situations in these places. In areas like Malaya, Singapore, and Sumatra, registration had less to do with protecting imperial armies from venereal disease than with concerns about colonial male labor migrating from China, Japan, and elsewhere. These male laborers, like the English soldiers of the early nineteenth century, were not expected to form families, but rather to engage in whatever kinds of sex and domesticity prostitutes (or other laborers) were prepared to offer. Elsewhere, as in twentieth-century India and South Africa, the issue was protecting the white nuclear families of colonists. The mode of transmission of venereal disease was vague; concerned citizens in the Cape Colony complained that "respectable families have become infected through their nurses and washerwomen,"[23] but it is unclear whether they were referring to casual contact or to wet nursing, rape, or seduction. As the nineteenth century progressed, however, it became imaginable for laborers to have families. As Lenore Manderson put it for the Malay states, "At the point at which the . . . colonial government decided that the cost of continued immigration of laborers was greater than the cost of public health interventions within the colony, the child was discovered."[24] In the discourse of maternal health and venereal disease circulated internationally by physicians—about which more will be said below—the interests of mothers were characterized as endangered by prostitutes, because syphilis and gonorrhea could be carried to the conjugal bed by soldiers and laborers, affecting maternal fertility and child health. Hence, the CD Acts and their analogues became a strategy for protecting the (supposedly internally racially homogeneous) families of both colonists and colonial laborers. Concerns about interracial sex (and reproduction) clearly were also at play in the impulse toward registration in different localities; one cross-cutting issue was the international migration of European Jews, spurred by a combination of economic hardship and pogroms. Reports of Jewish prostitutes engaging in interracial sex (variously defined) surfaced from India to South Africa to Argentina to the United States.[25] In Singapore, as in India, prostitutes were registered and distinguished based on the nationality of the men that they served, and were understood to be more or less responsive to the legislation: Japanese women were "clean," but Chinese women were "dirty," "backward," and had to be forced to undergo medical treatment.[26]

U.S. IMPERIALISM AND PROSTITUTION

While historians have sometimes suggested that regulation of prostitution did not exist in the United States,[27] in fact, military officials reliably instituted regulation outside the U.S. mainland and in border regions. Cuba, Haiti, Nicaragua, Santo Domingo, the Panama Canal Zone, Hawaii, and the Philippines all had some policy of regulation.[28] Likewise, towns in Texas, Arizona, and Florida where troops were garrisoned to fight foreign threats also implemented regulation policies.[29] Whether the character of these changes involved "the advantages and blessings of enlightened civilization," as the invading General Miles promised the Puerto Rican people within days of his arrival, was certainly a matter of perspective. The notion itself, however, was not idle or entirely cynical. Many North Americans were committed to this version of what they were offering to the "Latin races," whom they sought to convert in matters of government, culture, health, and most substantially, in their organization of family, sexuality, and reproduction.

U.S. colonial prostitution policies were not entirely consistent, nor were they uncontested. The Panama Canal Zone, a site of extensive U.S.

government management of a trans-Caribbean migrant labor force, had particular problems. The Canal Commission frequently paid the passage for West Indian laborers to the zone, a practice that got the commission in trouble when it was discovered that some of the laborers were women. In 1906 the New York Independent and the New York Evening Post ran articles accusing the commission of importing prostitutes from Martinique; commission members responded, in a congressional inquiry, that they were simply providing domestic servants and that sometimes these women entered into common-law marriages.[30] According to a later (1923) report by a military physician stationed there, after the canal was completed,

> the system of the segregated district was adopted. All prostitutes were to be forced to live in the section set aside for them; medical examination of the women was to be performed weekly; and men were to be examined prior to being permitted to enter the district. Chemical prophylaxis was to be compulsory for every man leaving the district, and police guards were to be so placed that only one entrance and one exit were available. . . . The objections, both moral and sentimental, in the States to a segregated district were recognized, but it was thought impossible to avoid such a district unless the military police could prevent prostitution.[31]

Along the Mexican border in 1916 (where there were troops stretched from Brownsville, Texas, to Nogales, Arizona), the military policy was to permit soldiers to engage in brief sexual liaisons with prostitutes, ostensibly to the exclusion of allowing rape, concubinage, or marriage. One officer explained the ideology behind the policy by saying, "If prostitution were not provided, these men would disobey orders, go to Mexican villages and get mixed up with [rape] the women and thereby possibly bring on war."[32] Within the borders of Mexico, General "Blackjack" Pershing organized prostitution inside the bounds of the military camp. A surgeon described its implementation: "The prostitutes were surrounded by a barbed-wire fence, every woman was examined, and only those found uninfected were retained for duty."[33] Reformers from the YWCA complained vigorously about the military situation on the border, on the grounds of both vice and race; although the brothels were as segregated as the military—often with black, white, and Mexican prostitutes occupying different neighborhoods—the soldiers could go where they liked. A popular magazine in the United States expressed reformers' discomfort with the policy, claiming that "intemperance and immorality" were the two things that endangered troop strength, and adding, "Although all may be quiet along the Rio Grande, as long as our regulars and militia are stationed there, yet they remain liable to the physical and moral perils that in camp life act as the enemy within the gates."[34]

While the 1916 Pershing expedition included actual camps for prostitutes, elsewhere the U.S. military merely restricted prostitution to neighborhoods where it was already common and instituted mandatory medical exams. When U.S. troops occupied the city of Veracruz, Mexico in 1914, the Red Cross helped the army undertake enforcement of a segregated district and medical inspection there. A writer for the social-work journal *The Survey* took pains to emphasize the superiority of U.S. oversight of the system. Whereas Mexican officials were all male, lax in locating clandestine prostitutes, and susceptible to bribery, the U.S. military was more efficient and the Red Cross more sensitive to the possible embarrassment or even abuse that might occur when only men conducted medical examinations.[35] In colonies like Puerto Rico, the Philippines, and Cuba, the U.S. military endorsed the existing Spanish policy of protecting the families of *gente decente* (respectable people) from rowdy women, unsanitary prostitution, and the danger of contagion through quarantine in segregated neighborhoods, weekly or biweekly pelvic exams, and mandatory medical treatment. During the receivership of Santo Domingo at the turn of the century, U.S. authorities restricted prostitution to certain neighborhoods.[36] In Cuba, the U.S. military government briefly repealed (1898), then reinstated (1899) prostitution regulation. Likewise in the Philippines, the American military established a "tolerance" zone, or segregated district, for prostitution in 1901.[37] There, the Woman Christian Temperance Union kept up a continuous and very public campaign from 1900 to 1902 to eliminate the army's issuance of health certificates to prostitutes. Ostensibly, they won: the Insular Affairs Division at the War Department agreed to stop issuing cards. In fact, as both the military and the WCTU knew, inspection continued, though without benefit of certificates.[38] (Indeed, as late as 1989, prostitutes near the Subic Bay naval base were still subject to registration and medical inspection, and base-related prostitution was among the reasons cited by the Philippine government for refusing to renew the lease for the base. But that is to get ahead of the story.)

Historians and politicians alike have had difficulty naming the United States as a colonial power.[39] It is customary to think of the events of 1898—when the U.S. seized the colonies of Puerto Rico, Cuba, and the Philippines in a war with Spain—as principally military in nature, and to suggest that the year 1898 marked the first insertion of the United States into the community of imperial powers. Neither assertion is particularly true. The U.S. had long since begun territorial expansion, and the military invasions of 1898 brought trailing after them substantial social and cultural changes. Whereas the British proudly called their territorial acquisitions empire-building, the United States—except among some people between 1898 and 1917—has been deeply invested in a notion of itself as opposed to imperialism, to the extent that even the Spanish-American War was justified as an anti-(Spanish) imperialist gesture, just as the overthrow of the Arbenz government in Guatemala in 1954 and the Allende presidency in Chile in 1973 could also be described as anti-(Soviet) imperialism. To speak of imperialism in the U.S. political context is to refer to an illegitimate, morally reprehensible form of power over a victimized people (hence the popularity on the left several decades ago of using the term *internal colonialism* as a model for making sense of anti-Chicano racism, or the description of African Americans as Third World people: to call it colonialism was to render it illegitimate within mainstream political traditions).

This elusive paradox of the United States as an anti-colonialist imperial power has impoverished our language and our analytic tools for understanding how to characterize U.S. expansionism and influence outside its borders.[40] Even that characterization—of an anti-colonialist imperialism—may be too precious, for it takes the rhetoric of U.S. imperial "difference" or "new-ness" (including the notion of a post-1945 "neo-colonialism," in which the U.S. is preeminent) too seriously, simply reiterating the notion of American exceptionalism which has authorized a great deal that is ugly in U.S. history, not least U.S. imperialism itself.[41] The rhetoric of newness refers not only to a structure of masking, but a structure of legitimation of the nation's imperial mission. We must take care, then, in referring to the discursive structure of North American imperial legitimation not to replicate its logic, not to be seduced by its sense of itself as "new." In the context of prostitution policy, U.S. imperialism was anything but exceptional; national policy simply reiterated British policy.

TROPICAL MEDICINE

The regulation of prostitution as a sanitary measure was continuous with a range of other imperial health concerns. Throughout the seventeenth, eighteenth, and nineteenth centuries, one of the crucial problems for both the imperialism of armies and the colonialism of settler-states was the health of whites in what was termed the tropics. One of the reasons "darkest Africa" was so mysterious to Europeans was that they usually died en route: the mortality of armies in central Africa was as high as 50 percent in the early nineteenth century; and the interior of Africa was known in the eighteenth century as the "white man's grave."[42] A usable medicine in the tropics was a necessary precondition for the success of colonialism.[43] Yet the immediate physical survival of white individuals was only the beginning of the colonial problem. In order to govern and perhaps even populate a far-flung empire, Europeans had to be able to survive in the tropics long-term, and to reproduce themselves (i.e., to reproduce white people), or so it seemed to colonizing Europeans. At a minimum, soldiers and colonial officials could not return to the metropolis so debilitated or diseased that they were incapable of reproduction even outside the colony; this would make the cost of imperialism dreadfully high. Increasingly, however, it seemed that a combination of venereal disease in men and "tropical neurasthenia," or simply "tropical sterility," in women was making reproduction by colonials impossible.

By late in the nineteenth century, tropical medicine had begun to provide increasingly useful information about tropical diseases, and by the early twentieth century sanitary measures were making real inroads into military and settler mortality associated with diseases like malaria, cholera, and yellow fever. Ronald Ross's discovery, in India, that the *Anopheles* mosquito caused malaria enabled armies to begin an aggressive program of draining and filling the low places where water pooled and *Anopheles* bred.[44] Imperial armies and bureaucracies became the greatest advocates of modern sanitary measures to destroy filth by building sanitary houses and water and sewer systems. While U.S. and European officials in the metropoles hesitated and debated measures to purify urban water supplies, imperial and military officials plowed ahead and developed a robust public health regimen in the colonies. The British Imperial Medical Service, the German Imperial Colonial Office, the French Institut Pasteur, and the U.S. Army Medical Corps were unrestrained in their power to interfere in the most private realms of personal life. They were given extraordinary latitude, and they insisted upon ways of cooking, dressing, keeping homes, and disposing of waste for colonizers and natives alike.[45]

Tropical medicine was also deployed in the service of protecting armies and colonial populations from venereal disease, in the sense of telling people what kind of sex to have. Concerns about diseases like "tropical sterility" declined as laboratory medicine gained the ascendancy (it came to seem that it was not so much the place as the microorganisms), but fears about venereal disease did not recede. If anything, they increased. Tropical medicine and its associated sciences were crucial for producing racial difference between colonizer and colonized. Tropical medicine constructed a singular, metonymic relationship among race, place, and disease, albeit newly triangulated by microorganisms: people were sick because they lived in the tropics and were infected by tropical parasites; tropical people were (racially) different from those living in the temperate zone.

Warwick Anderson suggests for the Philippines that tropical medicine was a defining discourse of the relationship between colonizer and colonized. "The Filipino emerged in this period as a potentially dangerous part of the zoological realm," he writes, "while the American colonizer became a resilient racial type, no longer inevitably susceptible to the tropical climate but vulnerable to the crowd of invisible, alien parasites newly associated with native bodies."[46] This description could equally apply to the way questions of venereal disease produced the (imperial) soldier and the (native) prostitute; he as susceptible and endangered, she is a source of disease and a threat. Indeed, this view helps us understand the implicit epidemiology of the CD Acts, one that many have pointed out made little sense: Why was it so important to diagnose and quarantine women, but not men? Did they think men incapable of giving venereal diseases to women?

This similarity in structure between the imperial logic of tropical medicine and that of venereal disease is not accidental. Rather, the science of syphilis derived from tropical medicine. Historians of prostitution and venereal-disease policy have long assumed that international changes in the ways prostitution was dealt with in the late nineteenth and early twentieth centuries were caused by the discovery of the microorganism that caused syphilis and the subsequent availability of a cure, albeit an imperfect one, in the development of Salvarsan.[47] However, as the Tuskegee syphilis experiment tells us, the availability of a treatment does not necessarily "cause" anything—public health officials can mobilize as much to withhold treatment as to provide it.[48] On the contrary, the evidence points the other way: the development of a science of venereal disease was "caused" by the colonial problem of dealing with prostitution. The scientific problem of syphilis was inserted into colonial questions of tropical medicine and of the organization of armies, labor forces, and the various forms of sanctioned domesticity. Indeed, without the colonial context, its scientific questions and conclusions were illegible.

Venereal disease research at the turn of the century developed within colonial medicine and research in two senses. First, colonies provided the raw material. German researcher Albert Neisser, for example, traveled to the Dutch colony of Java in order to work with apes in his search for the microorganism that caused syphilis. Similarly, French researchers Elie Metchnikoff and Emile Roux were able to induce the disease in nonhuman animals for the first time in apes imported from the tropics, hence facilitating further research on the disease. Equally important, it was governments' colonial offices that supported the research in order to protect soldiers and labor forces. Because of the problem of colonial prostitution and the fact of tropical syphilis, it was tropical medicine that provided the funding, intellectual models, and background for the discovery of the cause of syphilis. In March 1905 it was Fritz Schaudinn, a tropical medicine researcher working for the German Imperial Colonial Office, who discovered a microorganism that caused syphilis, working with a colleague, Erich Hoffmann, a dermatologist who ran a syphilis clinic in Berlin. Schaudinn's previous work was on trypanosomes, protozoans associated with sleeping sickness, a deadly problem for German colonists and their colonial workforce in East and Southern Africa. Hoffmann wrote later:

> We scraped the secondary lesions of the syphilitic and collected the serum for microscopic examination. One day we hit the jackpot. All at once Schaudinn let out a yell and said, "Here it is!" I crowded him away from the microscope and peering into the eyepiece saw a shadowy spiral form slowly turning like a gimlet and at the same time swimming like a fish in slow motion across the microscopic field. We were sure that the microscopic gimlet was the cause of syphilis, but we could not prove it at the time.[49]

Hoffman and Schaudinn argued that they had found a spirillum, a microbe intermediate between a bacterium and a protozoan. The notion that it was like a protozoan parasite, "swimming like a fish," provided a link to trypanosomes and other tropical disease agents.

This kind of account of what Schaudinn named the *Spirochaete pallida*—a disease agent similar to his African trypanosomes—as the cause of syphilis apparently appealed to biologists, because as Hoffmann noted, the claim to have found it was by no means proven. The usual standard of proof that someone had indeed found a pathogenic agent was that it produced disease when injected into an uninfected animal

(Koch's postulate). Such proof was not developed for Schaudinn and Hoffman's microbe until 1913, eight years later.[50] Sociologists of science have suggested that we can think of pathogens as things that are not so much discovered as invented, produced in and through engagement with the ideologies and politics inside and outside science.[51] It is instructive to note just how experimentally and intellectually fragile the original discovery was (as perhaps are all new discoveries), and therefore how much it depended on the extrascientific knowledge of the tropical dangers of syphilis to make it meaningful. Given the information Schaudinn and Hoffmann provided their colleagues, medical researchers today probably could not find a microorganism causing syphilis because they depend on different assumptions. The spirochete was subsequently relocated taxonomically from the spirilla group and today is understood to be utterly unrelated to trypanosomes or protozoans. Moreover, later researchers believed that the skin lesions where Schaudinn found his "spirillum" only rarely were a site of a syphilitic microorganism.[52]

The ideologies that identified syphilis as a tropical disease worked to cover over inconsistencies and incoherencies in the scientific papers and international scientific networks' belief in the truth of the discovery. Schaudinn's discovery was widely replicated, and historians of science continue to distinguish Schaudinn and Hoffmann's authentic discovery from earlier, specious claims. Physicians and biologists in Japan, England, France, and the United States found it easy to accept the authenticity of Schaudinn's discovery. Once the Germans' account of the cause of syphilis was taken up by other researchers, physicians, and colonial officials, it probably could not fail if was even close to accurate. The "discovery" had armies and organization behind it, to perfect it and make it useful. Among the powerful and respected German scientific establishment, there was initial skepticism about whether there was sufficient proof for Schaudinn's spirochete as the pathogen in syphilis, but one important figure did accept it. Paul Ehrlich, like Schaudinn, worked for the Imperial Colonial Office. He was also attempting work with trypanosomes, though his specific interest was in African relapsing fever, which threatened the labor force in German Africa. Ehrlich was intrigued by Schaudinn's report and began to work on syphilis simultaneously with recurrent fever, on the theory that they were similar diseases. He encouraged his lab assistant, Sahashiro Hata, to try the arsenical compounds they were using on recurrent fever on trypanosomes with syphilis. Based on their work, other researchers with the Imperial Colonial Office tested arsenic compounds on Africans with sleeping sickness

German East Africa and the Congo; these were the first trials of the chemical that ultimately became the standard treatment for syphilis. In Germany, Ehrlich persuaded colleagues to test it on human patients in insane asylums and pronounced the results successful. He publicly announced that "606" (for the 606th arsenical compound tested) was an effective cure of syphilis in 1909. In his paper, "The Experimental Chemotherapy of Spirilloses," Ehrlich acknowledged a debt to Schaudinn and tropical medicine, and specifically to the "discovery . . . that syphilis is a spirochaetal disease [and] Schaudinn's hypothesis that trypanosomes and spirochaetes are closely related."[53]

Researchers at the Institut Pasteur also accepted Schaudinn's finding and set out to produce a prophylaxis or vaccine against the pathogen, with the goal of inoculating the imperial army. In 1906, Metchnikoff and Roux, working first with apes and then with human volunteers, developed a mercurial ointment that they argued could prevent the disease in men after exposure. By 1907, the French imperial army and navy were using mercury ointment, and it was widely in use by World War I. Beginning in 1916 the U.S. military established prophylaxis stations, where men who had potentially been exposed could seek a friction treatment with calomel, a mercuric, applied to the penis.[54] Through a process highly mediated by the ideology of tropical medicine, then, medical researchers had at last found a means of protecting Euro-American soldiers from the dangers of colonial and foreign sex.

MARKING VENEREAL DISEASE AS OTHER

In the U.S. as elsewhere, syphilis was consistently troped as a "foreign" disease. As historian Alan Brandt has written, by the early twentieth century "venereal disease had become, preeminently, a disease of the 'other,' be it the other race, the other class, the other ethnic group."[55] Prostitution, considered the primary mechanism for the spread of venereal disease, was also construed as a practice of foreigners (at a time when unprecedented immigration was changing the "racial" character of major U.S. cities like New York, Chicago, and San Francisco). A particularly virulent version of this belief was published in a popular magazine article from 1909:

> Unless we make energetic and successful war upon the red light districts . . . we shall have Oriental brothel slavery thrust upon us . . . with all its unnatural and abnormal practices, established among us by the French traders. Jew traders, too. . . . Shall we defend our American civilization,

or lower our flag to the most despicable foreigners—French, Irish, Italians, Jews and Mongolians.[56]

While this notion of venereal disease as "foreign" was hardly new— some date it to fifteenth-century Europe—the colonial roots of the early-twentieth-century medicine of syphilis clung to it in the United States, in the same way that more recent efforts to produce an African-origin story for AIDS have constructed it as a disease of "them" (variously defined). The *New York Times,* in announcing Ehrlich's discovery to the lay public in the United States, specifically referenced the association of syphilis with tropical disease. Constrained by norms of propriety that prohibited the use of the word *syphilis* in public discourse, the *Times* article relied on Africa to make the point, saying that " '606' [treated] the blood disease, unconquered for centuries" and the "recurrent fever" common in Africa.[57]

Medical, reform, and public health writers explicitly compared venereal disease to tropical diseases like malaria and yellow fever, linking the vigorous public health measures associated with colonies to suggestions about what to do about prostitution in U.S. cities, and Salvarsan, to quinine. "To drain a red-light district and destroy thereby a breeding place of syphilis and gonorrhea is as logical as it is to drain a swamp and destroy thereby a breeding place of malaria and yellow fever," said a federal official.[58] A specialist at the Mayo Clinic wrote, "Medically speaking, [the prostitute] can be thought of as the intermediate host or carrier of *Spirochaete pallida,* just as the mosquito is host for the malarial parasite." Lavinia Dock, an advocate of the professionalization of nursing, claimed that prostitution "is now as certainly the abiding place and inexhaustible source of . . . venereal disease, as the marshy swamp is the abode of the malaria-carrying mosquito."[59] A genitourinary disease specialist arguing against regulating prostitution to control venereal disease suggested that "it would just be as rational to try to stamp out an epidemic of yellow fever by quarantining the women and allowing the men to run at large, as to expect to control the social evil by laws directed only against fallen women."[60] Another physician, writing about the efficacy of Ehrlich's "606," asserted, "I believe that it is a specific in syphilis, though it would be presumptuous to say that it will cure every case . . . any more than we can say that quinine will cure every case of malaria."[61] The American Social Hygiene Association issued an educational stamp that read, "We've Fought in the Open: Bubonic Plague—Yellow Fever—Tuberculosis, Now, Venereal Disease." The stamp personified and racialized the diseases in different ways. Yellow fever was figured as a young black man (most likely evoking the anti–yellow fever campaigns in Panama and Cuba), tuberculosis as an old white man, and bubonic plague as a skeletal, grim-reaper figure. Venereal disease was depicted as a brown-skinned woman, scantily draped in red—the picture of the "tropical" prostitute.[62]

THE ANTI-REGULATION MOVEMENT
AND DEBATES OVER PROSTITUTION

This particular kind of scientific marking of venereal disease as "other"—as tropical and colonial—had consequences for popular reform movements related to venereal disease and prostitution. In both Britain and the United States, a movement urged the suppression of prostitution (and trafficking) rather than medical inspection and regulation. Women campaigned to protect prostitutes (or prevent women from becoming prostitutes), while physicians tried to protect "innocent" wives and babes from venereal disease acquired through husbands' liaisons with prostitutes. The movement to repeal the English CD Acts and suppress prostitution everywhere was constituted through international conferences, through the coming together and breaking apart of political alliances, and through the opening of local chapters of various organizations around the world. The movement was organized first under the leadership of Josephine Butler and her English organization, the Ladies National Association (LNA), then subsequently, under the American Woman's Christian Temperance Union (WCTU) and Butler's Salvation Army. Alongside and in tandem to the women's movement for repeal, there were also other kinds of (mostly male) reform groups: the Protestant clergy and physicians, and, after the turn of the century, joint organizations constituted under the medico-religious rubric of "social hygiene." For Butler, the WCTU, and the clergymen, the movement was a social and missionary Protestantism, with a good dose of women's rights language thrown in. In the twentieth century, it took on the mantle of science, modernity, and the state without altogether abandoning the language of either Protestantism or woman's rights.

U.S. and British reform movements alike devoted considerable energy to India policy. The American WCTU sent missionaries to India to report on conditions there related to "white slavery" and "social purity," and published numerous exposés. Butler was the earliest and most visible leader of the cause of repeal in England, but her movement faltered in India; while Butler was committed to repeal there, English women were divided on the issue. It was the U.S. organization, the WCTU, that most prominently carried the fight for repeal into the twentieth century and around the globe. Unlike the LNA, the WCTU had already begun the work of establishing chapters throughout the world under the aegis of a missionary organization, the World WCTU, or WWCTU, which advocated an end to that "demon rum." Although we tend to think of suffrage and similar causes when we think of U.S. women's groups in the late nineteenth and early twentieth centuries, missionaries were by far the largest group of organized U.S. women, and their ranks grew rapidly until the First World War.[63] With local chapters around the globe, the WWCTU was better positioned to wage the locality-by-locality struggle to end "legalized vice," a struggle which continued until the Second World War.

Colonialism was a contentious issue within both the LNA and the WCTU. An irreconcilable break occurred between Butler and the WCTU over the issue of the CD Acts in India, with Butler calling for colonial repeal, and the U.S. organization taking the position that domestic repeal was sufficient.[64] Despite its years of opposition to medical inspection, the national (North American) WCTU had long entertained a certain ambivalence with respect to colonial contexts. When Butler pushed the campaign against the CD Acts into India in the 1890s, she encountered resistance from her compatriot, Lady Henry Somerset, who publicly endorsed regulation in the colonies. Frances Willard, the North American president of the WCTU and a close friend of Lady Somerset, expressed her ambivalence over the conflict between Somerset and Butler. "We in America have practically no standing army; we have no 'oriental difficulties,'" wrote Willard, whereas "the British Government must deal with 'a condition and not a theory.'" Willard's remarks were taken to be supportive of Somerset, causing Butler and numerous chapter leaders in the British colonies to openly break with the WCTU in 1897, ironically, only a year before America acquired its own version of "oriental difficulties" in the tropics.[65]

These questions also provoked a major conflict within the WWCTU. Willard's chief critics were Elizabeth Wheeler Andrew and Dr. Katherine Bushnell, two U.S. missionaries who traveled the world for the WCTU organizing against the regulation of prostitution. They sharply criticized an 1893 editorial that had appeared in the WCTU newspaper, the *Union Signal,* advocating the acquisition of Hawaii by the United States and suggesting that North Americans could do for the progress of

Hawaii what the British had done for India. Andrews argued passionately that the British authority in India was undermined by its support of vice. Together, Andrews and Bushnell published a book, *The Queen's Daughters in India,* that condemned British registration and inspection of Indian prostitutes. They subsequently traveled to South Africa and elsewhere to organize WWCTU chapters to oppose the CD Acts. Meanwhile, enterprising women journalists wrote stories of women's unwilling bondage to exploitative men in Hawaii, India, Hong Kong, and the Philippines for the *Union Signal.*[66] It was only after Willard's death in 1898 that the WWCTU was able to return to the issue of repeal of the CD Acts with all of its former zeal.

The English movement's successes and failures inspired others. For example, in 1888 one of Josephine Butler's Dutch correspondents wrote to her about the "social evil" in the Netherlands East Indies. There, she wrote, the military had considered "introducing the Anglo-Indian system of having separate tents inhabited by the licensed women in the camps. At present at a fixed hour in the evening the doors of the Barracks are opened in order to admit a certain number of these poor victims. . . . The fact stated here shows that the bad example set by the English government in India is infecting Java, and no doubt other Colonies of other nations. . . . If you should succeed in your next great attack upon India, it will be an immense lever for us."[67]

The repeal movement employed a language of women's rights to argue for an end to the CD Acts. In England, Protestant women noted, for example, that men accused of immorality were winked at, while women suspected of the same act were detained, arrested, and subject to a humiliating medical examination. Whereas proponents of the CD Acts focused on immoral women as the cause of vice, the LNA and later the WCTU looked to seduction and pimps as the cause, thereby turning the problem into one of innocent women and predatory men.[68] In the colonies, the British LNA and the WWCTU deployed a notion of sanctified womanhood that had been reduced from a natural dignity to a state of wretchedness because of men's cruelty and lust. Indian women, argued Butler, were "helpless, voiceless, hopeless. Their helplessness appeals to the heart . . . these pitiful Indian women, girls, children, as many of them are. They have not even the small power of resistance which the western woman may have." This sort of language cropped up, too, in the WCTU's official newspaper. While on the face of it, this may seem to be an essentially egalitarian argument, locating woman's rights on an international scale, it was also excessive and exaggerated. The language of sentimentality deployed in the Indian context indicated a fundamental mistrust of colonized women's ability to defend themselves. As a number of theorists have argued, the idiom of colonial women's victimization produced a logic in which English and American women were active, assertive, capable of controlling their bodies and defending others, whereas colonized women were passive, dependent, and in need of being defended.[69] Sentimentality was not an innocent language in the politics of colonialism; it produced the speaker as someone who was the master of her fate, while the spoken about needed her protection.

Defenders of the Acts, too, deployed a language of woman's rights. Prostitution was the bulwark of the family, they argued, protecting innocent women and girls from men's lust. Drawing on early Christian writings, some (especially Catholics) compared prostitution to a sewer, as a necessary outlet for filth that kept the rest of the city clean. In places like Singapore, where Chinese and Japanese labor migration was extensive, English defenders of the CD Acts and similar regulation argued that the CD Acts represented a progressive measure that prevented indentured servitude or other forms of forced prostitution. Within Japan, liberals defended the acts on these grounds as well. The state, they argued, could rescue women held against their will, but only if registration allowed governments to become an essential third party to the two-way contract between the pimp or brothel owner and the woman or her family.[70] Another kind of defense of the Acts was the assertion that they protected laborers' wives and children by preventing their fathers' and husbands' acquiring venereal diseases from prostitutes.[71] In places like India and the Cape, two types of woman's rights arguments in favor of the Acts held sway. The first followed the trajectory of tropical medicine's expansion into "native" areas and held that women were receiving treatment for their diseases that they otherwise would not, and furthermore that the possession of a registration ticket improved a woman's ability to entice soldiers and hence her earning potential.[72] The second argument was that white women and their families were endangered by nurses and domestic servants who might be carriers of venereal disease.

Others advocated "purity," employing a racial idiom. In South Africa, the Attorney General argued for repression rather than regulation of prostitution, telling the House of Assembly, "There are certain houses in Cape Town which any Kaffir could frequent, and as long as he was able to pay the sum demanded, he could have illicit intercourse with these white European women. This [is] a matter of the gravest importance, for once the barriers were broken down between the European

nd native races in this country, there was no limit to the terrible dan-
ers to which women would be submitted, particularly in isolated
places." In the Transvaal, Africans who had sex with white prostitutes
were punished. In 1902 the Aliens Immigration Act barred the immigration of Eastern European Jews to South Africa and virtually eliminated continental prostitution in the Cape.[73]

These struggles over who spoke for women, racial purity, public
health, and medical progress were complicated by the question of alliance with the state power of the colonizer. While on the face of it, defenders allied themselves with the state and repealers did not, their relationships to the state became increasingly indistinguishable. As one
historian points out, for England, "long before the Acts were repealed,
the hard core of the Antis had moved on to demanding 'social purity,'
censorship, legislation against male homosexuals and school crusades
against masturbation."[74] Furthermore, advocates of repeal of the CD
Acts also supported abolition of prostitution, a fact whose importance
increased in the twentieth century, when especially the Americans began
to advocate widespread imprisonment of prostitutes. Imprisonment in
state and federal facilities explicitly built upon the model of "rescue
homes," wherein Protestant women attempted the work of "reclaiming"
and rehabilitating the prostitutes who came to them, but they also bore
more than a passing resemblance to the lock hospitals that repealers had
spent decades condemning.[75]

The alliance of the anti-regulation forces with the state became increasingly prominent in the years leading up to World War I, when as
we shall see in chapter 2, the North American WCTU explicitly under-
took work under the auspices of the U.S. government and the U.S. military. Whereas registration certified and sanitized a variety of sexual and
domestic arrangements, the opposition it generated, a liberal repeal
movement, argued for putting everyone into nuclear families. Modernity
required "modern" families, the argument went, and prostitutes, soldiers, and unmarried laborers failed to constitute nuclear families. Liberalism of a variety of stripes—metropolitan, missionary, and Creole nationalist—envisioned an end to state-sanctioned vice, the seduction of
women, lecherous men, and other (archaic) forms of corruption in favor
of state repression of prostitution, healthy bodies, and racially homogeneous nuclear families. The movement against the CD Acts, strong in the
metropole and weak in the colonies, turned after 1900 to advocating incarceration of prostitutes as a women's rights measure.

The modernist languages of scientific progress and women's rights continued to certify the positions of both regulationists and repealers, authorizing extensive intervention into the organization of domesticity for colonizer and colonized. Whether pronouncing on the servant problem in South Africa or paying the passage for women in Martinique to provide Canal Zone laborers with sex, clean laundry, and companionship, colonizing governments and their liberal reformers disagreed with each other over the proper form of colonial domestic arrangements, but all agreed on the need for their management. In the international colonial system, there were only a handful of available positions. Prostitution and domestic policies were not organized in response to local situations, or only very generally. Instead, they emerged from a small number of boilerplate models, most of them drawn from the experience of the British Empire. The United States, far from belonging to this international colonial community only through its response to a series of accidents (paradigmatically, the explosion of the battleship *Maine*), was certainly part of a colonizing system, a membership evident in its adoption of British and other colonial norms for the organization of prostitution.

Sex and Citizenship

The Politics of Prostitution
in Puerto Rico, 1898–1918

In a decade, this island should be the test-tube experiment
which proved that syphilis need not be.
— Herman Goodman, Venereal Officer,
Camp Las Casas, Puerto Rico

In 1917, with little discussion and less consultation with the island's inhabitants, Congress made Puerto Ricans U.S. citizens. The cynical view
held that the Jones Act granting citizenship was passed in order to provide fresh cannon fodder for the coming World War I. Whether or not
this was the motivation, it was over and done before much in the way of
opposition, support, or even considered public opinion could form on the
island. A year later, the WCTU, the U.S. military, and U.S. officials on the
island worked together to bring a repressive prostitution policy to Puerto
Rico, one that required the incarceration of all prostitutes on the island to
control venereal disease among the newly drafted Puerto Rican/American
soldiers training on the island. As in other empires, U.S. prostitution policy on the island was a tremendously important arena for debate over the
nature of colonial modernity, and the struggle over the meaning of Puerto
Rican citizenship took place significantly with reference to prostitution.
The United States had two kinds of prostitution policies: one for domestic
areas and one for foreign territories and possessions. Shortly after the
conferral of citizenship in Puerto Rico, U.S. officials and reformers instituted the domestic version of the policy on the island. North Americans' support for the policy was expressed in two registers, both suggestive of the overall tone of the relationship between the island and the
mainland. One held that Puerto Rican women were dangerous to other
people's health, and the other, that Puerto Rican women were endangered,
sick, and in need of care. Both rationales argued for the continued inter-

vention of North Americans, indeed demanded that it be redoubled. Similarly, Puerto Rican protests over their new status as U.S. citizens took place indirectly, through objections to prostitution policy. Historians have argued that there was little controversy over the conferral of citizenship in Puerto Rico in 1917, but perhaps the issue is better framed through the lens of the question of who controlled the sexuality of the island's poor women. At a time when congressional legislation and Supreme Court decisions were rapidly redefining the relationship between the island and the mainland in confounded and contradictory ways, prostitution policy provided a concrete and limited forum in which to debate the merits of these new relationships.

Venereal disease and prostitution policy in Puerto Rico in this period was anomalous. As we have seen, medical inspection and licensing were U.S. colonial policy, whereas on the mainland, wholesale suppression and incarceration of prostitutes was the usual order of the day. Prior to 1918, Puerto Rico had a policy of reglementation, or registration. From 1905 to 1917 prostitutes in the port city of San Juan had been required to undergo weekly medical examinations at San Juan's Special Hospital for Women, and those outside the metropolitan area had been registered at local police stations.[1] In 1918, convicted prostitutes began to be incarcerated. These new measures represented a shift in that territory from the implementation of the foreign policy to the domestic one.

The WCTU led the effort to abolish reglementation in Puerto Rico. According to Edith Hildreth, president of the local chapter, their work began after she witnessed a shocking scene: an older Puerto Rican woman, apparently a prostitute, leading a young woman whom Hildreth took to be "feeble-minded" by the hand. For Hildreth, who had been schooled in "white slavery" alarm and the panic over the traffic in girls, this was an older woman leading a younger, defenseless one astray. Hildreth fetched the chief of police, a Colonel Shanton, but they could not locate the pair. Hildreth, an experienced and tireless campaigner, launched herself on the new cause, the suppression of prostitution. She organized a meeting that included Shanton, Governor Arthur Yager, and Attorney General Howard Kern,[2] and persuaded them to begin enforcing mainland laws requiring the suppression of prostitution within five miles of training-camp cantonments. Women found within this zone and suspected of consorting with soldiers would be arrested, incarcerated, and treated for venereal disease.

In July, it seemed that the WCTU had enlisted significant segments of the Puerto Rican elite and U.S. colonial officials in suppressing prostitution. The police in San Juan and the rest of the island arrested significant numbers of prostitutes and suspected prostitutes. The WCTU organized a "Police Women's Reserve Corp," a women's group that could help the police identify and arrest prostitutes.[3] As the WCTU had done in earlier, less successful efforts in the Philippines, the Puerto Rican organization enlisted local women's groups, like the Ponce Club de Damas.[4] They also facilitated the spread of police enforcement efforts outside the San Juan area to places thoroughly remote from the training camp, and distributed posters urging women to "Clean Up Your Town." They had the emphatic support of Attorney General Kern, who urged that accused prostitutes be vigorously prosecuted and sentenced to six months or more in jail. He even sent a circular to prosecutors and judges throughout the island, threatening them with removal if they failed to enforce laws against prostitution and adultery. Shanton demanded the ouster of the head of military sanitation, who disliked the idea of mass arrests. Thereafter, insular judges and prosecutors complied with Kern's request and gave prostitutes sentences of six months to a year. Local officials obligingly cleared the jails of male prisoners to make way for the women. Residents turned out in numbers to watch the women prisoners being transported in flatbed trucks to central jails at four sites around the island. Military physicians, like Dr. Herman Goodman, a urologist, and Dr. L. Yordan Pasarell, a public health physician, developed treatment regimens for the women in prison.[5] Newspaper editors of diverse political persuasions lauded the policy. *La Correspondencia,* the paper of the Union party, praised the dedication of prisons for women as a crucial modernization measure. "There has been a lack in our country of a special place for women sentenced by our courts," opined a front-page editorial. "We believe the time has come for the initiation of something that completely modifies the prevailing penal system in Puerto Rico, lifting it to the height found in the other nations of the world."[6]

The campaign also had the indirect support of the Catholic bishop, who urged Puerto Rico's newly minted soldiers to abandon the custom among rural people of common-law marriage and to formalize their unions before the state and the Church. The Puerto Rican Catholic Church and the U.S. military and legal system, using the access afforded them by the draft of Puerto Rican soldiers in 1918, seized the opportunity to make the working classes marry. Kern wrote to insular judges in June 1918 and again in July—periods of draft call-ups—to ask them to perform marriages free of charge, ideally at draft physicals, for soldiers who had lived with their wives for at least two years. General Chrisman of the training camp told new recruits to marry so they could designate beneficiaries for life insurance policies. Kern's circular on prostitution also urged the judiciary to curb adultery and concubinage. Priests circulated a letter among soldiers, telling them, among other things, to be faithful, loyal soldiers, to turn over their paychecks to their families, and "if there are any, among the Catholics who live shamefully in concubinage, they must sanctify and legalize their union by means of Catholic matrimony. The bishop has ordered the Reverend Fathers of the different towns of the island and principally those of San Juan to facilitate the means to unite legitimately those who live in sin."[7] One attorney who supported the anti-prostitution policy claimed that "this law extends protection to matrimony, and the young man, when he arrives at the right age, must fulfill his social duty, choosing a wife and contracting matrimony. To do otherwise is to risk infringing one of the sections [of the law]."[8] Colonial authorities and Puerto Rican elites agreed that the sexual practices of working-class people had become a scandal, their reproductive and sexual practices the subject of intense official scrutiny.

Then, in August 1918, women arrested for illicit sexuality became a different kind of issue: abruptly, some Puerto Ricans began to represent them as having been victimized by North American colonial excesses. ¡¡Basta Ya!! (Enough!!) screamed a headline in La Correspondencia, "The Attorney General is Violating the Laws of the Country." That evening, two prominent attorneys in Ponce held an open-air rally to denounce the Attorney General; they told the story of Susanna Torres, a young woman accused by a spurned suitor of having infecting him with venereal disease, but who, it was revealed after a physical examination, was a virgin. The following day, August 21, El Tiempo ran a front-page editorial decrying the policy under the headline, "For God's Sake, Mr. Attorney." The piece asked whether it was fair to incarcerate a woman for having a contagious disease. Would the same be done to a man? Of course not, the paper insisted. La Correspondencia ran the first of a series of columns entitled "The People Are with Us," containing letters objecting to the policy, some cast in terms of class politics. One announced, "One thousand workers of the Bayamón collective congratulate you for energetic campaign in favor of the people's rights,"[9] while another asked how Puerto Rico could be subject to measures "to imprison these innocents, with no greater crime than to protect their own lives and those of their children who are dying of hunger, who ask her, beg her for a morsel of bread to eat and a torn garment with which to cover their feeble bodies."[10]

A few days later, more than three hundred imprisoned women in Ponce staged the first of a series of riots. Incarcerated women had been distributed among four sites: San Juan, Mayagüez, Arecibo, and Ponce. In each, they experienced daily aggressive and painful treatments for venereal disease: repeated blood tests and pelvic exams, vaginal irrigations, and treatments with assorted mercurials and arsenicals (Salvarsan, neo-Salvarsan, and similar compounds, all courtesy of the Red Cross). While these treatments represented the best and most modern treatments in the arsenal of medical science, they were also painful, and, especially in the case of vaginal irrigations, humiliating, as even physicians understood. Dr. Pasarell wrote:

> The women all received [medical care] in six months they would not receive outside in two years. One of the reasons for this was that we had control of every case and they reported for injections every day, which would be impossible in private practice. The physician in private practice is confronted with the fact that he cannot make a patient continue treatment persistently. We have been able to push the treatment to the utmost.

It was in this context, then, that the women and girls rioted, cursing Kern, the Red Cross, and the bad food, upon the arrival of a physician, intern, and nurse at the Ponce jail on the afternoon of August 26. It is not clear whether they had agreed to the necessity of invasive biomedical treatment. Newspaper advertisements for patent medicines (mainly imported) to cure syphilis, venereal disease, "female illness," and *sangre impura* bears witness to a vigorous counterdiscourse on treatment options.[11]

Throughout the fall of 1918, *El Tiempo* and *La Correspondencia* kept up their criticism of the policy, both editorially and in prominently placed letters to the editor, the writers positioning themselves as populist voices against an unjust attack. Most criticism centered on Kern himself, though writers also attacked the double standard that required women, but not men, to be virtuous. It had the desired effect; fewer and fewer new arrests were made. On the other hand, most of the more than eight hundred women sentenced remained in jail, and the governor granted few pardons, though many were solicited. In early October, natural disaster accomplished what political protest could not. An earthquake destroyed the "hospital-jail" in Mayagüez, forcing authorities to move the women to the other three facilities and thereby taxing the available space. The move also further strained the financial resources of the Attorney General's office, which was already running a deficit. New arrests had to cease altogether.[12]

By winter, the factions were at an impasse. Governor Yager and Attorney General Kern were forced to request an emergency appropriation to pay for the continued incarceration of the extra prisoners. The insular House of Representatives, called into emergency session, refused to approve the deficit appropriation. Members of the House accused Kern of acting antidemocratically, of persecuting the press and judges who opposed his prostitution-suppression policy, and of imposing alien values on the island. They unanimously called upon the U.S. Senate to recall Kern. As one newspaper commented, "The Puritanism of the Puritan Mr. Kern is on trial."[13]

Kern responded vindictively. Unwilling to release the prisoners, the Attorney General cut appropriations for food "to the very minimum consistent with life." Even without funds, however, he maintained an aggressive program of biomedical treatment for the prisoners, with a special emphasis on testing and treatment for gonorrhea and syphilis. Gone, however, was the rhetoric that had previously undergirded the effort: a rhetoric of compassion and reform now took on a punitive tone. After the legislature adjourned, Kern wrote in his report to the governor, "Orders were issued by the Attorney General to reduce all rations for all prisoners . . . to an amount not to exceed sixteen cents a day. This ration can be increased as soon as the deficiency appropriations are approved." As local merchants cut off credit, women prisoners staged a fresh series of riots to protest the lack of food.[14] Members of the popularly elected legislature, notably those of the dominant Partido Unión de Puerto Rico (or Unionistas), associated with those who had been the local economic and political elite prior to the advent of U.S. rule in 1898, held firm against the incarceration and sent a delegation to Washington to demand Kern's dismissal. By spring, Kern had been recalled and the women had been returned to their homes. What had been front-page news and had consumed the energies of considerable segments of Puerto Rican society for a year had passed.[15]

What, then, was being enacted in this drama? In part, the conflict set the stage for what would become a constant feature of Puerto Rican politics: from eugenics to population policy to sterilization, the sexuality and reproduction of poor women would become the battleground—symbolic and real—for the meaning of the U.S. presence in Puerto Rico. An astonishing array of players, including scientists, foundations, politicians, nationalists, and feminists, weighed in on the management of the sexuality of poor Puerto Rican women. This policy expressed one of the ways "Porto Ricans" (as the U.S. colonizers baptized them)[16] were being made into "tropical American citizens," in the ironically apt terminology

of army physician Bailey K. Ashford—simultaneously "American" and
not, "tropical" and (oxymoronically) "citizens."[17] At the same time, the
production of stories about who prostitutes were, what effect they had
on families and the island, and who could best speak to the problem of
what to do about them was profoundly gendering work. Were they way-
ward daughters, diseased fallen women, or desperate mothers? Were
those who spoke on their behalf expressing tender maternal solicitude,
hard-edged masculine scientific expertise, or the distant but kind concern
of the patriarch, or *patrón?* Not only were North Americans working
out their ambivalent positions on how and whether to assimilate Puerto
Ricans through prostitution policy, but Puerto Ricans also were developing responses to the emergent U.S. positions.

Status was also clearly part of what was at stake. While the Jones Act
had been enacted in response to concerted efforts of Puerto Rican political leaders to regularize the island's status, it had embodied a compromise destined to suit no one: citizenship without the rights of U.S. citizens, such as voting in national elections—a blanket change in status
from above without a plebiscite or even much congressional debate. The
act, personified and riposted in the Puerto Rican press as "el Bill Jones,"
managed simultaneously to thwart aspirations for independence and for
U.S. statehood—two of the major political currents on the island, then
as now. To compound matters, in 1917 Kern argued two cases in the
Supreme Court, *In the matter of Tapia* and *Muratti v. Foote,* which succeeded in rendering Puerto Ricans as second-class citizens. In an exercise
in legal sophistry that had more to do with politics than precedent, the
Supreme Court agreed with Kern that Puerto Rico was not entitled to the
same legal status enjoyed by other U.S. territories. The court proclaimed
that the island was not a territory, in the sense of, say, Arizona, but was
rather an "unincorporated territory," a term invented by the Court exclusively for Puerto Rico.[18] The decisions in *Tapia* and *Muratti* and "el
Bill Jones" seemed ripe for Puerto Rican commentary and complaint, but
this was also the period of the Alien and Sedition Acts: those who objected to U.S. policy were at risk of being arrested for treason or prosecuted as dangerous radicals. Thus, at a time when the relationship between the island and the mainland was rapidly changing—in insulting
ways—prostitution policy provided a concrete and relatively safe forum
in which to debate these new relationships.

Science was used extensively to underscore the authority of the military and colonial officials, and of the Puerto Rican public health officials
who worked for them. It was used unevenly but not contradicted by the

women and Christian reformers who supported (and even prompted) the military policy. However, science was not a language that Puerto Ricans who opposed the prostitution policy used. The leadership of the opposition campaign was composed of lawyers and politicians who had come of age during the period of Spanish rule, and they had little interest in science as a language of statecraft. They also had little reason to think of themselves as racially different from North Americans, and tropical medicine and the science of empire were implicitly or explicitly a grammar of racial difference. Whether they were born in Europe or Puerto Rico, whether they were *peninsulares* or *criollos* (Spaniards or Creoles), Puerto Rican politicians conceived of themselves as at the top of a local racial and class hierarchy. They were landowners on an island where that was increasingly rare, either former plantation slaveowners or from families that had owned slaves in a racially heterogeneous society—in other words, they were white and elite. They understood themselves as in an argument with the American newcomers about who was going to manage the sexuality of working-class women, under what authority, and with what rules. North American colonizers, in contrast, largely saw themselves as managing a society of black or brown people incapable of self-rule. North Americans accomplished this sharp differentiation in no small measure through the idiom of science.

PROSTITUTION POLICY AND ECONOMIC TRANSITION BEFORE 1917

There were two coinciding processes that affected prostitutes and prostitution policies in the half century before passage of the Jones Act. First, hacienda slaves, free laborers, and bound ("white") workers from coastal sugar and mountain coffee plantations, as well as rural peasants and small-holders from inland *fincas,* were being made into a working class. This transition was a result of a contradictory tangle of both liberatory and repressive causes, from the freeing of slaves to the separation of peasants from their land, two processes with equally confounding effects, and from the building of a strong, class-conscious labor movement to periodic starvation. Increased migration, urbanization, and dependence on wage earning drew significant numbers of working-class women into prostitution. Simultaneously, the policy of prostitution registration and medical inspection as a scientific, bureaucratic, modern method of colonial administration came to the attention of liberal Creole elites in the 1870s. At the same time that economic transitions were rendering working people dramatically more visible as a "problem" for Puerto Rico's urban and rural elites, and something a modern nation ought to do something about, the technology of the CD Acts provided a solution.

As Puerto Rican historian Fernando Picó has shown, in 1900 Puerto Rico was a society that had already endured a quarter-century of economic upheaval. The market for Puerto Rican sugar had collapsed in the last third of the nineteenth century, shifting the bulk of the monocultural economy abruptly from sugar to coffee. The abolition of slavery in 1873 resulted in freedom for former slaves and the possibility of migration to cities, where they become wage laborers. San Juan, in particular, became the destination for a growing number of young women seeking domestic labor or sex work.[19] Creole and Spanish elites instituted an extensive system to limit the movements of freed laborers, both black and white, including the so-called *libreta* (passbook) system, which required all poor people to show that they were employed and by whom.[20]

U.S. colonialism did not bring the CD Acts to Puerto Rico; the Spanish did. In 1876 Spanish authorities had instituted a segregated "red-light" district in San Juan along with mandatory medical inspection. Prostitution arrived with a vengeance in the southern coastal city of Ponce in the late 1890s, along with a wave of repression; prostitutes were required to carry a *libreta* showing their medical stamp, and those who did not were thrown in jail. A Liberal Autonomist movement strongly endorsed prostitution registration as being essential to a modern nation, enjoining a sharp geographic separation between *gente decente* and prostitutes. As the movement's leader, Luis Muñoz Rivera, wrote in 1893, "We pity the fallen woman, but we must avoid at all costs her contact with the honorable woman. In this way, her contaminating spray will not reach our face, nor tarnish the purity of our society."[21] Police sweeps also rounded up women who were not prostitutes. Historian Eileen Findlay's careful reading of newspapers from the period finds numerous petitions from women demanding to be released from jail who claimed that they were married, in common-law marriages, and/or gainfully employed. That these would qualify as defenses suggest that police action was aimed at poor, unattached, disorderly women. In the case of both migrating laborers and prostitutes, the goal of the paternalist passbook policy was to ensure that everyone would be tightly bound within concentric circles of family and employer control.[22]

A second stage in the process of the making of a migratory, wage-dependent working class involved the dispossession of peasants from coffee and subsistence agriculture, and was greatly accelerated by the advent of North American rule. In 1898 U.S. military officials froze credit and devalued the currency, rendering life for *jibaros* (peasants) dramatically more precarious. (The U.S. replaced the centavo with the cent, at twice its value, effectively doubling prices, a policy that proved incredibly disruptive on an island where most basic foodstuffs were imported.) In 1899 Hurricane San Ciriaco ripped through the island's central mountain range (the *cordillera central*), destroying not only that year's crops but also the slow-growing coffee plants themselves. Coffee agriculture was left in tatters, and coffee farmers without a harvest for years to come. Well-financed North Americans bought up land, particularly in the sugar-growing coastal regions. Better capitalized than their Puerto Rican counterparts, they built *centrales* (sugar mills) that enabled them to refine sugar right on the island, thereby fetching a far higher price than the poorer growers' unrefined sugar. Many members of the former ruling classes returned to Spain, France, and elsewhere in Europe. The expansion of luxury crops for export also meant less food for working-class people. "Every advance of coffee or sugar entailed an increase in the mortality rate," writes Picó. "The reduction of the area dedicated to the cultivation of food crops meant the worsening of the workers' diet."[23] Sociologist Kelvin Santiago-Valles has shown that even North American observers noticed a difference in how successfully subsistence-level peasants were making their living. Whereas an observer in 1898 had complained that nature's "lavish bounty . . . reduces the necessity for work to its minimum," by 1900 another wrote that "people are dying of hunger by the hundreds."

Ironically, despite this growing landlessness and the marginal nutrition of working-class Puerto Ricans, the dominant discourse in the United States about the effect of the North American presence told a different story. It celebrated the arrival of the United States as a benevolent event that had made Puerto Ricans healthier. Science and public health were key to this story. As one traveler's narrative had it:

> When the Americans took possession of Porto Rico it was one of the dirtiest, filthiest, and most unsanitary of countries. Lack of adequate water supply, carelessness, and an utter ignorant disregard for the simplest rules of hygiene and sanitation had made the island a menace to human health, life, and comfort.

But by 1914, when this traveler's tale was published, the writer could confidently say:

> There is no greater monument or more lasting proof of the triumph of
> modern sanitation and science than the present condition of Porto Rico as
> compared to its past state. To-day Porto Rico is one of the cleanest, the
> most sanitary, and the healthiest of countries, and it is doubtful if another
> city in the world can compare with San Juan for cleanliness and health.
> There is every reason for a reasonably careful person to live free from all
> ills and die of old age.[24]

The core of this claim was the work by U.S. military physician Bailey K.
Ashford in diagnosing, identifying a causative microorganism, and treating hookworm-related anemia. Journalist Sylvester Baxter claimed that
"the island's record in sanitation has a world-wide import," writing that
in matters of public health, these "fruits of the War with Spain have a
value so incalculable that in comparison all other fruits of the conflict
seem insignificant."[25] By the second decade of the U.S. presence, this establishment of science and public health as the key feature of U.S. rule
in Puerto Rico made it much more difficult to argue against the benevolence of the U.S. mission. Even a writer for the leftist magazine *The Nation* was forced to admit that "it cannot be emphasized too strongly that
the Porto Ricans are a sick people," and he conceded the necessity of an
ongoing American involvement in insular affairs.[26] Despite these hearty
assertions of the benefits of U.S. rule, from 1898 to 1902, the death rate
increased steadily; and for the next twenty-five years, it remained more
or less constant.[27] In other words, in the context of international gains
in public health and longevity, the accelerated concentration of wealth
in a few hands—mostly American—effected by the U.S. presence probably made the health circumstances of the majority of the population
worse, the rhetoric of science notwithstanding.

Under the rubric of public health, the U.S. administration, like the
Spanish before them, enforced a version of the CD Acts to control venereal disease and prostitution. Despite weak efforts to abolish it, Puerto
Rican and U.S. military officials maintained in force the policy that required registration at the Special Hospital for Women in San Juan and
mandatory medical treatment of those sex workers found to be ill.[28] This
de facto state of things was formalized in 1905, and thereafter until
1917, prostitutes were required to undergo weekly medical examinations at the Special Hospital for Women—in permanent quarters beginning in 1905—and those outside the city had to register at local police
stations.[29] In the southern city of Ponce, a municipal reglementation or-
dinance had been passed earlier, in 1894, and it was backed by the institution of a "hygiene hospital" and the establishment of zones of pros-

titution, a system that U.S. officials not only upheld after 1898, but whose enforcement was intensified.[30] Just as the Spanish had, the United States endorsed a policy that attempted to segregate prostitutes from respectable folk as a bureaucratic and public health solution worthy of a modern nation.

In a similar vein, U.S. colonial officials also took up another Spanish colonial concern immediately after the invasion: the work of getting rural and working-class people to formalize their sexual and reproductive relationships through marriage, something many of them refused to do—the official marriage rate in 1899 was only around 50 percent. The attorney general for Puerto Rico, A. C. Sharpe, wrote that the significance of this low marriage rate was that it put civilization at risk.

> Family life is the recognized basis of true civilization. American law and institutions regard the relation of the husband and wife as one of the most sacred guarantees for the perpetuity of the state. Marriage is recognized as the only lawful relation by which Providence has permitted the continuance of the human race, and the history of mankind has proved it to be one of the chief foundations of social order.

With the future of civilization, the state, and the human race dependent on marriage, U.S. colonial officials in 1899 passed laws allowing civil matrimony—without benefit of a priest—and eliminating fees associated with marriage. When these did little to change the marriage rate, in 1902 the legislature passed a law allowing the full right to divorce—making Puerto Rico the first place in Latin America to permit it. What followed was not the intended acceleration of the marriage rate, but an explosion of divorce petitions by women who complained of marital infidelity and domestic abuse. Unintentionally, colonial officials had handed Puerto Rican women and feminists a potent new weapon in their struggles for equality.[31]

Missionary women, however, sided with colonial officials in the effort to produce respectable families. While the WCTU chapter in Puerto Rico was initially uninterested in the "purity" cause, members nevertheless located themselves symbolically and metaphorically in a story about families. The chapter, composed of both Puerto Rican and North American women of the respectable classes, was organized in response to a temperance referendum on the island and sponsored small morality plays in their ultimately successful effort to drum up support for temperance among Puerto Rican voters. Edith Hildreth, then vice-president of the chapter, reported that at a play held at the YMCA: "Uncle Sam, the twenty-six dry states, and the District of Columbia were featured. A small native boy, in tears, took the part of Porto Rico, and in response to a question from Uncle Sam he replied, 'I want to get in on this, too!'" She added, "Great applause greeted the words of the child."[32] This image, figuring Puerto Rico as a small child (in tears, no less)—here cast in the masculine, perhaps a response to the rather awkward problem that despite their campaigning, women could not vote—was a motif that was to be reiterated in the later anti-prostitution campaign. Members of the WCTU were mothers to those it sought to reform.

Among their first acts, then, U.S. colonial officials worked to organize domesticity in Puerto Rico, including "sanitary" prostitution and nuclear families. There was nothing unique or original about these acts; as we have seen, they belonged to an international organization of colonial militaries, laborers, and Creole families and represented substantial continuity with Spanish policies. Domesticity was both a lever for transforming and reorganizing the colonial state and an utterly banal exercise.

CONSTRUCTING A MORAL PANIC: VENEREAL DISEASE IN 1918

The transformation of prostitution policy from medical inspection and registration to suppression and jailing of prostitutes happened through a process that Stuart Hall has called a "moral panic": the production of an issue as a "crisis" that begins to function as an allegory for multiple social cleavages, conflicts, and antipathies.[33] The writing about this policy does not directly tell us the things we would like to know: What ideologies, what habits of mind supplied colonizers with the arrogance to believe that they, individually or as emissaries from the United States or as missionaries for a morality drawn from Protestant Christianity were the best governors of—or spokespeople for—Puerto Ricans whom they barely understood? What stories did they tell themselves that enabled them to see their collusion in the economic brutalization and increasing malnutrition of working-class people in Puerto Rico in general—and the imprisonment of women engaged in sex work in particular—as "doing good"? Or, similarly, how do we understand how former slaveowners positioned themselves as the sympathizers and defenders of "poor unfortunate" women, many of whom (particularly in San Juan) were black or of mixed race? Finally, if it is possible to ask this question without being melodramatic, how do we understand a political moment in which all sides purported to have the best interests of working-class women at heart, but in which those same women were effectively medically raped,

starved, jailed, separated from their children, and deprived of t..
livelihood? Languages of racial and gendered difference were highly
effective at creating the rhetorics that made these activities possible and
politically profitable. They also provide a tangible starting point for close
analysis that sheds light on these broader questions, and it is to the deployment of race and gender that this chapter now turns.

RACE

Passions were mobilized on the subject of prostitution and VD policy
around a series of interlocking narratives about sex and citizenship. On
the North American side, the simplest and most predictable narrative
was a racial discourse of purity, exclusion, and nationalism. Puerto Rican prostitutes were dangerous to soldiers and their women back home
on the mainland and had to be contained. Indeed, in this view the steamy
tropics of Puerto Rico fairly stank of sexual excess, rot, and germs. This
position was most evident in the writing of Gavin Payne of the Red
Cross. Payne insisted that a forceful VD policy was important because

> Porto Rico is one of our own back doors—and the back doors of our
> homes are the places where the germs come in. These fair-haired young
> sailors of ours come into these tropical ports. Thousands of these Porto
> Rican laborers have been imported into the states recently.

In this narrative, the important victims of the spread of venereal disease
were North Americans, who were held to be white—"fair-haired"—and
they might catch it through the contact of the U.S. Navy with the island
and through the immigration of contract laborers—who were associated
with back doors, blackness, and disease (recall, too, that this was the era
of Jim Crow). Payne claimed that Puerto Ricans, in contrast to North
Americans, did not fear venereal disease and were not necessarily even
cognizant of the discomfort it caused. Rather, the disease was ubiquitous
on the island, roughly coterminous with the ontological state of being
Puerto Rican. "Among a million and a half people [that inhabit the is-
land] . . . the disease has reached a saturation point," he wrote. The lack
of moral intelligence among the "natives," he thought, made them particularly susceptible. "We always have to bear in mind the large proportion of people down here who are unmoral, rather than immoral,"
Payne insisted. "The haunting fear of venereal disease is not as common
among Porto Rican young men as among men of our temperate zone."
If he rendered Puerto Ricans as oddly innocent of sexual wrongdoing, in

a patronizing sort of way, it was in the service of marking them off as sharply, fundamentally, different from North Americans, through race, disease, morality, and climate. Of prostitutes in jail, he remarked, "The element of remorse [does] not appear as often as it probably would among this type in the temperate zone. . . . This is attributable to a laxity in moral standards."[34]

This contrast between our "fair-haired" boys and a tropics in which the disease had reached a saturation point was clearly a racial distinction. In mainland medical writing, African Americans were held to have extremely high rates of syphilis (a subgenre of the writing that found them to be hypersexual). "The utter depravity, the sexual degeneracy, and degradation of these people is unprintable, and to the average person, unbelievable," wrote a U.S. physician about African Americans in Indiana. Venereal disease had been spread widely among African Americans by sexual immorality, argued Dr. Thomas Murrell. "Morality among these people is almost a joke and only assumed as a matter of convenience or when there is a lack of desire and opportunity for indulgence, and venereal diseases are well-nigh universal. . . . In clinic and private practice I have never seen a negro virgin over 18 years of age." (A Howard University physician wrote that black women's "immorality" was a result of white male depredations, claiming acerbically, "Virginity is as rare among this class of negresses as continence is among white men.") A substantial medical literature identified syphilis as rampant among African Americans, with estimates reaching as high as 90 percent. Among physicians, there was "a practical unanimity of opinion that this disease is far more common in the colored race than in the white." During the First World War, the army distributed educational posters for soldiers and civilians alike showing far higher rates of venereal diseases for "colored" soldiers than for whites.[35] Syphilis was so effective in making racial distinctions that information contradicting the association of African Americans with very high rates was rendered unimportant; two studies, one showing comparable rates among working-class whites and blacks and another showing lower rates for African Americans were ignored, even though they were published in a prominent medical journal.[36] Similarly, the army continued to publish its racial venereal statistics during World War I, even after an internal assessment which cited shoddy record keeping and "glaring inconsistencies" found them to be worthless.[37]

The effort to turn racially heterogeneous Puerto Ricans into uniformly dark-skinned "natives" rested on the belief that there were two, and only two, racial categories (white and black, or nearly so), with

North Americans taking up the white pole and Puerto Ricans at or near the black pole. However, even within the terms of the vocabulary of the medical discourse of syphilis, there were other options for thinking about race. Within the U.S. Army's medical division, for example, there were at least three entirely distinct sets of racial categorizations. The Surgeon General's office discussed venereal disease statistics using only two categories: white and "colored" (or "Negro," since the two terms were used synonymously). In contrast, medical journal articles by Herman Goodman about syphilis in Puerto Rico referred to at least three racial classifications. He described the island population as composed of whites, Negroes, and mulattos, and some articles also refer to a "mixture of the two races in varying proportion." A third variation was found in the postwar publication by the U.S. Army Medical Office, *Defects Found in Drafted Men,* which employed no fewer than fourteen racial categories, including the Irish, Scandinavian, and Hungarian races, as well as a single category that included Indian, Chinese, and Japanese people.[38]

The work of making Puerto Ricans into one or two races (in the latter case, finding "white" and "black" Puerto Ricans) was admittedly complicated since Puerto Ricans themselves were in a position to talk back. Senators from the nearby southeastern United States foiled efforts to bring Puerto Rican soldiers to South Carolina to train before going overseas, arguing that these young soldiers would be a problem for the laws and customs of Jim Crow. To Southern politicians already alarmed by the proposed concentrations of African-American soldiers with guns in their region, the notion of adding to their number black and "mixed race" soldiers untutored in the ways of Jim Crow—"not accustomed to our point of view on the racial question," as one Senator put it—was out of the question. These observations about the intolerability of Puerto Ricans for Southern racism proved true and self-fulfilling; Puerto Rican laborers sent north by the U.S. Department of Labor were drawn into some of the frequent race riots of the wartime period. Five were killed in a riot that was also directed at black soldiers, with whom the Puerto Ricans worked in a Georgia explosives factory.[39]

Puerto Rican soldiers did refuse to designate themselves as black or white in ways familiar to those from the United States. One Puerto Rican soldier, for example, Antonio Guzmán, who had been assigned first to a white and then to a black regiment at Camp Las Casas, insisted on a military hearing over his race. The differences in the way he and U.S. army officials presented his case speaks volumes about the differences in what constituted "race" for Puerto Ricans and Americans: he presented affidavits from neighbors and officials in his home town, which referred to ancestors, moral character, social standing, and the ownership of land. One wrote:

> I have as high an opinion of Sr. Guzmán as of all his family, with regard to their honor and morals. [They] belong to the white race; this belief that I have always had of them is shared by the community in which they live. [They] carry on social relations with all the families in Arecibo of the highest prestige and social worth.[40]

Guzmán lost his case. The army concluded that he was "of white descendent, but the observation and general examination of his person lead this Board to believe he is not of pure white race." For them, "white" was an impersonal, visual category—they knew it when they saw it—whereas for Guzmán and his neighbors, it was a social category, one maintained through gossip and the collective memory of who married with whom, and who was allowed into polite society.

Herman Goodman, the venereal officer for the training camp at Las Casas, reported extensively in the medical literature on treatment of the incarcerated women and chronicled cases of tropical diseases such as yaws and hookworm alongside syphilis and gonorrhea, construing them as closely related.[41] Venereal disease in Puerto Rico was understood within the terms and through the institutions of tropical medicine and sanitation (the blood tests for syphilis and smears for gonorrhea were even performed by the Institute for Tropical Medicine).[42] Just as the search for the spirochete had done in earlier decades, the science of venereal disease provided a particularly successful idiom for elaborating difference in Puerto Rico in 1918. But drawing attention to venereal disease also transformed the narrative of tropical disease, changing it from a problem of colonial labor—from the relentless focus on hookworm, the "germ of laziness," that had existed for the first two decades of the U.S. presence[43]—to an issue of colonial sexuality and reproduction.

In Goodman's articles, science and medicine, rather than simply offering a mechanism for describing the conditions of contact with foreign strangers, provided a means of thinking about their assimilation. For Goodman, Puerto Rico—and Puerto Rican women, more specifically—had to be sanitized, in a sense simultaneously moral, medical, and racial. Assimilation, however, was not the same as full integration. Puerto Ricans were not rendered as citizens in the same sense as mainland Anglos; rather, they were brought in as (docile, tamed, sanitized) second-class citizens. Scientific language was at once metaphoric and literal: Puerto

Rican prostitutes were in fact treated for disease, but the symbolic significance of a crusade against disease extended far beyond the limited number of women affected directly by the policy. North Americans understood what they were doing in two distinct registers—one conservative, one liberal. On the conservative side, the challenge was to keep (mainland) Americans safe from (foreign, female) dirt and disease. On the liberal side, physicians and WCTU members used their superior knowledge in the work of benevolence, of saving Puerto Rican women and children from their victimization by Puerto Rican men. In either case, however, the work of assimilating Puerto Ricans as ersatz citizens produced them, through a science of women's bodies, as fundamentally different from North Americans—"almost the same, but not quite," in Homi Bhabha's phrase, or, more pointedly, "almost the same, but not *white.*"[44] Goodman was much concerned about "virtuous" Puerto Rican women and children victimized by syphilis. In his view, they were principally endangered by prostitutes who spread the disease. The men who engaged in sex with both, he mentioned almost as an afterthought. Incarcerating prostitutes was key to promoting "community health" in his view; by this, he meant principally the health of women and children. Goodman left Puerto Rico at the height of the anti-VD campaign, and in writing about it later, he simply declared victory. "The main source of infection is the prostitute," he wrote. "With her isolation new cases of syphilis among the men of the community and from these to the women and children cease."[45] The incarceration policy, in short, could be considered an important measure to prevent the victimization of the wives and children of men, presumably (in Goodman's account) soldiers, who were prone to having sex with prostitutes. By treating soldiers and prostitutes, he could eliminate syphilis. "In a decade," he argued, "this island should be the example to all the world as the test-tube experiment which proved that syphilis need not be."[46]

Among North Americans, Goodman's ability to imagine Puerto Ricans as victims of syphilis (albeit, alongside Puerto Rican female "villains") made him a liberal, a sympathetic colonial who could imagine that the "natives," too, suffered. Puerto Ricans were not disposable bodies for him, and he did not insist too strongly on their difference. Although he argued there was a greater prevalence of venereal disease in the tropics, Goodman claimed there was a universality to its manifestation. "A theory as to the predisposition on the part of the colored race has been advanced; but reports of the disease among whites are sufficiently common to warrant the statement that race plays no essential part in the etiology of the disease," he wrote. Likewise, he insisted that in Puerto Rico, "the syphilitic lesions we have seen differ in no way from those seen in the United States."[47] He explicitly rejected the belief, common in the medical literature, that "tropical" or racially marked bodies manifested disease differently, or were particularly prone to venereal disease.

Nevertheless, it would be equally mistaken to say that Goodman regarded Puerto Rican bodies as the same as North American ones, even with respect to his limited script of disease. His medical articles on venereal disease all began by describing the racial composition of Puerto Rico as different from that of the mainland, emphasizing the presence of greater percentages of people of African, indigenous, and mixed heritage. He asserted that syphilis "had an early start" in Puerto Rico, locating its beginnings as early as the beginning of the sixteenth century, and he suggested that the Caribbean may, in fact, have been the origin point for the disease. He claimed the existence of exotic, tropical venereal diseases—yaws (strawberry-like skin eruptions, occurring anywhere on the body; not usually thought of as a venereal disease); ulcerating granuloma (healed-over, ulcerous growths on the skin, also not usually specified as a different disease in its venereal manifestations); and a filarial-involved hydrocele (fluid-filled enlargement) and elephantiasis (gross enlargement) of the scrotum and testes that rendered Puerto Rican genitalia enormous and diseased. "Hydrocele," he wrote,

> is almost an insular characteristic. In not a few, it is no exaggeration to say that the scrotum hung as low as the knees. Strange to say, a hydrocele of more than moderate size, and usually bilateral, gives the Porto Rican no apparent discomfort. For many years the trousers made on the island allowed for the extra mass. Many men wear suspensories, as might readily be supposed, but more for appearance than for comfort.

In making these claims, he placed Puerto Rican sexuality within the narratives of dangerous, racialized sex: the familiar huge genitals of the black male; the extraordinary, extravagant, and strange reproductive organs of the black female. He added a twist to this narrative by advocating a theory that there are uniquely tropical venereal diseases. Moreover, by asserting a Caribbean starting-point for the disease, he contributed to the argument that if the "truth" about syphilis was to be found in its origins, then it was "essentially" a Caribbean disease. And Puerto Ricans, with a syphilis rate that he represented to be possibly as high as 55 percent and with proliferating possibilities for venereal disease categories, were perhaps "essentially" a venereal diseased people.[48]

GENDER

Prostitutes—or rather, the ability to speak on behalf of prostitutes—became a symbolic battleground for the Puerto Rican nation (or colony, depending on one's point of view). This struggle mobilized ideology that functioned significantly through a grammar not only of race but of gender. The behavior of women prostitutes was at issue in a profoundly gendered way—male sexuality was not publicly scrutinized in the same way, and the "morality" or "disease" of men's sexuality could not be made to stand for the malaise of the island / nation. Moreover, the claim to be able to rectify and manage working-class women's sexuality and labor was made by embodying certain kinds of gendered behavior. North American military officials and scientists took up the masculine role of the expert, scientific, managerial knower in order to pronounce on prostitution policy and matters of governance in general. Spanish and Creole elites, in contrast, defended women by assuming the mantle of chivalrous manhood. As Ashis Nandy points out, establishing manhood as the grounding for claims to power can be said to constitute success for colonialism:

> When such a cultural consensus grows, the main threat to the colonizers is bound to become the latent fear that the colonized will reject the consensus and, instead of trying to redeem their "masculinity" by becoming counterplayers of the rulers according to the established rules, will discover an alternative frame of reference within which the oppressed do not seem weak, degraded and distorted men trying to break the monopoly of the rulers on a fixed quantity of machismo.[49]

Or, similarly, Kelvin Santiago-Valles makes this argument with Puerto Rico in mind:

> Colonialism reproduces a cultural consensus whereby broad sectors of the colonized population, particularly the literate and property-owning "native" classes of the colony, actively participate in the sign systems that constitute the various oppressed groups as subordinate: class exploitation, racism, paternalism, machismo, heterosexism, and so on. These are the structural trenches where colonial-capitalist relations are perpetually dug in, this being the site from which all possible expressions of reform, "home rule," neocolonial independence, and even anti-imperialism can be negotiated.[50]

Contrasting claims to manhood were not the only basis of this struggle, however; ideologies of womanhood were equally at stake. By the second decade of U.S. rule, Puerto Rico had a WCTU chapter determined to stamp out "the social evil," justifying its position in strikingly female terms: through what Peggy Pascoe calls "female moral authority," the notion that women as guardians of the hearth and keepers of the home occupied the moral high ground (particularly with respect to sex) and hence had an obligation to "clean up" the (dirty, military, and commercial) public sphere. North American women also invoked the notion of prostitutes as their (cross-cultural) daughters who, as both their age- and evolutionary-civilization superiors, they had an obligation to guide. The WCTU also successfully enlisted the support of Puerto Rican "ladies'" social clubs (though not of the working-class women's organizations), who extended a patrician concern for the poor unfortunates. Collectively, they constituted working-class women's sexuality as the ground for their various claims to power and authority.

Historian Gladys Jiménez-Muñoz has argued brilliantly for thinking of struggle over Puerto Rican woman suffrage in the decade following the incarceration of prostitutes as being fundamentally a fight over the nature of the civic body produced by "el Bill Jones." She argues that (male) genteel Creoles feared "that women's suffrage would blur the distinction between the Puerto Rican social body and Puerto Rican sexual bodies, thereby en-gendering chaos with the Island's political body. Such fears immediately conjured visions of political cross-dressing and gender uncertainty."[51] Moreover, she suggests that for the U.S. Congress, backing elite (literate) women's suffrage in Puerto Rico (albeit nearly a decade after woman suffrage was won on the mainland) enabled that body to take up the mantle of "democratic" reform for women against the island's (male) political majority—in other words, to advocate colonialism under the banner of liberalism. We can move this insight backward in time, to 1918, and explore what it meant to turn the Puerto Rican prostitute body into a symbol of the nation. This battle contrasts sharply with the struggle Jiménez-Muñoz describes, of bringing woman suffrage to the island in the late 1920s and early 1930s.[52] Whereas suffrage was about the question of the active entrance of women into citizenship, into the body politic, the prostitution reform battle of 1918 rendered the prostitute herself politically inert—rhetorically, by turning her into a symbol, and actually, by imprisoning her. In so doing, the struggle succeeded in solidifying a series of political positions. Colonizing men became chivalrous figures, defending virtuous women on the island from syphilis through prostitute contact with soldier-husbands, or protecting the mainland from infection by dirty women; in so doing, the violence of their role was erased, transformed into heroism. Women reformers from the mainland WCTU—in concert with elite Creole women from the island—enacted a maternalist, protective role, "saving" young women prostitutes from disease and immorality. Creole men, too, enacted roles as protectors, as benevolent *patrones*. Those who disappeared as agents were those around whom the debate swirled: working-class women who sometimes sold sex in order to survive, the female counterparts of the (male) urban disorderly classes.

The question of whether elite women—Puerto Rican or mainland U.S.—ought to play a role in politics was one of the ways that gender was at issue. On an island with little history of elite women's activism (and a tiny middle class), the activities of the WCTU and other well-to-do women reformers had the capacity to shock. There was little enough public support for the idea of a single standard of "purity" that would apply to men as well. On the other hand, the double move of WCTU-style reform, not only asserting a substantial divide between themselves and the prostitute women they sought to reform, but also embracing them as daughters, did draw elite Puerto Rican women into the WCTU. In calling for women to "enlist" in the Police Women's Reserve Corps, the WCTU specifically called on "the ladies of Porto Rico"—women of the elite classes whose morals were beyond reproach. One of the local groups participating in the "clean-up" campaign was the *Club de Damas de Ponce* (the Ponce Ladies Club). In a context where such questions as whether women in the public sphere were immodest per se were much contested, defining oneself as being against immodesty and promiscuity (and of the elite classes) was a productive discourse for the WCTU. This is perhaps most evident in the negative case—in the opposition generated by the Police Women's Reserve Corps, a group that was criticized for collapsing the social distance that they meant to establish. An editorial in *El Tiempo* called the proposal to enlist Puerto Rican women in such a project "very strange and abnormal."

> The Porto Rican woman, because of her natural timidity, her naiveté, her characteristic modesty; because of lack of experience with this special class of work and her absolute lack of knowledge about detective work, for lack of training in this new police sport, would not be able to be of much help in the persecution of clandestine prostitution, work very far from a lady's place and in opposition to the very delicate and pure feelings of our ladies.[53]

A lady's place, apparently, did not involve political activism. However, if women were going to make a case for themselves as political actors, it is clear that in some way they had to address the question of modesty. Taking up the mantle of sexual morality as a political position was not a bad way to start.

In contrast to the elite women with whom the WCTU sought alliance, Puerto Rican working-class women did have a substantial tradition of political activism. Especially in the tobacco trades—the largest source of employment for women—women had fought for and won the right to organize under the banner of the Federación Libre de Trabajadores (FLT) and had eventually moved into leadership positions in this, Puerto Rico's largest union. In 1908 it was the FLT that issued the first formal call for women's suffrage, followed by the Socialist Party (organized in 1915). The Puerto Rican Socialist Party articulated itself as the party advocating equality for women. In 1919 a male Puerto Rican labor leader put it this way:

> Women have always been the proprietary victims of the tyranny despotism, and authority of men and society over them. But, it is time to put an end to these practices. Working class women are our comrades, they share our misery and privations. The Socialist Party, through its struggles, recognizes and supports the right of women to a full participation in all social affairs; the party exists for the defense of women and humanity in general.[54]

From this milieu emerged radical women leaders like Luisa Capetillo, who wore pants, advocated free love, and bore three children while refusing marriage; and innumerable women's strikes and price riots directed at perceived gouging practices. In fact, just as controversy about the anti-prostitution policy was heating up, there occurred simultaneously a multi-sited strike of women tobacco strippers.[55]

To the extent that women's activism was associated with the labor movement and the Socialist Party, WCTU activity, first for temperance and then for prostitution reform, may have been a sort of entering wedge for the expansion of elite women's activism. At any rate, the founding manifesto of the Liga Femínea Portorriqueña (Porto Rican Feminist League, or Feminine League), an organization dedicated to winning suffrage exclusively for literate women (fewer than one-sixth of Puerto Rican women at that time), cited anti-vice activity as one of its precursors. It also drew on European and decolonization traditions, mentioning English, French, Italian, and Egyptian woman suffrage activities. The manifesto adopted a rhetorical style similar to the WCTU's, simultaneously embracing and rejecting prostitutes and other poor women:

The seed that the war sowed has begun to bear fruit, and the latent energy that came to manifest itself in the feminine camp, now free of the prejudices and vicious practices [practices of vice] that, for centuries, have impeded us from walking on the path to awaken not only our moral worth, but also our physical worth.

This circumlocution makes both the "energy" to put down prostitution and "vicious practices" qualities of the women that the manifesto includes. The manifesto's authors also locate their own activities firmly within the discourses of modernization and health.

The Porto Rican woman must have her own legal standing to aid in the progress of her country if she is going to be anything in the world, in line with what women in nineteen states of the American Union have, and of many civilized countries. It will never be a sin to make Porto Rican women as feminist as possible, if one succeeds in giving them the true and healthy feminism.[56]

After the war, a new kind of feminism took the stage in Puerto Rico, as the women incarcerated under the policy straggled home or were transferred to hospitals and mental asylums. As we will see in chapter 3, "health" was more than a mere metaphor. Questions of health, modernity, and reproduction were critical feminist issues in Puerto Rico.

Missionary women, in contrast, sided with colonial officials in the effort to produce respectable families. Like colonial bureaucrats and military officials, Edith Hildreth and the WCTU longed to make over the tropics, but whereas Goodman saw the island as a laboratory, they saw it as a middle-class American home. Members' activism was attributed to the WCTU's "motherly instinct."[57] For them, the women to be "saved" were not the innocent, but the sinners. Wrote Hildreth,

It is believed and hoped that these women can be committed to homes in isolated places and there kept until they are completely cured. The idea is to segregate all such women, to give them light employment and to make them as happy as possible during their internment and at the same time to carry on the work of social uplift among them in an effort to reclaim them.[58]

As in rescue missions, WCTU members began teaching the women and girls in jail skills for various kinds of working-class labor: needlework, lace making, hat making, basketry, and shoe making (they attributed prostitution to their belief that "practically none of these women know how to work.") They also taught English and literacy classes. One proposal, never implemented because of a lack of facilities, would have had the prisoners doing various kinds of agricultural work, including the production of castor-bean oil for airplane engines.[59] Incarcerated women were not being punished as lawbreakers, but healed, as victims of illness. Hildreth argued that "all are sick, and some are very sick," and under the policy, "they are receiving the best and most modern care for their particular diseases, under competent physicians, with the end in view of curing them if possible." Indeed, Hildreth at one point referred to the jails in which the women were held simply as "hospitals," and the desire to see them arrested as "the campaign for combating the ailments that inflict the unfortunate." Echoing Payne, she explained the need for missionaries in this way: "As in many Latin countries, public opinion has not been awakened as to the awful dangers and untold sufferings due directly to venereal disease."[60]

Forty years later, Edith Hildreth would write her memoirs. Of this period, she recorded only that she had raised children. While this would seem a direct abnegation of her political activism on the island, it could also be a veiled reference to what she believed was her "maternal" care for the girls accused of prostitution. In her autobiography, the children she recalled were mostly hers, but one was a Puerto Rican girl, Tula, left unclaimed for weeks at Presbyterian Hospital, the mission hospital where Hildreth's husband was medical director. It was the girl children that she dwelt on, especially one, Baby Ruth, who died. She wrote that the Puerto Rican mothers marveled at her sanitary practices, for "these poor natives had never seen a baby treated with such sanitary care," and she tried to teach them how to boil and scrub, too, forming a Mothers Club. Hildreth recorded her evangelical work, from Sunday School for children to persuading mothers to become Protestants. It was a chronicle written in a different era, the 1950s, when women's political activism was, if not harder to justify, then in search of a rhetorical justification, unmoored from the maternalist languages of the second decade of the twentieth century. Yet, while the memoir is evidently misleading, it also represents a kind of truth. Hildreth, it seems even from the contemporary record, never represented herself as being far outside the realm of family and Sunday School. She and the WCTU understood themselves to be teaching the "natives," explicitly or implicitly children, about sanitation and their kind of (evangelical, Protestant) Christianity.[61]

Between 1917 and 1918, then, gender and women's bodies became a significant idiom in which colonial relations were negotiated. North American politicians, reformers, and missionaries identified the victimization of women, or, conversely, the danger they posed, as an important reason for massive repression and intervention. The increasingly visible poor women of the dislocated rural classes appear in this literature as "loose" women in need of containment. Puerto Rican male politicians likewise cast themselves as the protectors of wronged womanhood in order to struggle with North American colonial officials and the federal government over questions of status, victimization, and citizenship. There were notable losers in this struggle: Attorney General Kern was recalled, and accused prostitutes spent six months in jail. The jailed women appear as authors of their own narratives only briefly in the written accounts, as the women who rioted.

CITIZENSHIP AND STATUS

Puerto Rican elite support for the policy had initially been couched in the language of propriety and polite society. Right living and social duty required right sexuality. Yet, with time, Puerto Rican opposition developed in the language of citizenship and the right relation between the island and the mainland. It also extended beyond the elite classes. In Caguas, a mob tried to forcibly free a few women briefly imprisoned there,[62] while unions issued statements of support for the women. One newspaper article argued that poor women were being falsely accused of prostitution, that the forceful circular issued by the attorney general had compromised the independence of the judiciary by threatening to remove judges who refused to enforce anti-prostitution laws, and that it violated the principles of the Organic Act to compromise individual liberty without due process. The article warned "citizen" Kern that he had disgraced Puerto Rico before the U.S. government, and the U.S. government before Puerto Rico, by "presenting us as incapable of ruling our own destinies" in promoting the policy so forcefully.[63]

The debate over the suppression of prostitution was simultaneously a response to the reconfiguration of the island as a geography of American citizens, a referendum on it, and a means for elites to achieve political realignments in relation to each other and to the governance of "the poor" in response to it. In one sense, the conflict between the legislature and the governor and attorney general over the suppression of prostitution was not about prostitution or venereal disease at all, but an opportunity to conduct a highly symbolic and stylized debate over status in and through the medium of women's bodies. The status question, although a central and defining preoccupation of Puerto Rican politics, was all but irresolvable on the island, since, as was evident in the federal Congress's manipulation of the Jones Act, a purely insular consensus could always be trumped by remote players in Washington. One could even say that the different political groupings were not very far apart in 1918: all advocated remedies for the perceived colonial status of the island. Precisely because the struggles over politics and economics were so often fruitless, medicine and public health policy became important battlegrounds. Far more often than in purely political matters, we find productive disputes, in which, unlike the case of politics, alignments of Puerto Ricans versus North Americans could actually result in victories for Puerto Ricans. From there, it is possible to see that in another sense, the argument was literally and importantly about prostitutes. It mattered who governed and controlled the working classes—their labor, their loyalty, their families and sexuality, their votes in insular elections.

Opposition to the policy solidified the rather tenuous position of the Unionistas as the voice of popular dissatisfaction with North American rule, at a time when massive unemployment, skyrocketing prices, and acute labor conflict were drawing many to the Socialists, already the second-largest party on the island. Puerto Rico had three major political parties in 1918, linked to different class interests. The Unionist Party was the banner of the old *hacendado* coffee elite that had been displaced by North American sugar interests. The Unionistas had opposed U.S. citizenship and contained a significant faction that advocated independence; its dominant tendency, however, favored a loose alliance with the United States and home rule, a solution similar in structure to that of Canada within the British Commonwealth. The tiny Republicano Party argued that the appropriate framework for a self-governing republic in the U.S. system was statehood. They termed themselves progressives and were associated with the emergent professional class. The party was led by a U.S.-trained, black physician, José Celso Barbosa. The Socialist Party was an agrarian trade-unionist champion of the largely black and mixed-race cane cutters and urban municipal workers. It embraced strong ties with the United States as a means of expanding workers' political rights and defending itself against local elites. Alone among the political parties, the Socialist Party contained a significant number of women in prominent positions and advocated woman suffrage.[64]

Moreover, when the legislature called for Kern's removal, more than his "Puritanism" was on trial, more than his ability to impose "alien values" was being contested. At issue also was his involvement in the *Tapia* and *Muratti* cases. The delegation sent to Washington to demand Kern's removal over prostitution policy was at least as angry about the Supreme

Court cases as about prostitution. Socialist Party leader Santiago Iglesias later made this issue clear, saying that his only real objection to Kern was not prostitution policy, but rather

> his attitude in the Tapia and another similar case. That our own legal representative should use the influence of his office and the people's money to upset the decision of our Supreme Court and the Federal Court in giving us the right of grand jury is, to my mind, enough of an indictment.[65]

Another faction urged Kern's ouster on the grounds of profligacy and waste, arguing that deficit spending represented poor administration.[66] The charge that Kern was "presenting us as incapable of ruling our own destinies" in so forcefully promoting the policy strongly echoed the status question. In short, the debate over whether to support Kern's enforcement of the prostitution policy was turned into a referendum on U.S. administration as a whole.

The incarceration of women was pressed into service as an allegory for the relationship between the island and the mainland for both Puerto Ricans and North Americans. For Puerto Ricans, the notion of a disrespected citizenry was translated into a description of upright womanhood defiled or humble womanhood mistreated. The circulation of the story of Susanna Torres was a metaphor for this relationship. The young lady was said to have been humiliated—and possibly "ruined"—by this outrageous North American policy, much as the Spanish elite had been reduced and embarrassed by the indignities of being subject to North America. The assertions that prostitutes were simply impoverished women desperate to feed their starving children resonated because both hunger and reduced economic circumstances were part of the landscape of Puerto Rico under U.S. rule. Prostitutes were transformed from the dangerous women of the U.S. policy to an emblem of the victimized Puerto Rican people. Through rhetorics of gender and race, both Puerto Rican elites and North American colonials worked to solidify their claims to power, to position themselves in relation to each other, and to develop a series of pliable, manipulable symbols for understanding each other.

CHAPTER 3

Debating Reproduction

Birth Control, Eugenics, and Overpopulation
in Puerto Rico, 1920–1940

The brazenness of the Yankee invaders has reached the
extreme of trying to profane Puerto Rican motherhood; of
trying to invade the very insides of nationality.

> —Pedro Albizu Campos, leader, Nationalist Party

I have always believed that some method of restricting the
birth rate among the lower and more ignorant elements of the
population is the only salvation for the Island.

> —James Beverley, Governor of Puerto Rico

I . . . cannot agree that B. Control clinics can help the
condition of the country when any woman can receive such
help. . . . So many of the natives are unmoral. We want to put
the status of the home and legally married women and the
legitimate children on a higher plan than they are at present.

> —Charlotte Bermúdez, Presbyterian Board of
> Foreign Missions

With the end of World War I, the "problem" of working-class women
shifted from prostitution to issues of reproduction and birth control.
Struggles over birth control on the island drew on and promoted a number of different and often incompatible beliefs: that insular poverty was
caused by overpopulation; that birth control was a genocidal, American
plot; that excess childbearing caused maternal ill-health; and that the future prosperity of the island lay in smaller, "modern," eugenic families.

Birth control provided the policy issue, and eugenics, overpopulation, and maternal health provided the terms in which a number of larger issues were debated: nationalism and the status question, modernization, poverty, capitalism. The discursive and ideological arena of reproduction and sexuality became particularly important in the 1920s and '30s as the weak consensus for American rule deteriorated both on and off the island in the face of widespread poverty and hunger, and rapidly shifting alliances for change took shape and gave way to new ones. While the contest over nationalism in this period is usually recalled in terms of the dramatic events involving the Nationalist Party—the growing independence movement associated with Pedro Albizu Campos and the harsh measures used to put it down, including the 1936 Ponce massacre, where the police fired on a peaceful march[1]—it is helpful to note that there were at least three nationalisms being struggled over, and that questions of motherhood and birth control were crucial to all of them. One, of course, was the *independentista* nationalism of Albizu, which longed for a return to a pre-American Puerto Rico, imagined to some extent as an agrarian utopia in which everyone had enough to eat, where family was the bulwark of society, and where Spanish-ness was preeminent. This ideal of nationalism was not an egalitarian vision exactly, and gender was a defining inequality; it identified women with motherhood, which in turn became "the insides of nationhood"—mothers made citizens, reproducing both bodies and culture. A contrasting ideal of nationalism was the North American version that sought protection for the (white, U.S.) nation from too many of "them"—working-class and/or dark-skinned people. It was an exclusive nationalism derived from "hard" eugenics, which feared the reproduction of the lower classes, Puerto Ricans in general, and, indeed, all non-"Nordics." A third, modernizing nationalism was associated with missionaries, social workers, reformers, and public health professionals—both Puerto Rican and North American. It suggested that the state of the family was the key to the well-being of the island, and that reducing large families, the number of irregular marriages, and the high maternal and infant mortality rates of the (increasing landless) rural subsistence farmers and urban and agricultural working classes was crucial to improving the economic status of the island. The latter two nationalisms informed the supporters of birth control, while the nationalism of Albizu (and the multifaceted opposition to birth control from the island's Catholic bishops) provided the opposition. Nevertheless, it would be a mistake to describe these as mutually exclusive positions, particularly when it came to feminists. While concern over modernizing the family was an explicit motivating force for insular feminism, many of the most visible feminist leaders and birth control supporters on the island were also *independentistas,* however much the nationalism of the party was predicated on equating motherhood and nationhood. Even so, these same people had considerable dealings with the most conservative eugenicists and overpopulationists from the mainland. What emerges from all this boundary-blurring among supporters of birth control is not so much ideological muddiness as a group of strong-minded and pragmatic women, most but not all of whom were Puerto Rican, who championed birth control as an unmitigated good thing in the face of ongoing attempts by both colonialist and nationalist men to manipulate woman, and woman-as-mother, as a symbol.

NATIONALISTS AND CATHOLICS

In the 1930s the Nationalist movement of Albizu began to argue that the existence of birth control on the island was part of a U.S. federal policy of genocide, a position taken up by the Catholic Church throughout the next several decades. As many Puerto Rican feminists have pointed out, the Nationalist Party relied on an ideal of a pre-U.S.-intervention family that was large and dominated by fathers and husbands. Albizu argued:

> The brazenness of the Yankee invaders has reached the extreme of trying to profane Puerto Rican motherhood; of trying to invade the very insides of nationality. When our women lose the transcendental and divine concept that they are not only mothers of their children but mothers of all future generations of Puerto Rico, if they come to lose that feeling, Puerto Rico will disappear within a generation.[2]

In the Nationalist Party of Albizu, nationalism, motherhood, and a Hispanophilic, conservative Catholicism were closely entangled. With the only "non-colonized" moment in Puerto Rican history being more than four hundred years distant, Albizu looked to Spain for models for the independent Puerto Rican nation, a longing predicated in part on a nostalgic narrative of an originary family, a story that glorified maternity.

Albizu's Puerto Rican Nationalist Party emerged from obscurity in 1932. It briefly occupied center stage by accusing a Rockefeller Foundation doctor of gross medical malfeasance in perpetrating deadly experiments with cancer on the island. The evidence was a bitter, vicious letter written by North American physician Cornelius Rhoads, in which he heaped abuse on Puerto Ricans as a group and claimed to have killed several "and injected cancer into seven more" in his capacity as a physician. Rhoads, with characteristic insensitivity, shrugged the letter off as a "joke." Ultimately, an investigation of the health status of Rhoads's patients exonerated both the Rockefeller program and Rhoads (who went on to an illustrious career on the mainland, including the directorship of the Sloan-Kettering Institute and medical oversight of the now-infamous chemical weapons tests on unprotected U.S. soldiers during World War II).[3] Nevertheless, the incident generated considerable discussion in insular newspapers and (appropriately) cast a long shadow over the integrity of U.S. philanthropic efforts on the island and the benevolence of North Americans' intentions more broadly.[4] The Rhoads affair—remembered to this day on the island—also left an odd and little-noted legacy. It marked the first time that Puerto Ricans construed efforts to enact birth control measures as part of a genocidal plot by North Americans. The U.S. government, the Nationalist Party argued during the Rhoads affair, "counsels such measures as will finish the work of extermination and displacement: emigration and birth control."[5] Not only did economic exploitation work to impoverish Puerto Ricans, the party suggested, but the mainland government was also actively trying to kill insular citizens by inducing disease, to displace them through emigration, and to prevent their reproduction through birth control. The irony of this charge is that, at the time, there was little mainland support for birth control on the island; in 1932 it was almost exclusively Puerto Rican women who were promoting such a program. But by the party's account, motherhood was equated with Puerto Rican-ness, and birth control, in this dualistic universe, could only be a North American plot.

A few months later, in the spring of 1932, a struggle between Nationalist Party and U.S. colonialist accounts of "overpopulation" on the island took place in the pages of Margaret Sanger's *Birth Control Review.* This argument suggests a great deal about how compacted a symbol birth control really was, at once an argument about economics, poverty, nationality, and U.S. political and military intervention. A mainland writer, Theodore Schroeder, offered an impassioned piece on "Porto Rico's Population Problem."[6] He painted a bleak picture of life on the island and suggested that for a host of ills—hunger, homelessness, lack of educational opportunity, unemployment, disease (especially syphilis), poor housing—"the largest contributing factor is overpopulation." (Although for Schroeder this was a timeless condition of the island, it bears remembering that he was writing during the depths of the Depression.) Overpopulation, he suggested, had been exacerbated by U.S. public health interventions, which, he claimed, had lowered the death rate (as we have seen, they had not). His recommendation was birth control, imposed by force if necessary; he suggested the federal government employ the military. Schroeder warned darkly that the growing population on the island meant that if the alternative was "pillage as the only means of getting food," then the U.S. army would be forced to restore civil order brutally: "There will be, of course, American soldiers and machine guns to reduce the population. Perhaps this is the best method of solving the problem, but if the time for machine guns should ever come, where will the major responsibility lie?" Sooner or later, he warned, the force of the military might be required to put down Puerto Ricans' unruly reproduction.

This rhetorical threat of the deployment of the U.S. military against Puerto Rican civilians did not go unanswered. José Enamorado Cuesta, secretary of the Nationalist Party, shot back a pointed reply to the *Birth Control Review* article.

> As a Porto Rican who feels himself a freeman, I cannot help taking exception [to the article. The author] does not tell your readers that it is directly at the door of American capitalism that the blame must be laid for everything that is wrong in Porto Rico today. . . . He does not tell that in thirty-four years of American intervention, the people have been dispossessed of their land and brought to the condition of paupers. . . . Our real problem lies in the actual control by American capital of practically all our wealth. . . . We may, and we may not enact birth control laws (I think we would) as soon as the American flag is lowered from our public buildings. The main thing is that it be lowered, the sooner the better.[7]

Enamorado read Schroeder's concerns about "overpopulation" as an economic theory in drag, which pointed to sex and reproduction to distract from a discussion of the role of North American corporations and the federal government on the island. Enamorado's letter, demanding an end to U.S. intervention on the island, makes legible the apocalyptic vision offered by Schroeder, of North American military might violently putting down an uprising. The nationalist movement had made the possibility of an anti-American uprising a real concern for many people from the mainland, and a hope for some Puerto Ricans. In the condensed space of an article and a letter responding to it, these two men managed to turn birth control and motherhood into the grounds for a debate on the legitimacy of North American military and economic dominance of the island, as well as the remedy for the increasingly desperate hunger and landlessness of the island's peasant and working classes.

This Nationalist position on birth control had its roots in the Catholic opposition of the 1920s, which was every bit as preoccupied as the Nationalist Party with questions of economy and motherhood. While Puerto Rican supporters of birth control—like those in the neo-Malthusian movement internationally—cited overpopulation as a key reason why birth control should be decriminalized, the bishops assigned to Puerto Rico turned to both economics and motherhood to oppose the neo-Malthusian arguments. As Annette Ramírez de Arellano and Conrad Seipp have shown, in the 1920s the Catholic response to the overpopulation argument followed the contours of European depopulationists. Bishop Joseph Caruana warned Puerto Ricans against the sin of "race suicide," which is to say, the problem of exterminating themselves as a people by failing to reproduce.[8] Two Dominican priests, Martin Bertsen and Marcos Martins, criticized the Malthusian logic of overpopulation, saying that, historically, populations had not grown in exponential proportions, and that wealth had tended to grow more quickly than population. They added, "The Italian economist Ferrero, in diametrical opposition to Malthusian theory, arrived at the conclusion that a country in which the population continued growing exponentially, runs the risk of becoming too rich." An article in the Catholic weekly, *El Piloto,* cited France as a nation committing suicide and argued that depopulation there was contributing to France's failure to compete economically with Germany.[9]

The two priests also based their arguments on the romanticized image of the Puerto Rican mother with many children. Physician José Montenegro, arguing in defense of the Catholic position, warned against birth control use, arguing that interference with reproduction would result in madness. "There is no greater folly," he wrote, "than exposing the queen of the home to such tortures, depriving her of the natural satisfaction of seeing herself surrounded by all her rosebuds."[10] Modern life, including the use of birth control, was rendering women delicate and neurasthenic. Birth control could upset physical and emotional balance, disrupt the nervous system, even cause cancer. The bishops took up the health argument in a slightly different vein, suggesting that contraception "has always been condemned for reasons of moral health, as an abominable crime, gravely immoral." The eugenic emphasis of the mainland birth control movement, they argued, was "repugnant and unjust." Later children, the bishops insisted, were usually healthier and stronger than the first, and there was no way to predict whether children would be physically or mentally unsound. Indeed, the reduced number of children of the families of the well-to-do suffered, for "is it not a fact that such children, pampered by the exaggerated attentions of their parents, are almost always ill-behaved, nervous, egotistical, discontented, selfish, and lacking in energy and self-sacrifice?"[11]

Another significant uproar over birth control on the island developed in 1935 and equally turned on issues of nationalism. Ironically, however, it was organized within the Catholic Church, largely by Irish clerics. This time, the charge that there at least *was* a North American–directed birth control program stood on firmer ground; various New Deal agencies had lent material aid to the birth control effort. Insular Catholic activists and bishops abruptly put an end to this federal effort, however, arguing that birth control was a "foreign" (non-Catholic) practice. Catholic Action, a group in Ponce, wrote President Roosevelt to demand an end to the program on the grounds that birth control was "contrary to the Principles sustained by the Catholic Religion which is professed by the great majority of the people of this island." Similarly, Bishop Edwin Byrne of San Juan privately accused the head of the Department of the Interior of "foisting birth control in this Catholic country."[12] A few months later, when supporters failed to end the project, the Catholic opposition went public. Bishop Byrne warned Carlos Chardón of the Puerto Rico Reconstruction Administration (PRRA) by telegram: "Today's *El Mundo* [newspaper] states that the PRRA is reopening *centros maternales* . . . Said Centros abetted artificial birth control . . . If PRRA does so, the Catholic Church will publicize same throughout United States and make public opposition here."[13] The program continued, and a month later Bryne did as he had threatened by arranging for an article to appear in the New York City Church organ, the *Brooklyn Tablet*. It was timed for maximum damage to the Puerto Rican program. Franklin D. Roosevelt, with only a month to go in his reelection campaign, acted to protect his base of Catholic support on the mainland. The program was hastily canceled.[14]

By the late 1930s, Catholicism, motherhood, and Puerto Rican-ness had become so conflated in birth control rhetoric that mainland Catholics could use such rhetoric to speak on behalf of the Puerto Rican mother—even against the island's elected representatives. In 1937 the insular legislature passed a bill removing legal impediments to birth control (which had been illegal under the island's version of the Comstock law, as well as under the federal act). Bishop Aloysius Willinger of Ponce, while stopping short of the "genocide" argument, nevertheless insisted that birth control was an immoral American practice that was being imposed on Puerto Rico. The charge was echoed by the Puerto Rican chap-

ter of the Catholic Daughters of America, who confronted the then-sec-
retary of the legislature and one of a significant number of Puerto Rican
women in public life, Maria Luisa Arcelay, arguing that Arcelay's support for the legislation was anti-Catholic, anti-woman, and anti-Puerto
Rican.[15] The manifest irony of members of a mainland-based organization like the Catholic Daughters (or a North American bishop like Willinger) insisting that the elected legislature was un-Puerto Rican was apparently lost on them.

If necessary, bishops in Puerto Rico could use the contrasting nationalist rhetoric of "American-ness" as well. Bishop Byrne warned the colonial governor, Blanton Winship, that if he signed the bill legalizing birth
control, "then our [U.S.] Government will be following the lead of Communist Russia." Governor Winship, if unimpressed by charges of communism, was nevertheless concerned about the argument that birth control was un-Puerto Rican. He sought the advice of U.S. Secretary of the
Interior Ernest Gruening, who wrote back, "Leave Puerto Rico and ap-
point Rafael Menéndez Ramos, the Commissioner of Agriculture, as acting governor. . . . He's a devout Catholic, but he'll sign the bill. Then it
will have been the work of a Catholic House, a Catholic Senate and a
Catholic Puerto Rican governor.[16] Menéndez did indeed sign the bill,
though the Church argued all the way to the U.S. Supreme Court that the
act was un-American, violating federal obscenity statutes. The Court in
1939 upheld the law nevertheless. That year, birth control in Puerto Rico
finally did become a permanent U.S. federal government program
through funds made available under the Social Security Act. Paradoxically, the Church dropped the charge that birth control was an American plot at precisely the moment when it became a stable, federally
funded program.

MAINLAND OVERPOPULATIONISTS

The roots of the idea of overpopulation for commentators like Schroeder
in his *Birth Control Review* piece were complex; it was a concept with a
tangled history born of politics, statistics, and struggles over professional
legitimacy. As other historians have pointed out, two groups began to
sound alike and work together to popularize such ideas in the 1920s: reformers associated with the birth control movement and academic demographers and population experts with roots in the eugenics movement.[17] In the context of Puerto Rico, another thread was interwoven,
as José Enamorada Cuesta noted: overpopulation was also an economic

theory and a defense of the continued rule of the United States in the face
of the apparent failure of U.S. policy. Beginning with the inauguration
of the British Malthusian League in the mid–nineteenth century, birth
control advocates had been popularizing the notion that excess reproduction caused poverty.[18] In the 1920s, birth controllers, or neo-Malthusians
as they were called, gained new stature from the overlapping sciences of
eugenics and population demography. Eugenicists like Guy Irving Birch
and C.C. Little began to publish in both the *Birth Control Review* and
in places like the biologists' *Journal of Heredity*. While historians of eugenics have noted a steep decline in the popularity of eugenics among biologists in the 1930s, feminist scholars have commented that eugenics
did not so much disappear as go into the work of population demography.[19] While there is a distinction worth making here about kinds of
eugenicists—social workers and public health workers thought of eugenics differently than biologists—this feminist insight is quite helpful in
following the career of eugenics in Puerto Rico.

Population demography stressed class, racial, and geographical differences with respect to reproduction. The writings of people like Madison Grant, who was concerned about low "Nordic" birth rates, and
Lothrop Stoddard in *The Rising Tide of Color* are notorious examples
of a kind of reproductive racism that held that the high birthrates among
non-"Nordics," or "Anglo-Saxons," constituted a threat to their America, but much of the work in population demography was more explicitly about class than racial difference. Raymond Pearl, for example, edited the eminently respectable *Journal of Heredity*, which in the 1930s
ran articles on topics like the "Implications of Current Demographic
Trends For Birth Control and Eugenics," which argued that those reproducing the most were the least wealthy and educated, or "Overpopulation" and "The Differential Birthrate," which investigated causes for
higher birth rates among working-class people, or the elitist "New England Puritans: An Obituary," which argued that the old stock had been
overrun—to cite a few examples.[20] Another important outlet for scientific research on human difference was the more mainstream, less hys-
terical, and arguably, therefore, more insidious, *Human Biology*, which
over the course of three issues in the 1930s ran articles on "The Population Problem in Japan" (class differences in fertility), "Factors Associated with the Growth and Nutrition of Porto Rican Children," the
"Common Cold in Jews and Non-Jews" (racial differences in children's
growth rates and illnesses), and an article on "The Negro Infant" (which
canvassed everything from twinning, to skin pigment in the tropics, to

assertions that the Negro birth rate was sharply higher than that for whites).[21] By 1937, the paradigm of reproduction as a significant form of racial, class-based, and geographic difference was firmly established. A review article in the *Journal of Heredity*, in which Guy Burch asked the disingenuous question, "Overpopulation or Underpopulation?—A Review of Conflicting Opinions," captures this shift. The article concluded that no serious scientist could any longer believe anything other than that the global population was growing alarmingly, and that the segment that was increasing was of the worst sort. Native-born whites, demographers concluded, were declining dramatically in numbers, largely through the combined effects of birth control, high taxes, and unfair numerical competition from the worst quarter of the population.[22] During the Depression, a related notion of overpopulation was popularized in the concern over "relief babies," as social workers and popular writers scrutinized the habits and morals of those on relief and found them wanting. "Relief babies" entered the lexicon of headline writers as an unnecessary and unwelcome drain on the public coffers, a commentary on the immorality of the poor, and a critique of New Deal programs.[23]

In Puerto Rico, the word and idea of overpopulation first emerged early in the century. Its initial usage was not to describe a condition of the island as a whole, as it would later come to be used, but rather to refer specifically to the idea that the working class was reproducing too much. It was first used in policy debates to explain off-island labor contracts, where agents from U.S. business or agriculture would offer transportation to places like Hawaii, Arizona, or Georgia in exchange for work contracts, often involving very low wages. Such agents were welcomed by colonial governors, but not by Republicano and Socialist leaders, who charged that the arrangements were little better than legalized slavery. Governor Yager in 1914 and others thereafter responded to such charges by arguing that they were helping to relieve the island's unemployment and its "overpopulation."[24] Socialists on the island also began to use the term at about the same time, though to different ends. They used it to refer to the birth control movement and to describe a deliberate strategy by the laboring classes to limit the number of workers. As one socialist commentator put it, "The density of the rural population makes the situation of the peasant more difficult and painful daily, which, by increasing itself [*desdoblarse*] prolifically, creates new and numerous competitors in labor and sustenance."[25]

Beginning in the mid-1920s, and decisively by the 1930s, however, the term *overpopulation* had acquired another meaning, one that blamed excessive sexuality and fertility for the poverty of the island as a whole.

In public health journals and newspapers on the island, North American researchers and Creole officials alike blamed overpopulation for a multitude of ills—poverty, delinquency, homelessness, prostitution, disease.[26] Where earlier, even health professionals who supported birth control had routinely argued against the overpopulation thesis ("Our social life requires both quantity and quality of men with distinct roles," wrote one physician in 1917[27]), by the 1920s arguments for diminishing poverty through birth control had become quite common. Popular, health, and policy writers began to characterize the problem of overpopulation as a matter of simple arithmetic—as a statistical relationship between the birth rate and the death rate or as a relationship between total population and resources. By 1926, the annual report of the Bureau of Vital Statistics had begun routinely to comment on the island's overpopulation in these terms. That year's report—distributed widely through the newly founded *Porto Rico Health Review*—devoted its first pages to commentary on population density and the excessive birth rate, and noted, "Industrially undeveloped and still backward agriculturally, Porto Rico has been, however, steadily increasing its population at an astounding rate."[28] Modernization and progress, in this sort of account, required a change in both production and reproduction. Other writers compared population figures to acres dedicated to food production.[29]

Ironically, however, by making an argument that on the one hand was obsessively interested in working-class and *jíbara* (peasant) women, but that on the other collapsed distinctions between classes by relying on statistical generalizations about the entire population of the island, public health and governmental officials produced an argument that was often untrue on its own terms. It ignored the fact that most crops on the island were—and had been for centuries—grown for export, while most food consumed on the island was imported; it saw the relationship of population to food as unmediated by power, politics, and the island's place in the world economy.[30] The discourse of overpopulation invoked a nostalgia for self-sufficient communities whose stability was threatened by a sudden rise in population caused by the imposition of modernity, especially medicine and science. Yet the targets of overpopulation rhetoric were never communities historically isolated from modernity, but colonies and former colonies, active participants for centuries in the world economy. Food supplies and populations do not exist in stable, simple relationships. Food is a commodity, exchanged for cash through elaborate networks of trade, transportation, and political relations. In the Puerto Rican colonial context, arable land was often devoted to cash crops like sugar, and food was imported from other places. It was social and economic relations, not the ratio of population and acres of land, that caused some people to get more than others, yet this arithmetic logic provided the idiom in which the problem was often posed.

Overpopulation, as an explanation for insular poverty, would have had to refer to a population growing faster than wealth. However, according to the same official statistics overpopulationists used, the per capita incomes of Puerto Ricans underwent spectacular increases from the second decade of the twentieth century through the late 1920s; most of this, however, was in sugar exports (largely, then, increases in wealth were in the hands of North Americans on the island).[31] At the same time, however, one study found that male unemployment had increased from 20 to 30 percent from 1920 to 1926 (and the governor's report indicated that overall unemployment had increased to 60 percent by 1930).[32] This fact points up the limitations of per capita income as a statistical device and the problem with the overpopulation argument: wealth is, of course, not evenly distributed among the population, so a rise in overall wealth can occur at the same time that poverty increases among the working classes. Indeed, as many Puerto Rican historians have pointed out, in the insular economic context of the 1920s, sugar production was increasing precisely at the expense of *jíbaro* subsistence farming, and even local elites were losing their land because of changes in tariffs and credit.[33] On its own terms, the overpopulation argument often failed to explain widespread hunger on the island.[34] To follow out the logic of the statistical data the Bureau of Vital Statistics offered: per capita income began to decline sharply in 1928 and 1929, following the island's devastating experience with Hurricane San Felipe, which destroyed that year's sugar crop; the lowest point was in 1933, after another major hurricane. Per capita income on the island largely followed mainland trends throughout the Depression (which arrived early, hastened by hurricane damage to agricultural infrastructure) and did not return to 1930 levels until 1940. Then, in the 1940s—as the rhetoric of overpopulation intensified—population grew, but per capita income grew much faster, doubling between 1940 and 1944, and tripling by 1952.[35] Population, in other words, failed utterly as an explanation of the *cause* of insular poverty; it did not even correlate with it. Nevertheless, the argument that uncontrolled Puerto Rican sexuality and reproduction were dangerous had sufficient force that it persisted even in the face of evidence that flatly contradicted it.

For mainland North Americans, the discourse of overpopulation also expressed a sense that something had gone terribly awry on the island.

In the 1920s, popular, policy, and public health writing on the mainland about Puerto Rico was marked by a deepening pessimism about the ability of the United States to bestow well-being and prosperity on Puerto Rico. After 1930, articles in the mainland press spoke of the "troublous isle," "a complex of extremely difficult problems," of poverty, "rebellion," "sedition and students." Gone was the naive, cheerful tone of earlier years, when it was thought the simple presence of Americans would bring health and well-being; suspicion dawned among liberals and leftists that poverty and disease remained, that their cause was U.S. corporate sugar plantations, and that "imperialism" might be the proper name for U.S. policy on the island.[36] The nationalist movement, by 1933 fully outside the limited electoral system and advocating armed rebellion to secure independence from the United States, dealt another serious blow to North Americans' belief in the benevolence of the U.S. mission there. Ernest Greuning, Roosevelt's Director of the Division of Territories and Island Possessions of the Department of the Interior—a liberal but certainly no radical—could write in the *New York Times* in 1936 that Puerto Rico's

> long-growing economic distress account[s] for the agitation for independence. . . . A section of Puerto Rican opinion holds the United States responsible for the absorption of the lands of formerly small independent proprietors by absentee sugar companies. . . . It is undoubtedly true that the large profits of these companies—some as high as 100 per cent in a single year—profits which, as the Puerto Ricans complain, are promptly exported from the island, derive not from the legitimate returns from sugar processing but from the corporate ownership of land and the onerous conditions imposed thereby on the "colonos" and farm workers.[37]

Similarly, another mainland observer wrote in 1930,

> It is estimated that following the Spanish-American War the actual number of farms decreased by 30,000 while the large sugar and tobacco plantations increased their acreage by buying out the neighboring small farmers. . . . They sold because the large tobacco growers, and in still higher degree the sugar planters, were able to offer . . . unprecedently [*sic*] high prices for land. Having sold his farm, the small farmer, faced by rapidly rising land values on an island already thickly populated, was unable to buy another farm; and usually was unable to find a steady job, for the large planters naturally tend to the use of labor-saving machinery.[38]

Governors Theodore Roosevelt and James Beverley popularized a new discourse about the island, that insular residents were desperately poor.

Increasingly, even those responsible for carrying out the work of colonialism felt there might be some justice to the nationalist movement's economics.

In many ways, overpopulation served as a reply to and encapsulation of this policy concern: something was wrong in Puerto Rico, but it could not be entirely the fault of the United States. As *Literary Digest* summarized it in 1932, "The Porto Rico stork is . . . a prodigious producer. And his 'overproduction' is blamed for a series of evils—unemployment, low wages, malnutrition, and disease."[39] Governor Beverley confided to Margaret Sanger in 1933,

> I have always believed that some method of restricting the birth rate among the lower and more ignorant elements of the population is the only salvation for the Island. The tragedy of the situation is that the more intelligent classes voluntarily restrict their birth rate, while the most vicious, most ignorant, and most helpless and hopeless part of the population multiplies with tremendous rapidity."[40]

By 1932, responding to the problem of overpopulation had become the cornerstone of federal policy in Puerto Rico, as the memoir of one of Franklin Roosevelt's close advisors makes clear.[41] Whereas a decade and a half earlier, the military and federal government had identified the "problem" of making Puerto Ricans into proper citizens as residing in prostitution—nonreproductive sexuality that threatened the "legitimate" reproduction of the nation—now even marital sexuality was dangerous. The Puerto Rican family had to be reformed.

The extent to which overpopulation was not only an economic theory but a kind of nationalism can be seen in how an additional question consistently informed the twentieth-century North American popular and political perspective on insular status: the question of race. While Puerto Rican *mestizaje* confounded North American efforts to describe race in terms of black and white, it also increased the range of possible descriptions. The question of whether the island population was characterized as mostly white or black—and, one suspects, as therefore *essentially* black or white—was closely imbricated with questions of status. Writers who described the island as mostly white favored independence; those who saw it as black argued for continued U.S. rule. By extension, then, the question of overpopulation intervened in a debate about Puerto Rican race in subtle (and not so subtle) ways. For instance, two public policy studies from the early 1930s, The Brookings Institute's *Porto Rico and Its Problems* (1930) and Justine and Bailey Diffie's *Porto Rico: A Broken Pledge* (1931),

took opposite views of Puerto Ricans' race, and made quite different rec-
ommendations about status and population. The Brookings Institute report concluded that Puerto Rico's problems could be alleviated only
through reducing the population and strengthening U.S. rule on the island.
It also had the following to saying about the race of Puerto Ricans:

> Racial statistics in Porto Rico are only approximations to the truth, as the
> population is extremely intermixed and there are not only two colors, but
> an infinity of shades. It is next to impossible, in many cases, to determine
> whether a person is white or slightly colored. In such cases, of which there
> are thousands, the strictness or tolerance of the census agent determines
> how the person is to be classed.[42]

While beginning with a description of a "mixed" race, this passage
quickly reasserted that people, in fact, were either white or "colored,"
though it was "next to impossible" to determine which. The insistence
that this difference still mattered, even in the absence of visually distin-
guishable markers, seems the reductio ad absurdum of the notion of
white (though not black) racial "purity." *Porto Rico: A Broken Pledge*
reached opposite conclusions. Overpopulation was not a problem on the
island, the authors argued, but U.S. capitalist extraction was, and the
United States had no legitimate role to play in the governance of the island. In accounting for the race of Puerto Ricans, these authors, too, began with a historical narrative of racial amalgamation. They, however,
resolved the issue in the opposite way:

> Despite this racial mélange, however, there are two classes in whose
> composition there is scarcely any foreign blood. The *jibaros*, or peasants,
> are of pure Spanish extraction, and inhabit the interior of the Island. The
> pure blooded Spaniards of the higher class have remained the leaders
> socially and politically, and largely retain the characteristics of their
> ancestors.[43]

In this text, Puerto Rico was characteristically Spanish and capable of
self-rule, whereas for the Brookings Institution report, the writing em-
phasizes an African presence and the need for U.S. governance.

Travelers' tales likewise contained contrasting theories concerning
what ailed Puerto Rico, the value of the U.S. presence, and the "race" of
Puerto Ricans. *Dynamite on Our Doorstep* (1945) was written by a
teacher who had spent two years on the island. It is a pro-intervention
book, arguing, among other things, that the North American presence
had been an unambivalently good thing for the island, and that most of

Puerto Rico's troubles could be attributed to its birth rate. The author, Wenzell Brown, was also even more certain than the Brookings Institute about the race of Puerto Ricans:

> The Puerto Rican will tell you that only 30 per cent of the island is colored. This means that only 30 per cent answer "colored" when asked by the census taker. Some place the figure with colored blood as high as 85 per cent.[44]

Nationalist discontent was fomented by "Negroes," Brown argued, and the nationalists systematically misrecognized the cause of Puerto Rican poverty—they lay it at the feet of the North Americans, when, he insisted, it was caused by overpopulation.

White Elephants in the Caribbean (1936) reached opposite conclusions. Its author weighed in emphatically against the "meddling" U.S. social policy in Puerto Rico and read the "race" of Puerto Ricans in terms of the absolute dominance of Spanish "blood" over African (the precise opposite of the "one-drop rule" of African hyperdescent sometimes operative in the mainland United States context).

> The crux of the whole American problem in Puerto Rico [is] "Spanish blood." Purity of racial blood is all that is left guarding the time-honored strain, tradition and legend of the Spaniard. Curiously, this racial endurance and hardihood persists in whatever corpuscles are communicated through a few drops of white Spanish blood to an African, through miscegenation. They, too, carry on vicariously the Spanish tradition. One steadfast manifestation of Spanish blood is its antipathy to and repellence of the domination of the upstart American.[45]

These four books spanned a decade and a half and policy and popular genres, telling two typical stories. In one, overpopulation was produced by dark-skinned people who needed to change their reproduction in order to be made into proper U.S. citizens. In the other, Puerto Ricans were white and Spanish and entitled to self-rule. In short, overpopulation, by virtue of being aligned with the status question, became also an argument about race, since Puerto Rican status was always entangled with narratives about the race of the island's inhabitants.

THE BIRTH CONTROL MOVEMENT:
LEFT AND FEMINIST NATIONALISMS

If the Nationalist Party on the one hand and U.S. colonialists, overpopulationists, and conservative eugenicists on the other were mirror images of each other, arguing for and against U.S. rule through the idiom of birth control, there was a third position. Liberal professionals—Puerto Rican and North American, women and men—forged a modernizing nationalism that was equally hinged to maternity and reproduction, but that rested neither on an uncritical glorification of Puerto Rican motherhood nor an equally adamant revulsion to it. Instead, through discourses of maternal health, illegitimacy, and a progressive eugenics, modernizing middle-class professionals sought to reform motherhood, to render both material aid and (often patronizing) advice to working-class women. This "soft" eugenics stressed that the excessive childbearing of working-class women was involuntary, unwanted, and detrimental to the health of the mother, the children, and the nation. By reforming working-class families, these professionals hoped they could improve the economic, social, and to some extent racial foundations of the island. Their story is important, for while their victories were few and contingent in the 1930s, by the end of the 1940s, this political formation would gain access to power in the form of control of the office of governor and populist economic reform.

While the origins of a movement probably tell us little about its nature, it bears repeating that the nationalist charge that the birth control movement was North American in origin was untrue. An insular birth control movement had begun in the 1920s under the auspices of the Puerto Rican Socialist Party—before most places on the mainland (outside of New York City) even had an active birth control movement. The ideas came as much from Europe as from the United States,[46] and there was little involvement by North Americans in the Puerto Rican birth control movement until the 1930s, yet the merits of birth control were widely debated in insular newspapers beginning in the second decade of the twentieth century. Birth control was endorsed by the Socialist Party in 1920; and a bill to decriminalize its promotion was first introduced in 1923.[47] In 1925, socialist José Lanauze Rolón founded the island's first birth control group, the Liga para el control de natalidad de Puerto Rico, or Birth Control League of Puerto Rico.[48]

In the 1920s, the modernizing nationalism of birth control rhetoric was explicit, and leftist. In this formulation, birth control was quite divorced from sex, and even families; birth control programs would be passed by the insular legislature and would begin immediately to minimize the number of barefoot, undernourished, and uneducated children hanging about town squares and inhabiting the thatched *bohíos* of the countryside. In 1922 Luis Muñoz Marín, then a backer of the Socialist

Party, described overpopulation as a problem that victimized the nation, and he urged birth control as its solution. "If there is any country on earth that needs the practice of practical Malthusianism [birth control] more, in order to save itself economically and spiritually, than Puerto Rico, I have not been able to find it on the map" he wrote.[49] A year later, he added that the island had become "a raft adrift with 1,300,000 victims who scratch, bite and kick to obtain the few supplies on board, [where] there is more hunger than there are meals." He continued, "The problem can be attacked in two ways; reducing the population or increasing wealth. . . . I believe that reducing the population is the most important, the most practical, and the cheapest. Scientific methods of avoiding conception should be taught to all poor families who wish to learn them."[50] An editorial in San Juan's largest daily, *El Mundo,* argued:

> These endless offspring of our *jíbaros* are the misfortune that retard our advancement. The standard of our peasant families goes down every time a new child arrives to make the subsistence problem more difficult to resolve, and thus, little by little there arises a rural generation undermined from their childhood, destined from before birth to pass unprofitably through life, victims of themselves, of the fatal inheritance bequeathed them by their progenitors. We would be grateful if the government sought a way for our country to stop being so overcrowded—and with residents without the opportunity to succeed in life.[51]

A modern nation ought to have fewer such children, and better prospects for their thin, overworked, and sometimes desperate parents. The two most visible leaders of the birth control movement were perfect symbols of this modernism: Muñoz Marín, heir of Puerto Rico's most respected (if somewhat conservative) political family, himself a socialist and poet living in New York's Greenwich Village and advocating radical new ideas. The second, José Lanauze Rolón, was Afro–Puerto Rican, a Communist, and a physician trained in the United States at Howard University, the embodiment not only of new scientific ideas but, like that other black physician and political leader José Celso Barbosa, a symbol of the new opportunities for black Puerto Ricans made available through North American education. Birth control thus became a symbol of things not done by an older, conservative, Church- and tradition-bound generation who lacked the imagination for progress or a commitment to ending the poverty of the laboring class.

Members of Lanauze's Liga understood themselves to be trying to

produce happy families, a healthier working class, and a wealthier nation through birth control. Its statement of purpose identified "practical
procreation" as a "first step towards social eugenics," which was a
means for "combating ignorance, poverty, and crime," a way to producing "healthier, better educated, and happier children" and improving the lot of the working classes.[52] Shortly after the group's founding,
editorials in El Mundo and the Times of San Juan supported them, calling theirs a progressive and enlightened cause. El Mundo suggested one
of the reasons why their campaign would necessarily focus on working-
class people, while reiterating themes of family, progress, and national
improvement:

> For part of the population, the legislation [prohibiting birth control] is a
> dead letter; for the rest, disgracefully those who most need it, those who
> most need to try to limit their offspring, those who do not have the means
> to feed, instruct, and allow their children to progress, this law has a fatal
> importance: they are completely ignorant of something that could serve as
> the foundation for their domestic happiness.[53]

The movement was particularly concerned with contributing to "allevi-
ating the desperate poverty of the home of the working classes" and
helping them to produce "children healthier in body and soul," because,
"in almost all civilized countries there exist today robust movements of
public opinion to instruct the masses in prudent and scientific birth control."[54] Theirs was a modernizing, civilizing nationalism.

The early movement embraced the notion that it was the nation, not
individuals, that required birth control. The Times suggested that "perhaps there is no other place in this world where birth control would be
more beneficial and should be [more] greatly encouraged than in Porto
Rico . . . this rapidly overpopulated island." Liga member Alfredo Bern-
abé wrote to Margaret Sanger that there was a real urgency to birth control propaganda in Puerto Rico, "as it is the most thickly populated
country in the whole world and I dare to say the poorest."[55] Lanauze
Rolón, publicly debating the group's position on birth control on the island with the Catholic Church in insular newspapers from December
1925 to September 1926, argued principally that "prudent birth control
contributes to the happiness of the home and the progress of the community."[56] A legislator reintroducing a bill to decriminalize birth control
told a newspaper: "In my judgment this legislation is essential to the desire [afán] that encourages everyone to construct a better nation, healthier and happier for us and our descendants."[57] A civic leader pronounced

to the League of Women Voters in San Juan that "the major obstacle that retards our culture is the excess of population that tends to maintain a low standard of living, relative to the continent."[58] Muñoz Marín linked the individual, the nation, and overpopulation most eloquently, saying,

> The influence of this horrifying situation [of overpopulation] on our customs and moral sensibility is more disastrous every day. We carry generous blood in our veins, and now we must not be generous; we harbor in our souls instincts of kindness, and the struggle for life does not permit us to be kind. All that is elevated and noble in our collective soul is starving to death in this damnable and grotesque circumstance.[59]

According to Lanauze, though, the mere existence of a birth control movement represented progress, as it put Puerto Rico in the company of the "civilized nations of the world," all of which he characterized as being centrally concerned with the quantity and quality of its population.

From 1932 to 1936 the birth control cause was taken over from these left groups by nurses and social workers, who were feminists equally possessed of a modernizing nationalism. The wider political agenda of this group of Puerto Rican and North American women included the consolidation of social work and nursing as autonomous professions, the creation of maternal and child health programs, the ending of illegitimacy, obtaining suffrage for literate women (exclusively), and the extension of mainland minimum-wage legislation to the working classes of Puerto Rico.[60] While the historiographical literature has (correctly) emphasized the distance between the interests of these (petit bourgeois, professionalizing) women from the robust working-class feminism in the socialist and trade-unionist camps,[61] the members of the modernizing middle classes themselves would have perceived no such a split. Precisely because their political orientation was organized as a nationalism, they did not see class in the European sense, but understood themselves to be seeking the good of the nation as a whole. That is, class was not for them a fixed characteristic; one was not essentially, or permanently, working class. From the perspective of the nation, it was perfectly consistent to advocate minimum-wage legislation and restricted suffrage; both a minimum wage and education were necessary for the improvement of individuals, and hence for the forging of a modern citizenry. Birth control— and motherhood—were crucial to this feminist nationalism. Unlike the left nationalism of Lanauze and Muñoz Marín, for this feminist nationalism birth control operated precisely in the realm of the family, producing modern nuclear families and healthy mothers able to educate their small number of children and transmit the values of progress and modernization. Their goals—like those of feminists in the United States and elsewhere—were to link maternalism, the state, and social advancement. (Puerto Rico's difference was that birth control, state maternalism, and suffrage were a unified feminist agenda, in contrast to the mainland, where these were the goals of women's groups very much at odds with each other).

Nurses and social workers were the main players in the beginnings of a clinic movement on the island, and in most cases, they were Puerto Rican by birth or ancestry. In 1932 a birth control clinic was opened in San Juan by Violet Callendar,[62] a nurse who had trained in the Harlem clinic of Margaret Sanger's Birth Control Clinical Research Bureau. Sanger violently disliked Callendar; she had not only dissuaded the Bureau from supporting her efforts, but had discouraged the Holland-Rantos company from supplying her clinic with free diaphragms.[63] With no support on the mainland and little ability to raise funds on the island, Callendar's clinic failed within months. Another clinic, opened in Lares by feminist leader Rosa González (also an activist for woman suffrage and the professionalization of nursing) failed as quickly.[64] There was a third attempt that same year, in Mayagüez, this one supported by Sanger, Protestant missionaries, a local women's group, and the prominent Puerto Rican physician Dr. Manuel Guzmán Rodríguez (active in the island's AMA and editor of its journal), but it too was short-lived.[65]

The intended clientele for these birth control clinics was working-class women; whatever the unmet need for birth control may have been among the middle and elite classes, they were not the target (and this undoubtedly was a factor in why these clinics so often failed; by intent, they were not self-supporting). Callendar told her funders, "The operation of birth control clinics where poor women may receive free, or for a nominal fee, reliable medical assistance would stop at its source the causes of much unhappiness and destitution."[66] Large families were a cause of poverty, and birth control could make the lives of working-class women happier. Birth control was, even more emphatically, a means of solving islandwide social problems. Callendar and her supporters wrote in their statement of purpose that they intended "to promote and propagate sexual education especially among the poor people . . . so as to able to develop strong and healthy future generations, and thus avoid the grave social [problem] of . . . dependency."[67] Not only could birth control reduce the burden on public and private charity, but it could ensure the health and well-being of the island's citizenry as a whole in the future.

Birth control was key to constituting the right sort of working-class family—small, nuclear, and legitimate. Charlotte Bermudez, a North American who started the Mayagüez clinic, stated this commitment in the negative: she was not interested in birth control if it did not promote legal marriage and legitimate birth. "Personally," she wrote Margaret Sanger,

> my interest declined when I discovered that the large majority of people here were mainly interested in helping most particularly the most un-fortunate women—those living in "concubináto" [as mistresses], which state is recognized by society as perfectly alright. I . . . cannot agree that B. Control clinics can help the condition of the country when any woman can receive such help. . . . So many of the natives are unmoral. We want to put the status of the home and legally married woman and the legitimate children on a higher plane than they are at present.[68]

The goal here is as much to "help the condition of the country" as it is to improve the lives of individual women; in Bermúdez's case, perhaps more. Birth control programs, in her mind, ought to strengthen the legitimate family; there was considerable danger that it would have the opposite effect unless clinics restricted their clientele to married women. Violet Callendar expressed a similar concern about men's lack of regard for marriage in their familial arrangements, albeit with more sympathy for the "other woman." She argued that men who had more than one family contributed a great deal to the harsh poverty in which women bore and raised children. As she wrote to Sanger:

> Some men here have as many as ten women. I know of one young man 26 years of age, who earns $10 a week; he has three women and 14 children with another child expected in the Spring. In the heart of San Juan I saw a pregnant woman walking the streets seeking admission into a hospital, and was finally told that there were no vacant beds. She finally dropped in a doorway after the membranes ruptured and a policeman called an ambulance.[69]

For these women, the irresponsibility of men and their habit of taking mistresses contributed a great deal to economic distress and "the condition of the country." Legitimate nuclear families, birth control, and male fidelity could strengthen the island nation.

The proper sort of family could also be implicitly white. A study sponsored by the University of Puerto Rico's School of Social Work gave a racial cast to the phenomenon of illegitimacy, noting that "the problem of illegitimacy is especially serious among the colored people." It correlated a host of ills with illegitimate birth, including poverty, hunger, and disease. The casualness with which working-class people, and perhaps working-class people of color in particular, treated the formation of households and their lack of regard for the institutional forms of church and state had frustrated all efforts of Spanish and U.S. colonial authorities to rectify it, and modernizing Puerto Rican social workers fared little better. "Illegitimacy," however, did not refer to women raising children without a man. Rather, according to a School of Social Work study, the overwhelming majority of "illegitimate" children lived with both their mother and their father; however, their parents' union had not been consecrated as a "legal" marriage and the children were therefore "illegitimate." It found that 43.5 percent of rural children under the age of 15 were illegitimate; however, a mere 9 percent of households were female-headed.[70] Living in "consensual unions" was not at all unusual in rural areas, where people had fairly circumscribed access to the institutions of church and state (and perhaps not a great deal of concern for them, either, since formalizing marriages was nevertheless possible, and secular and ecclesiastic authorities routinely urged it). The ubiquity of such arrangements made them no less prominent as a "social problem" that ought to be rectified for the good of the nation.

In 1935 a birth control program run with federal monies briefly replaced these underfunded and short-lived clinics. The federal program, however, was no less under the control of social workers and nurses. Initiated by two friends of Eleanor Roosevelt, Dorothy Bourne and Gladys Gaylord, it marked the success of the broader agenda—on the island and the mainland—of maternalist politics, which sought state support for mothers and their efforts, particularly those of working-class mothers, to provide for their families. A few years earlier, the (North American) governor James Beverley—a personal friend of Bourne's—had publicly supported the use of birth control. While Beverley's statement had elicited a considerable outcry from the Catholic press, on the island and off, it had also paved the way for the federal birth control program.[71] Run largely on the strength of the social workers that Bourne trained at the University of Puerto Rico, the program involved staff members' visiting birth control clients at their homes, initially to screen for eligibility, and afterward to ensure the clients' continued use of the method.[72] It also encompassed at least one diaphragm clinic, run out the School of Tropical Medicine at the University of Puerto Rico by gynecologist José Belaval.[73]

For Dorothy Bourne and the staff she recruited to be part of the
Puerto Rico Emergency Relief Administration (PRERA) birth control
project, the "overpopulation" of the nation was a dominant problem
that birth control promised to solve. Overpopulation provided the logic
whereby birth control could be a New Deal program—lack of it was not
an individual difficulty but a regionwide economic problem. For social
workers, "Population Problems" was a required course for the graduate
curriculum Bourne initiated at the University of Puerto Rico; the professionals trained there supplied most of the staff and impetus for the federal initiative. The course description included:

> Population doctrines since Malthus; growth and industry; population
> changes and international relations, migration and its control. Control of
> population growth, trends in births and deaths with their social and eco-
> nomic consequences. Emphasis on Puerto Rico.[74]

However, courses also included "Health Problems of Puerto Rico."
Theirs was not a conservative eugenics concerned exclusively with ensuring that working-class, potentially unhealthy people not be born. The
Social Service Section of PRERA, which Bourne also ran, was concerned
with multiple "environmental" social problems. She wrote that it carried
on "activities" in child welfare, maternal health, recreation, probation
and parole . . . medical social work, nutrition and home economics."[75]
This wide-ranging agenda made the formation of modern, small families,
and the health, recreation, criminal rehabilitation, and nutrition of
working-class families part of the same program of the economic and social development; it represented the material, moral, and familial improvement of the island, from the bottom up.

This Puerto Rican and U.S. feminist nationalism was neither intrinsically pro-U.S. nor pro-independence. For all that it saw the federal government as a potent ally to further its own agenda, it also had a significant *independentista* faction. Bourne put two Puerto Rican social
workers in charge of the birth control project. One of the principal participants, and a leader in her own right, Carmen Rivera de Alvarado, was
an *independentista*.[76] (It is a measure of her centrality to the movement
that when the legality of the insular measure decriminalizing birth control in 1937 was challenged, Rivera de Alvarado was among those who
were arrested to provide a test case.) Yet theirs was not the nationalism
of Albizu, of nostalgia for large families. For most Puerto Rican feminists, support for the cause of independence could never rely on
"mother" as the iconic representation of the nation. From the North

American side, Bourne also expressed a certain ambivalence about colonialism. Of the colonial question, she wrote:

> Social workers . . . see it as their obligation to work toward a solution of this problem which will be compatible with a satisfying political program. This complicates the ethical position of the conscientious social worker. Can the economic needs of the clients and the future of professional social work in dealing with those needs, be faced as a part of a general social-economic problem; or does the fact that the client as well as the social worker is a part of an emotional situation, motivated in many cases by rebellion against a colonial psychology, greatly complicate the issue for Puerto Rico?[77]

Bourne wrestled with the question of whether she was trying to solve a regional economic problem or whether she faced an essentially colonial one. Other, similarly positioned women in the political network around Eleanor Roosevelt (like Ruby Black) openly supported the movement for independence.

PROGRESSIVE EUGENICS

Another complicating factor in assessing the politics of these modernizing professionals, feminist and otherwise, is that they were enthusiastic supporters of eugenics. Violet Callendar, for example, cheered the passage of a eugenic sterilization law in Mexico,[78] and the birth control legislation they all supported also contained a provision for the eugenic sterilization of the "unfit." Edna Lonigan, a North American policy advisor, recommended the

> organization of a Race Betterment Association, to unite moderate Catholics and Protestants in a program to improve racial stocks in Puerto Rico, and to provide better care for children in their formative years, by emphasizing the responsibility of fathers in caring for their children, and raising the family's standard of living.[79]

Like Bourne and other social workers and nurses, Lonigan urged a contraceptive plan based interchangeably on eugenic, health, and familial considerations. Should we, then, understand their desire for working-class families to use birth control as a wish for the elimination of these people—as the Nationalist Party and some later feminist historians and activists did indeed read them?[80] I think not, taking into consideration the broader context of public health in Puerto Rico, but such an argument requires at least a slight revision of the historiographical tradition of eugenics, on the mainland as well as the island.

Locating the eugenics movement politically and culturally in Europe, North America, or Latin America is a surprisingly difficult task; eugenics is all over the political map. One early-twentieth-century physician complained, not inaccurately, that the term *eugenics* was "a mere catch phrase which covers any rubbish which any crank chooses to inflict upon the world," and which brought together "all the neo-Malthusians, anti-vaccinationists, antivivisectionists, Christian Scientists . . . vegetarians, and the rest."[81] A quick survey of historical work suggests that historians of eugenics, although well aware of this heterogeneity, have often preferred neater stories uncovered by following a single professional or intellectual strand through the thicket of eugenics rhetorics and practices. Hence, we have histories of eugenics in biology, for example,[82] or of eugenics among physicians and public health workers,[83] or of eugenics in psychiatry and mental testing,[84] or of eugenics in the birth control movement,[85] or in public policy, or its use in sterilization laws and immigration restriction, or by the directors of institutions for "the feeble-minded." Work on the infant and child health movement shows that the language of eugenics was used in Progressive, child-feeding programs aimed at keeping immigrants' children alive through the killing summer months in cities in the northeastern United States.[86] Edward Larson, writing about the U.S. "Deep South," and Nancy Leys Stepan, writing on Latin America, both suggest how thoroughly eugenics could be wed to Progressive programs designed to promote infant and maternal health. These are the networks and intellectual currents in which we ought to locate Puerto Rican eugenics. Eugenics does not always fit into a teleological account that ends with the Nazis and the Holocaust. While the connections and echoes between North American, Latin American, and Nazi eugenics are real, to take them to be the whole of the movement underestimates the banality of eugenics, masks its wide appeal, and renders it so radically different from contemporary culture as to make its continued survival and ongoing influence invisible.

Puerto Rican eugenics—like eugenics in the U.S. South and in Latin America—was an agenda of liberals and leftists advocating progress. Eugenics, like birth control, was a program for making working-class families healthy, for improving the condition of the country, and it stood in contrast to the racialism of tropical medicine. It was a project of the modernizing middle classes—women and men, Puerto Rican and North American—who sought to modernize the island. Tropical medicine, dominated in Puerto Rico by North Americans associated with the Rockefeller Foundation, was, among other things, a racial theory that posited a metonymic relationship among race, place, and disease: the tropics were inhabited by dark people whose bodies were a wellspring of disease. Eugenics and overpopulation, in contrast, told a story of a reformable (white) people, who through a program of right reproduction, could become a modern nation. Pedro Ortiz, Puerto Rico's commissioner of health through the mid-1920s, told a North American audience of the need to correct the discourse of the tropics, as it referred to Puerto Rico, and replace it with a language of modernization and public health:

> Wrong ideas that have settled in the minds of non-residents need to be corrected. [These include an image of the tropics inhabited by] an inferior stock, poor, ignorant and degenerated, of a physical and peculiar mental structure, under a red-hot sun. . . . Wild and fierce animals and beasts, poisonous and annoying insects of all denominations . . . and in this immense wilderness, people mixed and blended, of all races and creeds, without a definite personality, full of vice, degraded, and incapable of rising above this level. A queer and inferior people, lazy and indolent and powerless to organize a civilized community. . . . The question is raised whether the stronger races through a natural instinct of selection occupied and inhabited the regions north and south of the tropics and the powerless inferior races with no ambition and no initiative have remained in the tropics.[87]

Similarly, Antonio Fernós Isern, at that time Ortiz's deputy, also complained about how understandings of tropical medicine and health construed the "tropics" as incompatible with civilized and white communities: "We are living testimony to the fact that 'the tropics' belong more to the realm of the imaginary than to this practical world. In fact, we are evidence in favor of the contention that the white man breeds so rapidly in the tropics that excessive population results, thus constituting a problem itself."[88] Whereas tropical medicine constructed a non-white "race" based on geography, public health constructed classes—those people in need of intervention and those whose education enabled them to intervene.

Maternal health and progressive eugenics developed in reaction to, and built on, the infrastructure provided by the Rockefeller Foundation in Puerto Rico. In 1919 the Rockefeller Foundation had been invited to the island to address the extensive problem of tuberculosis there. After a brief study, however, members of the Foundation's International Health Division, or IHD,[89] decided instead to focus their initial work on tropical parasites instead: hookworm, malaria, and dysentery. The reason for this decision speaks volumes about how the IHD understood its purpose, its strengths, and the things it was not willing to do. Tuberculosis was a disease of poverty, but parasitic diseases were a consequence of geography. The IHD was far more comfortable with altering geography—filling in places where water pooled, putting down tile in irrigation canals, building latrines—than with engaging in the politically fraught activity of trying to improve poor people's standard of living. As an IHD report put it, the advantage of treating tropical diseases rather than TB was that "success in their control [is not] dependent upon the improvement in the economic condition of the people."[90] Direct charity, they regarded as an utter waste of money; and like all Republicans, they loathed the New Deal. As a member of the IHD wrote, "We can but dimly perceive the tremendous amount of money involved in this sporadic, poorly advised attempt to make the world over in a day."[91] Well into the Depression on the island, the IHD could insist, "We do not agree that any phase of the situation in Porto Rico today demands the employment of emergency relief measures, nor do we believe that such emergency relief measures as are proposed can lead to permanent betterment of the conditions toward which they are directed." Labor was the key—healthy laborers, and the efficient, scientific management of both government and health concerns.

The eugenics model provided an alternative view. Already voiced in Puerto Rican public health journals beginning in the 1920s, eugenics became a dominant paradigm in public health on the island in 1933, when New Deal funding started to reorganize health care on the island. The sources are better at showing what these eugenics advocates did than what they thought, but that is revealing enough. Under very eugenic division names, like the "Department of Social Medicine and Puericulture," an influx of women and some men into the *Salud Publica* launched programs to improve child health through school-based nursing, to address tuberculosis, and of course, to promote birth control to reduce overpopulation. Other projects included the establishment of programs like supplementary feeding for infants and young children, "milk stations" to provide fresh and unadulterated milk for infants and new mothers, child nursing and dental clinics, visiting nurses and child welfare social workers, and a tuberculosis sanitarium that could minimize contagion and provide wholesome food, rest, and respite from labor and overcrowded living conditions.[92] In this model, disease and poverty could not be meaningfully separated, nor could they be attacked in pieces; poverty was an integral part of ill-health, and social hygiene and disease an integral part of poverty.

The promoters of this paradigm were more likely to be liberal and female, and drawn from the ranks of social workers or nurses than conservative, male, and laboratory researchers. The Public Health Department welcomed women, as, of course, did Bourne's social work program at the University of Puerto Rico. The IHD, in contrast, had vigorously guarded the gates against women, even going so far as to demand their money back when a Harvard researcher in Puerto Rico intimated that some of his data had been collected by a *nurse*.[93] In Puerto Rico, eugenics was the language of a modernizing middle class, female and male, of public health advocates who sought an alternative to the racialism of tropical medicine.

CLARENCE GAMBLE AND THE TRIUMPH
OF MAINLAND OVERPOPULATIONISTS

The era of nurse and social work control over birth control programs was short-lived. Their modernizing nationalism and moderate eugenics was ultimately replaced—albeit incompletely—by a program more closely aligned with conservative eugenics and the colonial impulse to protect the United States from too many of "them." While the election-year row by the Catholic Church abruptly put an end to the federal effort, the pieces of the project were picked up in 1936 by private philanthropist, physician, and researcher Clarence Gamble, heir to the Proctor & Gamble soap fortune. Gamble immediately founded a new group, the Asociación pro Salud Maternal e Infantil (Maternal and Child Health Association), which contained many of the same people, but which was reorganized to put physicians (and ultimately, Gamble himself) in charge of the previously autonomous nurses and social workers. Through this group, Gamble established a network of clinics throughout the island from 1936 to 1939. The most important change was technological: the new clinics promoted spermicidal jellies and creams rather than diaphragms for birth control. Gamble believed these methods were more suited to the abilities of impoverished women; the diaphragm, he felt, was too difficult for their limited skills and intelligence and so would not be widely used. In making these changes, he inaugurated a program that would persist through the 1950s and would have a lasting impact on how birth control was practiced on the island: he replaced a fairly effective method (the diaphragm) with one (foams and jellies) that had much lower success rates, thereby paving the way in later decades for the widespread use of sterilization and the contraceptive pill, which, whatever their dangers and limitations, worked.

Gamble was principally concerned with limiting the number of Puerto Ricans of the lower classes, and this desire to minimize the number of "them" was linked to an elitist nationalism. He was quite blunt about his interest in supplying contraception only to very poor people, and ultimately he used a house-to-house canvas in rural and working-class communities in order to pressure them into using birth control methods.[94] In an article in *Human Fertility* on the declining fertility of the college educated, Gamble expressed particular concern about what he considered to be the abuse of birth control by "the fittest" and the danger that they would be outreproduced by lower types.[95] Gamble's understanding of the island, and the kind of reproduction it required, did not include poor Puerto Ricans. As he wrote in the *Journal of Heredity:*

> In this intricate technological age, highly trained specialists in large numbers are required to man the great complex of delicate organizations, industrial, political, educational, etc. that constitute a modern nation. The greatest single reservoir of those possessing the requisite abilities, the ability to plan, to guide, to execute with intelligence, is the group of college-trained citizens. . . . By reason of these considerations, the fecundity of this group is a matter of great significance. Since children tend to inherit the intellectual capacity of their parents, the average of the children of graduates will be above that of the nation as a whole.[96]

His vision of reform was of the hard-line eugenicist sort, and his control of the birth limitation program allowed him to more sharply target working-class women, with little concern about whether the program was fitted to their needs or even welcome. The Puerto Rican project was one of several Gamble established. Similar programs were developed throughout the rural South in the 1930s, particularly in Appalachia.[97] Gamble saw birth control as a tool for reducing overpopulation and poverty, and the unit he was interested in affecting was not the individual or the heterosexual couple, but communities and populations. Thus, acceptance rates (the number of people willing to use his chosen birth control methods) were more important for him than failure rates. Though he had no data to suggest that it was true, he believed that impoverished people were more likely to use jelly, foam, or creams than diaphragms. To him, unintended pregnancies, however important to an individual woman or family, were not so significant at the level of population if the tradeoff was a larger percentage of people willing to use the method he prescribed. This framework assured that individual outcomes were unimportant. Gamble did not waver in this conviction, though he might have had occasion to consider its wisdom when he lost two of his eight field workers to accidental pregnancies begun while using the methods he promoted.[98]

The early socialist backers of birth control had focused on removing barriers to access to birth control rather than on trying to encourage anyone to use it. They had tried to make the condoms, douches, and patent medicines then in use available to a wider group of people. The primary impediments they had identified were local and federal laws that prohibited the advertisement, sale, or mailing of these articles, as well as the opposition of the Catholic Church to their use. Later, social worker and nurse programs differed from socialist programs in that they proactively delivered birth control to working-class women. These projects, in promoting the diaphragm, selected the most effective contraceptive device available and the one most often used by the upper classes and by North American and European women. The logic of a diaphragm clinic, however much it might be trying to manage the reproduction of the working classes, was at least clear. It required trained medical personnel to fit a diaphragm, and it was assumed that working-class women lacked the resources to visit a personal doctor.

Gamble took the logic of clinics and stood it on its head. He promoted simple methods through activist, interventionist clinics. He opposed the diaphragm as being too expensive and too difficult to use for the poor people he intended to target. Social workers who had previously worked in the program found the shift distasteful. Gladys Gaylord wrote him that "my experience in Puerto Rico leads me to believe that it would be unwise to use any but the most approved methods. . . . When I was there, leading physicians were loathe to back anything that was not guaranteed a high percent of success . . . in the critical situations which come to such a clinic."[99] As Gaylord noted, Gamble had knowingly substituted a fairly effective method for one known to be much less so. In favoring methods other than the diaphragm, Gamble was outside the main currents of thought of the American Birth Control League (ABCL) in the 1920s and 1930s.[100] Indeed, Gamble's instructions for organizing the Asociación were intended to block the insular group from affiliation with the ABCL, as that group backed diaphragm methods and required that its clinics use only "recognized methods."[101] Moreover, even Gilbert Beebe, the demographer Gamble ultimately hired to collect the results of the field trials, repeatedly emphasized the superiority of the diaphragm;

he wrote that it was more effective, was used with greater consistency, and that social workers reported that it was easier to teach.[102] Being independently wealthy, though, and unwilling to donate funds to projects he did not control himself, Gamble was able to promote whatever projects he thought worthy. Moreover, the physicians' group on whose board he sat, the National Committee on Maternal Health (NCMH), was enthusiastic about promoting simple methods. The idea that other methods—even less effective ones—would be necessary for particularly impoverished and colonized people was not original with Gamble; it was, in fact, foundational for others, particularly scientists involved in birth control.

Robert L. Dickinson, the founder of the NCMH, was among the early advocates of a different kind of birth control program for colonized people. Indeed, Dickinson was the first to identify an effective rationale for the involvement of biologists in contraceptive research: the need for something simple that could be used in colonial regions. In 1927 he had advised Marjorie Farrer of the Investigation Committee on birth control in London that research on very simple methods was the next great research project needed. "The requests which our Committee receives from foreign lands like China, India, and the Near East and from some of the slum districts here," he wrote her, "stresses the need of protection much more simple than the vaginal cap, or even . . . jelly."[103] He also wrote the Rockefeller Bureau of Social Hygiene and urged that they fund such work (though he recommended the work be done in Britain, as legal difficulties seemed to him to block birth control research in the U.S.). "Do you care to discuss a possible program of investigation in England?" he inquired. "The situation in India among the overly prolific poor was brought up to me several times, and advice concerning methods adapted to the wives of dull-minded natives was asked for."[104] The Bureau was indeed interested, and Dickinson wrote the proposal for the first contraceptive research project by biologists that Rockefeller money funded: the F. A. E. Crew study on spermaticide effectiveness. In it, he reiterated the need for something that could be used by colonized peoples, and added that it should work to stop venereal disease as well, repeating the conventional wisdom that these were populations particularly afflicted with such diseases. He stressed the need for "some simple measure which will be available for the wife of the slum dweller, the peasant or the coolie, though dull of mind. . . . It [also] should be effective against the gonococcus and the spirochete."[105] While the Crew study itself produced little of note, it provided a model for both the Rockefeller Foundation and biologists at large for biological investigation of contraception. Since the Rockefeller Foundation was the major funder for biological research between the wars and was invested in setting the agenda for the profession as a whole (in style if not in content), this was a significant event. As Merriley Borell and Adele Clarke have argued, Crew's work marked the beginning of what subsequently became the normative involvement of biologists in contraceptive research.[106]

Under fire from the ABCL and Dr. José Belaval, the obstetrician Gamble was trying to recruit as medical director for his program, Gamble eventually agreed to a single demonstration clinic in San Juan that would provide diaphragms. His other projects—ultimately more than sixty of them—would, however, promote only simpler methods.[107] Others conceded to the Gamble program. The two Puerto Rican women he put on staff were quite formidable people: they were Rosa González, who did not suffer fools gladly and who publicly did battle with prominent physicians and was successful in her effort to professionalize nursing in Puerto Rico,[108] and the feminist *independentista* Carmen Rivera de Alvarado. Still, the two women had no resources to run the project themselves, and insular-funded birth control programs had failed.

Gamble, though outside the mainstream of contraceptive activism, read the research climate well. Biological research on contraceptive methods had developed and remained firmly within the paradigm of concern about the overpopulation of colonized and formerly colonized regions, alongside the profligacy of "slum dwellers" within the United States and Britain. The motivation for this research rested on a notion that it was better to prevent poor or dark-skinned people from being born, and it maintained a quite ambivalent relationship to the idea of white, affluent women voluntarily limiting their own fertility. Before the Second World War, this emphasis was largely the responsibility of the Rockefeller Foundation.[109] Rockefeller money also supported the activist and diaphragm-focused (efficacy) efforts of Sanger and the Sangerists at the Birth Control Clinical Research Bureau and the American Birth Control League.[110] However, this funding was consistently accompanied by Rockefeller efforts to incorporate all the divergent birth control organizations—Sangerists, the NCMH, eugenicists, and demographers—under the banner of population, not individual or familial, birth limitation. Even Sanger, who consistently advocated the compatibility of these approaches, finally balked at what she saw as the complete erasure (not merely the overshadowing) of her goal of women's reproductive autonomy.[111] As a frustrated but sympathetic staff member of the Bureau of Social Hygiene recorded, following a meeting with Sanger and Dr. Henry Pratt Fairchild over a proposed merger of the BCFA and his American Eugenics Society, "Mrs. Sanger views birth control essentially as a woman's right with medical responsibility for meeting it. Would regret seeing basic principle upset by doubtful claims of therapeutic population control arguments."[112]

Gamble's influence in insular birth control programs was long-lived. Even when the funding for his project was taken over by the health department, the methods, the staff, and even the forms for recording information remained unchanged, and Gamble maintained regular contact with the staff, who continued to treat him as their director and make data available to him.[113] By using experimental methods, Gamble was able to interest pharmaceutical companies in donating materials. Even after his withdrawal of financial support, his Puerto Rican contacts correctly assessed that his continued involvement was crucial to the availability of free supplies. Gamble used the project to generate medical papers under his name on spermicidal effectiveness, based both on laboratory research and field trials in Puerto Rico.[114] From the mid-1930s through the early 1950s, Gamble reconstituted birth control in Puerto Rico on North American terms by making the island into a laboratory. Not least among his successes, he showed that Puerto Rico had a class of highly trained medical, nursing, and other professionals who could competently collect data for researchers, which would significantly influence decisions to hold future clinical trials on the island.[115]

At the end of the 1930s, sterilization became available as an alternative to foams and jellies. In 1937 the legislature passed a bill that made distribution of birth control legal and assigned the task to the health department. While the bill was challenged, a federal ruling in 1939 permitted the rural clinics of the health department to prescribe birth control to protect the life or health of the (potential) mother, a treatment local medical professionals were prepared to administer quite liberally. At the same time, the legislature passed a eugenic sterilization law which included poverty as a legitimate reason for permitting sterilizations. A Eugenic Sterilization Board was authorized to review and enforce involuntary sterilizations, but only a total of forty-eight cases were decided in the decades that followed. Far more significant, in light of Gamble's insistence on highly ineffective methods and the resultant scarcity of diaphragms on the island, was that women who sought to control their fertility in a reliable way turned increasingly to sterilization, legalized under this bill, in the decade that followed.

To summarize this multifaceted and rather complex story of the "problem" of Puerto Rican reproduction in the 1920s, '30s, and '40s, then: overpopulation, eugenics, and birth control programs intervened in debates about whether the island was entitled to independence, and whether the "race" of the island's inhabitants was "black" or "Spanish." The notion that through overpopulation poor women were responsible for the economic ills of the island simultaneously served to mask U.S. capitalist extraction and to provide an occasion for further U.S. involvement. The draconian figuring of the Puerto Rican woman by Gamble (and earlier, in writings like Schroeder's) as a source of danger to the United States laid the foundations for postwar population control policies. In its more immediate implications, it made certain kinds of reproductive autonomy impossible for many Puerto Rican women, even or especially those of the middle and elite classes, as condoms and jelly were just not effective enough to be used for reliable child spacing. This same understanding of the colonized family in India as "dull-witted" and dangerous, as described by R. L. Dickinson, underwrote the involvement of biologists and the Rockefeller Foundation in birth control research. In Puerto Rico, it was fundamental to the establishment of a pattern of using the island as a laboratory for such research: Puerto Rico would go on to become the test site for Depo Provera, IUDs, and the pill.

The milder account of the working-class Puerto Rican family offered by socialists, liberals, and feminists had different consequences. The view that the ills of Puerto Ricans had been produced not by the tropical climate but by poverty, that they had been caused by working-class women through overpopulation, illegitimacy, and bad diet and housing—a view won through eugenics—permitted more substantial federal interventions during the Depression in state-run industry, child-feeding programs, and birth control. In the long run, it was also this view of Puerto Rican poverty as remedial—not inherent in degenerate, tropical bodies—that authorized the limited home rule (the election of Luis Muñoz Marín as governor in 1948) that passed for decolonization in Puerto Rico. In this view, working-class Puerto Rican women were a danger, but a reformable one, to the future of the island, and they were often themselves victimized—through weakened health and exhaustion—by the overpopulation that reformers wished to end. In the decades that followed, liberals and conservatives would continue to disagree over which view of the Puerto Rican working-class woman was correct. But they did not doubt that she was a key to understanding what was wrong in Puerto Rico.

CHAPTER 4

Demon Mothers in the Social Laboratory

Development, Overpopulation, and "the Pill," 1940–1960

Puerto Rico has been a headache to the United States for 40 years. Its poverty is a disgrace to the Stars and Stripes. From the economic point of view the overwhelming problem of Puerto Rico is the relation of population to the land. The orphan island teems and bristles with crowded thousands. . . . Puerto Rico's poverty is caused first and overwhelmingly by overpopulation, which is in turn caused by several factors— natural fecundity for one thing, the influence of the Roman Catholic Church, and the efficiency of the United States Health Service.

—John Gunther, *Inside Latin America,* 1945

There they are, the teeming millions of the little island of Puerto Rico, ready to serve as handy examples for anyone who wants to damn American policies in public health. And it is a difficult example to argue away, because there is no denying the existence of the Puerto Ricans, and because there is equally no denying that most of them continue to live under deplorable, substandard conditions, despite all of the capital, experts, and technologies that have been lavished on the island during a period of fifty years through a paternalistic American policy.

—Rockefeller Foundation document, January 1952

After World War II, Puerto Rico and the Third World in general emerged as visible problems, albeit soluble ones, for U.S. philanthropy and foreign policy. Cold War social science and policy rendered poverty and communism, envisioned as two sides of the same coin, as issues that the nation needed to address. If Third World populations were too poor, they might "go over" to the Soviets, but social science—sociology, economics, history, and demography—held solutions to poverty. One of the most important was that overpopulation needed to be addressed through family planning. This analysis of the Third World, as victimized by poverty and as endangering U.S. interests through its actual or potential relationship to communism, rationalized an abrupt expansion of U.S. social, political, economic, and military roles in the colonized and formerly colonized world. Following President Truman's call to ameliorate Third World poverty through technological assistance (then termed the Point Four initiative, named for the fourth point in his inaugural address, and later termed, simply "development"), science and technology, too, became important components of this new policy of development. Whether development constituted a radical break with colonialism is debatable. Arturo Escobar and James Fergusen have argued, I think persuasively, that it did not.[1] As decolonization movements throughout the Third World demanded national autonomy, the United States replaced colonialism with development. International family planning was deemed key to its success.

This chapter explores how arguments about overpopulating, working-class mothers came to undergird development policy. Puerto Rico was explicitly a "laboratory" in which development—foreign aid, industrialization (a.k.a. the "global assembly line"), import substitution, and population control—was being tested as a global policy. The relentlessly fertile Puerto Rican mother provided an interpretive key for (post)colonial poverty, communism, and the role of the United States in the Third World. For liberals, she was victimized by her endless children, and they longed to rescue her from her own ignorance and "macho" Puerto Rican men who proved their virility through her suffering maternity; for conservatives, she was a "demon mother" whose dangerous fecundity could only be halted by strong measures—sterilization, high doses of hormones, perhaps a contraceptive agent in the water. In either case, poverty was caused by reproduction, and U.S. experts had answers. Puerto Rican reproduction and its responsiveness to family-planning interventions was intensively studied by social scientists since it was intended to provide a model for the rest of the world. In this period, the work of producing authoritative knowledge about overpopulation shifted from biologists to social scientists, and economists, demographers, sociologists, and historians claimed the "problem" of working-class women's reproduction as their own, transforming it from an issue of race suicide and maternal health to the cause of economic underdevelopment. Birth control programs assumed an international significance. Reproductive biology research was deeply influenced by this ideology of overpopulation, as a handful of researchers—first maverick, then mainstream—tested and developed the birth-control pill as an antidote to "overpopulation." Puerto Rico continued to occupy the forefront of birth control research; the model established by Gamble, of using Puerto Rican researchers to conduct the work, began a new phase with the rise of endocrinological and other high-technology approaches, especially the pill and IUD. Once again, working-class women's bodies were the loci of struggle over insular class relations and the relationship of the United States to the island.

The backdrop for these developments was the fashioning of Puerto Rico as the jewel in the crown of U.S. development policy in the 1940s and 1950s. Puerto Rico played a key role in the elaboration of meanings of development because, as John Kenneth Galbraith wrote in 1953, "At precisely the moment when the United States proclaimed its interest in Point Four, the people of Puerto Rico constituted themselves as a kind of pilot plant to demonstrate the process."[2] The New Deal came late to Puerto Rico but arrived with a vengeance, in the form of a New Deal economics professor ousted from his prominent role in the Roosevelt administration. Rexford Tugwell (Communist "Red Rex" to his enemies in Congress, who were legion) became governor in 1941 and aggressively attempted to institute liberal policies to address the widespread landlessness and joblessness of Depression-era Puerto Rico, including land reform and state-operated farms and industry, measures that were retrospectively described as early development programs. Tugwell was concerned with rational, efficient management and planning in government as key to state reorganization of the economy. In these projects, Tugwell was complemented, pushed, and sometimes contradicted by the progressive populist Luis Muñoz Marín, elected to the insular Senate in 1940 under the banner of a new party, the Partido Popular Democrático (PPD, or just the Populares), with the slogan *"Pan, Tierra, Libertad"* (Bread, Land, Liberty) and a promise to do something to help the rural working class. In the following election, Muñoz Marín became head of the Senate, and by 1949, he was the island's first elected governor. As the island's leading senator,

he envisioned and enacted a compromise on the issue of independence—
a status termed Commonwealth on the mainland and Free Associated
State in Puerto Rico (a phrase that incorporated all three available status
options)—that gave the island increased self-rule in the form of a home-
grown governor, but continued the U.S. military presence, the authority
of the U.S. federal government, and ultimately expanded North American economic influence by offering huge tax breaks to companies who
brought factories to the island through a program termed Operation
Bootstrap. Together, Tugwell, Muñoz Marín, and Muñoz Marín's economic advisor, Teodoro Moscoso, forged a plan for insular economic improvement that spanned two eras of U.S. liberalism, beginning as the New
Deal and ending as Third World economic development.[3]

Addressing overpopulation was key to plans for economic improvement for Muñoz Marín and others of his generation of young Puerto Rican politicians. Their plans had two facets. One was the encouragement
of emigration to the mainland, which ultimately resulted in half the insular population living on the mainland. This divided families, created a permanent dependence on good relations between the island and mainland,
produced a low-wage labor force on the mainland that could be pushed
back to the island in times of hardship, and spawned a literature of exile.
The second facet addressed reproduction; members of the younger, professional class of Puerto Ricans (not, notably, high government officials,
but others—social workers, public health officers, small-town mayors,
hospital administrators) encouraged the use of birth control and surgical
sterilization. Equally important, U.S. academics, missionaries, and philanthropists pushed these measures to limit fertility. Numerous sociological studies of women's reproductive behavior provided the Populares with
models for social change on the island,[4] and offered mainland social scientists a laboratory—often explicitly so-called—for testing birth control
and other development proposals. Puerto Rico was the site of what one demographer termed "experiments in social change,"[5] and its birth control
program was "An Experiment in Population Control."[6]

MUÑOZ MARÍN, THE POPULARES, AND OTHER MODERNIZERS

Two things distinguished the Populares from previous generations of
Puerto Rican leaders: their belief in the value of scientific, expert knowl-
edge and their faith in a plan of "development" in concert with the
United States. Their pro-Americanism was deeply rooted, if ambivalent.
Muñoz Marín, Moscoso, who headed the economic development agency

Fomento, and Antonio Fernós Isern, head of the Department of Public Health and later, Puerto Rico's liaison to the U.S. Senate, were all educated in the United States, spoke excellent English, and had lived on the mainland for extended periods of time. Muñoz Marín, though an *independentista* in his youth, had come to power following his break with the Liberal Party over the party's support for the Tydings bill, which would have offered a plebiscite on status and the promise of independence. Muñoz Marín felt that the terms of independence in the bill would have condemned the island to starvation, and he sought an alternative that preserved both freedom for the island and a road to economic well-being. His party promised New Deal–style reforms: old age pensions, unemployment benefits, disability and maternity insurance, government control of sugar mills, slum clearance, and land reform. The PPD's rise to power on the "Bread, Land, and Liberty" slogan encapsulated the priorities of these modernizers: bread first, then land reform, and freedom later. If that meant an unholy alliance with the United States for bread, so be it. As Muñoz Marín put it later, he was only interested in "self-government without the slavery of the threat of hunger."[7]

The PPD vision was popular, not only among the rural working class but also among young, college-educated elites. Tugwell, himself a former professor of economics, had a passion for brain-trust-style administration and planning, and he readily promoted young intellectuals with good ideas into positions of real power. Rafael Picó, a geographer from Clark University, became head of the Planning Board, and Enrique de Toro (age 25) was appointed head of its finance division; Jaime Benítez became chancellor of the university, and Roberto Sánchez Vilella, an engineer from Ohio State, organized the city bus service. They were young, on average thirty-one years old, and with few exceptions, like Muñoz Marín had mainland educations.[8] For this youthful group, sociology would become a key element of public policy; they trusted in the University of Puerto Rico for answers, and that institution's Social Science Research Center functioned as an advisory body to the government.

Through the decade of the 1940s, these politicians began to forge a new political, economic, and social structure for the island. Economically, this meant export-led industrialization: first, government-run factories, then privately owned ones recruited from the mainland were to produce export goods that would provide the engines for economic growth. These factories employed disproportionate numbers of women. The number of employed women on the island increased an average of 21 percent per decade between 1940 and 1960, while labor force participation

ates for men dropped, from 80 percent in 1950 to 60 percent in 1975.[9]
industrialization had other effects. Agriculture fell off sharply, and a
combination of rural unemployment, cheap airfares, and increased in-
terconnection between the mainland and the island spurred massive emigration to New York, especially among men.[10] Among women, the shift
from homework jobs—particularly in the needle trades—to reliance on
factory wage-labor meant that it became far more difficult for mothers
of young children to be employed. Despite the creation of new jobs, the
enterprise relied to a significant extent on federal transfer payments; federal aid jumped from $3 million in 1933 to $43 million in 1943 (which
represented an amount as great as the yield from the island's largest
crop), and aid increased steadily through the 1940s.[11]

   The political conundrum for the PPD in general, and Muñoz Marín
in particular, was that as U.S. aid reached significant proportions and resulted in real improvements in standards of living, independence would
have meant killing the goose that laid the golden egg. The status the PPD
adopted in compromise, that of the Estado Libre Asociado, stopped far
short of actual independence, but attempted to simultaneously increase
autonomy and economic well-being. In short, the island agreed to become a showcase for Cold War, U.S.-style development. There were victories to be claimed for development policies, Commonwealth status,
and Muñoz Marín's dream of economic improvement. Infant mortality,
which had remained at very high levels from 1900 to 1939, began a
steady and sharp decline, from an average of 122 per 1,000 in the period
1935–39, to 105 per 1,000 in 1940–44, and 79 per 1,000 in 1945–49.[12]
Per capita annual income likewise began a steady rise, from $121 in
1940, to $576 in 1960 in constant dollars, which represented a 476 per-
cent increase.[13] Overall mortality rates declined as well, from 20 per
1,000 in the 1930s, to 15 per 1,000 in the 1940s, to 8 per 1,000 in the
1950s.[14] *Independentista* critics argued that the architects of development in Puerto Rico did nothing remarkable, that they merely hitched
Puerto Rico to the rising star of the U.S. economy but in a permanently
inferior position. They pointed to a different statistic: per capita income
in Puerto Rico has stayed more or less constant vis-à-vis the United
States, with Puerto Rico permanently in the poorest position, at an income level half of Mississippi's average.

   Limiting population became a cornerstone of development policy for
its architects on the mainland. On the island, it had a more ambivalent
status. As we have seen, Muñoz Marín had been an early advocate of
overpopulation as a description of what ailed the island, and in later

years would even argue that overpopulation was one of the most important reasons why Puerto Rico could not be independent.[15] Still, during the 1940s and 1950s, he was insistent that addressing overpopulation was not the way to bring economic prosperity to the island. "Our aim must be to increase our production more rapidly than our population," he wrote. "To achieve this, several solutions are offered. It seems to me that the principal solution lies in . . . the 'battle of production,' which the government has already begun in industry and agriculture."[16] Tugwell, Muñoz Marín, and health department head Fernós Isern were all uneasy supporters of birth control as an economic panacea. This may have reflected the difficulty of governance where the Catholic Church was a major political player, though one ought not exaggerate the Church's influence. In 1960 the Church challenged Muñoz Marín directly in an election, running its own candidates, with birth control as the issue, and Muñoz Marín won by a landslide. At a roundtable sponsored by the health department on "Puerto Rico's Population Problem," many PPDers, including academics, government officials, and public figures pronounced that overpopulation was a serious problem that Puerto Rico had to face. Despite the considerable support within the PPD for the overpopulation thesis, though, and the general accord between the scientific modernizing bent of the party and that of the overpopulationists, the PPD was also genuinely committed to economic growth and industrialization, and unwilling to accept birth control as a simpler and cheaper alternative. In this respect, the PPD approached overpopulation like it approached the status question: if the *independistas* were lined up one side and North Americans on the other, the PPD steered a middle course.

MAKING SENSE OF OVERPOPULATION ON THE MAINLAND AND THE ISLAND

After World War II, the Malthusian argument was reinvigorated as the problem of the "population explosion." Previously a minority position—the dominant line of thought on the mainland had been that the United States and European nations suffered from underpopulation and were in danger of committing "race suicide"[17]—in the postwar period the "population explosion" became an article of faith. (As late as 1950, sociologist David Riesman argued in *The Lonely Crowd* that the American character was fundamentally shaped by the problem of population decline.[18]) Through the image of the prolifically fertile Third World mother, social scientists, biologists, and pundits told a simple story about decolonization and communism: too many of "them," with their uprisings, their poverty, and their unchecked fertility menaced "us." This narrative generated vast quantities of print. In the late 1940s, the number of scholarly journals in the United States devoted to population issues doubled, from two to four. By the mid-1950s, there was a fifth, *Eugenics Quarterly,* in addition to two new international journals with substantial North American participation.[19] Even more remarkable was the expansion of the bookshelf of popular writing on the subject, a virtual population explosion of its own.

Overpopulation was a key economic narrative. The president of the World Bank, Eugene Black, wrote, "There are movements in the less developed countries which vitiate all efforts to raise world living standards. . . . One of the most massive of these obstacles is the tremendous rise in the populations of the already crowded countries. . . . Cities are crowded to bursting, and are still getting bigger."[20] Excessive, uncontrolled reproduction was an obstacle to capital formation—the concentration of wealth among a few people that economists (and popular economics) deemed necessary for industrialization (which is to say, development). All these extra babies frittered capital away on education and shoes instead of permitting the concentration of funds among investors. As noted liberal biologist Julian Huxley wrote, population growth in Asia and Latin America

> makes their development much more difficult. To develop an underdeveloped country . . . needs a great deal of capital, technical skill, and trained manpower. If too many babies are born, too much of that capital and skill and manpower will be used up in providing food, housing, education, health, and other services for them.[21]

Although this narrative was a story of class, of too many working-class people taking from the more important entrepreneurial class, it is also a gendered tale, a parable of the 1950s middle-class U.S. household—of the sober, income-generating husband (possessor of capital and technical skill) and of the profligate wife (demanding ever more money for food, housing, and health care for children).

In this discourse, those most responsible for overpopulation were women, and Puerto Rican women functioned prominently as examples for mainland social scientists. These difficult women included, in Alan Guttmacher's phrase, the "Puerto Rican woman . . . [who] refuse[s] to be bothered by birth control techniques."[22] J. Mayone Stycos wrote that many Third World women simply never thought about contraception, and the tone was one of outrage that they had neglected this matter of international importance. "While we have seen that the average woman wants only three or four children," he wrote, "high proportions of the same women say they have never thought of the matter before." Although he did not say so, Stycos, too, was thinking of Puerto Rico, the place where he did his fieldwork. He also complained that "women become seriously interested in birth control only after several births and then want to *stop* having children. However, contraceptive activity at this late date tends to be relatively inefficient because of lack of experience and because sexual patterns have become fairly routinized and difficult to change."[23] The most intimate details of the sexual habits of working-class women in Puerto Rico became an important subject in an international academic discourse. Third World women's sexual behavior was rendered dangerous and unreasonable, the cause of poverty and hence of communism, and needed to be made known, managed, and regulated.

Even more sharply than in the 1920s and 1930s, the contradictions of postwar overpopulation discourse suggest that it responded more to the cultural logic of anxiety about Third World women than that it was coherent on its own terms. Again, if overpopulation caused poverty, quality of life would have to be declining by some standard, such as per capita income or health status, as population increased. In virtually all parts of the world the postwar period showed the opposite trends: per capita income rose as population rose. If overpopulation was a measurable economic claim—and hence falsifiable—then the macroeconomic trends of the postwar period disproved it. If, instead, it was an article of Cold War belief, like "democracy" or "America," then it was entirely coherent: Third World underdevelopment was caused by having the wrong sort of family.

In Puerto Rico, overpopulation had already long since been available to policy makers and health professionals as a description of the island; in this period, it also became the language of social science. The postwar period saw the massive involvement of social scientists in Puerto Rico. There was a joke that circulated about this time that asked: Who are the members of the Puerto Rican family? The answer: Mom, Dad, the kids, and the sociologist. Already by 1955, one historian was warning that the proliferating academic studies had to be taken with a grain of salt, since rural people had become savvy to social scientists and were wary of having their foibles paraded across a world stage.[24] Overpopulation was crucial to the representations of the island to the mainland; as a Rockefeller

Foundation official wrote, "The words 'population problem' call to mind situations like Puerto Rico."[25] The modernizing forces of Operation Bootstrap and Muñoz Marín were represented—as in a 1949 *Time* magazine cover story—as pitched in an epic battle against the backwardness (of women in particular) that was characterized by overpopulation.[26]

Economists, historians, demographers, political scientists, anthropologists, and sociologists arrived on the island in considerable numbers to study Puerto Ricans in the postwar period. In the 1940s, first demographer Clarence Senior, then historian Milliard Hansen served as director of the University of Puerto Rico's Social Science Research Center, which provided the infrastructure for extensive social science research on the island. The Center attracted considerable funding and large numbers of well-known researchers from the mainland.[27] Hansen attributed the interest to the belief (which he shared) that Puerto Rico was "virtually a social science laboratory where in the compactness of 3,435 square miles and two and a quarter million people the scholar may study all of the facets of rapid social change as well as the fusion and conflict of cultures."[28] Hansen neglected to mention another attractive feature: the interest and attention of local government. The Populares and academic researchers offered each other considerable mutual support. Largely because of its relentless academic promotion, Operation Bootstrap came to stand for successful, technologically based social and economic change. In 1953 the *Annals of the Academy of Social and Political Science* devoted an entire issue to Puerto Rico; its subtitle was "A Study in Democratic Development." The volume laid out the research agenda of North American academics in Puerto Rico, which consisted of four parts: politics, particularly anticommunism and an evaluation of the Commonwealth status; economic development (namely, industrialization and the establishment of low wage rates in the context of a historically militant labor movement); the fusion of Latin American and North American cultures on the island, including patterns of labor and family; and finally, the problem of overpopulation and birth control on the island. In this final section, readers learned that economic and social progress rested on women's willingness to use birth control.[29]

In the 1950s sociologists and demographers associated with the Social Science Research Center produced several monographs and a prodigious number of articles on the attitudes of working-class Puerto Rican families (especially women) toward birth control. These works concluded that working-class Puerto Rican families wanted fewer children, and they blamed (or pitied) women to account for the discrepancy. The earliest book, Paul Hatt's *Backgrounds of Human Fertility in Puerto*

Rico, found that there was surprisingly little opposition to birth control among the five thousand people he interviewed. He had assumed that the Catholic Church would be a significant factor, but more than 80 percent of his sample were either unaware of or disagreed with the Church's position on birth control. In general, most people told his interviewers that they wanted small families, between two and three children. Later studies, including J. Mayone Stycos's *Family and Fertility in Puerto Rico* and Reuben Hill et al.'s *The Family and Population Control: A Puerto Rican Experiment in Social Change,* reiterated these findings. These studies tried to explain the gap between what people told their interviewers and what they did, and they attempted to design policy initiatives that would persuade people to use birth control.

In each of these studies, large families were attributed to the backwardness of women. J. W. Combs wrote that the problem of overpopulation developed in the following way: "So early do large numbers of women start childbearing in Puerto Rico and so quickly do they follow up with higher order births [second and third children] that each thousand women bear more second order births by age 25 than do the same number of women in the States by age 35."[30] Likewise, Hill et al. describe Puerto Rican fertility rates in terms of ratios of women to children. One might think women had children by themselves. The studies explained women's attitudes differently, in terms either of a narrative of victimization—they lacked information of the right sort, or oppression in the family or the society prevented them from using birth control—or of demonization—that "culture" or poverty had rendered women's behavior pathological, so they behaved in irrational ways. Hatt reported an imminent breakthrough in the progress of women. Fashioning himself as an advocate of Puerto Rican women's rights, Hatt correlated support for birth control use in his sample with support for women working outside the home, and he suggested that low levels of birth control use were caused by women's oppression. This Hatt attributed to cultural backwardness, but he believed progress was imminent. He felt the trend was toward improvement in the status of women, including growing support for women working, growing secularization and rejection of the Catholic Church, and a desire to marry later and more formally. The next study, Stycos's, told a less sanguine story. In his account, women's backwardness was particularly prominent among the lower classes and showed little sign of changing because it was strongly enforced by men. Stycos told a story of machismo and a cult of virginity, in which the only available rebellion for girls and young women was early marriage, which then entrapped them in endless childbearing. He, in particular, pursued the demonization narrative. He wrote that birth control use was impeded by "the complex of superstitious beliefs harbored principally by women . . . the phobic mechanisms frequently constructed by the uneducated as defenses against a technical world."[31] Whereas Hatt told a story of reasonable people, Stycos's figures were grotesques, caught in complex oedipal triangles and motivated to produce many children by a deep psychology dictated by culture and folk customs. In the final study, Hill et al. found little impetus to change women's reproductive rates within Puerto Rican society. However, he thought well-directed interventions by social scientists and experts from the mainland could succeed in managing and changing sexual and reproductive behavior.

As in the 1920s and 1930s, this story of the "problem" of women succeeded in making the case that overpopulation caused poverty even when the explicit demographic and economic data ran counter to that conclusion. All agreed that beginning in 1948 and continuing through the 1950s, birth rates in Puerto Rico were dropping. Life expectancy continued to lengthen, and per capita income tripled in the 1950s.[32] In short, though population density continued to rise, quality of life improved markedly and there seemed no real case to be made for the need for U.S. consultants to establish population control programs. However much the threat of overpopulation might be deferred to the future or used to account for the past, these issues constituted a problem for the overpopulation argument. As Kingsley Davis put it, referring to the plausibility of the prediction of future population disaster, "To many observers, Puerto Rico already appeared hopelessly overpopulated in the 1930's. Yet the population has continued to grow, and the level of living has risen. . . . Puerto Ricans were living better in 1950 than they were in 1940, despite the fact that there were 342,000 more of them. Does this mean," he asked, "that the island was not overpopulated in the 1930s, or that it is not overpopulated now?"[33] He answers no, of course, but it is hard to say why; at this point in his argument, the contradictions seem apparent even to him. Likewise, Hill et al. in 1959 began their book with the remarkably unpersuasive observation that Puerto Rico's population density was so dangerously high as to put it in the company of England, Wales, the Netherlands, and Belgium, and to make it quite unlike Haiti, Jamaica, or Brazil. In an argument attributing causal relationships between demographics and poverty, these comparisons sound like an argument *for* population density. The authors went on to note improvements in health, life expectancy, and standard of living, particularly among the poorest residents, alongside a continued high (though admittedly declining) birthrate. These authors, too, had to ask:

> The foregoing outline of Puerto Rico's economic and demographic position and development is such that the following question may legitimately be raised: does Puerto Rico have a population problem? Opponents of controlled fertility programs can justifiably point to the very real advances Puerto Rico has made during periods of high rates of fertility.[34]

Again the reply is no, but the authors accomplished this only by pointing to the continued existence of poor families with many children, as if their mere existence signaled that the problem could be blamed ipso facto on women's disorderly, excessive reproduction.

In this way, the question of the relationship of colonialism and capitalism to Puerto Rican poverty—particularly volatile in its context of being a Cold War model of "development through democracy"[35]—was once again deflected onto working-class women's bodies. Once more, working-class women's problematic reproduction became the ground on which U.S. intervention was justified, and North American academics secured their authority by defining the island's "real" problems. This process is most evident when these social scientists account for the contradictions in their argument. Hill et al., writing about an economic and political situation that did not self-evidently require a shift in population demographics—or at least not one induced by them—changed the terms of discussion. "A first step in investigating the population problem while assuming a practical result," they wrote, "is to rephrase the phenomenon of overpopulation of the island in family terms—the pressure of numbers of children upon the resources of individual families. When we do this we see that there are as many population problems for the island as there are families with more children than they can support satisfactorily."[36] Why some sectors of society had more resources than others was no longer a question that needed to be asked. Instead, the issue became, why do some families have more children than they can support? Answering this question preoccupied the remainder of the study. Through this ideological sleight-of-hand, the question of the cause of poverty raised in the opening chapter became one of attitudes toward contraception. Instead of examining the effects of colonial capitalism, Hill et al. wrote instead about the intellectual and psychological peculiarities of the Puerto Rican family. For exoticized reasons like a "modesty complex" in women and machismo in men, this family was ambivalent about whether they wanted many children.

Economists, historians, demographers, and political scientists used the work of the sociologists of the Puerto Rican Family Project to describe obstacles to capital formation, to examine changing patterns of rural/urban life, and to characterize Puerto Rico's capitalist route out of poverty. The only significant dissent from the overpopulation thesis among this era's social scientists can be found in Eric Wolf and Sydney Mintz, who were mostly impressed by the rationality of having large families in the context of labor-intensive agriculture, which required workers on family plots or supplemental wage-earners.[37] With the exception of these chroniclers of "folk cultures," the academic sector spoke with one voice in recommending policy: encouraging emigration was necessary but not sufficient, and birth control had to be widely implemented.

POPULATION CONTROL

The discourse of overpopulation and the social science projects on birth control that it generated ultimately had the hoped-for effect: the decade of the 1960s found vastly more women using birth control than had done so in 1940 (to the extent that the studies are reliable, we can see the trend: a 1939 study found 34 percent of women used contraception, while a 1968 study found 74 percent).[38] However, this change did not occur as a result of centralized planning, although Tugwell, Muñoz Marín, and Gamble might have wished they could institute such programs. The fortunes of state-sponsored fertility and population control projects were various, but they garnered considerable opposition from an activist, Irish-Catholic clergy on the island in these decades, and ultimately they had little impact on fertility rates.[39] While these governmental efforts were embattled, however, an ultimately more successful project began. A huge array of Puerto Rican modernizing middle-class professionals took up the banner of overpopulation, advocating the idea that familial poverty was caused by too many children, and through a combination of educating, cajoling, and pressuring working-class women, succeeded in raising the rate of birth control use, and more especially, the reliance on surgical sterilization. Teachers, newspaper editors, small-town mayors, social workers, nurses, hospital administrators, and some physicians relentlessly promoted birth control, surgical sterilization, and small families. Still more importantly, factories opened under Operation Bootstrap began to employ significant numbers of young women, thereby increasing the pressure on them to limit their fertility.

Central planning of birth control programs did not fail for want of trying. Gamble consistently tried to organize rural population control hands of the Health Department in 1939, Gamble's role continued to include soliciting regular reports on its evolution and interceding with the pharmaceutical companies to have them supply free materials. He helped the Asociación pro Salud Maternal e Infantil transfer a number of nurses trained in birth control and Dr. José Belaval to the Health Department. Continuity in personnel and the Health Department's broad infrastructure made it possible at first to radically expand services, and about 160 rural health units and subunits continued to increase the provision of free birth control services until 1942, when World War II was extended to include the Caribbean. At that time, birth control became more difficult to obtain—along with food, fuel, and all kinds of imports—as German submarines patrolling the Caribbean disrupted supply lines from the mainland. At the same time, a new commissioner of health evidenced considerably less commitment to the birth control program, split up the group of nurses from the Asociación, and left birth control in the hands of local clinic officers, many of whom were inclined to neglect it. Thereafter, relatively few women obtained birth control from the rural health units.[40] In 1946 Gamble tried to initiate another project, described as "an experiment in population control," to make birth control intensively available to residents of a rural area. For nine years, Gamble and his employees, Christopher Tietze and Wilson Wing, tried unsuccessfully to enlist the support of the insular government in, or even simply win permission for, a regional birth control project. They were refused.

Certain programs were carried out on a smaller scale with governmental approval, however. In 1955, after nine years of effort, Gamble's population control project was finally sited in Trujillo Alto, on the outskirts of San Juan. Its goal, never reached, was to reduce the overall birth rate in a single, small community. In 1959 Gamble withdrew from the area, but not before he had steered Joseph Sunnen, a St. Louis businessman interested in doing something about the population "problem," to Puerto Rico to try something with "simple" methods. Beginning in 1956, Sunnen supported another similar project that distributed a single birth control method—a product he had developed called Emko, an aerosolized foam—to residents of a slum, ironically named Los Bravos del Boston (the Boston Braves).[41] Gamble also participated in a third project that was to have huge repercussions: he teamed up with G. D. Searle pharmaceutical company in the testing of the birth control pill.

With or without government support, however, neither Gamble nor Sunnen was the most important benefactor of birth control on the island; that role was taken up by the pharmaceutical companies. Not only Searle, but all the major companies—Youngs Rubber (and Holland-Rantos, its parent company), Ortho Pharmaceutical (and hence Johnson & Johnson), Eaton Labs, Lanteen Medical Laboratories, and Durex Products—sponsored contraceptive research on the island in the 1940s and 1950s.[42] Hoffman-Laroche sponsored a brief trial of an oral contraceptive in 1941, and Searle sponsored two larger-scale trials of steroid oral contraceptives beginning in 1956 and 1957. Gamble was reduced to little more than a coordinator of grants from the various pharmaceutical companies. Sunnen, on the other hand, started a pharmaceutical company, Emko Corporation, and used Puerto Rico as the testing ground for his new product.[43] As we will see, corporate sponsorship produced research that was glowingly positive about its products, yet scientifically flawed. Still, as Adele Clarke has argued, there was a sense of controversy and illegitimacy that clung to reproductive research,[44] and this made it difficult to find funding for it through the traditional routes. When funders like the Rockefeller Foundation refused to support direct research on contraceptives in Puerto Rico (or elsewhere), the pharmaceuticals were ready and willing to step into the breach.

The local partner in these various projects was a group known by different names through the years, but led by many of the same people throughout the name changes: the Asociación pro Salud Maternal e Infantil (Maternal and Child Health Association), the Asociación de Estudios Poblacionales (Population Association), and finally, the Asociación Puertorriqueña pro Bienestar de la Familia (also known as the Family Planning Association of Puerto Rico, which exists to this day as a local affiliate of the International Planned Parenthood Federation). These organizational names registered the sea changes in how Puerto Ricans of the middle classes thought about and argued for birth control—from maternal health and eugenics, to overpopulation, to the more sanitized "family planning." These organizations provided the labor, facilities, and organization that made all these projects possible. These included such disparate and necessary things as the recruitment and training of the 1,500 volunteers who distributed Emko throughout the island, the hiring and supervision of nurses and social workers who did home visits for both the Trujillo Alto and the Searle projects, the storage of medical records, the provision of a jeep for visits to rural residents to collect information, and the provision of physical space and clerical support for compiling results when the principal investigators appeared for one of their irregular trips to the island. They also gave encouragement and funding for sterilization for their patients, about which more will be said in chapter 5.

The various *asociaciones* also provided the incalculable benefit of putting a Puerto Rican face on North American projects. Even so, their leaders and members were also autonomous actors. The North American funders were very specific about the design of programs, and these organizations were constrained in their ability to modify them. However, members of these groups were passionate believers in and supporters of the virtues of birth control and sterilization, and formidable people in their own right. For most of the twenty years under discussion here, these organizations were led by Puerto Rican women who were feminists, social workers, and *independentistas,* first by Carmen Rivera de Alvarado and then by Celestina Zalduondo. For a while, too, the Asociación Puertorriqueña was largely led by its medical director, a North American feminist and former social worker, Dr. Edris Rice-Wray, who at the time also held down an important post at the health department.[45]

Although overpopulation was the theory that provided the critical driving force for all promoters of birth control and sterilization in Puerto Rico in this period, its specific meaning and the desired outcome it was intended to produce differed between Gamble and the members of the *asociaciones.* For Gamble, the driving force in his involvement continued to be eugenic concerns. While many segments of the scientific community had changed positions with respect to eugenics by the 1940s and 1950s, Gamble's remained the same. He wrote that the Trujillo Alto project was

> designed to discover whether our present means of birth control, intensively applied, can control the dangerously expanding population of an unambitious and unintelligent group. . . . It has been said that birth control has been injurious to the race since it has been used by the intelligent and foresighted. It seems to me that only by some . . . demonstration can this accusation be refuted and our nation protected from an undue expansion of the unintelligent groups.[46]

He was flatly contemptuous of working-class people in Puerto Rico (and elsewhere) and of their ability to help themselves. Of a contraceptive program carried out through home visits, he wrote that "the jibaroes [*sic*] may not have enough energy to use the method, but if this doesn't per-suade them I feel that nothing will."[47] In the 1950s Gamble could still publish in *Eugenical News* and *Eugenics Quarterly,* writing more than twenty articles on the virtues of eugenic sterilization for mental defec-tives and the failure of the college educated to reproduce sufficiently be-tween 1945 and 1954.[48] However, the existence of eugenics journals in the 1950s, and the willingness of major journals like the *Journal of the American Medical Association* to publish this work, also suggests that he was not alone.

Again, we find that the ways we usually think of eugenics does not enable us to understand the Puerto Rican story very well—or, perhaps, the mainland story, either. Historians have suggested that eugenics, in the 1920s and 1930s sense of the term, had essentially disappeared from the U.S. landscape by 1945, one reaction to the horror of Nazi eugenics.[49] While this may characterize some scientists and popularizers, eugenics as a word and idea with positive appeal nevertheless died a slower death. An editor of the *Journal of the American Medical Association* quoted the following with approval in 1961:

> Who can doubt that human eugenics will eventually overcome the resis-tance of social traditions and ethical scruples and will make it possible to plan parenthood not only in time and quantity, but also in quality. A day may come when children can be made almost to order, with perfect fitness for life . . . in the foundry or in the presidential chair.[50]

The Milbank Memorial Fund continued to give support to the American Eugenics Society throughout the 1950s,[51] and some state eugenics boards, including those in North Carolina and Iowa, continued to meet and recommend sterilization throughout the 1950s. The postwar period, with its vastly expanded governmental and medical establishments, was in many ways more frightening than the period before the war, with its (hardly benign) neglect of poor people and people of color.

The end of eugenics is perhaps more appropriately dated to the early 1970s, and it is associated with the political movements of people of color. The ability to make an issue of the Tuskegee syphilis experiment in 1972 was a moment marking such a shift. In that year, a series of newspaper articles "exposed" that the U.S. Public Health Service had sponsored a natural history study in which syphilis had been left un-treated among black men (and hence also among their wives and fami-lies) who were part of the study. The exposé created a public outcry that put an end to the experiment. However, it was more importantly the case that the political climate had changed than that new knowledge had been revealed. As James Jones has shown, the experiment had been well documented in the public health and medical literature and well known to the local public health community, white and black, for forty years.[52] Likewise, the revelation that doctors were sterilizing U.S. women on welfare without their consent, including some well-publicized lawsuits charging abuse and coercion (like that concerning the Relf sisters of South Carolina, sterilized without their or their mother's knowledge at the ages of 13 and 14), condemned the practice. On the mainland, the civil rights and feminist movements ultimately did more to end eugenics practices than shifts in biology.

In Puerto Rico, Gamble's eugenics found echoes in the various *asociaciones,* but in the 1950s—after two decades of Gamble's control of birth control programs—we still find significant differences between his politics and those of someone like Celestina Zalduondo. When Gamble sent her the draft of an article that suggested that poor people in Puerto Rico were a problem, Zalduondo wrote back that she "would not accept that because a person is landless she is a social problem."[53] She understood her politics to be allied in a populist way with the struggles of working-class people. She offered a clear statement of her own strategy in her advice to a birth control champion in Argentina: "Explore with the leaders of the workers and see if you find support for your cause among them. Among the people themselves, who need and want the service, you will find your most ardent followers. Go to them."[54] At the same time, they were to her "the little people" and "the masses of poor and ignorant families," who had trouble understanding the simplest instructions.[55]

Gamble's plans for population control and eugenics were hampered by the fact that the products he backed did not work; subsequent laboratory and statistical data established that these foams and jellies were all but useless as spermicides.[56] Nevertheless, Gamble persuaded corporations to donate vast quantities of them to programs on the island, facilitating these companies' involvement in ultimately more effective, if sometimes quite dangerous, birth control research on the island. Ortho, for example, contributed considerable amounts of the contraceptive cream Preceptin extensively to the insular Health Department, and it was vigorously promoted in health units around the island.[57] In the Trujillo Alto project, Gamble insisted that the workers in that project urge women to use only the jellies of the companies supporting it.[58] Gamble also offered contributing pharmaceuticals access to a new method of spermicide rating he was developing a year in advance of its publication.

This was a powerful lure, since Gamble was on the AMA standards committee for contraceptives.[59] Gamble was as good as his word; their products ranked high when he reported his results.[60] The most significant corporate abridgment of women's choice of contraceptives came from Joseph Sunnen, who insisted that only his product, Emko foam, would be distributed along with the more than $300,000 he contributed from 1958 to 1961. Gamble encouraged and directed Sunnen, a newcomer to the field of contraception who was willingly guided. Unfortunately, Gamble's test for spermicidal effectiveness found Emko to be virtually inert. Favors are favors, however, and Gamble revised his procedures and published information that in at least one test Emko worked well.[61]

From the Emko program we know that many women also came to the conclusion that the foam didn't work well, even without benefit of laboratory data. The program for the product's distribution was brilliantly conceived and demonstrates Zalduondo's incredible organizational skill. The island was divided into twenty districts, each including three or four towns, with each overseen by a social worker. These social workers recruited, trained, and supervised a total of about 1,500 volunteers—usually teachers and social workers, but including three mayors, two policemen, twenty-four professional spiritists, one high priestess of a sect, twelve janitors, and two tenders of fighting cocks—who held meetings, gave out printed literature, importuned their neighbors, and generally used whatever methods they deemed appropriate to distribute Emko to women who wanted to use it.[62] Storefront clinics were set up to distribute Emko and handbills; a short film on contraception, *Los Tiempos Cambian,* was distributed to all the movie houses on the island, and in one town where a priest prevented the opening of an office, the program was run out of a van. To varying degrees, they succeeded in saturating the island with knowledge of the method. Unfortunately, it was pretty ineffective as a contraceptive. When a few years later Dr. Penny Satterthwaite wanted to keep her patients from switching frequently between the IUD and the pill, she told them they would have to use Emko for three months in between these two methods. It proved a good way to dissuade them. Wrote Satterthwaite, "Our area had been well covered by the Family Planning Association and most of the 40 percent of our patients who had had previous contraceptive experience claimed to have tried it and failed."[63] The Population Council reported a 29.6 percent failure rate for the method.[64]

DEVELOPING CONTRACEPTIVES

The other work in which the Asociación Puertorriqueña Pro Bienestar de la Familia (Pro Familia) and Ryder Memorial Hospital (a Congregationalist mission project) participated were high-tech and "scientific" projects to promote fertility limitation, developed by U.S. researchers in keeping with the spirit of the Point Four goal of technological assistance. Businessmen and scientific researchers, thoroughly familiar with the idea that development required industrial and technological inputs to increase economic well-being, also sought technological change as a means of social change on population questions. As a *New York Times* editorial put it in the 1960s, "If significant reductions in population growth are to be achieved there must be a technological breakthrough in contraception similar to that in food production."[65] In the 1950s and 1960s, physicians and pharmaceutical company researchers ran studies in Puerto Rico of the hormonal birth control pill, Depo-Provera, and of several IUDs, and Pro Familia and Ryder provided the support and did all the actual fieldwork and patient care.

One of the interesting questions about the development of "the pill" is why it happened when it did. To make the point that Adele Clarke has made so provocatively about all reproductive research, it happened very late.[66] If we proceed along a narrative of basic science breakthroughs followed by technological innovations that made them usable, then clinical trials of the estrogen–progestin contraceptive pill should have begun in the early 1940s, not 1956. The idea of hormonal, systemic contraception had been around since the turn of the century, and a number of studies in the 1920s and '30s found that estrogen and progesterone were effective in inhibiting ovulation. German biologist Ludwig Haberlandt showed in the 1920s that material from the corpus luteum (the "yellow body" left on the ovary after ovulation has occurred) could induce sterility in rabbits, and he proposed that such research could lead to a contraceptive for human females.[67] In the early 1930s, Corner and Allen isolated an extract from the corpus luteum in crystalline form, which they termed progestin.[68] A. W. Makepeace and collaborators conducted successful animal tests on the inhibition of ovulation with progestin in 1937.[69] On the estrogen side of the equation, Raphael Kuzrock reported in 1937 that estrogen caused ova to remain in the fallopian tubes and not descend into the uterus for implantation. He too suggested that this held promise for "hormonal sterilization" in humans.[70] Admittedly, the only commercial source for steroidal hormones was still the distilled urine of

mares and pregnant women (as historian Nelly Oudshoorn's account of
its collection and the neighbors' complaints of the smell at the Dutch
pharmaceutical company Organon have made unforgettably clear),
which was costly to produce and was certainly a drag on development
of hormones for contraceptive use.[71] Yet even this problem was solved
by 1940, when Russell Marker announced that he had created a synthetic progestin from Mexican yams.[72] By the mid-1940s, Fuller Albright, who had been working on estrogen therapy for painful and irregular menstruation,[73] had even proposed a method for clinical
application—in a textbook, no less—where he wrote:

> Since preventing ovulation prevents pregnancy, one could employ the same
> principles in birth control. . . . Thus, for example, if an individual took 1
> mg. diethylstilbestrol [DES, a synthetic estrogen] by mouth daily from the
> first day of her period for the next six weeks, she would not ovulate.[74]

When Gregory Pincus presented the earliest results from the line of research that became the first contraceptive "pill" at a conference in 1955,
the session's chair, Solly Zuckerman, felt that he had shown nothing that
was not already well known: that is, that progestin inhibits ovulation.[75]
Yet, if the scientific obstacles to producing a birth control pill had been
solved by 1940, and the point seemed obvious by 1945, why was it another decade before there were clinical trials? Forces other than the
purely scientific were at work, both in inhibiting and in promoting birth
control research.

A widely shared analysis of Third World overpopulation as a pressing social problem was a critical precondition for the development of the
pill. As the editorial from the *New York Times* quoted earlier suggests,
systemic hormonal contraception was a product of postcolonial development every bit as much as the Green Revolution in agriculture was.
This fact has been obscured by the tremendous (and unexpected) impact
of the pill in the mainland United States, and by researchers' desire to de-
emphasize it in response to sustained criticism during the 1960s of dangerous contraceptive testing with genocidal intent in the Third World.
While accusations of genocide seem to have been no more accurate in the
1960s than they were in the 1930s, they point up two interesting things.
First, as we have seen, women's sexuality and reproduction were crucial
to both Third World nationalisms and to the postcolonial development
apparatus; once again, the struggle was over who would regulate and
manage the bodies of working-class women. Second, while genocide may
not be to the point, the larger framework of overpopulation was; only

the dangerous figure of the demon mother could launch the research enterprise of the pill across the shoals that were so self-evidently there.

Researchers had no way to know whether or not the pill was safe. If
many people were aware in 1940 that it was possible to make a contraceptive pill yet sat on their hands, it was because it seemed impossible to
predict what the side effects would be. Indeed, this was Zuckerman's
warning to Pincus at the 1955 Tokyo conference where his results were
first presented:

> We need better evidence about the occurrence of side effects in human
> beings. It is not enough though . . . that we take presumed negative
> evidence about the lack of side-effects from animal experiments to imply
> that no undesirable side-effects would occur in human beings. There is an
> urgent need for prolonged observation before we draw any firm
> conclusions.[76]

Three pharmaceutical companies—Searle, Parke-Davis, and Pfizer—
possessed patents and animal studies in 1955 that would have enabled
them to begin clinical trials with the hope of turning a considerable
profit, but there was no competition. The corporate leadership at Parke-
Davis and Pfizer believed that clinical trials would be too dangerous and
unethical; at Searle, they went to Puerto Rico. In the 1970s, a member
of the World Heath Organization's Contraceptive Task Force described
the context in retrospect. While he meant to praise Searle, the hesitancy
of other players is remarkable.

> Full credit should be given to the Searle Company for their sang-froid,
> vision and courage in marketing the first oral contraceptive preparation in
> 1959 [when FDA approved it for treatment of "menstrual irregularities"]
> in a hostile atmosphere controlled by restrictive and conservative societal
> forces influenced by traditionalism, strong taboos (and still popular) belief
> that technological progress can be stopped by ideological forces and politi-
> cal determination. This was a period in history when several drug houses
> declared that it was and always would be incompatible with their ethical
> principles to manufacture fertility regulating agents.[77]

While we should not underestimate the extent to which this context was
informed by an ethic that was simply anti-sex, or more precisely, opposed to nonreproductive sex, there was also a subsequent explosion of
concern about possible side effects when the pill became widely available
on the mainland, including from physicians. It ought to alert us to the
palpable concern present in the 1950s, following the thalidomide
tragedy (in which a tranquilizer prescribed for pregnant women had

caused severe limb deformities in their offspring), about side effects. Common sense dictated that caution was appropriate in giving steroidal compounds with powerful, systemic effects—many of which were unknown—to a population of healthy women. Pharmaceutical companies had plenty of reason for concern about clinical trials in healthy, reproductive-age women. Even considering opposition to contraceptives on anti-sex grounds alone, we still must account for what made this resistance surmountable for some researchers in the 1950s.

In Puerto Rico, as we have seen, the road to the clinical trials was inaugurated with the founding of the Population Association and its transformation into Pro Familia. These groups were composed mostly of women and operated within the tradition of feminism that believed strongly in modernization, technology, and science as a road to social progress. On the mainland, the project was launched in a similar way: Margaret Sanger, champion since the Progressive Era of technology as the means to better contraception, guided heiress Katherine Dexter Mc-Cormick toward funding endocrinological research on hormonal contraception. In 1951, at Sanger's urging, Gregory Pincus, already known for maverick work in reproductive biology (he had lost his appointment at Harvard following his well-publicized claim to have induced parthenogenesis in rabbits), began work on hormonal contraceptives under a small grant from the Planned Parenthood Federation of America (PPFA). In 1953 McCormick took over the funding of his work, and even as PPFA lost interest in it, began to fund it as extensively as Pincus could find use for the money.[78]

Pincus and a postdoctoral fellow in his lab, Min-Chueh Chang, had discussed working on hormonal contraception before; Pincus wrote later that "a recognition of the population explosion" prompted him to consider such research.[79] Chang also recalled that overpopulation had been a critical issue in their laboratory. He told one writer on the history of progestin contraceptives that he and Pincus had often discussed methods of contraception, "particularly after the 'population explosion' made the headlines after World War II."[80] These concerns certainly informed their decision to apply for a PPFA grant, and too, PPFA's decision to grant it; its director in this period was none other than William Vogt, author of *People! Challenge to Survival*. After leaving Harvard, Pincus had had to struggle for funding for his Worcester Foundation for Experimental Biology. A biological entrepreneur par excellence, he had worked for numerous funders, including Searle pharmaceutical, the Rockefeller Foundation, and PPFA.[81] With McCormick's interest, however, hormonal contraceptive research became lucrative as well as an appealing line of work for addressing the social problems of the developing world. The latter continued to be a serious issue in Pincus's writing. He began a 1959 *Washington Post* piece on hormonal contraceptive research with the following words:

> The control of the population explosion now upon us by the limitation of births is particularly demanding in countries where the birth-rate pressure curtails already limited economic development. Conventional contraceptive methods have been known and publicized widely in these countries, but the acceptance of them has been most unremarkable. . . . Accordingly, there has been an increasing demand for a simple, easily practiced, generally acceptable, inexpensive means of contraception. Generally this demand has been for some easy medication.[82]

Urging that in the wake of the atomic bomb, scientific research must take responsibility for its social effects, Pincus wrote in another context that biologists had a positive social responsibility to address overpopulation. He called for biologists to form a Federation of Population Scientists and to undertake further research on limiting fertility.[83]

After completing animal studies with progesterone and a host of other steroidal compounds obtained from various pharmaceutical companies,[84] Pincus (through PPFA) approached Dr. John Rock, who was working with progesterone on human subjects in an infertility clinic at the Free Hospital for Women near Boston.[85] Margaret Sanger initially opposed Pincus's collaboration with Rock, as the latter was a devout Catholic. Yet Rock ultimately proved a staunch ally of contraception, principally because he too was concerned about the threat of overpopulation. He was the author in 1965 of a crusader's book addressed to the Catholic hierarchy and laity, *The Time Has Come: A Catholic Doctor's Proposal to End the Battle Over Birth Control,* which defended the pill as a natural contraceptive (because its action mimicked pregnancy) and as an essential response to the threat of overpopulation.[86] While all the principals involved in the development of the pill suggest that concerns about overpopulation were a major factor in undertaking research on hormonal contraceptives, the most dramatic example is John Rock. Rock was, by all accounts, a man for whom moral and ethical considerations were paramount. Unlike Pincus, he never became rich from the success of the pill—he refused to invest in Searle stock because he disliked the idea that people would think he had become wealthy from risks taken with others' bodies—and he had no love of the role of maverick.

He was known as a physician who was elaborately kind to his patients, had a faithful following, and who as a researcher was particularly concerned about side effects.[87] In short, he provides an excellent study—not of the unethical handling of the pill trials—but of precisely the opposite, of how global political concerns made the pill trials *ethical* for many North Americans, and later, for the burgeoning Puerto Rican middle class.

Rock and his group of graduate physicians (Drs. Angelika Tsacoma, Luigi Mastroianni, and John Kelley) were initially using steroids for the opposite ends of Pincus's lab: to try to induce pregnancy in women who were inexplicably infertile. These clinicians used synthetic estrogenic and natural progesterone treatments, hypothesizing that the problem might involve underdeveloped reproductive organs and that simulating pregnancy could help. After four months, they stopped the treatment, and thirteen of their eighty previously infertile subjects became pregnant.[88] Working with Pincus's group (which included Chang, Robert Slechta, Anne Merrill, and J. Choiniere), Rock's group of clinicians began in 1954 to use those researchers' more active synthetic steroids, and they tried to measure whether infertile patients were ovulating during the administration of these compounds. They initiated a regime of urine testing and basal body temperature monitoring to look for secondary effects of ovulation (pregnandiol in urine, a sharp rise in morning temperature) in patients they believed were normally regular ovulaters. Tsacoma even did laparotomies on ten patients who were already scheduled for hysterectomies, during which she looked for corpus lutea (yellow bodies) evidence on the ovary of recent ovulation.[89]

This research suggested that ovulation was inhibited, particularly with two steroids, initially reported to be 19-nor-17-ethinyl testosterone and 17-ethinyl estaeneolone. These names, although laborious, are interesting; the first is related to testosterone, the second, to estrogen. Later, among both historians and scientific researchers, the story came to be told that Pincus and Rock were interested only in progesterone-related compounds. This story was important, because it described a "natural" mode of contraception in which chemicals merely simulated pregnancy, inhibiting repeated ovulation in the same way many mammalian females do during pregnancy, through excreting progesterone.[90] (In Rock's word's, "They provide a natural means of fertility control such as nature uses after ovulation and during pregnancy."[91]) This also had implications for the kinds of side effects that were considered (Pincus argued that few were to be expected, since the human female body was "naturally" adapted to large amounts of progesterone[92]) and supported an ethical argument about the morality of this sort of contraception since it mimicked a natural process. Moreover, testosterone and estrogen had and have profound social identities beyond their chemical character as steroids.[93] They have been reified as "sex hormones," and, indeed, have been frequently rendered in popular culture as the essence of maleness or femaleness.[94] That both are present in men and women, and that both are systemically active—not just affecting secondary sex characteristics—has historically been less important than other cultural meanings. Yet all hormones are closely related steroids, and once chemists began to tamper with them, it was probably more appropriate to consider all of them simply as steroids, as Pincus's early papers did, than to try to name them as related to a particular hormone. For, as every introductory organic chemistry student knows, there is more than one way to name a carbon ring. In fact, that is precisely what happened. The 19-nor-17-ethinyl testosterone mentioned above came to be referred to as norethynodrel—a progestin, no longer a testosterone—and became the basis for the first pill. As time went on, the pill's character as a progestin became increasingly a part of its identity, although throughout the 1960s, no one could say for sure how it worked—whether in fact it simulated pregnancy or did something else. By 1963, a reviewer for a medical journal article noted in the margin of his review that norethynodrel could just as easily be named as a testosterone, an estrogen, or a progestin—but commented, "Testosterone looks funny in print . . . Nah, we'd never print it."[95] Whatever the nature of global concerns about excessive population, those targeted to receive steroidal contraceptives were still importantly *women,* and the compound simply could not be named testosterone.

The responses to the next set of small-scale trials suggests again how fundamentally the targets of this project to offer a technological fix for overpopulation were women. In the next group of female patients, no new information was gleaned, and Pincus and McCormick showed themselves willing to utilize less-than-consenting populations—a "cage of ovulating females," in McCormick's phrase.[96] In these clinical trials, one targeted female students at the new medical school in Puerto Rico and another utilized mental patients in Massachusetts—female and male—at a facility where McCormick had been a regular contributor. (There was also a short-lived effort by Pincus to use Puerto Rican women prisoners.) For the medical students, the demanding daily regimen of pill-taking, temperature-measuring, vaginal smear and monthly urine collection and endometrial biopsy proved impossible to keep up with, even though their grades were apparently held hostage to their participation in the study. No meaningful data were collected. Although the mental patient group could be more successfully monitored on a daily basis, female contraceptive effect was difficult to gauge in a population that were presumed not to have sexual intercourse. These studies, then, offered little except the general information that these steroidal compounds posed no immediately appreciable systemic danger to users. However, they once again raised the flag of side effects; as with Rock's infertile patients, quite a number of the participants complained of dizziness, nausea, headache, and menstrual irregularities.[97]

Researchers also followed another lead in this series of cases: steroids had previously been documented to cause male infertility, too. Among the psychotic men in Massachusetts, urine samples and biopsied testicular tissue showed—albeit inconclusively—that the steroidal compound they were testing stopped sperm production.[98] The implications of this were never pursued; no effort was made to develop or further test the pill as a contraceptive for men. Something about giving steroidal compounds to men was less appealing than controlling women's fertility. This choice was probably overdetermined. A number of explanations come to mind, including the fact that McCormick and Sanger, as funders, were interested specifically in a female-controlled method and the fact that the discourse of overpopulation targeted women. However, another issue was noted that probably also contributed: one of the male mental patients was described by a nurse as acting "effeminate" during treatment. Although no physiologic effects like breast development were reported, the suggestion that these steroids could make men act like women, or like homosexuals, was apparently enough. It is hard to guess what behavior a psychotic man who was unable to cooperate with researchers could have exhibited to make him seem "feminine" to the nursing staff. But such possible side effects dovetailed with the perception of hormones as powerfully the essence of maleness or femaleness, and seem to have been sufficient to deter further such research.

The next round of testing in 1956 involved a much larger series of cases, and these, too, were organized in Puerto Rico. Two groups of women, one residents of a housing project in Río Piedras, and another, patients of Ryder Hospital (usually, women turned down for sterilization because they had fewer than the three children required[99]), were enrolled in an effort to understand whether the pill prevented pregnancy and whether it was acceptable and could be used effectively by those who "most needed" contraception, specifically working-class women living in overpopulated and underdeveloped countries. By 1957, each group consisted of between 200 and 300 women. Many feminist scholars and activists, as well as popular writers, have argued that the Puerto Rico trials were shoddily conducted, in that they took inappropriate risks with women's health.[100] It might also be said that they failed on their own terms; they neither lowered the birth rate among trial participants nor were they acceptable. Half the trial participants in both groups dropped out, and a good percentage of these left the trials because they found the side effects—severe headache, nausea, vomiting, mid-cycle bleeding—too unpleasant and not worth the trouble.[101] There were also a significant number of pregnancies in both groups. In the first year and a half, there were twenty pregnancies among the 295 participants from Río Piedras, or a percentage of 14 per 100 woman-years of exposure.[102] (Pincus misreported this as five pregnancies in the text of his article announcing the success of the pill. He acknowledged another fourteen pregnancies in a footnote.[103]) Moreover, the pregnancy rate among those who stopped using the pill was 79 percent within four months, a very high rate caused by the "rebound effect" of heightened fertility post-pill.[104] All of this was close enough for Pincus—the pregnancies during the study were explicable in terms of pills missed, whether under orders from a physician to relieve side effects or because of forgetfulness—and most occurred after women were no longer enrolled in the study. Those who were truly miserable with side effects were quickly out of the study. However, its real effect on the community of women who took the pill was a rate of side effects (including those so severe as to require hospitalization) high enough that new recruitment for the study became quite difficult,[105] and an increase in the pregnancy rate.

The trials—and the pill generally—have also been criticized as an example of male and masculinist science being callous about women's bodies.[106] But it bears underlining that the people most directly involved with these trials were women and feminists. Sanger and McCormick supported and shepherded the work of Pincus and his lab, even when PPFA dropped it. Although Pincus was subsequently embraced by the medical community and sharply criticized by feminists, it is interesting to note where he sought out sympathetic audiences in the late 1950s. The first public venue in which information about trials of a contraceptive pill was published was not a scientific journal, but the *Ladies Home Journal,* and the first conference at which the results were presented was an annual Planned Parenthood conference.[107] In Puerto Rico, two North American women doctors—who, one suspects, found a wider field for professional credibility and work on the island than on the mainland in the 1950s—conducted the trials. Dr. Edris Rice-Wray, medical director of the Asociación and director of the Health Department work in Río Piedras, and Adeleine (Penny) Satterthwaite of Ryder Hospital were the primary physicians recording the effects of the pill. Each had a Puerto Rican female counterpart who was even more intimately involved in the trials: in Río Piedras, nurses Mercedes Quiñones and Iris Rodríguez of Pro Familia, and in Humacao, social worker Noemí Rodríguez from Ryder. These women were no mere lackeys in this process; they were well educated professionals who had come to birth control work because they believed in the cause. Both Rice-Wray and Satterthwaite continued contraceptive research elsewhere after they left Puerto Rico—the former with the pill in Mexico, the latter, with the IUD in Thailand.[108] Like their male colleagues in the study, both also cited concerns about overpopulation as the motivating force that brought them to this work. Satterthwaite, a missionary, told the following story:

> On my way to Puerto Rico . . . [I met] Dr. Ralph Allee. He said to me, "Here you're going to Puerto Rico, out to save lives and to deliver babies, and full of enthusiasm. Have you ever thought about what you may be doing to complicate the future of the [island]." Here was an agricultural man . . . worrying about food supply. And so he was perhaps the first one that really faced me up to a responsibility.[109]

Rice-Wray, similarly, wrote, "Puerto Rico is one of the most densely populated countries in the world. We are all interested in finding some reliable contraceptive which is cheap, acceptable to the people, easy to take and something the people themselves would be interested in taking."[110] She later also used similar language to characterize the situation of Mexico.[111] Of the motivation of Iris Rodríguez, Noemí Rodríguez, and Mercedes Quiñones, it is more difficult to say anything definite, since they wrote no letters or articles for the study, making it harder to guess at their frame of mind. Nevertheless, they acted in a way consistent with both the leadership and membership of Pro Familia and the other *asociaciones* during the previous twenty years. From one point of view, they practiced the art of the possible, seeking to promote birth control and hence jumping onto whatever project some North American group or company was willing to fund. From a more cynical perspective, they collaborated with North Americans in the project of making over the "backward" working-class into modern families, through coercive means if necessary.

To notice the cooperation between feminists and Searle Pharmaceu-

tical is not to say that they behaved in precisely the same way. Both Satterthwaite and Rice-Wray treated side effects with much greater seri-
ousness than Pincus or Searle. They were very concerned, and both recommended that the pill not be used further. In her initial report to the
company, Rice-Wray wrote that Enovid "causes too many side effects to
be generally acceptable."[112] Satterthwaite wrote to Gamble repeatedly
that she was "a little alarmed by the marked changes . . . which I have
noted in the cervices of these women who have been taking the pills,"
particularly those who had begun the study with cervical erosions that
subsequently worsened.[113] She continued to insist on regular endometrial biopsies to test for any signs of reproductive cancers, even though
the biopsies had to be sent all the way to Boston to be read, due to lack
of facilities on the island. Pincus played fast and loose about the distinction between "his" cases—those directly under his supervision at Río
Piedras—and Satterthwaite's in Humacao, reporting her results together
with his (as if it were a single group), even though she felt the results were
not yet ready for public scrutiny.[114] The final straw for Satterthwaite was
when, after her considerable concern about reproductive cancer risk associated with the pill and three cases within her sample, Pincus announced at a news conference that he believed the pill had a *protective*
effect against cancer and that he had gotten a grant from the American
Cancer Society to study it.[115] Even under pressure from Pincus, Satterthwaite refused to back down from her belief that the side effects reported by women were real and significant.[116] Pincus, meanwhile, ran a
placebo trial, and concluded that the suggestion of the possibility of side
effects was what was causing them, due to "the emotional super-activ-
ity of Puerto Rican women." Thereafter, potential participants simply
were not warned.[117] By the mid-1960s, Satterthwaite had decided firmly
that the IUD was more acceptable, safer, and easier to use, and advocated its use over the pill.[118]

In sum, an underlying logic of risk brought the clinical trials of the pill
to Puerto Rico. Researchers had been motivated initially to do research
on the pill because they were concerned about overpopulation, and
Puerto Rico stood as one of the paradigmatic examples of overpopulation. When Thomas Parran, head of the U.S. Public Health Service,
thought of overpopulation, he mentioned "such countries as China or
India (or Java or Puerto Rico)."[119] Whereas most groups of researchers
had been deterred in developing a steroidal contraceptive by concerns
over dangers associated with its systemic effects, the threat of overpopulation was a factor that overrode such concerns. Medical researchers

were accustomed to cost-benefit thinking: the risks of a drug ought to be less significant than the danger posed by the disease it was used to treat. The cost-benefit ratio of contraceptives was harder to figure within this calculus; no side effects were worth the risk if the people taking the drug were healthy. However, overpopulation shifted this equation: the dangers of overpopulation were construed as life threatening, and hence worth a great deal of risk.

There is still another reason to think of pill research as overdetermined by the colonial context. There were actually very early trials of an oral contraceptive proposed for Puerto Rico. In 1941 the pharmaceutical company Hoffman-Laroche, apparently in collaboration with Sanger and Gamble, tried to test an oral contraceptive designed in Africa in Puerto Rico. Sanger proposed it to José Belaval on a trip to the island and he readily accepted.[120] Belaval even went so far as to arrange for facilities with Presbyterian Hospital,[121] but he found no takers for the drug, a problem Gamble, unsurprisingly, attributed to his "working too high on the social scale."[122]

In the two decades at mid-century, then, the "dangerous mother" popularized in the rhetoric of overpopulation in the 1920s and 1930s came to occupy center stage, not only in Puerto Rico but as a characterization of the problems of the Third World generally. The reproduction of working-class women in Puerto Rico contributed to launching a new form of international power and relations between the United States and the Third World: economic development. Puerto Rico, having been characterized as a "laboratory" of one sort or another since World War I, was transformed into a "social laboratory" for anti-poverty development programs intended to stave off communism by transforming backward women. Development on the island was characterized on the one hand by a program of industrialization, and on the other by population control programs that made women their target. In keeping with a theory of reproductive research and activism stretching back to the 1920s that working-class and colonized women required contraceptives different from those used by affluent or U.S women, the programs specifically encouraged "simple" contraception. Simple contraception in this period included jelly and foam, and later other methods, including sterilization and ultimately the pill and IUD as well, that gave physicians and population control workers increasing control over working-class women's reproduction. The model was designed to be exportable, and there were subsequently many population control programs throughout Asia, Africa, and Latin America sponsored by U.S. and European development agencies.

Overpopulation provided a sociological explanation for Third World poverty, one that denied a role for international capitalism or colonialism in producing these conditions. It rested on an implausible, oversimplified, and often frankly untrue theory of economics and public health that went something like this:

> In the many areas of the world where the standard of living is at subsistence level, each specific improvement in death control serves to depress that standard. As the living standard goes down, malnutrition grows, ill health increases, and the death rate rises. . . . In these areas widespread provision of effective and acceptable methods of pregnancy spacing is essential to further health improvement.[123]

Though it was written about the island in 1961, this was of course a preposterous description. Puerto Rico was urban and industrial, and at the time health, wealth, and income were increasing at astonishing rates. The evocation of a "standard of living at subsistence level" seems designed to conjure up visions of a remote agricultural village, rather than of a colony and economic outpost that had endured for five hundred years, first under Spain and then under the United States. The most interesting thing about these lines, however, is that they come not from sociology or economics—though they could have—but from a gynecology journal, and they served to introduce an article on the pill. Reproductive research produced the pill as a specific technological fix to the Third World problem of overpopulation. In so doing, it rendered the account of overpopulation more plausible by associating it with science and technological solutions at the height of the Cold War belief in them.

CHAPTER 5

The Politics of Sterilization, 1937–1974

If the politics of birth control engaged multiple nationalisms, sterilization in Puerto Rico did so to a still greater extent. It became an issue around which questions of insular status, economy, race, and gender swirled—or, to put it differently, as the words themselves were called into question—colonialism, capitalism, racism, and sexism. The burgeoning of Third World nationalist, feminist, and racial justice movements brought the never neutral questions of sexuality and reproduction to the forefront of these struggles, and Puerto Rican sterilization was important far beyond the boundaries of the island. By the 1970s, the debate over the question of sterilization had stretched across four decades and multiple places, from the island to the mainland to Latin America. As it did so, it also doubled back on itself, and claims about sterilization policies in Puerto Rico in the 1930s came to stand in for concerns about coercive sterilization of Native Americans in Bureau of Indian Affairs hospitals or of Chicanas in Los Angeles in the 1970s. As the history of sterilization became so important in the 1970s—as if it told the essential "truth" of the policy in that decade—it becomes difficult to make sense of the earlier policies and practices without having the story refracted, however obliquely, through the lens of the questions of the later period. That being the case, it is ultimately more straightforward (and perhaps simply honest) to tell the narrative of this chapter backwards, to begin in the 1970s so as to understand how Puerto Rican working-class women's sterilization became crucial to the politics of liberation movements.

On the mainland in the 1970s, reproductive rights activists in groups like the Coalition to End Sterilization Abuse (CESA) in New York and the Coalition for Abortion Rights and Against Sterilization Abuse (CARASA) in California and some socialist feminist scholars began to explore questions of the racial and international politics of birth control and contraceptive sterilization. Repeatedly, Puerto Rico emerged in this literature as an exemplary case study of how birth control could be used for capitalist social engineering with racist ends. Sterilization rates in Puerto Rico—about one-third of women of childbearing age, a figure that remained constant through the 1980s—were among the highest in the world at that time.[1] Bonnie Mass's *Population Target,* Linda Gordon's *Woman's Body, Woman's Right,* Angela Davis's *Woman, Race, and Class,* and filmmaker Ana María García's *La Operación* purported to show the existence of a U.S. corporate and government policy, begun in the 1930s, to eradicate "excess" Puerto Rican workers through the mass sterilization of women. For Bonnie Mass, Puerto Rico was the most advanced case of a U.S. foreign policy of population control and capitalist expansion in Latin America.[2] Linda Gordon took up this argument and placed it in the context of Margaret Sanger's support for eugenics and the question of whether Planned Parenthood—particularly its international wing—was a racist organization.[3] For Davis, this narrative became an example of racism in the women's movement: white women continued to urge freedom from reproduction, even in a context where it was coercive.[4] García folded the story into a film that was also about the mistreatment of Puerto Ricans in New York, and equated women's lost fertility with land stolen by U.S. colonialist invaders.[5]

This chapter explores some of the limitations of this analysis. While there seems little doubt of the intuition guiding this reading of Puerto Rican policy—that reproduction was a site of coercion, violence, and U.S. genocidal impulses—the mainland reproductive rights movement, in adopting a politic that insisted that the sterilization of Puerto Rican women amounted to genocide, self-consciously allied itself with Puerto Rican nationalism but failed to recognize the extent to which nationalist pro-natalism in Puerto Rico had historically been associated with conservative Catholicism and anti-feminism. In so doing, mainland feminism disabled potential alliances with feminists on the island, who negotiated far more complex relationships with the various nationalist ideologies, and adopted their anti-colonialism while refusing their pro-natalism. Ironically, mainland anti-colonialist feminists ended up pronouncing on the failures of impoverished Puerto Rican families, particularly

women, and the necessity for (U.S. women's) intervention—precisely
the same terrain occupied by liberal U.S. colonialists and Puerto Rican
elites.

The debate over Puerto Rican sterilization among mainland feminists probably had more to do with the politics of race on the continent
than with Puerto Rico. Through scholarly books and political organizations, multiracial groups of feminist activists and scholars in the
1970s took up questions of race and poverty and insisted that they
were sufficiently important to modify the feminist demand for freedom
from reproduction (through birth control and abortion) to encompass
also the freedom *to* reproduce without state or other social intervention.[6] Nevertheless, the mainland feminist effort to articulate an anti-
colonialist politics with women at the center inadvertently recapitu-
lated the terms of a U.S. colonialist narrative: Puerto Rican women are
victimized and need to be saved. As a result, the movement failed to
generate significant political alliances with feminists in Puerto Rico,
who were among the people, after all, it was intended to help. This
kind of political relationship was certainly possible. In the 1920s and
'30s, without benefit of planes or phones, suffragists and New Dealers
had managed to create lasting, effective alliances with Puerto Rican
women's organizations that had resulted in measurable change for insular women on the island, including the right to vote and, briefly, a
minimum wage law.[7]

Mainland feminists turned the Puerto Rican sterilization story into an
allegory for a continental U.S. issue. They attributed high sterilization
rates on the island to the apparatuses of social control: the U.S. military,
the federal government, and corporate capitalism. What disappeared in
these accounts was the Puerto Rican feminist and birth control movement. For example, Mass turned the continuous, fifty-year-old insular
feminist and birth control movement into a pawn of corporate and U.S.
governmental interests:

> In response to these "demographic pressures" [as identified by U.S.
> demographers], private birth control clinics were set up under the auspices
> of *La Asociación Puertorriqueña Pro Bienestar de la Familia*, first supported
> by Planned Parenthood, and later by the Sunnen Foundation . . . .
> [Subsequently,] funding of the private *Asociación Puertorriqueña Pro
> Bienestar de la Familia* was taken over by the Health, Education and
> Welfare (HEW) Department's Office of Economic Opportunity as part
> of Lyndon Johnson's Great Society anti-poverty program.[8]

Mass ignored the fact that some Puerto Rican feminist activists had supported Pro Familia and its precursor organizations for thirty years before Planned Parenthood did, and that it had never received all its funding from any of these sources. Her use of the passive voice ("clinics were set up") misleadingly attributes responsibility for birth control and sterilization activities to mainland instruments of social control, neglecting all the Puerto Rican women who fought to establish them. Ana María García's *La Operación* tells a similar story, of coercive U.S. efforts to sterilize working-class women, through alternating testimonials by women and authoritative voice-overs. Yet the women in the film who have been sterilized tell a story of decisions they made based on health, family economies, or beliefs about modernity, while the voice-over inscribes a narrative of the state and social control. For example, in the opening minutes of the film, a woman tells the interviewer, "We didn't have much money and the doctor told me I couldn't have many children. I talked to my husband and got myself the operation [*y me operé*—the meaning is subtly changed in the English subtitle to "and got sterilized"] . . . Nobody forced me." Where "nobody forced me" is clearly a reference either to the prevalent Catholic discourse of "forced sterilization" or to something the interviewer said off camera, the narration that follows tells a subtly different story: "In 1937 sterilization was approved by Governor Blanton Winship, based on the principles of eugenics, advocating the breeding of the fit and the weeding out of the unfit, namely the poor and the non-white." Again, Puerto Rican feminist activism is excised from this account. In fact, women's groups lobbied for the bill (which also legalized birth control) and, as we have seen, feminist leader and *independentista* Carmen Rivera de Alvarado allowed herself to be arrested in order to test the bill's standing under federal law.[9] In these and the other accounts, any attempt to limit fertility is part of a genocidal U.S. plan, and Puerto Rican feminists simply drop out. Puerto Rican women stand en bloc for the problem of women's oppression, and as proof-text for the importance of (mainland) feminism. Gayatri Spivak has argued that this problem is endemic to left politics and left intellectuals; she terms it the problem of speaking on behalf of the subaltern. Here, the ventriloquist trick is one of forcing a narrative from the bodies of working-class Puerto Rican women in order to authorize U.S. feminist politics.[10]

There was, nevertheless, something significant at stake for feminist antisterilization politics: the mainland dynamics of race and reproduction. In the 1970s mainland socialist feminists began to respond to conservative efforts to force working-class and non-white women to limit their fertility. Paradoxically, every significant success of white, middle-class women in the United States to limit their fertility has been answered by this kind of reactionary repressive effort against working-class and/or non-white women, from the Social Darwinism of the mid–nineteenth century, to "race suicide" at century's end, to eugenics in the early to mid–twentieth century. In the 1960s and '70s, the liberalization of birth control and abortion laws and the widespread use of the pill prompted some policy makers and scientists to begin calling for compulsory birth control measures for working-class people. More than ten states saw legislation proposed (albeit unsuccessfully) requiring women on welfare to use birth control.[11] Meanwhile, progressive groups began to investigate whether the various new Department of Health, Education, and Welfare (HEW) health care and anti-poverty programs were covertly enacting what these policy makers were recommending: compulsory birth control and sterilization. In 1973 the Southern Poverty Law Center broke the news of the case that seemed to confirm the worst fears: that of Mary Alice's and Minnie Lee Relf's unwilling and unwitting sterilization.[12] Significantly, this story emerged hard on the heels of revelations that in nearby Tuskegee, Alabama, the U.S. Public Health Service had knowingly and deliberately withheld treatment for syphilis from a group of black men in order to monitor the "natural" course of the disease.[13] A picture of alternating neglect and malevolent governmental health activities in communities of color began to emerge. Within months, Congressional hearings revealed that in 1972, sixteen thousand women and eight thousand men had been sterilized with federal government funds, and that more than three hundred of these patients had been under the age of 21.[14] Further lawsuits followed. In 1977, ten Mexican-American women tried to sue the Los Angeles County Hospital for obtaining their "consent" for sterilization while they were in labor, and in English, though they spoke only Spanish. Bureau of Indian Affairs hospitals were believed to be particularly egregious in their abuse of sterilization, and Norma Jean Serena, a Native American mother of three, attempted to sue officials in Armstrong County, Pennsylvania, for civil rights violations for conspiring to have her sterilized when her third child was born.[15]

True, there was also a kind of international politics being struggled over, but again it had mostly to do with U.S. foreign policy. As we have seen, liberal academics and State Department policy makers had made the Cold War case for intervention in the Third World family: communism was caused by overpopulation and could be halted with birth control. While the Malthusian argument was bad economics and doomed policy, it nevertheless sold well on the mainland—it identified the cause of Third World poverty not as the history of colonialism but as ignorant women and too-large families, and it found the solution in suburban American-style domesticity and liberal democracy. Thus, it provided a response to the Soviet Union's accusations of U.S. imperialism and a grounding for a patriotic American nationalism. In Indochina, the U.S. Agency for International Development distributed birth control pills to halt the spread of communism in South Vietnam, while the Defense Department dropped napalm on the North.[16] Meanwhile, scientists like biologist Paul Ehrlich of Stanford University and physiologist Melvin Ketchel of Tufts Medical School suggested putting sterilizing agents in the water and rice supplies of Third World countries.[17]

Mainland leftists and feminists joined the debate over sterilization as part of essentially local struggles over internal U.S. politics. Black power movement figures, taking up a pro-natalist position that had been debated in African-American communities since early in the twentieth century, argued that HEW birth control programs in ghettoes and working-class neighborhoods constituted genocide.[18] The Young Lords and La Brecha—young Puerto Ricans inspired by the Black Panthers—heard in this genocide argument echoes from their own nationalist tradition and took it up as well. Thus, when members of the Puerto Rican Socialist Party (PSP) and the Independence Party (PIP) testified before the United Nations special committee on colonialism that "North American imperialists" were embarked on a "plan of genocide" in Puerto Rico that had led to the sterilization of 200,000 women,[19] many leftists and feminists in the mainland United States were appalled but not greatly surprised: the testimony echoed what they already knew about African Americans in the South, and Native Americans and Chicanos in the Southwest.[20]

Questions about population control in Puerto Rico became central to a major debate about U.S. politics within feminist circles. The question of sterilization abuse divided mainland feminists in the 1970s, separating those who believed that working-class people should at times be strongly encouraged to remedy their economic situation by limiting the number of children from those who regarded the suggestion as racist and elitist. This conflict emerged sharply over the efforts of CESA in New York to make and enforce guidelines related to contraceptive sterilization. With Puerto Rican physician Helen Rodriguez-Trias as spokesperson, CESA and others developed guidelines whereby New York municipal hospitals could perform tubal ligations only under limited and restrictive circumstances, including a thirty-day waiting period and an interdiction on obtaining consent for the operation at the time of other medical procedures such as abortion or delivery.[21] These guidelines were particularly important, they argued, given that population control enthusiast Antonio Silva had recently moved from his public health post in Puerto Rico to one at New York's Lincoln Hospital.[22] The proposal generated substantial opposition from obstetricians and gynecologists, who charged that it limited their free speech, and more significantly from segments of the feminist community. Planned Parenthood, long the chief advocate for birth control and a major provider of services, refused to accept either the analysis or the guidelines and emerged as the principle, if unsuccessful, opponent of a bill to implement them. Subsequently, the fight went national, and in 1978 the HEW guidelines on sterilization in hospitals were sharply amended, despite the opposition of some chapters of the National Organization for Women.[23]

This division also appeared, albeit on slightly different grounds, in scholarly journals. Puerto Rican sterilization specifically gave shape to the issue of whether women's history counts as "real" history. Gordon's discussion of sterilization in Puerto Rico and population control policies was passionately opposed by historians James Reed (and less vociferously) Doone Williams and Greer Williams. Reed and others argued in favor of the Malthusian economic equation and contended that Puerto Ricans suffered badly from an imbalance between population and resources and would have been far worse off without the aid of U.S. birth controllers.[24] The differences between Gordon and Reed became a cause célèbre in history and feminist journals in the late 1970s. Reed's champions insisted that he was writing "objective" history, whereas Gordon—and women's historians in general—were writing "ideology" for a feminist political movement.[25] Feminists and leftists responded that it was Reed who wrote ideological history—as an apologist for a racist, capitalist state.[26] These questions were never resolved. They were rehearsed all over again in the late 1980s and early 1990s when Gordon and Reed's books were reissued with new introductions in which each claimed they had been wronged by the initial reviews.[27]

THE GENOCIDE ARGUMENT: THE HISTORY OF A DISCOURSE

While the politics of sterilization abuse defined the antiracist left in the mainland context, it made a very different set of political distinctions in

Puerto Rico. The discourse of sterilization as genocide and social control had a long history on the island and tended to demarcate a position that could be quite conservative. As we have seen, the Nationalist Party of Albizu Campos had begun insisting that birth control was a genocidal American plot long before there was North American support for the island's birth control movement. Albizu's formulation of birth control and sterilization as "trying to invade the very insides of nationality," was rearticulated in the 1960s by Puerto Rican literary figure René Marqués in his famous essay, "El puertorriqueño dócil" (The Docile Puerto Rican), which argued that one of the effects of U.S. colonial rule was the imposition of an Anglo-Saxon matriarchy, with women controlling the family and taking inappropriate roles in civil society, replacing a strong Creole machismo, Spanish honor, and the Roman paterfamilias.[28] Celestine Zalduondo, feminist, *independentista,* and sterilization provider, expressed the critique of Albizu's politics in these terms: "In some areas of the island, the notion of the heroic child bearer is very important. You can go back to Pedro Albizo Campos, the head of the Nationalist Party for many years, who argued against birth control, and who exalted the peasant woman who bore many children for her homeland."[29]

After 1937 Nationalists abandoned their concern with birth control and the genocide argument began to turn almost exclusively on sterilization. As we have seen, the 1937 birth control bill included provisions for eugenic sterilization. Following the model established by numerous U.S. states and Latin American nations, the bill created a Eugenics Board. Puerto Rico's board functioned quite differently from those in the high-sterilization-rate states like California or North Carolina. It ordered only ninety-seven involuntary sterilizations, in contrast to tens of thousands in California.[30] Unlike the mainland, there were two kinds of legal sterilization in Puerto Rico in the 1930s: eugenic and contraceptive (which was presumptively voluntary). On the mainland, voluntary contraceptive sterilization did not become legal until the 1970s (when it rapidly became the most popular birth control method on the mainland, by far). As the number of surgical sterilization procedures done in Puerto Rican hospitals increased steadily from the 1940s through the 1960s, the overwhelming majority were *not* ordered by the Eugenics Board. The controversy in Puerto Rico was over the nature of what was happening in municipal hospitals—how voluntary the operation in fact was—but was never over officially ordered, involuntary eugenic sterilization. The comparison with the mainland in works like García's film, which argued that sterilization was always a eugenic measure, was to compare apples and oranges. However one interprets the activities of municipal hospitals in this early period, they were not engaged in eugenic sterilization in the same sense that mainland institutions were.

From the early 1940s through the early 1960s, the Church waged a continuous campaign against contraceptive sterilization and its supporters, insisting that there was a secret, genocidal mass sterilization policy being carried out in Puerto Rican clinics and hospitals. The charge emerged first in 1944, when the Bishop of Ponce wrote a pastoral letter accusing a missionary-run clinic in the mountain town of Lares of trying to eliminate the next generation, having done 400 sterilizations in two years in a town with a population of only 17,000. (According to supporters of sterilization, the pastoral letter had the opposite of its intended effect: it instructed women on the existence and availability of effective birth control—from the pulpit, no less.[31]) The rumor of secret mutilating procedures done on women was resurrected in October 1947, when the main insular newspaper, *El Mundo,* reported that North American researcher Christopher Tietze had published very high figures for sterilization rates. The article began with a Health Department denial that there was any organized sterilization campaign, though the official, Dr. José Belaval, was forced to agree that indeed 3,373 women had been sterilized at public hospitals.[32] A few days later the bishop of San Juan denounced the decline in popular morality in general, but especially that of "the ostensible defenders of public health [who] have transgressed the limits of their competence and professional authority, pretending to resolve the economic problem of Puerto Rico [by] making it so there are fewer Puerto Ricans."[33] In 1949 Public Health Commissioner Dr. Juan Antonio Pons played into the Church's hands, telling the Puerto Rican Public Health Association that he supported an intensive program of voluntary sterilization, saying "I don't see why the District Hospitals don't dedicate one or two days a week to do 50 voluntary sterilizations a day."[34] Despite a hasty amendment by Pons in the press,[35] the island's two Catholic bishops issued a joint pastoral letter claiming that Pons had as much as admitted the existence of a state-sponsored program of involuntary sterilization.[36] In 1951 *El Mundo* claimed that University of Puerto Rico economist Emilio Cofresí's *Realidad Poblacional de Puerto Rico* proved once and for all that there was no official sterilization program. Catholic officials denounced this conclusion as unjustified,[37] and a month later formed a group, *La Unión pro Defensa de la Moral Natural* (the Union for the Defense of Natural Morality), declaring themselves to be against "the government's genocidal campaign . . . [of] sterilization."[38] This group, along with others like the Pious Union of Christian Wives and Mothers,[39] kept sterilization on the front pages of the newspapers throughout the next several years, as allegations flew back and forth between the Public Health Department and the various Catholic groups over whether there was in fact a state-sponsored sterilization campaign.[40] The debate was even carried to the mainland, as a delegation of priests and a physician from Puerto Rico persuaded a national Catholic men's organization, the Society of the Sacred Name, to denounce the "Governor's sterilization campaign in the territory of Puerto Rico,"[41] and an insular physician told a medical seminar in Birmingham, Alabama, about a "campaign of mass sterilization and birth control" on the island.[42]

In the same period, the new political formation that emerged under the leadership of Luis Muñoz Marín and the Partido Democrático Popular offered a new reading of the sterilization debate. As ever, Muñoz Marín steered a middle course. Like the supporters of birth control and sterilization, he worried about overpopulation in his public pronouncements; but like the Catholic Church, he condemned birth control and sterilization, at least officially (though unofficially he tolerated and even encouraged private efforts). Governor Muñoz Marín's response to the Church's charge that Pons's statement in support of sterilization demonstrated the existence of a secret mass sterilization campaign was typical: he insisted that "it is not the policy of the government of Puerto Rico to solve the problem created by the imbalance between the resources and the population of the country by contraceptive means and much less by sterilization."[43] Muñoz Marín's "both-and" position on sterilization succeeded in delaying confrontation for nearly twenty years, until his power was fully consolidated. In 1960, when the Catholic Action Party—including considerable numbers of *independentistas*—ran a candidate against Muñoz Marín, they lost by a landslide.[44] Thereafter, the island's controversial, Irish bishops were recalled and replaced with milder, Puerto Rican clerics. In 1963 an agreement was quietly struck between the government and the Church, that as long as patients were advised about the church-approved rhythm method the church would not oppose the existence of birth control and sterilization programs. With that agreement in hand, the Muñoz government for the first time *did* begin to use local public health funds for birth control and sterilization programs.[45]

At the same time, a new Nationalist *independentista* formation emerged, this time on the mainland and again with anti-sterilization politics. The Young Lords Party and similar groups composed largely of mainland-born youth in their late teens and early twenties were inspired by mainland racial justice movements, the legacy of Albizu, and the insular independence movement. They adopted the pro-natalist, anti-sterilization rhetoric of all three groups. They also instigated a militant movement for social change in mainland urban barrios, including regular municipal garbage removal, children's breakfast programs, drug treatment, job training, and an end to police brutality.[46] The combination was powerful. For many, the desire to end racism, disrespect, and economic discrimination against mainland Puerto Ricans became synonymous with nationalism, independence, and an end to sterilization abuse. Repeating the pattern of the island, some in the Young Lord's women's caucus opposed anti-sterilization politics, suggesting again the persistence of *independentista* Puerto Rican women's refusal of pro-natalist maternalism.[47] Other members of the women's caucus adopted a similarly split position: opposition to sterilization, but support for abortion rights.[48] Nevertheless, many North American feminists and Marxist-Leninists, especially in places like New York, Chicago, and Boston where the influence of the Young Lords was significant, adopted the anti-sterilization position as an inescapable part of the package that a commitment to antiracism and support for national liberation struggles entailed.

THE EVIDENCE AGAINST FORCED STERILIZATION CAMPAIGNS

If indeed there was no official policy on the part of the U.S. federal government or in Muñoz Marín's Populares government in the 1930s, 1940s, or 1950s to support a mass sterilization or birth control program, what of the possibility that there was a secret campaign, as the Catholic Church charged, or widespread pressure on women to use birth control methods or have the operation? There are good reasons to treat such charges with skepticism. First and most simply, the island lacked the medical infrastructure that would have been necessary for any government to carry out a serious campaign to limit women's reproduction against their will. From the 1930s through the 1960s, the most significant reproductive health problem most women faced was that they were not getting any treatment at all, not that they were overwhelmed with unwanted services. Second, Clarence Gamble, encouraged by the newspaper accounts of "mass sterilization," offered to support and fund them, but was regretfully unable to find evidence of their existence, as private reports to him from his researchers on the island testify. Third, survey data consistently found that women were overwhelmingly pleased with having obtained sterilization. However flawed these studies might be, it seems unlikely that if there had been a concerted campaign of involuntary sterilization it would have left no traces at all in these reports.

In the 1930s, when the Nationalist Party and Catholic Church charged that birth control was being abused, the majority of the medical services were urban, while the majority of the population was rural. In the 1920s and 1930s, the Rockefeller Foundation International Health Division built twenty-four rural health units serving fifty-four of the island's seventy-seven municipalities, but the program's head, George Payne (by 1936 also working for the insular Health Department) consistently refused to support birth control and denied permission for birth control to be made available through the only vehicle of rural health care, the public health units.[49] Throughout the 1930s, the demand to separate birth control from both rural and urban public health services severely hampered efforts. As late as 1937, birth control was available only through a small network of fifteen clinics associated either with private hospitals or run on plantations by sugar producers.[50] In 1939 the service was taken over by the Health Department with federal Social Security Act funds.[51] Briefly, in 1940–41, a significant program was run out of the public health units, but it was short-lived: a new administration demanded the destruction of all birth control brochures and allowed the program to languish through the period of wartime shortages.[52]

Government officials and physicians also lacked the access to women they would have needed to carry out a mass sterilization campaign. Before 1940, most women gave birth at home, attended by a midwife. Midwifery became a licensed profession in 1931, and throughout the 1940s continued to be the government's only significant plan for rural reproductive health care.[53] In 1940, by one estimate, only 10 percent of women gave birth in a hospital, though by 1950 this number had climbed to 40 percent, and by 1960 it was 77.5 percent.[54] Figures for the island as a whole, though, can be misleading, for the trend was very uneven and most hospital births were in the major cities or represented women in extremis. In rural Lajas, for example, the municipality registered 2,956 births in the period 1941–45, and only 10 of them were in a hospital or attended by a physician. The access to hospitals, moreover, depended on income; midwives charged about $5 in 1945, compared with $25 for in-hospital delivery.[55] Women were not, then, routinely present in hospitals to be subject to improper pressure; those who had hospital sterilization operations went to some trouble to get there. Some women apparently traveled considerable distances to obtain the operation at hospitals known to do it. In Fajardo, where the municipal hospital had performed more than 2,000 operations by 1951, the mayor claimed that "there have been cases of Puerto Ricans who came all the way from New York just to be operated on."[56]

Little wonder, then, that Gamble could find no mass sterilization campaign to support in the 1940s and '50s. Gamble sent his fieldworker Christopher Tietze in 1946 to interview government officials and birth control activists (some of them Gamble's friends and allies for more than a decade) to find those responsible for the mass-sterilization campaign and offer his support. Not only could he not find one, but Tietze was urged by governmental officials not to let Gamble start such a campaign because it would stretch the limited number of hospital beds even further.[57] Indeed, José Belaval, on hearing from Tietze that Gamble would like to institute such a program, wrote Gamble himself to complain:

> It is true that our poor women ask to be sent to the hospital for delivery and post-partum esterilization. Fifty per cent of the cases coming to the prenatal clinics are willing to submit themselves to esterilizations. [But] our present Commissioner of [Public Health] does not believe in the existence of a population problem in the island and no official provision for the esterilization of women has been set up in the District Hospitals of the island.[58]

Wilson Wing of Johns Hopkins, making inquiries five years later, wrote Gamble with the same conclusions:

> The attached confidential report . . . indicates what I believe to be true; that the demand for sterilization is very much a lay drive. There is no official program to popularize it. In fact the demand for beds for this purpose is a source of anxiety to the Insular authorities who plan a general medical care program.[59]

In short, private, confidential offers to fund a sterilization program by a well-known, long-term supporter of birth control on the island—indeed, the philanthropist to whom government officials and activists had turned when the governmental birth control program on the island had been defunded fifteen years earlier—yielded flat denials that such a program existed. Belaval, a strong supporter of sterilization and the single most influential birth control advocate on the island for several decades, also believed, to his distress, that there was no mass sterilization program.

Finally, the sociological and demographic studies through which various social scientists have sought to make working-class Puerto Ricans speak have provided no evidence of forced sterilization campaigns. For example, in a 1982 study of women who had had tubal ligation dating as far back as 1954, only 16 of 846 reported that someone other than themselves had made the decision; of these, 13 were relatives, and only 2 women reported that neither they nor her husbands were consulted about the operation.[60] Another study found that 94 percent of women sterilized between 1956 and 1961 at the Asociación Pro Bienestar de la Familia, the local Planned Parenthood affiliate, were satisfied with the operation. Of those who were unhappy, only a few remotely implied that they had been misinformed or pressured into having the operation. Out of 519 interviewed between three and ten years after the operation, 3 reported that they had only later learned that there were temporary methods of contraception, and 2 felt that sterilization was in conflict with their religious beliefs.[61] Even Peta Murray Henderson, a believer in the forced sterilization thesis, was forced to admit that according to the 33 women she interviewed in the early 1970s, "in the majority of cases, the decision was made by the woman who then sought the approval of her husband and the co-operation of a doctor. . . . The demand for sterilization results from the expressed desires of women and not from coercive pressure from the health system."[62] Only one study reported a significant rate of dissatisfaction with the operation. José Vázquez Calzada's 1973 report that 36.1 percent of sterilized women (if only 12 percent of their spouses) were unhappy about having had the operation—a point to which we will return.[63]

The class data in the social science literature put an additional spin on the argument. If sterilization were principally involuntary, one would expect that working-class women, as the most socially vulnerable group, would show the highest rates, especially since this was the group whose fertility and contraceptive skill most worried physicians and administrators. However, the opposite was true. At least at first, the more affluent, those who would be favored in stiff competition for beds, were most likely to be sterilized. Hatt found in 1948 that, of all women, 6.6 percent were sterilized, and that the greatest proportion of them— 8.3 percent—were in the highest income category, compared with only 2.7 percent—for the lowest income category.[64] In 1954 Stycos reported that

> this method [female sterilization] is more frequently practiced by the better educated. Of all urban cases, only 12% of those with no education are

sterilized, whereas over 28% of those with six years of education or more [are]. In the country, the relationship is less marked, rising from 16% to 24%. This relationship is understandable in light of the requirements for sterilization. In private hospitals a fee is required; in public hospitals "pull" is often necessary to acquire bed space.[65]

Hill et. al. also recorded that the operation was more popular among women of the wealthy classes.[66]

THE POLITICS OF SUPPORT FOR
BIRTH CONTROL AND STERILIZATION

Sterilization had multiple sources of support on the island, from those who wished to give Puerto Rican women increased control over their own reproduction, to those who sought to bring it under state control. Some insular feminists in the 1950s and '60s drew on the available anti-natalist discourse, the rhetoric of overpopulation, to promote their long-standing goal of making safe and effective means of birth limitation available to Puerto Rican women. They worked alongside and took money from overpopulationists with different goals, including those like Gamble who believed that sterilization could get rid of working-class Puerto Ricans whom they saw as undesirable. The larger context, in which the diaphragm was unavailable and Gamble and various companies were promoting worthless jellies and foams, meant that there was good reason for women in general and birth control advocates in particular to see sterilization (like the pill) as useful and pragmatic alternatives. While promoters of sterilization lacked the access and the means to undertake a mass sterilization campaign, Gamble for one clearly wished for such a campaign with his offer to fund what the Church was calling genocide if someone would tell him where to send the money. This wish is what feminists like Mass and Gordon documented. The other group Puerto Rican feminists worked with included insular health professionals and administrators who believed that sterilization was the only birth control method that working-class women could use effectively, and some no doubt hoped that the operation would make them rich. What the politics of these diverse groups had in common was that for different reasons they saw the fate of Puerto Rico as linked to women's wombs.

The major institutional backer of sterilization was the Asociación Puertorriqueña pro Bienestar de la Familia (Pro Familia). Beginning in 1956, Pro Familia provided advice and financial assistance to women who sought sterilization.[67] While its leaders were always scrambling for funding by courting mainland philanthropists, as we have seen, they were nobody's dupes. Rivera and Zalduondo in particular were formidable activists, well-educated, well-connected participants in international scholarly and professional conferences and journals and believers in sterilization as an important part of birth control services. When funding for the free sterilization program flagged, Zalduondo cobbled together monies to enable it to continue, lobbied the government public health service to support it, and eventually began doing sterilizations in Pro Familia clinics, an action that prompted the Catholic Church to fly black flags from the church towers of town squares throughout the island.

Promoters of birth control and sterilization backed it for economic as well as political reasons. Many physicians and reformers believed that the island would be better off if working-class people could simply be persuaded to stop reproducing themselves. The trend among women toward increased reliance on sterilization was matched by a growing enthusiasm for the operation among physicians and increased awareness that there was money to be made from it. Many hospital officials believed that working-class Puerto Ricans were incapable of using birth control successfully. John Bierley, director of Presbyterian Hospital in San Juan, insisted that the hypersexuality of Puerto Ricans made birth control impossible. He complained, obscenely, that he had seen few virgins over 11 years of age and added that "the old man comes so fast that the wife does [not] even have a chance to slip in a dose of jelly."[68] Only slightly less offensive was Roy Stokes of St. Luke's Memorial Hospital in Ponce, who told his staff that "contraceptive devices are not practical for the majority of people, only for the more intelligent."[69] In 1952, 80 percent of the physicians who returned a questionnaire survey said they were in favor of sterilization for reasons of health, 66 percent were in favor for reasons of poverty, and 63 percent favored the operation when women had more children than they desired.[70] In private hospitals, sterilization was a very lucrative procedure, with some hospitals opening simply to provide the operation.[71] Many had policies urging maternity patients to have tubal ligations after delivery. The most extreme of these was Presbyterian Hospital, where in 1947 it was the unofficial policy of the hospital to refuse to admit women for their fourth delivery unless they agreed to sterilization, provided the pregnancy was uncomplicated.[72] While this policy was certainly unethical, it resulted only in about 263 tubal ligations a year. Since most women delivered at home with a midwife, and even those who wished for the comfort and prestige of a private hospital delivery were often turned away, the effect of the policy was to award those limited beds only to those who would also pay for the operation or who experienced complications in labor.[73]

For those women who sought sterilization, many claimed it was difficult to obtain at the low-cost municipal hospitals, many of which refused to do the operation at all. However, mayors of rural municipalities could often be persuaded to help, and many agreed to pay for the procedure when the local Municipal Hospital would or could not do it, either because of policy or lack of beds. An official of the Puerto Rican Development Office, in a confidential report, related that in the course of his travels exploring the parameters of sterilization in 1951, he had gone to Juncos: "When I spoke to the ma[y]or Víctor Lanza concerning this problem, he showed me two women who were waiting their turn to speak to him to determine the dates for their operation." In town after town, he reported either that the municipal hospitals were doing large numbers of sterilizations for surrounding areas, or that mayors were paying for them out of discretionary funds.[74] Medical patronage, however, was not unique to sterilization. Although these two decades saw a rapidly expanding medical infrastructure, the island continued to have an extremely inadequate number of beds, and access to medical services was often best obtained through the favors of politicians, which of course worked to politicians' benefit, too.

It is important to say that the insular government did make sterilization available for free or for a nominal fee for a few years in the late 1960s and early 1970s in response to lobbying by Zalduondo's group and the overpopulation establishment. The one study showing high rates of sterilization regret was done during this period. This program was sharply curtailed in 1972 because of increased federal scrutiny; those who worked in municipal hospitals report that the new rules resulted in a sharp drop in sterilization rates in Puerto Rican public hospitals. It is possible and even likely that government policy in these years influenced women's decisions to be sterilized, especially since this period corresponded with the rapid entry of women into the factory workforce. This quite limited claim—that sterilization was easy to get and quite possibly even improperly urged on working-class women in municipal hospitals for a period of fewer than five years—is, I think, the only plausible case that can be made for the sterilization-as-social-control thesis. Ironically, it was over before mainland feminists ever demanded that it be stopped.

MAINLAND FEMINISTS: PLAYERS IN A COLONIAL FIELD

In the mainland feminist accounts, the possible understandings of sterilization are reduced to either social control—the women were forced—or to its mirror, a liberal version of "authenticity"—they really wanted to be sterilized. This dualism is self-sustaining; each argument evokes the other. The continued claim to "know" the desires and subjectivities of working-class Puerto Rican women has been an authorizing force in the continued iterations of the colonial and anti-colonial project: the women were forced; the women desired to be sterilized. Speaking through the subaltern body renders the speaker invisible; speaking of outrages on the subaltern body authorizes intervention. The women desired sterilization; they lacked the ability to control their fertility, which missionary and development-project hospitals could provide. Or, they were forced; they required the protection of "our" political movement, be it nationalism, socialism, or feminism.

By championing the politics of illegitimate sterilization, mainland feminism reiterated the colonialist move rather than providing an alternative. U.S. feminists erased the history of Puerto Rican feminist support for birth control and sterilization and insisted on the authority of U.S. feminist and Puerto Rican nationalist claims of wanting to "save" working-class Puerto Rican women. They used concerns about sterilization abuse on the island as a vehicle to express political views on a host of other subjects. They attempted to produce a feminist politics inclusive of racially marked, "non-white" women in the United States and in the Third World, develop a critique of physician influence over women, and sought to repudiate the history of white women's missionary work. But they did so without regard to what such efforts meant for the Puerto Rican circumstances they sought to improve. Puerto Rican feminism was erased from mainland feminist concerns.

This is not an argument that working-class women chose to be sterilized; it is an argument that there is no evidence that there was a repressive campaign to force them. The former is an unsubstantiable claim about subjectivity, the latter, a falsifiable claim about the activities of a repressive state apparatus, to use Althusser's term. There was no singular subjectivity, an impoverished Puerto Rican women's "class consciousness," if you will, that could speak from within the multiple iterations of this discourse: "woman as mother to the nation," "woman as destroyer (through fertility) of the nation," and "woman as the hyper-victimized (through inability to realize her fertility)." It was extremely difficult for mainland feminists to find an alternative to the apparently opposing camps of nationalist pro-natalism versus colonialist anti-natalism. Despite good intentions, feminists were caught up by the terms of U.S. national, colonial, and racial discourse. Yet, to borrow again from Spivak, if we assume that "our" (not–Third World, middle-class) subjectivity is complex, discursively written, and divided against itself, we cannot then also assume that that of the subaltern is simple, producing a singular "authentic" and readily knowable position or choice. There is no such subaltern subject. With respect to sterilization, the only function of such an imagined subject is to authorize the speaker as the possessor of true knowledge of the subaltern, whether we are speaking of Puerto Rican nationalists, U.S. (colonialist) social scientists, Puerto Rican health professionals and feminists, or mainland feminists. When mainland feminists like Mass accepted the nationalist version of the subaltern—the women are victimized—while rejecting or ignoring the perspective of feminists like those in Pro Familia as duped, bourgeois pawns of colonialism, they accepted a pro-natalist anti-feminism because it carried the banner of the subaltern.

In recent years, Puerto Rican feminists have begun to produce an alternative version of the forced sterilization narrative. In *Política sexual en Puerto Rico,* Margarita Ostolaza Bey writes of the necessary erasure, or rather, impossibility, of Puerto Rican feminism in the opposition between nationalism's "woman" (which she identifies with Puerto Rican social science) and overpopulationist rhetoric, "the ideological discourse of colonial politics." She writes:

> Puerto Rican social science has conceived of the control of the woman's body from within the . . . frame of sterilization. . . . Some have even gone to the extreme of insisting that sterilization was designed to exterminate Puerto Rican-ness itself, as if *puertorriqueñidad* depended on the number of times Puerto Rican women give birth. . . . [In contrast, in] the ideological discourse of colonial politics, the fact that the labor force is reproduced in the woman's body . . . makes her responsible for the rise in unemployment . . . the increase in poverty, the increase in the public debt. . . . According to this ideological discourse, it seems that women are responsible for having given birth to two million surplus Puerto Ricans, Puerto Ricans in excess.[76]

Ostolaza Bey argues that "the anticolonialist discourse is also hispanophilic, antifeminist, and reactionary because it is based on the idea that the past—any past—was better." She shows that the wombs of Puerto Rican women were intensely politicized, that the argument between nationalism and colonialism over whether women are too prolific or not prolific enough serves to write these very women out of existence, to make women's political agency unimaginable.[77] Annette Ramírez de Arrellano has pointed out the considerable involvement of Puerto Rican women in the movement to make birth control and sterilization available. Yamila Azize-Vargas has underscored that the women involved in the Puerto Rican birth control movement were also leaders in the feminist and suffrage movements[78] (a politics that sets them apart from mainland feminism, where suffrage supporters largely were uneasy with birth control, seeing it as divisive and anti-family[79]). Finally, Iris López has insisted that we need a more sophisticated conception of why Puerto Rican women chose to be sterilized; while the economic pressures and other constraints on choice were real enough, it is also critical to conserve an awareness of Puerto Rican women's agency. In her helpful formulation, sterilization ought to be thought of as the "constrained choice" of women in need of safe and reliable contraception and pressured to believe it was a moral and civic duty.[80]

Insular feminists' ambivalent politics of strategic alliance were described in the nationalist account as disloyal to the nation because they were disloyal to motherhood. Improbably and absurdly, the charge was echoed by mainland feminists. The colonial logic that located working-class Puerto Rican women's sexuality and reproduction at the very center of debates about Puerto Rican nationhood carried over into the very movements that struggled to produce an alternative: feminists, anti-colonialists, and racial justice movements. To make Rey Chow's point, the logic of U.S. left anti-colonialism demanded that the only "authentic natives" were those that could occupy the position of "the people."[81] Puerto Rican feminists failed to fit the bill because they were middle-class professionals and intellectuals who differed with charismatic nationalist leaders. In short, they were too much like mainland feminists to fulfill the role appointed for (romanticized, victimized) Third World women. While the ostensible target of this historical account was mainland exploitation, it in fact rendered Puerto Rican feminists as dupes and puppets of North American colonialists and recentered the debate over working-class women's reproduction.

CHAPTER 6

"I like to be in America"

*Postwar Puerto Rican Migration, the Culture
of Poverty, and the Moynihan Report*

When I was being raised in East Harlem, I was frequently
called a 'spik.' I am now referred to as being culturally
deprived, socially disadvantaged and a product of the culture
of poverty.

> —Joseph Monserrat, Commonwealth Department of
> Migration, 1973

In 1961 long-time Puerto Rican labor activist Jesus Colón commented
on what people in New York City were hearing about Puerto Ricans.
There were the "voluminous studies" and "official reports" and

> elaborate highly-documented "surveys" of the "difficult" problem of the
> "unwanted, unassimilable Puerto Ricans" who live in the great metropolis
> of New York. . . . We Puerto Ricans have even been subject to treatment
> in the Broadway drama and fabulously successful musical show. But
> invariably this treatment harps on what is superficial and sentimental,
> transient and ephemeral, or bizarre and grotesque in Puerto Rican life. . . .
> Years ago, it was the "brutal and uncouth" Irish; then it was the "knife-
> wielding" Italians; later it was the "clannish" Jews with "strange" ways;
> yesterday it was the Negro; today, it is the Puerto Ricans—and the
> Negroes—who are relegated to the last rung of New York's social ladder.[1]

Colón was among the early Puerto Rican migrants to New York, part of
a small but politically active community dating back to nineteenth-century political exiles, traders, and laborers.[2] As he watched New York respond to a flood of new Puerto Rican migrants in the postwar period,
Colón read his times with a certain prescience. A decade later, these ways
of representing Puerto Ricans would reach hyperbolic proportions: "vo-

162

luminous studies" about Puerto Ricans as a problem would fill library shelves; the Broadway play *West Side Story* would reach a national audience as a film; the "bizarre and grotesque" would increasingly define Puerto Ricans in the mainland press and social science literature, and the process that linked together Negroes and Puerto Ricans and assigned them to the bottom "rung of the social ladder" would have succeeded in persuading an extraordinary number of people in the United States that this was a natural, or at least inevitable, order of things.

These characterizations of Puerto Ricans were effective because they were founded on the narratives of family, sex, and reproduction that came from the island. If the liberals who constructed the edifice of development in Puerto Rico put birth control at the center of their project, and nationalists, leftists, and mainland feminists put anti-sterilization politics at the center of theirs, the story of reproduction that shaped the response of mainland institutions to the postwar migration of Puerto Ricans was the "culture of poverty." The culture of poverty, as elaborated by anthropologist Oscar Lewis and taken up by political neoconservatives and a sensation-seeking press, represented a transformed but recognizable form of the trend begun in the anthropology and sociology of overpopulation on the island: a tendency to see most of what ailed the island as rooted in reproduction. An ambivalent but influential account of the culture of poverty was promoted by Lewis's *La Vida,* a story of a Puerto Rican family with branches on the island and the mainland. In it, the culture of poverty was characterized by absent fathers, matriarchal families, women having children while still very young themselves, poor work habits, violence, and obsession with sex. By the time children were six or seven, they had been so damaged by the effects of this culture that they were unable to take advantage of opportunities to escape poverty. The family Lewis studied, whom he called the Ríos, were in a sense modern-day Jukes or Kallikaks. Like those earlier, eugenics-literature exemplars of multigenerational degeneracy, the Ríos family stood as an explanation of the cause of poverty and as a significant threat to the society at large.[3] Not incidentally, most of the major protagonists in *La Vida* were prostitutes. While Lewis's intentions were evidently more complex, the book ultimately provided an alibi for all those who wished to suggest that cultural, sexual, and reproductive causes were responsible for Puerto Ricans' poverty.

This social science of the Puerto Rican family was also a significant contributor to the sociology of the racially marked working-class family that reached its pinnacle (or nadir, for its opponents) in the Moynihan

Report. The Moynihan Report, the Department of Labor's 1965 *The Ne-gro Family: The Case for National Action,* was—and remains—tremendously controversial. Appearing at a critical juncture in the fashioning of federal programs in response to the civil rights movement, the Moynihan Report blamed African American family structure for racial differences in educational and economic achievement. Debate over it has continued to be incredibly productive of racial meanings in the United States, from questions of the relationship of ethnicity and race to public-policy struggles over AFDC mediated by the figure of the "welfare queen." This chapter explores the relationship between two things we usually think of as separate—the impact of development projects on politics and the relationship of such policies to African Americans and other racialized minority groups in the United States. To the extent that we link these things at all, we generally argue it the other way: racism, developed at "home" in relation primarily to African Americans, structured the United States's patronizing (at best) or exploitative relations with what used to be termed the Third World. This chapter makes the opposite argument: racial meanings—specifically those promulgated in the extensive literature in Puerto Rico of (pathological) Puerto Rican families as an obstacle to economic development—developed in the Third World, and then returned to the mainland United States as a way of understanding both Puerto Rican migrants and African Americans. Of course, these relationships were highly mediated and complex. Oscar Lewis's notion of a culture of poverty, for example, was also developed in relation to Mexican families, not just Puerto Ricans, and Moynihan drew extensively on sociology from the 1930s on the black family. Nevertheless, by tracing the evolution of two ideas through the social science literature—that there was a (highly racialized) class called "the poor" beneath the working class, and that "chaotic families" described certain members of this class—it is clear that Puerto Ricans and "Negroes" were strongly linked in the social science literature and that the sociology of Puerto Rican families had a tremendous influence on the development of the Moynihan Report.

The culture of poverty, as applied to Puerto Ricans, was a social science solution to a political problem. Hundreds of thousands of largely working-class Puerto Ricans migrated to the mainland in the postwar period, initially mostly to New York, where they were conspicuously under- and unemployed, poorly fed, and often without sufficient warm clothing. New Yorkers greeted this mass migration—the first since immigration restriction laws had halted the influx of Europeans in the 1920s—with hostility. Newspaper headlines in the late 1940s heralded a "New Airborne Invasion," the "Puerto Rican problem," and, when inadequate housing forced Puerto Ricans to live in basements and coal bins, "A New Race of Cavedwellers."[4] Politicians turned to social scientists to explain, and thus to solve, the "problem" of working-class Puerto Ricans. One answer was bad mothers, who passed along the pathology of being poor to their children. As a solution, the culture-of-poverty thesis had the benefit of separating the problem of families' poverty from labor and housing markets, rooting it instead in sex and marriage. This narrative of mothers and cultures was self-fulfilling: employers, by the mid-sixties often unable legally or morally to use race as an explicit criteria for hiring, came increasingly to rely on culture as the reason they could not hire African Americans or Puerto Ricans.[5] Together with the Moynihan Report strand of sociology of African Americans, the idea of a culture of poverty accomplished for the mainland what overpopulation had for the island: it provided a terrain on which to debate poverty policy that was based on ideologies of gender, insulated from economics, and tremendously productive of difference, race, class, liberal discourses of rescue, and conservative demonization of the poor. Puerto Ricans were not poor because of racism, job markets, or colonialism, but because they had the wrong sort of family.

Ultimately, this literature both reflected and encapsulated the process through which the idiom of race shifted from biology to social science. As we have seen, until the 1930s Puerto Rican difference was marked chiefly in terms of biological race, degeneracy—or, in the case of progressive eugenics, positively, in terms of the (never complete) possibility of race improvement. Through the 1940s and '50s, the biologism of experts' knowledge of Puerto Ricans appeared to soften somewhat; overpopulation had social science roots. However, though apparently a product of statistics and economics, overpopulation was also a product of eugenics, as we have seen, and had at its core the biological racialism of Raymond Pearl's *Human Biology*, and its solution was medical and scientific, in "the pill" and sterilization. It is in the 1960s, really, that one encounters a fully developed, culturally saturating social science of Puerto Rican difference in the culture-of-poverty thesis. The key to it was still reproductive—one could even argue that biology never fully disappeared from the grammar of difference—but "culture" now did the work of "race." Joseph Monserrat captured this sense memorably when he wrote, in the lines that serve as an epigraph for this chapter, that in the course of his lifetime the "culture of poverty" came to do the cultural work that "spik" had in his boyhood.

Puerto Rican activists on the mainland were well aware of these characterizations and by the 1960s were actively responding to them. This response included labor activism, from the socialism of those like Jesus Colón to the workplace unionism of the International Ladies Garment Workers, as well as the development of Puerto Rican political and cultural groups on the mainland, like the Young Lords Party and the Nuyorican Poets, and women's groups like the Young Lords' Women's Caucus and the Welfare Rights Organization. These groups argued for an economic interpretation of their situation. Puerto Ricans were not poor because of culture, family, sex, or child rearing, but because of their international economic location. Puerto Rican migrants were the casualties of Operation Bootstrap, unwilling and unwelcome expatriates. As poet Martín Espada wrote, they were exiles in "cit[ies] of coughing and broken radiators,"[6] where the climate and the people were cold, where being poor inflicted unexpected cruelties and humiliations, where work was well paid by Puerto Rican standards but unreliable, exhausting, boring, and unforgiving of days when one needed to stay home with sick children or rest. Homesickness for *Borinquen* was a constant companion, but so too was knowledge of the lack of work there and the growing hostility on the part of those who remained on the island toward the people derisively termed "Nuyoricans." People found they could neither stay on the mainland nor return to the island, and their constant shuttling back and forth generated a whole genre of wry but poignant descriptions of this new kind of labor migration—a "commuter nation," taking the *"guagua aérea"* (air bus) and finding "Puerto Rican identity up in the air."[7]

Policy-making, however, does not thrive on irony or nostalgia, and U.S. political debate did not embrace terms like *colonialism* or *international division of labor*. Instead, Puerto Ricans and their problems were duly enumerated by censuses, quantified by sociologists, and rendered into newsprint as numbers. From this work, we learn that there were 53,000 Puerto Ricans living in the United States in 1930, a number that declined during the Depression and did not increase significantly during the early 1940s.[8] The end of the Second World War coincided with the advent of cheap air travel, an economic boom on the mainland, and development policies on the island that resulted in better jobs for some and an increasingly sparse subsistence for others. Substantial numbers took the *guagua aérea* north. By 1969, according to the Census Bureau, there were 1,454,000 Puerto Ricans residing in the states and Washington, D.C., an increase of 1.4 million over 1930. Puerto Ricans invented the air migration, and cheap airfares made it accessible even for working-class people. Figures developed by the Commonwealth of Puerto Rico's Migration Division are suggestive about the extent to which it was a circular migration; in 1953, the Division claimed, 304,910 people had left the island and 203,307 had returned.[9]

PUERTO RICAN MIGRANTS, 1947:
THE MAKING OF A MORAL PANIC

Puerto Ricans became a problem for policy makers in New York City (in Colón's sense) in 1947. The *New York Times* published no articles about mainland Puerto Ricans in 1946, but almost thirty, all focused on the new migrants as a problem, in 1947. The tide began in January, with an article whose subtitle read, "1,500 a week from island and social agencies map action."[10] The *Times*'s numbers were huge, and wildly inflated. In October, the *Times* reported that there were 600,000 Puerto Ricans in New York—400,000 more than the census could find in all of the mainland U.S. in 1950, after three more years of a considerable influx.[11] Indeed, official numbers identified 1947 as a low year for Puerto Rican migrants, with only 25,000 that year, compared with 40,000 the year before.[12] But the level of panic evidenced in the newspapers in 1947 rapidly outstripped anything that could be the doing of even a hundred times as many Puerto Ricans.

For the newspapers and magazines—and hence a significant number of New Yorkers and other readers—Puerto Rican migrants were always already inserted into the idiom of policy, problems, and poverty. There were no articles on the explosion of *plenas* written about the migration, nor on the flourishing of this transplanted music in *Nueva* York, nor on the expansion of Spanish Harlem or the cultural transformation that was taking place on the Lower East Side, previously a home for European immigrants that was now becoming Puerto Rican barrio. No one even wrote of the significant boon for the garment factories of the appearance of thousands of new women workers trained in Puerto Rico's needlework industry just as Italian and Jewish women were leaving in significant numbers to follow the American dream as it moved to the suburbs. Rather, Puerto Ricans were simply a social work and public agency problem. One ethnographer told the following story:

> A photographer from a New York daily newspaper came to East 100th Street with an assignment to get a picture of "the children playing in the garbage. It was Sunday morning, and the children were scrubbed and dressed in their finest clothes. . . . None were playing in the garbage. The

photographer went to . . . [ask] a minister to help him carry out his assignment. The minister explained that it was Sunday, and the children didn't play in the garbage. The photographer, getting anxious now, said, "Look—there's some kids—over there." He ran to a garbage can, yanked off the lid, and motioned to the silent, staring children. "Hey kids— c'mere—over here. Let's play.[13]

Headlines spoke of curbing migration, of calling on Congress to halt the flow, of tropical diseases and poverty on the island.[14] Puerto Ricans were not the largest group of internal migrants in the United States in this period, but along with African Americans leaving the South, their migration was most thoroughly rendered a problem. When a city commissioner with a political bone to pick issued a report slamming the Welfare Department for a lack of safeguards against fraud, he wrote that the influx of Puerto Ricans had caused a sharp rise in caseloads and costs (and, implicitly, fraud), even though an earlier survey by the department had found that less than 8 percent of the city's Puerto Rican population had applied for relief and that "on the whole they were industrious, hardworking and willing."[15] Notwithstanding the incredible paternalism of that statement, these two reports, four months apart, make it clear that even before there were Puerto Ricans on relief, Puerto Ricans were already a welfare problem. That fall, when another Welfare Department study found that fewer than 4 percent of relief cases were Puerto Rican migrants,[16] another newspaper reported, "New York's relief cases have increased 54 per cent in areas where Puerto Ricans tend to congregate."[17]

In a pattern that was to be repeated again and again, the rising panic about excessive Puerto Ricans and the (utterly undocumented) strain on city services was ameliorated with an announcement that sociologists had been called in to study the problem. The cycle of this particular panic crested in the first week of August, when the *New York Times* ran daily exposés about the problem of Puerto Rican migration: officials worried, children abandoned in the airport, disease, substandard housing, rising crime levels. The series spawned letters and editorials demanding that "something" be done.[18] Within days, "something" was: the governor of Puerto Rico asked Columbia University to do a study of the "problem" of Puerto Rican migration. Paul Lazarsfeld, Director of Applied Sociology at Columbia, accepted the commission.[19] The uproar in the newspapers died down, and a cottage industry for social scientists in and around New York was born. A photo essay in *Life* that month, titled "Puerto Rican Migrants Jam New York," solidified this account: it featured pictures crowded to the edges of Puerto Ricans arriving on planes, filling welfare offices, overcrowded apartments, children swarming city streets, and—in the only picture in the essay that contained empty space—"Puerto Rico's Governor Jesus T. Pinero [*sic*] discusses the problem with sociologist P. T. Lazarsfeld."[20]

THE SOCIAL SCIENCE OF THE GHETTO

Given its subsequent career, it is hard to recall that the culture-of-poverty thesis was originally a liberal concept. Many have pointed out that, as deployed by neoconservatives in the 1980s, the thesis argued that the greatest cause of poverty was the poor themselves—or, more precisely, their families. Historian Robin Kelley is acidly funny about what the neoconservative social science of the ghetto said and did:

> I grew up in a world in which talking about somebody's mama was a way of life, an everyday occurrence. For all of us . . . it was a kind of game or performance . . . "your mom's so fat she broke the food chain." You would think that as a kid growing up in this world I could handle any insult, or at least be prepared for any slander tossed in the direction of my mom—or for that matter, my whole family, my friends, or my friends' families. But when I entered college and began reading the newspaper, monographs, and textbooks on a regular basis, I realized that many academics, journalists, policymakers, and politicians had taken the [verbal game of the] "dozens" to another level. In all my years of playing the dozens, I have rarely heard vitriol as vicious as the words spouted by Riverside (California) county welfare director Lawrence Townsend: "Every time I see a bag lady on the street, I wonder, was that an A.F.D.C. mother who hit the menopause wall—who can no longer reproduce and get money to support herself?" I have had kids tell me that my hair was so nappy it looked like a thousand Africans giving the Black Power salute, but never has anyone said to my face that my whole family— especially my mama—was a "tangle of pathology." Senator Daniel Patrick Moynihan has been saying it since 1965 and, like the one about your mama tying a mattress to her back and offering "roadside service," Moynihan's "snap" has been repeated by legions of analysts and politicians.[21]

Moynihan's report was certainly important to the story of ghetto social science. But as his friendly commentator, Lee Rainwater, observed in a 1967 book on the massive controversy the report generated, it contained no new news.[22] Moynihan was relying on an already established body of the social science of the ghetto (and, *pace* Rainwater, it was not just Negroes, but at a minimum Puerto Ricans as well—and arguably the Irish, Jews, and Italians.) To understand the evolution of Moynihan's "snap," we need to start earlier.

The culture of poverty was not a transhistorical idea that meant the same thing in the 1960s as it did in the 1980s, but a trope, a powerful set of images whose meanings moved and whose political effects ran the gamut from radical to liberal to conservative. Its key component—the thing that was probably responsible for its consistent power to mobilize people and produce public policy effects—was its narrative about the deviant sexuality of poor, usually non-white women. The story that "backwardness" and "poverty" were caused by something about women's sexuality and reproduction followed Puerto Rican migrants to the mainland, producing a literature about the "chaotic families" of Puerto Ricans in New York. The work of Lewis in *La Vida* marked Puerto Rican families as considerably worse than those portrayed in his earlier work on Mexico, and it joined with the sociology of African Americans' disorganized families to produce a particularly powerful synthesis. Both relied on a trope of non-white, working-class women's promiscuous sexuality, her illegitimate children, and the theory that her bad mothering produced poverty in the next generation.

In order to trace a genealogy of this linkage between African Americans and Puerto Ricans, we need to follow the line of descent through the social science of Puerto Ricans. The context for the development of this syncretism between overseas development and domestic welfare or poverty policy was, first, the intensification of the links between social science and policy makers on the mainland. Just as the University of Puerto Rico's Social Science Research Center provided the brain trust for the PPD, Northeastern universities offered extensive consultation on how to address the twin "problems" of poverty and Puerto Ricans. For a time in the 1940s and 1950s, it seemed that every urban institution of higher education in the Northeast—New York University, City College of New York, Princeton University, Columbia, Hofstra, Rutgers, Fordham, Harvard, MIT—had a significant research project on Puerto Ricans in New York City. East Harlem was almost as studied as the island itself.[23] There was close collaboration of policy makers and social scientists; not only did Governor Piñero fund the Columbia study, but its authors, in turn, allowed him to approve the detailed plan for it.[24] Five other studies were commissioned at about the same time by New York agencies, including the Board of Education and the Welfare and Health Council of New York City.[25] Even when foundations like Rockefeller and Ford began offering private monies for the development of a social science of Puerto Ricans on the mainland, it was assumed that such studies would maintain close relations with policy makers.

The first crop of studies did not use sex and morality as a lens through which to make sense of Puerto Ricans. Quite the opposite. Their authors saw themselves as resisting the sensational tendencies of the newspapers and magazines. They found, in general, that Puerto Ricans were doing well, by their definitions—assimilating, finding jobs—and that what problems there were would pass away with time. The initial social science of Puerto Ricans in New York simply had little to say about families or family structure. C. Wright Mills, Clarence Senior, and Ruth Goldsen published the results of the Columbia research in 1950 as *A Puerto Rican Journey*. The sociologist's role, in this text, was to defend Puerto Ricans with facts against the unfounded and unwarranted assertions in the popular press, including that Puerto Rican women had "loose morals" or were involved in prostitution.[26] The monograph's assessment of sex and gender stressed the story of the modernization of gender relations: Puerto Rican women coming to the United States were achieving greater independence from home and husband, freedom from male dominance, usually through work outside the home. In the study's terms, this was straightforwardly a good thing. Other books on Puerto Ricans on the mainland—including an ethnography, the work of a New Left journalist, and the studies by the Welfare Council and the Board of Education—found either close-knit families or heterogeneity with respect to family among Puerto Ricans in New York.[27] Unlike several of those that followed, they were based on research in the community—surveys and ethnographies—rather than derived from published sources.

The fashioning of a liberal, "expert" consensus in the late 1940s and early 1950s about the assimilability of Puerto Ricans, given the right public policy measures by groups like the Board of Education, happened side-by-side with massive McCarthyite repression of the Puerto Rican left in New York. The Puerto Rican Nationalist Party, the Communist Party U.S.A., and the International Workers Organization (IWO) had mobilized thousands of Puerto Ricans in 1947, but in the 1950s their leaders were harassed and jailed and membership dwindled. Jesús Colón and nine other Puerto Rican labor activists were forced to testify before the House Un-American Activities Committee.[28] After Truman signed Public Law 600 in 1950, clearing the way for permanent U.S. possession of Puerto Rico (a few years after the Philippines had been given independence), Nationalist leader Pedro Albizu Campos led a short-lived uprising to declare the Republic of Puerto Rico. On the mainland, Nationalists responded with an attempt to assassinate Truman. The resulting repression effectively put an end to the Nationalist Party at the same time that Communists were driven underground both on the island and the mainland. In New York, the FBI visited the homes and workplaces of suspected Puerto Rican radicals.[29] The Puerto Rican left on the mainland was decimated and would not again emerge as an effective political force until the *nueva despertar* (new awakening) of the late 1960s.

By default, centrist, middle-class "experts"—mostly but not exclusively North American—emerged as the interpreters of the Puerto Rican experience in *Nueva* York, including as well Puerto Rican anthropologists like Elena Padilla and Rosemary Santana Clooney.[30] There was no shortage of organizations designed to help Puerto Rican migrants and make them respectable in middle-class terms. In 1948 the Commonwealth's Migration Division opened offices in New York City. In 1949 the Mayor's Committee for Puerto Rican Affairs was established, which included many long-term "ethnic" activists and a number of Puerto Ricans, and in 1951 the Hispanic Leadership Forum was founded. In 1956 the Puerto Rican Association for Community Affairs was organized (composed primarily of young social workers), and in 1960 the Puerto Rican Family Institute.[31] For the most part, these groups stressed the politics of respectability and found working-class people to be something of a scandal. In a series of publications, the Migration Division endorsed the position that the migrants were, by and large, respectable: they had well-organized families; were originally urban residents on the island, not peasants; were eager to find jobs; and contributed positively to the economy of the mainland. At the same time, these groups urged Puerto Ricans to make the most of their opportunities and avoid behavior that would reflect badly on the group as a whole.[32] The one exception to this assimilationist emphasis was the *desfile puertorriqueño* (the Puerto Rican Day Parade), which was a cultural event rather than a political group per se and hence not (deliberately) organized to change political institutions.

WEST SIDE STORY

These efforts at respectability were dealt a serious blow by Broadway, where the play *West Side Story* portrayed Puerto Ricans as delinquents engaged in teenage sex and street gangs. The play is also evidence of the popular reach of social science to "explain" Puerto Ricans; at the time, Martha Gellhorn called the Broadway musical "a sociological document turned into art."[33] It offered both an explanation for why Puerto Ricans left the island and an analysis of their situation in New York. To account for their presence, the 1957 play relied on what had become common sense through the work of social scientists on the island in the 1940s: poverty, caused or exacerbated by overpopulation. *West Side Story* also borrowed from the assimilation-cycle paradigm in sociology, which argued that there was one path to incorporation into the citizenry of the United States, and that when a new immigrant group came to the U.S, the first step of that process was conflict and confrontation.[34] Like the social science it drew on, this was a liberal account: it stressed the inevitability of improvement and assimilation. The stories that the play's promoters told about it underscored its supposedly universal character. The play was described as a re-writing of Romeo and Juliet (after the film won ten Academy Awards, one enterprising publisher even put the two plays in the same volume),[35] and Leonard Bernstein and Jerry Robbins were said to have originally conceived it as "East Side Story," with the conflict centering on Jewish and Catholic gangs.[36] Montagues, Capulets, Jews, Catholics—the play was about irrational hatreds and their consequences, not the narrative of any particular group; it reiterated contemporary sociology's trope of the universal immigrant experience.

Yet the play and film managed simultaneously to point up Puerto Rican difference: it is about gangs, delinquency, and teen sexuality. While gangs and delinquency also characterize the "American" boys (also termed "Polacks" and "Wops," pointing out that the "Americans" in the play are only barely removed from their own immigrant ancestry), the explanation for criminality works differently in each case. For Puerto Rican youths, it is simply a feature of what it means to come to New York—that they are forced to fight for their right to be there, propelled from home by poverty and overpopulation. While this may be a sympathetic explanation, it is also a homogenizing one: they are delinquents because they are Puerto Rican. The "American" boys, in contrast, describe the competing discourses in which their criminality is inserted in one of the play's cleverest songs, "Dear Officer Krupke"—police and courts stress individual responsibility, psychiatrists blame family dynamics, social workers see them as a sign of sociological dysfunction, a "social disease." While the lyrics make fun of them all, the song points up the need for explanation and individualizes the boys' situations; the play even makes a few such gestures itself, pointing to the boys as the products of broken homes, alcoholism, or prostitution. Furthermore, whereas "American" girls are effectively nonentities for the play and film (except for the tomboy Anybodys, who perhaps stands in for the discourse of lesbian deviance and criminality[37]), it is Puerto Rican girls who are relentlessly heterosexualized. "American boys only want one thing from

Puerto Rican girls," María is warned, and her friend Anita is described in the stage directions as "knowing, sexual, sharp."[38] Both Anita (played in the film by Rita Moreno, whom Hollywood named "the Puerto Rican Firecracker") and María have sexually suggestive scenes, implying that they are or soon might be sexually active, and the American boys attempt to rape Anita. When Puerto Ricans who grew up the 1950s and '60s complain that everywhere they went, *West Side Story* provided the lens through which mainland Americans saw them,[39] this is part of the complaint—all the boys are criminals, all the girls are sexualized, and the island is "overpopulated."

Interestingly, the Broadway play was met with controversy in the Puerto Rican community on opening night, but not for any of these reasons. The objection was to a line that termed Puerto Rico an "island of tropic diseases." As we have seen, "tropical disease" ceased to be a politically viable paradigm in Puerto Rico in the 1930s, replaced instead by eugenics and "overpopulation." "Puerto Rico / You ugly island / Island of tropic diseases . . . / Always the hurricanes blowing / Always the population growing," sang a group of Puerto Rican girls in the play, listing the things they were glad to leave behind on the island. Lyricist Stephen Sondheim's failure to notice that the term *tropic diseases* was passé raised considerable ire in the Puerto Rican community (though the term *overpopulation* did not). People were infuriated by the lyric and demanded its removal. As Bernstein recounted later,

> Opening night . . . we had a . . . message from *La Prensa* [a New York Puerto Rican newspaper] saying that they heard about this song and we would be picketed when we came to New York unless we omitted or changed the song. They made particular reference to "Island of tropical diseases," telling us everybody knows Puerto Rico is free of disease. . . . We were insulting not only Puerto Rico but the Puerto Ricans and all immigrants. They didn't hear "Nobody knows in America / Puerto Rico's in America."[40]

The *New York Times* repeated the complaint two days later and assured its readers that there was virtually no tropical disease on the island.[41] As critic Alberto Sandoval notes, the "island of tropic diseases" lyric was changed when the play was made into a film. The process begun by New Deal liberals and Puerto Rican public health experts in the 1930s was complete; "overpopulation" was an acceptable framing of the island's difficulties, "tropical diseases" was offensive.

A SOCIAL SCIENCE OF DEVIANT FAMILIES

Oscar Handlin's *The Newcomers* was the first social science work to link Puerto Ricans and Negroes together as facing (and causing) similar problems in New York City, and also the first also to argue that they shared "chaotic families." He suggested that immigrants to New York City had always come in pairs: the Germans and the Irish, the Jews and the Italians, and now, the Negroes and the Puerto Ricans. If some of these groups had done better than others, he argued, it was because of differences in the groups themselves; Jews, for example, succeeded because of their strong commitment to education (not, say, because of the infusion of government funding into the Jewish community after World War II through the GI Bill and the Immigrant and Refugee Resettlement Act). The thing that distinguished Puerto Ricans and Negroes, unfortunately, was deviant sex and family life. Handlin wrote, "The number of illegitimacies and abortions, the frequency of homosexuality and sex crimes, and the generally lax attitude toward sexual behavior is certainly related to the chaotic family life prevalent in these groups."[42] Handlin argued that patterns of women's wage-earning emasculated Puerto Rican and black men: "In both groups, the woman's role as a wage-earner and the second-generation child's aggressiveness weakens the man's authority as husband and father."[43]

Another work reiterating this theme was a book that Moynihan himself was involved with, one that relied extensively on an account of Puerto Rican families as troubled. Like *The Newcomers,* Nathan Glazer and Moynihan's *Beyond the Melting Pot* saw Puerto Ricans and Negroes as different groups exhibiting more or less the same features, particularly disorganized families. Moynihan and Glazer reiterated every single complaint ever made against working-class Puerto Rican families on the island. There was "not much strength in the Puerto Rican family," yet the multiple children it produced accounted for poverty on both the island and mainland. "The" (singular, homogenized) Puerto Rican family was patriarchal and authoritarian, on the one hand, but marked by unstable consensual or common-law marriage, "and as a result about one-third of the births were illegitimate." The virginity of girls was sharply guarded by the family, but girls eloped at night with suitors they barely knew. Women were simultaneously overprotected and too independent; their sexuality and reproduction were overly guarded by husbands and fathers, but at the same time women made their own choices of whom to make their families with, and they often raised their children alone.

Marked both by excessive patriarchy and matriarchy—victimized *and* dangerous women—Puerto Rican families were fundamentally unable to support healthy children or a healthy community.

The sources for these assertions are interesting. For Puerto Ricans, Glazer, Moynihan, and Handlin all drew from the development literature of backward families on the island, ignoring the more positive studies of Puerto Ricans in New York. For Negroes, Handlin turned, astonishingly, to the bodice-ripping world of romance fiction, citing the existence of stories of unmarried sex in the black periodical *Tan*.[44] While he also cited the work on the black family of sociologist E. Franklin Frazier from the 1930s, *Tan* was his source for the 1950s. The idea that Handlin found stories with titles like "We Had to Have Each Other" and "Anything to Keep His Love" indicative of a normative, homogeneous culture of black courtship and sexual behavior suggests not so much the flimsiness of the evidence—although it is flimsy—but more importantly the certainty with which he approached the question of the pathology of black and Puerto Rican families. One is not persuaded by romance stories unless one wants to be.[45]

In addition to familial disorganization, Handlin argued that Puerto Ricans suffered from an absence of communal, labor, or political organizations or philanthropies—an argument that few historians of Puerto Ricans would now accept. His reasoning is revealing of the methodological and political assumptions of his social science. Handlin had to write off some fairly extensive organizations—the Nationalist Party, the socialist and communist groups, union locals, the mainland affiliates of insular political groups, the Migration Division of the Department of Labor of the Commonwealth, philanthropist Arturo Schomburg—as well as the wholesale repression of a number of these groups by the federal government. Handlin did not consider the Nationalist and socialist groups (or the Garveyites for Negroes) legitimate political or social organizations, but rather they acted as "agitators," preying on a "narrow, self-defeated hatred of the outsiders."[46] The union activism of Puerto Ricans was illegitimate for the opposite reason: it was not separate enough, but took place in interracialist locals. Similarly, active Puerto Rican support for Democratic Party candidates like Congressman (and Mayor) La Guardia, Vito Marcantonio, and Mayor O'Dwyer—who were at least superficially responsive to their concerns, to the endless irritation of more well-heeled New Yorkers—was dismissed as the mindless activity of the party machine.[47] Handlin also complained that "the welfare state assumed many social obligations earlier immigrants had borne themselves," citing, for example, the absence of Puerto Rican hospitals and orphanages.[48] (Did he mean that Puerto Ricans should have built "ethnic" hospitals next door to the municipal ones?) In other words, Handlin's notion of a benevolent organization was definitionally one that produced proper subjects of the liberal state, engaged in interest-group politics—neither nationalist nor interracialist. If Puerto Rican organizations did something else, Handlin saw a landscape characterized by the *absence* of civic groups.

This straightjacketed version of the correct path for families and communities in the social science literature set the tone for seeing ghetto communities as a "tangle of pathology" in later scholarship. Derived from the work of immigrant historians and sociologists in the 1920s, this scholarship looked for evidence that Puerto Ricans were engaged in the steps of the assimilation cycle or the race-relations cycle and oriented social scientists to see difference as deviance, deficiency, and pathology. This notion resonated in (what social science imagined as) the consensus 1950s: those who deviated from the path to assimilation were dooming themselves and their communities to lives of alienation from mainstream society, and hence to drug addiction, crime, and deviant sex. They would be individually unmoored to either the wider ("American") culture or located in thriving, assimilating immigrant communities—morally adrift, a social problem.

THE SIXTIES: INVENTING "THE POOR"
AND SOLVING THEIR PROBLEMS

In 1947, when Puerto Ricans first became a "problem," "the poor" did not exist in the United States. Everyone was lower class, upper class, or middle class. There were "unskilled laborers" to be sure, and "juvenile delinquents," a "criminal element," even (hereditary) "paupers." But while there was social pathology, often associated with an immigrant group or a particular class of native-born whites (like "Okies" or "hillbillies,") "the poor" was not a stable concept. One spoke of "poor people," and while "the poor" would not have sounded odd to most people, it was not in use in the U.S. social science literature, nor was "the underclass." At precisely the moment when the labor department, the media, and some social scientists were saying that "the working class" was being absorbed into the "middle" through improved wages and a greater access to consumer goods, another class, largely non-white, emerged: "the poor."

Although there were undoubtedly multiple sources, Oscar Lewis was credited in the scholarly literature as originating the rigorous usage of "the poor" as a group distinct from the working class, beginning with a conference paper he gave at the American Anthropological Association in 1961 that described a "culture of poverty."[49] That same year, he published *The Children of Sanchez,* based on Mexico research, in which he summarized the culture of poverty as follows:

> In anthropological usage, the term implies . . . a design for living which is passed down from generation to generation. . . . I want to draw attention to the fact that poverty in modern nations is not only a state of economic deprivation, of disorganization, or the absence of something. It is also something positive in the sense that it has a structure, a rationale, and defense mechanisms without which the poor could hardly carry on. In short, it is a way of life, remarkably stable and persistent, passed down from generation to generation along family lines.[50]

This is a striking definition: in three sentences, Lewis mentions that poverty is "passed down from generation to generation" twice. What distinguished "the poor," what made them different from any other class was not their relationship to labor or the means of production, but a set of behaviors and the reproduction of these patterns in children. It is about bad mothering— fathers are definitionally absent. Indeed, an early, approving commentator noted its behavioral features, "the ill-defined group referred to as 'the poor' does not include the stable, respectable working class."[51] Like Mayhew in the nineteenth century putting London prostitutes in the class of "those that will not work," Lewis's redefinition served to place whole groups of people doing remunerative work, even waged labor, outside the working class, specifically through their family structure and sexual behavior.[52]

A review article about "the poor" two years later is even more revealing about the work of the culture-of-poverty thesis: it clarifies that this is a class that relies on race for its definition. Social science, it argued, has identified three key characteristics of the poor:

1. There is a culture of poverty.

2. The family and sex patterns of the poor differ from those of the middle class.

3. The family and sex patterns of poor Negroes differ from those of whites on the same socioeconomic level.[53]

Here not only are "the poor" identified by their "sex patterns," but "sex patterns" are held to be a proxy for race: Negroes are identified as outside the working class at an income level where whites would be within it. Unsurprisingly, this new class proved notoriously hard to define—by the 1970s, social scientists had dismissed neighborhood, work history, and even income levels as reliable identifiers of the poor. Neighborhoods were heterogeneous, work history changed, and income levels were erratic. This did not discourage believers in a class "below" the working class. Rather, this flexible class of the impoverished seemed to remain what it was when Oscar Lewis wrote in 1961: describable predominantly in terms of behavioral characteristics, either heroism or pathology, depending on who was doing the defining. Among those who favored pathology—and even among the considerable number of liberals who preferred to split the difference, heroism but with a bit of pathology thrown in—the poor were distinguished primarily by their disorganized families and female-headed households. There was a tautology at the heart of the social science of the ghetto: the poor were those with disorganized families, and the cause of poverty was familial disorganization, which, in turn, was a feature of non-whites. "The poor," in short, made race into class, and class into immorality. In so doing, it made it possible to respond to race-based calls for social and economic justice in terms of sex—both gender and sexuality.

The invention of the poor (and their disorganized families) provided both a diagnosis of urban problems and suggested certain kinds of answers to them. On the one hand, Michael Harrington's journalistic book that relied centrally on the culture-of-poverty thesis, *The Other America,* is widely credited with producing the political momentum for the cluster of anti-poverty programs that were collectively given the name of the War on Poverty.[54] The defining of "the poor" as a distinct class in general, and the War on Poverty in particular, have a mixed history. At first, these social science and policy initiatives seemed capable of radically transforming people's educational, political, and economic situation, all the more so since they attracted the interest and energy of considerable numbers of activists. At the same time, these policies initiated the professionalization of the organizations that people were able to build, made them hostage to federal funding, and ultimately raised questions of who owned them—the community, social workers, or the federal government. There was something intrinsically peculiar about the federal government sponsoring community action programs in *el barrio* a few years after that same government had effectively crushed the Puerto Rican left. Historian José Sánchez argues in this vein that "they usurped for themselves an empty language of resistance as well as the

very real pain of Puerto Rican suffering in the interest of funding proposals and service delivery quotas."[55] In addition, urban renewal programs tore down—literally—the communities that community action
projects were trying to empower. These projects raised tremendous
hopes—that rundown neighborhoods would be rebuilt, that no one need
be poor in the United States, that community action projects would inaugurate an era of grassroots democracy—but, in fact, they were "over-
sold and underfinanced to the degree that their seeming failure was almost a matter of design," in the words of Moynihan, hardly a radical.[56]
It may be that the greatest legacy of the War on Poverty was discour-
agement and disillusionment.

THE MOYNIHAN REPORT AND *LA VIDA*

Given the marked politicization of social science in the postwar period,
it is not surprising that two of the most import social science texts about
race were written in relation to public policy problems. The Moynihan
Report was written about the civil rights movement. *La Vida* was written about two familiar problems—Puerto Rican migrants in New York
and La Perla in San Juan. La Perla was a famous, long-standing slum, located conspicuously along the road between El Condado, the luxury ho-
tel where overseas visitors often stayed, and La Forteleza, the Puerto Rican governor's mansion, and its endurance had taunted generations of
Washington administrations. Moynihan and Lewis both drew on a
trope borrowed from the newspapers as much as the social science literature: the promiscuous mother (that original Madonna / whore complex). In these texts, the story of the ghetto was not about legal or organized exclusion from American political and economic life (as the
borrowing of the term *ghetto* from Eastern European Jewish history
would seem to imply); rather it is about matriarchy (in Moynihan's
terms) or matrifocal households (in Lewis's), illegitimacy, and sexual
immorality. Lewis and Moynihan gave the social science of the ghetto
and its assertions about disorganized families new, important audiences:
Moynihan offered it up to policy makers at the highest levels in the Johnson administration, and Lewis wrote a bestseller. *La Vida* told the story
of poor Puerto Ricans in the most compelling way possible, without
footnotes, essentially as a novel, full of titillating sexual details. The
Moynihan Report, encountering the black civil rights movement, was
roundly (if not entirely successfully) refuted; *La Vida,* a politically more

multivalent book that encountered an even poorer, less organized community, became a liberal social science classic.

The story of the Moynihan Report is well known. Moynihan wrote *The Negro Family* while he was Assistant Secretary of Labor, as an advisory document for cabinet members about where civil rights policy ought to head next. The 1964 Civil Rights Act had just been passed, and some people inside and outside the Democratic Party were trying to understand from where, with Jim Crow legally dead, the next challenge from the civil rights movement was going to come. Suspecting that they would not like the answer—the Black Power movement was on the rise, there was rioting in cities, and even people like Martin Luther King Jr. were talking about economic equality—some white liberals were trying to seize the moment and channel the next phase of the movement in what seemed to them a reasonable direction. The Moynihan Report was written in response to these circumstances. It carefully made the case that American slavery had been the worst in history, and that unemployment rates for African-American men were unconscionably high, twice that of whites. The result of the former and cause of the latter, Moynihan argued, was family breakdown. Illegitimacy, black matriarchy, emasculated black men, and a familial "tangle of pathology" were together responsible for the limited educational and economic achievements of African Americans.[57] The next target of civil rights activity needed to be governmental action to save the Negro family.

The only concrete political outcome of the report was a speech, written by Moynihan and given by President Johnson at Howard University. Somewhat after that, there was a tremendous political uproar over Moynihan and his report. The speech was vetted beforehand by a handful of civil rights leaders and was initially received well. However, Moynihan's enemies inside the administration leaked word that there was a high-level, secret report that cast aspersions on the black family. Some people got copies of the report, and it set off a firestorm. Left and civil rights groups objected strenuously; hundreds of columns of newsprint, glossy magazine pages, and hours of time in political meetings were filled with denunciations and defenses of Moynihan, mostly denunciations.[58] Three things happened as a result. The event made Moynihan's political career and he became a long-term senator from New York. The controversy left an enduring mark on social science, one that continues to the present, with few scholars able to work in areas even tangentially related without having to take a position on Moynihan.

No monograph on the history of black women under slavery, contemporary black families in the United States, or ethnography of the Caribbean can escape the imperative to respond to Moynihan's assertion that slavery made the black family eternally and irremediably dysfunctional. The sociology of women and poverty was also dominated by this paradigm. The final thing the debate did was ensure that the figure of the sexualized black woman would be an enduring feature of the U.S. political landscape, affecting political debate on things as divergent as the existence of the "welfare queen" and Anita Hill's insistence that she was sexually harassed by Clarence Thomas.[59] Almost immediately, the Moynihan Report became an Ur-text of gender, race, and poverty.

Debates about development, decolonization, and the Third World were important to the report. It contemplated Brazilian slavery—and Latin American slavery more generally—at length. Nathan Glazer, Moynihan's earlier collaborator and ally, pointed out that international projects of development and decolonization in general became quite important to the social science of the black family in this political moment. "The period of lower-class romanticization came to an end," he wrote, because of

> the explosion of independence movements in colonial areas. . . . Thus the cultural relativistic stance in sociology and anthropology went into eclipse. The question now was: How do we get development. . . . In this perspective, of course, the lower-class family came out rather badly.[60]

For both Moynihan and Glazer, then, Latin America and the problem of international politics became the launching point for a new critique of the African-American family.

La Vida came out the year after the Moynihan Report and made a similar argument, explicitly in a development context. Like the over-population argument, Lewis's culture-of-poverty thesis shifted the terrain of debate about poverty and colonialism from the economy to sex. *La Vida* made essentially the same argument as Moynihan did about who the poor were—bad mothers, illegitimate children, broken homes and their products (who were unsuccessful in the labor market)—but with a different policy gloss. Lewis's introduction suggested that either war-on-poverty-style liberalism or Cuban-style radicalism could end poverty, but the book that followed told a completely different tale. It is the story of a prostitute, Fernanda ("a good-looking, dark Negro woman of about forty with a stocky, youthful figure . . . [who] had dull black eyes, heavy eyebrows and full lips"[61]) and her four children, three daughters—two of whom also become prostitutes—and a son. All three girls had been fostered out as small children. Three of the children had moved to New York, although there is considerable travel back and forth. With the exception of a long (forty-page) introduction, the book is narrated in the first person, and is based on the transcripts obtained by Lewis's research assistants in their interviews with members of the family. Lewis's editing produced a story that is intensely scatological, sexual, and violent. In the opening pages, readers encounter Fernanda, in her forties, and her teenage lover, Junior. Within the very first paragraph, Fernanda comments on shit, toilets, dirt, drinking, and how she dislikes children. Her struggle to find a new home is rendered in terms of its inadequate privacy and what that means for sex. "Junior and I like to neck all the time and that looks bad in front of children. . . . I'll have to hang a curtain over the bedroom doorway, too, but it won't do much good. The neighbors can hear the whole thing through the wall."[62] The book is obsessed with sex, but not love. In the course of two pages, the edited transcript has Fernanda relating the stories of two husbands and a lover; of the lover, she says, "Benjamín wanted to set me up in a room of my own and everything. He offered to pay a month's rent in advance so I could get a room. But I told him, 'No, don't do it. I'm only doing this in revenge' [against her husband]. I didn't love him or feel anything for him. Nothing at all."[63] In the same two pages, we find her cutting her husband's face with a knife, passing a night in jail, and engaging in prostitution. The narrative portrays nothing of how people manage food and housing with very little income, but sex is present in endless detail. One reviewer described the content of La Vida as "sex in a thousand forms, minutely described, until the world seems a gigantic, monotonous brothel."[64] The husbands, wives, and lovers of Fernanda and her children enter the narrative only for the briefest interludes, as numbers rather than people. The text constantly reinscribes what Lewis says in the introduction: Fernanda and her children have collectively had twenty marriages—only three of them legalized by church or state.

The book left little doubt about the fact that this was a depraved, unhappy existence. These people's lives, argued Lewis, are lonely, violent, tragic. People were sociable without real human connection. They were profligate with money, engaged in petty criminality, worked irregularly. ("I've made lots of money and I've spent it all," said Fernanda. "What would I want to keep it for? We're not made of stone and we all must die, right? Suppose I save money in the bank and then I die. Who is going to enjoy that money?"[65]) Many decisions seem inexplicable, if not downright self-destructive. Fernanda and her daughters reported shame and self-loathing associated with prostitution, but persisted in that work even when they had other options. Women end perfectly good relationships and stay in degrading and violent ones. Poor people seem incapable of holding on to money from one day to the next, spending their last dollar on beer or making a loan unlikely to be repaid. They are explosively violent, including with their children. Other times, with little logic, they are lenient to the point of neglect; their parenting seems to leave everything to be desired.

Parenting, sexuality, and the visibility of the body and its functions are co-mingled in ways intended to shock U.S., middle-class readers. Visiting Fernanda's daughter, Cruz, the ethnographer walks in on the following scene: Cruz's ex-husband is sitting in the corner of a room with his fly open. Their three-year-old daughter, Anita, is there. "Ay, you just saved me," Cruz tells the ethnographer.

> Emilio came in like a wild man with such an erection I swear it could have torn out any girl's insides. Listen, right in front of Anita he grabbed me, ripped off my blouse, and at one stroke I landed on the bed. He began killing me and kissing me, and telling me to lock the door at this hour of the day. . . . I get mad but Emilio said, 'I like it better when you're angry.' So I told him, 'You son of a great whore! You queer!' "[66]

Anita, listening, finally says to her mother, "Crucita, want titty." So Cruz picks her up and begins to nurse her, with a baby boy on the other breast. Cruz's sister's two children, ages 7 and 4, are also hanging about, as Cruz says she found them wandering the street at 11 p.m. the night before.[67] She finds a basin of urine under a cot, and asks

> "Whose piss is this? Oh, it's Anita's and mine." She took the basin to the toilet to empty it, closing the door behind her. The door slowly swung open and [the ethnographer] could see her urinating. When Cruz came out of the bathroom, Anita went in, pulled off her drawers and urinated on the floor. She came out naked. "Put your *panties* on, you hear me?" Cruz said.[68]

Then, in a scene a few pages later, Cruz teaches Anita the following poem:

> My cock went and died on me,
> He's in mourning, the stupid jerk,
> Open that cunt, woman,
> To put the corpse inside.[69]

Later, Cruz plays with her baby boy's genitals. The children are hungry, dirty, poorly toilet-trained, poorly weaned, knowing about sexuality;

most have been raised by people other than their parents for at least some period of their youth. They are, in short, for many readers the shocking antithesis of the 1960s middle-class American nuclear family.

La Vida brought the culture of poverty to a wide audience. It was published in a popular edition, priced at ten dollars, below most "serious" books, and ultimately released in an inexpensive paperback edition—intending, and finding, a wide audience. *La Vida* presented a version of the culture of poverty that located female sexual promiscuity as at the heart of community breakdown, violence, and poverty (Glazer commented that, in comparison with *Children of Sanchez* it had "weaker men, more immoral women, more irresponsible fathers, and mothers all too often grossly indifferent to their children."[70])The amount of sex in the book probably goes a long way toward explaining the book's popularity; one reviewer complained that in the book's public relations promotions, it had been "discussed as if this were a cheap piece of pornography."[72] It is a pornography of poverty, whose chief pleasures are voyeuristic. Nevertheless, it won the National Book Award for nonfiction in 1967.

Lewis's policy proposals were strangely at odds with the way the book makes its case for who "the poor" are. In the introduction, Lewis argued that two kinds of things can help the poor: either participation in some kind of revolutionary activity—he cited the civil rights movement or the Cuban revolution as good examples—or gradually raising the income of the poor, possibly combined with psychotherapy. Yet nothing about the story he tells suggests that these were realistic solutions. He describes participants in the culture of poverty as apolitical (despite evidence in the text that the members of the Ríos family are not), and further, that their poverty is self-perpetuating because it was passed down from mothers to children—in short, that it was not amenable to simple fiscal solutions. Furthermore, it seems that Lewis saw it as strengthening his call to action to paint the family in terms that were as depraved as possible. That he could have told a compelling story about their political *engagement* and their extensive theorizing about poverty, its causes and consequences, seems to have occurred to Lewis, because he includes a great deal of such material in the text, though he also seemed consciously to have submerged it. He apparently also chose the most chaotic family among those he studied to portray at length in the book. It emerged in *A Study of Slum Culture*—sort of the extended footnote to *La Vida*—that of the fifty families he studied at length, only 16 percent were female-headed. All the families he explored in *La Vida* were female-headed.[73]

Lewis's studies were dogged by controversy. His Mexican books had caused a scandal in Mexico, where they were criticized as "obscene beyond the limits of human decency," defamatory of Mexico and Mexicans, and perhaps the work of an FBI agent attempting to destroy Mexican society. While the government eventually cleared him of charges of subversion, he was roundly criticized. *La Vida* was a still harsher book. Lewis explicitly and disparagingly compared Puerto Ricans to Mexicans, complaining that Puerto Ricans had no revolutionary tradition to speak of, no knowledge of their own history, and were far more deviant than Mexicans by virtually any standard.

Political scientist Susan Rigdon, after extensive review of Lewis's papers and field notes, argues persuasively that the culture-of-poverty thesis was contradicted by a great deal of Lewis's own research and convictions, which suggested that there were many, many ways of being poor and Puerto Rican, or Mexican. Nevertheless, the thesis imposed a rough coherence on sprawling material by making a particular family "typical," following similarities across generations, and hence concluding that the book said something about poverty in general. Rigdon notes that on the Puerto Rico project,

> Lewis essentially processed all the data in his head. No attempt was made to do a content analysis of the interviews—more than 30,000 transcribed pages—even though they contained the great bulk of the data. Working in this manner there was virtually no way to produce generalizations about the material that were anything more than impressions or intuitions.[73]

The Puerto Rico project, funded by the Johnson administration, was incredibly unwieldy. It employed a staff of about fifty, and Lewis did little of the actual interviewing and spent little time in Puerto Rico. He was in failing health, and, according to Rigdon, people closest to him noticed an impact on his memory and thinking. A number of his collaborators on the Puerto Rico project also suggested alternate ways of interpreting the data: psychiatrist Carolina Lujón argued that most members of the Ríos family were mentally ill, and so what he had produced was a multigenerational study of mental illness, not poverty. In speeches and lectures, Lewis admitted the fragility of the culture of poverty, suggesting that the Ríos family might not be typical of anything. In 1967 he told an audience:

> I'm afraid that some people take certain constructs or models more seriously than I do. My whole thrust is to try to show that no matter what generalization social science comes up with, be it the folk society or the subculture

of poverty . . . [there is a] range of variation of human conditions and family life.[74]

Later, in a letter, he claimed that his work was never intended to support the culture-of-poverty concept.[75] While this combination of soft-peddling and disingenuousness about the claims made in La Vida distanced him personally from the controversy over the culture of poverty, Lewis never repudiated it in print.

The reception of La Vida was as divergent as the text itself was contradictory. It was widely reviewed, and the responses of the reviewers reflect the multivalence of the work itself. One of the most important reviews was Michael Harrington's in the New York Times Book Review, which hailed Lewis's latest work as destined to persuade middle America of the need for a renewed commitment to ending poverty.[76] Manuel Maldondo Denis, a sociologist at the University of Puerto Rico and a Marxist, was similarly enthused, characterizing the book's critics as "defenders of the status quo."[77] Some of the most negative reviews came from education activists on the left, including some associated with the Puerto Rican Department of Migration, who saw the book as libelous. Reviewers Gertrude Goldberg and Francesco Cordasco argued that the book was a treasure-trove of misinformation, telling the story of a mentally ill family as if it were representative of something, and they suggested that it reiterated the major fallacies of the Moynihan Report about the immoral poor.[78]

Two other reviewers who raised questions of representativeness—Handlin and Glazer—did so from the neoconservative side of the political fence. Handlin suggested that on the one hand the Ríoses were not representative of the poor (especially not "the poor of Europe and America before 1940") and were undeserving of pity. Those who did fit into Lewis's culture of poverty, he stressed (quoting Lewis) were non-white or marginal whites: "very low-income Negroes, Mexicans, Puerto Ricans, American Indians and Southern whites." He concluded that La Vida should make Americans question the War on Poverty. "The evidence runs counter to the simple assumption that subsidizing these families will transform their lives and introduce order and self-sufficiency into their existence." He points out as representative of the poor in general that in Lewis's text,

Simplicio cannot understand his bosses, who have "the custom of saving money. . . . They kill themselves week in and week out.". . . . Simplicio and his friends are proud to be poor. When they have money they spend it on clothing or immediate gratifications.[79]

Bad decisions, bad work habits, and bad morals account for why the poor are poor, and the federal government ought not to be subsidizing them. *Newsweek,* also quoting Simplicio saying "I am proud to be poor," suggests that this sentiment among the poor is exactly why it is so difficult for many people to support war-on-poverty programs.[80] Glazer anticipated a "storm that is certain to accompany the distribution of this book," no doubt based on the experience of Moynihan. It largely did not appear.[81]

From the left, *The Nation* also reviewed the book as a critique of liberal solutions such as income supports as a solution to poverty.

> New housing projects quickly become skyscraper slums, and when a trickle of affluence sweeps down to the lowest strata of society it sometimes enables a slum dweller to feed a narcotics habit or buy a Cadillac instead of paying the rent. An explanation of why some of the poor behave as they do, and why handouts and social work are inadequate, has now been formulated neatly, concisely, even brilliantly. . . . Poverty may be ameliorated or even eliminated, [Lewis] says, without necessarily modifying the vast and horrible "subculture of poverty"—a way of life that spits at middle-class values.[82]

However, *The Nation*'s reviewer, Elmer Bendiner, notices the same split in the book that Handlin does. In contrast to Handlin, he prefers the politics of the introduction to the politics of the text. "It makes a harrowing book, certainly, but I do not know what it means. It is not needed to support the argument in the introduction and it does not strengthen it."[83]

One thing that virtually every reviewer included was some fairly extensive quote encapsulating Lewis's account of the culture of poverty from the introduction. This was *La Vida's* chief legacy: the widespread availability—for popular, policy, and academic audiences—of the notion of the culture of poverty as wedded to a sexualized, dark-skinned woman, Moynihan's "matriarch." Both Lewis and Moynihan undoubtedly believed that they were making a strong case for improving the lives of working-class people.[84] The difference between them was that Moynihan became controversial, whereas *La Vida* never became a cause célèbre.

ALTERNATIVE FORMULATIONS

There were essentially three kinds of responses among Puerto Ricans in the 1960s to the culture of poverty. Some groups, composed significantly of social workers and other professionals, accepted that although there might be things that could be reformed about the family lives and personal decisions of working-class Puerto Ricans, poverty was largely driven by forces outside the community. A second group included the radical left anti-poverty activists, who saw the entire cause of Puerto Rican poverty as racism and discrimination. The third group saw mainland Puerto Rican poverty as rooted in colonialism and worked for the independence of the island. (The difference between anti-poverty and nationalist Puerto Rican groups had to do with emphasis, not with goals; they tended to agree in the broad strokes). None, however, accepted the argument that the primary cause of poverty was women's sexual behavior, matriarchy, or matrifocal households.

An example of the first type is the Puerto Rican Forum, a group of young professionals who won an anti-poverty grant to design a plan for a culturally appropriate Puerto Rican self-help plan (other examples include groups like Aspira—an education-reform organization that eventually won a lawsuit in 1974 to force the Board of Education to stop tracking Spanish-speaking youngsters into the lowest classes based solely on their English-speaking ability.) The Puerto Rican Forum argued that the issue of poverty was as much about discriminatory activities of Anglo employers as about impoverished Puerto Ricans.

> Because there is a culture of poverty that shapes personality and reaches into job behavior, family structure, community and political action, all of these are legitimate and vital concerns of programs to combat poverty as the new poverty legislation acknowledges for the first time. Because the culture of the poor is part of a larger system including persons whose actions may be more decisive than those of the poor themselves in altering the conditions of poverty, it is also vital to fight poverty by allocating funds to work among the non-poor—employers, landlords, educators, government officials, politicians, labor leaders, and others whom the poor accept as leaders.[85]

The Forum argued that poverty was a cycle—poor people were poor because bad educational opportunities led to lousy jobs, and bad education was caused by being poor. Its members were among the first to argue that the immigration cycle, in which things would inevitably get better for the next generation, was not happening for Puerto Ricans. "It is necessary to know that Puerto Ricans are *not* 'making it' once they learn English; that the children born in the city of Puerto Rican parents are *not* becoming successful New Yorkers once they go through the city's school system; that the story of the Puerto Ricans will *not* be the same as the story of the groups of immigrants that came before."[86] While they included "to strengthen family life" among their goals, they refused to make family causal.

The Young Lords's analysis of the problem of poverty was even sharper: jobs and services failed to reach the Puerto Rican community. In this, their analysis was much like that of the artists collectively known as the Nuyorican poets; or of the Puerto Rican Student Union; or El Congreso del Pueblo, a working-class group that united New York's more than eighty Puerto Rican social clubs and that led mass demonstrations about housing, police brutality, racism, and discrimination; or similarly, that of El Comité–MINP (Movimiento de Izquierda National Puertorriqueña), which began as an anti-urban-renewal group. The Young Lords used direct action tactics both to dramatize the problems of discrimination and to work to alleviate them. In New York City, the Young Lords began with a protest about municipal garbage collection, piling up trash in the middle of city streets and blocking traffic. They took over a church and started a breakfast program, organized clothing drives, commandeered an X-ray machine and ran a TB-screening program. Not only did their analysis point steadily beyond the poor themselves, but they were also noteworthy for their analysis about women and gender. They made equality for women a key plank in their platform (in response to a demand from the Women's Caucus). In the revised program and platform written in 1970, their fifth point could not have been further from Moynihan and Lewis's fear that matriarchy—too much power for women—led to poverty:

> We want equality for women. Down with machismo and male chauvinism. Under capitalism, women have been oppressed by both society and our men. The doctrine of machismo has been used by men to take out their frustrations on wives, sisters, mothers, and children. Men must fight along with sisters in the struggle for economic and social equality and must recognize that sisters make up over half of the revolutionary army: sisters and brothers are equals fighting for our people. Forward sisters in the struggle![87]

When the Lords took over Lincoln Hospital to protest mistreatment of workers, lack of service to patients, and lack of repairs to the building, they also started a daycare center.[88]

The third kind of group was exemplified by several organizations: the Movimiento Pro-Independencia (founded in 1960), renamed in 1971 the Partido Socialista Puertorriqueña or Socialists Party (MPI–PSP); the Partido Independentista Puertorriqueña or Independence Party (PIP); the

Movimiento para Liberación Nacional or Movement for National Liberation (MLN), founded in 1977; and the clandestine Fuerzas Armadas de Liberación Nacional, or Armed Forces of National Liberation (FALN). The mainland wings of these groups relied on a variety of strategies and tactics. They successfully sought to reopen the question of Puerto Rico's colonial status at the United Nations; kept alive concern about imprisoned Puerto Rican political activists, arguing that they were political prisoners; kept Puerto Rican independence a priority for the mainland U.S. left; and focused attention on U.S. bombing tests at Vieques. Some advocated armed struggle for Puerto Rican liberation, which drew massive repression from COINTELPRO, in particular, and the FBI and local police forces in general.[89] (While virtually all Puerto Rican groups on the mainland were the targets of some level of infiltration and repression in the 1960s and 1970s, some of it brutal, the harassment of the independence groups stands out.) Their only passing nod to even engaging the culture-of-poverty question was their continued focus on the question of sterilization abuse.

FROM LIBERALS TO NEOCONSERVATIVES TO NEOLIBERALS

Over the course of four decades, the trope of the dangerous mother as the cause of poverty made its way, in both overseas development projects and domestic welfare policy, from liberal to neoconservative to neoliberal projects. After the initial phase, marked by the contribution of the social science of Puerto Rico (and to a lesser extent, that of Mexico), there were multiple cross-fertilizations between welfare and development policies. The status of the "welfare queen" has sometimes differed from that of the mother of Third World overpopulation, but they continue to be in conversation with each other. What remains constant is the centrality of ideologies about women—victimized or dangerous—to provide the cause for policy intervention, and reproduction and sexuality to provide the core of a discourse of racial/national/class difference.

In the 1970s and '80s, Moynihan, Glazer, and Handlin's search for the pathology of black and Puerto Rican families became a core ingredient of neoconservatism, as did their belief that such pathology was absent from white, Catholic and Jewish "ethnics." At least as much as feminists, neoconservatives like Charles Murray and Irving Kristol have insisted that family politics are central to national public policy.[90] For them, these politics are racialized; there are good (male-headed, male-dominant) families and bad (female-dominant, disorganized) families, the latter almost always non-white. With the decline of the influence of the Civil Rights, Nationalist, and New Left traditions, this position has at times flowered into punitive consensus. Charles Murray's 1984 *Losing Ground: American Social Policy, 1950–1980* argued that AFDC itself was causing poverty by rewarding female-headed households and that it should be eliminated. In 1994 Republican House Speaker Newt Gingrich proposed that the children of young, single mothers be put in orphanages, and many liberals agreed that it was a proposal worth considering.[91] Or, with less striking imagery but more immediate effect, liberals and conservatives worked together to eliminate the AFDC "safety net" for poor women with children in 1996, largely in response to Murray's critique.

The power of discourses of gender to launch interventionist political agendas in Puerto Rico followed the migrants to the mainland and become part of a generalized race and class agenda. This is not to say that there was not a sociology of the "deviance" of the black family prior to the postwar arrival of Puerto Ricans; there was, of course, a continuous tradition from E. Franklin Frazier to Eugene Genovese.[92] The two traditions have reinforced each other's authority and emerged again with renewed vigor in recent years. This book, in a sense, represents a genealogy of the demonization of poor women in the welfare reform debates of 1994–97. One branch of their descent comes not from the mainland but from Puerto Rico.

Ghosts, Cyborgs, and Why Puerto Rico Is the Most Important Place in the World

While most books raise their methodological questions at the outset, here they serve as epilogue. History is about change, narrative, movement; the things this book tries to understand—gender, reproduction, and sexuality with respect to the U.S. relationship with Puerto Rico—are relationships that can only be made sense of over scores of years. The ways *Reproducing Empire* grapples with questions of representation, colonialism, race, and science—its theoretical premises—are entitled to defense and interrogation only at the end, after the narrative has worked out some of their virtues and limitations. Methodological questions do not necessarily make sense at the beginning, where they may represent an inherently incomplete effort at the outset to warn and prepare a reader about the framework that informs the choice of narrative elements. They sometimes make more sense afterward, where they provide an opportunity to reflect on what the presences and absences of the narrative have been, what it confirms, contradicts, and is silent on about what we thought we knew about culture, the past, power, or human beings. Some historians go so far as to push questions of historiography, epistemology, and the nature of culture out of the text altogether, as belonging in separate books and articles from our narratives of what happened. There is wisdom in this, though some of our colleagues in other fields complain that history suffers from being atheoretical. The truth is, history is always theoretical. For historians, narrative is the site of our theoretical problems. To says that two events are related to each other,

that they belong in the same narrative, to name what is "important"—
these are meaning-making activities, which is to say, they rely on and
produce an account of culture and how it works. The ongoing, stale-
mated debates historians engage in, about "the literary turn," or the status of something that gets called "theory," or about objectivity and
representation, often produce a much impoverished version of historical
work: such scholarship is neither *just* relating what happened nor just *relating* what happened. It is understanding what happened, in the full,
rich, human sense, requiring all our faculties—discernment, compassion,
analysis, insight, empathy, humility, recognition. We are neither so far
from our history that it is "presentist" to ask what it can teach us about
how we live, nor so close that it holds any simple lessons or facile analo-
gies. But the essence of history is movement, change over time; an historian's theory is never static. Narrative is key.

This epilogue, then, explores some of the theoretical issues that this
book has tried to work through. Specifically, it looks at three questions.
It begins by exploring the relationship among a series of large and abstract concepts, things which are simultaneously more delicate and more
dense than they first appear: globalization, the state, and culture; race
and gender; and imperialism and U.S. identity. Second, it asks how we
might think about the significance of science to culture, history, and politics. Finally, there is the question we might describe in shorthand as
"What about the real women?"—which raises a host of issues about
representation, epistemology, subjectivity, and colonialism.

PUERTO RICO

One of the benefits and burdens of teaching in the Southwest, where
there are few Puerto Ricans and fewer scholars of them, is that I am constantly asked to explain why Puerto Rico is interesting or important. I
have started to answer, with tongue only partially in cheek, that Puerto
Rico is the most important place in the world. Many of the contemporary processes that we would like to understand under the rubric of *globalization*—global economic restructuring and the feminization of the
"global assembly line"; the racialization of immigrant labor forces in the
United States; contemporary anti-poverty and welfare policy, from
AFDC to "empowerment zones"; the questions of whether the U.S. rhetoric of "doing good" overseas has any truth to it, or whether the U.S. is
"essentially" imperialist—any satisfactory answer to these questions
must inevitably trace some of its roots to Puerto Rico.

Puerto Rico offers a rich field for analysis for the contemporary world-political situation because most of the processes we associate with globalization and the intellectual moves that constitute its analysis—the fundamental instability of racial categories; the importance of U.S. imperial politics; the impotence and ultimately insignificance of the state (at least the Puerto Rican state); the permeability of national cultures; and the prominence of diasporic labor migration—began sooner and have lasted longer on the island and among its population overseas than in most other places. A handful of examples suggest some of the ways Puerto Rico is a place where political conditions and its people brilliantly theorize current global instabilities. First, a literary exchange. In 1975 Miguel Algarin and Miguel Piñero published an anthology of what they termed "Nuyorican Poetry," written in a New York, and specifically a Lower East Side "Spanglish," which was smart, political, working-class, and breathtakingly vernacular. As Puerto Rican literature, it was an affront to hispanophilic "high culture," to say nothing of the fact that it was written by New Yorkers; as American literature, it was problematic for mirroring reasons—too working-class, too vernacular, too political, and written by Puerto Ricans. From the Puerto Rican side, although responses included shocked dismissal, there was another intriguing response: the novelistic sensibility encompassed by *La guaracha del macho Camacho*. *Macho Camacho* incorporated many of the same hybrid elements: "slang" as literature; an emphasis on American TV and cartoons as resources for Puerto Rican working-class culture; sex; an emphasis on Afro–Puerto Ricans as representative Puerto Ricans. A third volume, written a few years earlier, was Piri Thomas's *Down These Mean Streets*, which underscored the relationship of black Puerto Ricans in New York to the emerging African-American struggle for racial justice. Here, in snapshot, was an account of racial, national, political, and linguistic hybridity and inventiveness that theorized with elegance and economy the various "post-" moves that had become so prominent and problematic in academic worlds.

Second, consider the tradition of political labor radicalism in Puerto Rico. The Puerto Rican Socialist Party solidified its power in the early twentieth century through the American decision to grant universal suffrage to men on the island, ensuring a position in the legislature for Socialist Party candidates as representatives of working-class men. This, combined with the significant alliance between the PSP, as it was called,[1] and the American Socialist Party and other labor radicals on the mainland, cemented the pro-Americanism of the working class on the island, already nascent in their dislike of the Spanish and Creole elites. The "American" tradition they claimed, however, was so wildly optimistic as to be embarrassing: "rights of man" liberalism, antislavery and political rights for African descendants, unionization, socialism. Out of this unlikely fusion, the PSP and its successors fashioned a politics far less socially conservative than many other labor movements, supporting woman suffrage, birth control, feminism, free love, and anti-racism. This peculiarly pro-U.S. yet enduring and radical labor movement—one of a handful that can still bring the workings of a country to a halt with a general strike, as it did in 1998—has been a key resource for the politics and persistence of feminism, gay rights, student movements, and similar social movements on the island. This linkage of labor and social movements is something that the left in the United States and much of Latin America can only dream of, something that "cultural studies," "postcolonial studies," "women's studies," and other leftist interdisciplinary academic formations have tried to achieve in recent years, echoing the political longing that has informed them at least since the 1960s.

A third and final example. In Puerto Rico, the things we normally think of as necessarily aligned to constitute a nation or a region—its people, language, geographical borders, government, economy, and myths, stories, histories, literature, and/or imagination—can be radically discontinuous, occupying entirely different spaces. Puerto Ricans are more or less evenly divided between the mainland and island, speaking Spanish, English, and Spanglish; its state apparatus and economy are ultimately controlled by the United States, yet its literature and histories constitute it as no less of a nation for all of that, and as many politicians on and off the island have discovered, one neglects the Puerto Rican-ness of those on the mainland at considerable peril. Here one finds the explicit disalignment of the components of a nation, and Frances Negrón, Chloe Georgas, and Ramón Grosfoguel have argued for a notion of Puerto Rican nation as an "ethno-nation," composed by its people, diasporic and insular. Puerto Rico's situation is not unique in this respect, but arguably typical of many of the regions formerly termed the Third World. What is unusual is the transparency of its condition; as one of only a handful of places that did not win a national state in the waves of decolonization, either in the late eighteenth and early nineteenth century or after World War II, Puerto Rico cannot look to the national state to provide an imaginary unity to gloss the contradictions of its situation. Puerto Ricans have long taken a somewhat ironic view of the contradictions of "nation" and "identity."

U.S. COLONIALISMS

William Faulkner reminds us that "the past is never dead. It's not even past."² While the history of the United States in Puerto Rico provides no allegories for current struggles over globalization, it does suggest something about the legacies that haunt it. *Reproducing Empire* is an argument for thinking about ideologies of family, sexuality, and reproduction as animating U.S. imperial and racial projects. It suggests that discourses of domesticity and science, reproduction and sexuality organized U.S. colonialism. These imperial projects were consistently yoked to one of the two great modernist narratives—women's rights or scientific progress—and often both. This dimension of the relationship between island and mainland is deeply familiar to consumers of popular press accounts of U.S. foreign policy; it represents neither the rapacious capitalism suggested by Marxist accounts of the economy, nor the alternately benevolent and Machiavellian world of diplomatic history. The book has attended to the care and maintenance of the accounts in which the United States is "doing good" overseas, fostering women's rights, economic development, public health and scientific progress, and to their deeply ambivalent legacies. It is not the contention here that these arguments were or are cynical; quite the opposite, they were deadly earnest and acutely felt. One has only to recall the sheaves of newsprint devoted to Fawzia Kasinga's request for asylum in the United States to avoid a genital operation—relentlessly termed "female genital mutilation" by the press—in 1995 (which resulted in a great deal of U.N. NGO activity); the partisan browbeating over whether the United States would "do something" (read: send troops) to halt the rape of women in Bosnia in 1993; or the angst over the fate of women under the Taliban in Afghanistan, including by those usually quite unconcerned with women's rights, after September 11, 2001, to understand that defending women and restoring a proper domesticity can be an urgent matter. The point is not that these are bad things to be concerned about. Rather, this book is interested in another question. What kinds of interventions do they authorize?

Another thing *Reproducing Empire* gestures toward is the idea that the term *globalization* is only the most recent name for a process that began with a similar world system called colonialism. The official ideologies of the United States have always imagined the nation outside of the system of colonialism, while its domestic opponents have, since the U.S. war in Indochina, imagined most of what is bad in the world to be a product of U.S. domination. More recently, postcolonial studies has added a peculiar twist to these opposing but symmetrical views by emphasizing British colonialism as the author of all or most bad things in the world. These narratives demand certain correctives. Self-evidently, there is a problem with celebrating and shoring up the role of the United States as arbiter of all international (and national) disputes, as the enforcer of justice in the world, and as an economic superpower, while denying that this self-appointed role has any relationship to the British understanding of the "white man's burden." What remains radically underhistoricized by those on the left is the role and function of development as the historical transition away from frank colonization in Asia and Africa. Following decolonization by Europe was the elaboration of an infrastructure termed *development*. This is the Cold War story, the narrative of the Pax Americana and of U.S. dominance and definition of the colonial contexts. Yet development involved the elaboration of quasi-statist structures that fundamentally made over the economic, political, and even international relations of Third World nations—a not bad description of the work of its predecessor, colonialism. The chronology of the Latin American story, of course, is different, as it precedes the "development" narrative. The process that some began to call *neocolonialism* by the United States began much earlier. The end of formal colonization by Spain in the eighteenth and nineteenth centuries was rapidly followed by U.S. territorial annexation in California, Texas, elsewhere in the U.S. West, Colombia / Panama, and the Caribbean islands. Other places—Haiti, Nicaragua, the Dominican Republic, Cuba, Guatemala, Chile—were subjected to repeated invasions and U.S.-authored coups or other changes in the heads of state; or, like Mexico under the Porfiriato, or Guatemala under the United Fruit Company, U.S. business interests dominated politics and the economy. That said, however, obviously a great deal of what is good and bad in the world is not caused by colonialism, development, globalization, or anything to do with the United States; internal power relations of gender, race, class, age, and so on, may be worked out through the structure of colonialism (what structures are untouched by it?) without being in any meaningful sense determined by them. Finally, the lacunae of postcolonial and subaltern studies are not caused by its Asian and African émigré theorists, but by the substantial unwillingness of those of us who study the United States, particularly historians of the U.S., to engage substantively with its challenges and invitations.

This book, then, has been an effort to fill these gaps, an Americanist's engagement with subaltern studies; it is an attempt to tell the story of "development" in light of what came before and after; an effort to wrestle with U.S. colonialism in Puerto Rico from the point of view simultaneously of the mainland and, following the excellent work of Puerto Rican scholars, of the island and its diaspora. It is, moreover, an effort to grapple with race in the United States that does not take the relations of African Americans and whites as its starting point, nor do I reduce what happens overseas to an "effect" of domestic racism, but rather I argue that the meaning of race in the United States was sometimes profoundly transformed by colonial relations. And it is, finally, an effort to take seriously the prominence of language about women, gender, reproduction, and sexuality in the rhetoric of empire, nationalism, and various liberalisms and modernization efforts.

There is no apologia for U.S. colonialism here, no triumphalist account of the extended life spans of Puerto Ricans as justification for the violence of modernization and development. If the island has a thriving tourist economy and its people have an unlimited right of immigration to the mainland that is enviable to its neighbors, it is also always subject to the whims and vicissitudes of U.S. policy, such as, for example, the abrupt decline of manufacturing as a result of Bill Clinton's decision to end tax breaks for U.S. corporations on the island. These were the tax breaks, it must be remembered, that ensured the success of investments in manufacturing while decimating agriculture on the island. Puerto Rico finds itself now with neither tax breaks, nor agriculture, nor half its population. If Puerto Rico seems to have prospered more under U.S. sovereignty than many of its independent neighbors in Latin America that labor under staggering debt, it may well be because virtually nowhere in Latin America is it possible to be outside the influence of the U.S. economy nor immune from its political and military pressure to organize states in ways favorable to the U.S.

CYBORGS

One of the major confluences of scholarly work that informs the shape of this text, the subjects on which it speaks and on which it remains silent, is science studies, particularly as refracted by feminists and anticolonialist theorists. In "A Manifesto for Cyborgs," Donna Haraway argues forcefully that we face a transformed landscape that requires fundamentally new politics. Not since the industrial revolution, she says, have we so needed to re-theorize our situation. The old forms thrown up

by the industrial revolution—the victimized worker and the rights-bear-
ing citizen, particularly female—no longer populate our world, and
hence socialist feminism runs the risk of fighting the last war. Instead, she
proposes a cyborg radical politics that operates in three key arenas. First,
the economy has been globalized, and we need to think in those terms;
there are no more national economies and hence a national politics will
necessarily fail. Second, the key thing operating both the economy and
the production of identities/subjects is technoscience; radical politics
needs to embrace this terrain and abandon its mythic fantasies of organic
wholeness—hence the "cyborg." Third, the family has been transformed
by the economies of "homework," not only in Third World free-trade
zones, but also in Silicon Valley; the organization of production organ-
izes child care, living arrangements, the number of children one can have.

What is fascinating about this argument is that in its telling, Haraway
has rearticulated and changed the three "pivots" around which one can
spin the story of colonialism. The state, the economy, and the family have
been replaced with technoscience, economy, and family. This may well be
right, may in fact be the nature of the transformation we have seen in the
twentieth century. In Haraway's account, technoscience operates the other
two. Although not consciously a response to this formulation in Haraway,
these are the narrative centers of this book—technoscience (and medicine),
family (reproduction and sexuality), and of course, economy and economic change. While this convergence is not entirely an accident, one
could also suggest that perhaps it is just true that, armed with a *New York
Times* and a few other tools, these are simply the interpretive keys to our
world that emerge. Perhaps this is not even a particularly surprising claim.

Given the prominence of technoscience in organizing the world, however, it is surprising how rarely historians or other analysts have much
to say about it. Science studies is a distinct subfield in any discipline, and
a slightly obscure one at that. On the left, to the extent that we have
much of anything to say about technoscience at all, it is generally that it
is bad (even as we celebrate the Zapatista movement's use of the Inter-
net). Yet when we pronounce science bad, we do not turn those same analytic lenses on ourselves, do not equally judge the social sciences and humanities as participants in world-systems of power. This hubris, more
than anything perhaps, is at the heart of the "science wars." Scientists,
often our most idealistic colleagues in academe, do not recognize themselves in our accounts. While it is true and troubling that modernity and
backwardness, civilization and savagery, the right to colonize and the
"need" to be colonized have often relied on science for definition, it is

also true that science lengthened life spans and relieved suffering. If we want to accuse technoscience for its complicity in colonial projects—and obviously we should—we have to do so in the context of the insights of subaltern studies, which suggest that we must also accuse ourselves.

Sympathies for science notwithstanding, though, "real facts" are a specter that haunts this text. In taking the work of scientists and social scientists to be one of its archives, this book treats their realist represen-tational work as a source for elucidating politics, specifically the politics of knowledge about Puerto Rico. For some readers, this apparent lack of interest in the facticity of these "facts" is irritating, even infuriating; is the point that they are wrong, or what? This question is compounded by the fact that, at times, *Reproducing Empire* takes pains to point out inaccuracies or inconsistencies in the way data was produced or inter-preted. The guiding motivation is not to play "gotcha" (though I am not unaware of its pleasures), but rather to uncover a point of view. When scientists and social scientists ignore their own data or the standards of their fields, these are particularly illuminating things about the ideologies that animate their knowledge production. Following a tradition stretch-ing from Claude Lévi-Strauss to Jacques Derrida, this book is interested in contradictions. The contradictions that a community, culture, or text can contain elucidate its myths, its ideologies, its worldview. Things that appear opposed from one perspective can be consistent and coherent from another point of view, much as two objects can blend into one when the observer stands at an angle that aligns them precisely. Thus, I explore what appear as contradictions to discover the angle of vision that can hold these seeming incongruities as consistent and coherent. Yet even where I do not follow researchers' missteps as a guide, I am interested in the politics of their questions, their knowledge-claims. I do not, finally, care how many Puerto Rican infants were born out of wedlock, but I am very interested in what made this such an important question for such a long period of time, and what that tells us about those who asked it.

Another context in which this book has been more than usually dis-inclined to ask whether something is a "good fact" or a "bad fact" has to do with statistics. In the humanities and social sciences, there are two principle lines of thought in relation to statistics: those who hold that they are the sine qua non of truthful or verifiable knowledge claims, and those who reject them altogether as providing only the most simplistic kinds of information. This text takes a rather different tack, under-standing statistics as a particularly compressed narrative. Numbers are the outcome of a set of activities by a researcher involving collecting data from different sites (in ways we must be persuaded are both reliable and commensurate), aggregating this information, manipulating and transforming this aggregate through various mathematics (which themselves have histories, and hence narratives of their production), and finally, the condensation of all this activity into a singular number, produced for some specific end, in order to compare the objects or people under study to others (and hence political, in the broadest sense that all ends-oriented meaning-making activity is political). Statistics can be more or less useful, more or less interesting, but they are intrinsically narrative and they can be analyzed as such.[3] There is nothing mysterious about decoding the elements of this narrative; its form is the scientific or social scientific paper, for which statistics often provide the punch line—the rest of it can be read as the story of how these numbers were arrived at. They only become complicated to understand once they are reified and abstracted from this specific narrative, which is to say cited from one paper to the next. For example, the production of statistics about the racial distribution in the Puerto Rican population, taken up in chapter 3, lends itself to analysis about how race is perceived and measured—always subject to debate in the Puerto Rican context—and what kinds of arguments statistics showing a preponderance of one "race" or another serve as prooftext for. But even less inherently murky subjects lend themselves to this kind of analysis; per capita income, for example, requires us to accept as reasonable the assertion that five people earning $500 and five people earning nothing is equivalent to ten people earning $250 (and that income earned in certain "informal" or "illegal" sectors does not count at all, and that methods of gaining information from all sectors of the "formal" economy are reliable and reasonable). All of these may be worthwhile assumptions under certain circumstances, yet it is evident that the more information one has about data collection and the results of alternative assumptions (where informal or illegal sectors are particularly large, e.g.), the better able one is to consider the value of such numbers. At any rate, the point is simply that statistics are most usefully treated not so much as "wrong" or "right," but as the result of a knowledge-creation process with its own dynamics, one that can be told and understood as story.

SUBALTERN STUDIES

Another major theoretical current shaping this book is subaltern studies. Subaltern studies is by and large not well understood by U.S. historians, nor by a significant segment of another community that this book would speak to, feminists and others on the intellectual and activist left in the United States. The best example of this is the ongoing misreading of Spivak's article "Can the Subaltern Speak?," which engenders the kind of passionate, sentimental defense of the maligned subaltern that Spivak's critique means to call into question as a self-interested ventriloquist trick. In this brilliant article, Spivak points to an interview in which theorists Michel Foucault and Giles Deleuze, whom she characterizes as revisionists of the Marxist and Freudian traditions, respectively, engage in a move she identifies as characteristic of contemporary intellectuals: the assertion that the dispossessed—the prisoner, the worker, the homosexual—has perfect knowledge of her social position and an uncomplicated ability to articulate it. This, Spivak argues, is far from Marx's understanding of class and representation, and even farther from Freud's notion of subjectivity, both of which rely on a certain "productive bafflement," in her phrase, which is to say, they assume that neither class structure nor subjectivity are transparent, but mystified, requiring analysis both by those interpellated into a class (or gender or race) and by intellectuals. By requiring the oppressed to "speak for themselves," she argues, intellectuals hide behind the dispossessed, obscure their own analytical and ideological work, and pretend that the production of knowledge itself is not a political and dominative process. One does not become a producer of authoritative knowledge by being dispossessed. To pretend otherwise, far from counteracting vanguardist politics by inviting in the voices of the oppressed, is to lie, to engage in vanguardist politics without taking responsibility for one's position as a middle-class intellectual authoring these texts, to be accountable for one's participation in the imperialist structures and histories of academic disciplines. This is not, however, a disavowal of the possibility of radical academic work, but merely its precondition; her critique of Foucault and Deleuze is hardly that they are intellectuals, but rather that they fail to see their complicity—and that of the subjects that they analyze and the availability of the theory that they write—to the projects of international capitalist exploitation and colonialism. There is no place of innocence for intellectuals, but there are many possibilities for anti-imperialism.

If this critique, and the work of the subaltern studies historians in general, has not been widely taken up by U.S. historians and feminists, it is perhaps because this is a potentially devastating critique of a great deal of the academic work of the "new" social history and of feminist and ethnic studies scholarship in general. We have come to rely rather extensively on the axiomatic belief that "recovering lost voices" or "women's experience" is always possible and self-evidently liberatory. To call this into question is to break faith, despite the evidence that leftists and feminists head academic departments, edit scholarly series, and get tenure, and that the power of labor, the independence of Third World nations, racial justice movements, and the ability to combat the gender segregation of labor markets are on the decline. In other words, since at least 1980, the economic and cultural power of academic leftists and feminists and those they purport to defend have had radically different careers. While this is not necessarily the fault of intellectuals, it does suggest that we ought to withhold confidence about the success of our strategies and be willing to revise them.

However, this is not necessarily a call to abandon scholarly leftist projects. The other thing that subaltern studies does is reveal and make available for analysis the political consequences of knowledge production, or more precisely, knowledge production *as* politics. If we can no longer hide behind the subaltern and perform the trick of making the oppressed speak, we can write about the ways our disciplines, our colleagues, and we ourselves have been enlisted into imperialist projects. This book has benefited enormously from this insight; it has made it possible to study the work and words of physicians, scientists, and social scientists as politically effective tools, which of course they precisely were. Sterilization, eugenics, birth control research, statistics about birth rates, marriage rates, syphilis rates are never politically neutral—how could they be? When Foucault writes about the statistical work of producing "the population," he begins to get at this. Subaltern studies pushes this insight much further.

One group of U.S. historians who have welcomed the work of subaltern studies and other analysis that privileges knowledge production, not incidentally, are Puerto Rican historians and analysts. Kelvin Santiago-Valles, Gladys Jimenez-Muñoz, Arlene Dávila, Alberto Sandoval Sánchez, and Arnaldo Cruz-Malave, to name a few, have in the last decade been at the forefront of scholarship that takes up the implications of subaltern and postcolonial studies for the United States, and it was they who taught me how to read this sometimes difficult Asian and African scholarship. This is a bit of a reversal for those of us who initially learned how to think about imperialism and international capitalism through the lens of Ché Guevara, liberation theology, and Cesar Chavez to find ourselves turning from Latin America to Asia to read a Latin American situation. Yet this is perhaps rather precisely the dream of a

"Third" World promulgated at Bandung in 1955: the possibility of a geographical "South" that was, if not united, then mutually conversant, and that would serve as the alternative, the conscience of the others. Without romanticizing, it bears noticing that "First" world scholarship could be immensely improved by paying attention to this possibility.

GHOSTS

Nevertheless, silent subalterns are troubling, and should be; they haunt texts as the victims of violence, the bad conscience of imperialism and racism. Their ghosts are the site of a conundrum at the heart of this one. One of the key arguments of this book, following Spivak, is that the sexuality and reproduction of poor women has been ceaselessly appropriated. Women reformers, U.S. officials and policy advisors, scientists and physicians, Puerto Rican nationalists and many others, all have claimed to know and speak for poor women who have been victimized by one or another kind of abuse of their sexual or reproductive vulnerability. In other words, representations of the issues surrounding the sexuality of working-class Puerto Rican women have never been innocent. Yet this very project is crucial to telling the story in this book. The task, then, has been to narrate these events without reiterating the colonialist move: the appropriation of these women's stories to mobilize pity, outrage, or contempt in order to further one or another agenda in relation to the island.

Recovering "real women" or "the oppressed" is not always possible, nor is it always a good thing. The ventriloquist work of the colonialist and nationalist forces in the stories in this book also purported to "recover" women's voices. Questions of subjectivity and representation are inescapably crucial to studies of colonialism. As Martín Lienhard among many others has argued, colonialism at its heart is always an inscription process.[4] Not in the weak sense of "just" representation, as if it floated free and had no consequences, did not kill people and take their livelihood, but rather in a stronger sense. Leinhard reminds us that *conquistadores* read aloud to uncomprehending Incas and Aztecs proclamations that gave the sailors title to the New World from God and Isabella just before they began their killing; or, to end where we began, Said tells us of Napoleon's research institute in Egypt that instructed his imperial army in how to rule, where to apply violence, producing grammars, censuses, citizens and non-citizens, the real and the fabulous, the familiar and the utterly strange. In the nineteenth century the British Imperial Office employed anthropologists; in the late twentieth century, would-be

CIA operatives majored in U.S. universities' Area Studies. As Mahmood Mamdani observed about the usefulness of academic histories of the Tutsis for the Hutu perpetrators of the Rwandan genocide, "post-geno-cidal sobriety compels a growing number of historians to take seriously the political uses to which their writings have been put."[5] This should be a strong warning to those of us who would attempt to write about the colonial: such knowledge has long served well the repressive goals of states, militaries, and militias.

Yet if the desire for knowledge of the subaltern is never innocent, nei-ther is its absence. When people in the religious left speak of "bearing wit-ness," it is to elucidate a morality of mutual human obligation to refuse to accept silence as an outcome of violence. Michel Rolph Trouillot writes about Haiti in this way, in a book called, significantly, *Silencing the Past,* saying that the absence of knowledge about the tremendous violence of the colonization and decolonization of Haiti has consequences in bloodshed and inequalities of power in the present.[6] In the historical moment in which this is being written, the imperative to overwrite and overlook the historical fact of U.S. colonialism seems very strong, as those in academe, in politics and business try to teach us to talk about "globalization" or "ending terrorism" as if these were benign processes, not rooted in histo-ries of colonialism and forms of capitalist domination. Ignorance as well as the obsessive production of knowledge about Puerto Rico by people in the United States have both been part of its political domination, with its concomitant poverty and foreshortened lives, dreams, and destinies.

There is no answer to these questions; to respond to one half of this problem is to court the opposite trouble. There are those who will won-der if I should have written this book. I am a U.S. Anglo whose ties to the island are only love and a relentless sense that just as the history of the island is inescapably tied to that of the mainland, so the mainland's history is reciprocally tied to the island. A certain version of identity pol-itics would go so far as to ask to know by what right I arrogate what should only belong to Puerto Ricans: the authority to represent the island and its people. Yet the silence about Puerto Rico in our history textbooks and newspapers does not serve the cause of economic, political, and so-cial justice for Puerto Ricans, either. And the island's history is also the history of U.S. colonialism, which is very much the business of U.S. An-glos. Others would challenge this work in the opposite way: why can't *Reproducing Empire* say more about the subjectivity of the working-class women whose bodies, reproduction, and sexuality were at the cen-ter of so many scientific, social scientific, nationalist, colonialist, and feminist projects? Yet as a story about how narratives of these women's subjectivities launched countless agendas, authorized so many people's political projects, how could it, without investing itself in the precise problem it means to begin to dislodge?

History and anthropology—the two fields to which this book is most indebted—have both grappled with these issues in the last two decades and come to opposite conclusions. Anthropology and history seem to be in the process of trading job descriptions. Anthropology has typically been charged with the work of studying "down" the social/economic/cultural ladder, looking at the "native," the "savage," and other voiceless peoples. Contemporary critics, noticing how this scholarship has been used to render its subjects "exotic" at best and pathological at worst, argue for studying "up." "Don't study the poor and powerless because everything you say about them will be used against them," enjoins Laura Nader.[7] At the other end of the spectrum, history, sometimes caricatured as the story of great men and wars, has been engaged in the opposite process: of recovering the stories of those it traditionally overlooked, particularly (but not limited to) the working classes, women, and people of color. We speak of "recovering the agency of the oppressed." It is impossible to choose between these critiques; both tell the truth. There is finally no single answer; as the preceding pages record, neglect and obsessive interest have both worked in the service of the imperial project in Puerto Rico.

This, then, is a haunted text, as sociologist Avery Gordon would say, naming the significant silences in a text in the same way novelist Toni Morrison did in *Beloved,* where she delicately but devastatingly narrated the violence of U.S. slavery as a ghost story.[8] These problems of subjectivity and subjection, structure and agency, history, anthropology, and postcolonial studies, studying "up" and studying "down" lead me to think of the women at the center of this book, the ones so much spoken about but seemingly speaking so little on their own behalf, as ghosts. They are inescapably and very much there, active and possessed of agency, with their own motives—heroism, resistance, indifference, pettiness, cruelty, the whole spectrum of human motivations—but elusive and hard to pin down. This is not their story, but they haunt it.

At first, when people who had read parts of this book began asking me, "But what about the real women?," I didn't know what they meant. For me, the book was very much peopled by real women who were being spoken to and spoken about at great length, women who suffered by virtue of being the subject of other people's narratives about backwardness, modernity, or overpopulation. They were put in jail as prostitutes, forced to (or compelled to refuse to) greet the birth or death of a child as part of the island's story of nationhood or modernization, denied jobs by those who perceived them as carrying the marks of a "culture of poverty." There is a place in Oscar Lewis's *La Vida* where a man explains why he signed the paper for his ex-wife, who needed the permission of a man (husband, father, or lover) to get a sterilization operation. At first he refused; then, on consideration, he concluded, "The best thing for Puerto Rico would be to sterilize all the women to keep so many vermin from being born."[9] This is a book about the kind of stories, told and retold, that could make it possible for a husband to say—and perhaps even to believe—such a thing about someone he loved, or at least had loved. Then there are the other "real" women who appear in this book—missionaries, nurses, social workers, activists. What made them not count? *Reproducing Empire* takes account of the same kinds of sources other histories do, often more—manuscripts, letters, newspapers, surveys, censuses, economic data, scientific articles, newsletters, magazines, essays, fiction, music. The difference is, this book understands the subject of these texts to be the author, not the women they wrote about. The decision to read this way opened up worlds, revealed something about power, but it also closed down other possibilities.

One day, I came to understand that this is an unsettling way to tell the story, to feel myself the absence of the "real" working-class women. The book could have said more. It is also true that the women in these narratives are never reducible to the sum of the representations about them. They were prostitutes who preferred their work to the alternatives and also those who hated it, criminals, women who gave birth to "illegitimate" children in the context of consensual unions, participants in riots, "backward" folk who had many children despite the birth controlling and modernizing projects of the state, and unwelcome migrants with female-headed households to the mainland United States. They were gamblers, thieves, practitioners of *santería,* adherents of a Catholicism at once more ecstatic and more pragmatic than that envisioned by the Church hierarchy, passionate lovers of "shocking" music, hard-working, often exhausted rural women who gossiped with their neighbors over very strong coffee with milk, modest and reserved women, those who hated sex and disliked their husbands, delighted mothers of "inappropriate" children, grieving parents of dead infants. Their interests were not those of elites, their perspectives not encompassed by hegemonic ideologies. While it would be a mistake to romanticize all refusals to accede to conventional, middle-class morality as forms of political resistance, neither could we say that women were necessarily passive or happy about being "rescued" from their failures to attain it. These refusals, while not recorded faithfully in the archives and public discourses of the period, are nevertheless recorded reliably, in the sense that they are always there. The effort to produce an authoritative story about these women, like the archive itself, is the product of a struggle for power and mastery, and such struggles leave traces.

Nevertheless, I feel a profound reluctance to try to tell the "truth" about these women, against the representations of scientists, social workers, nationalists, development officials. The representations in this book are a burden, a violence done to working-class women; they have been the basis of policy decisions about what to do to them that have affected employment, health, life, and fertility. It feels wrong to do it again, to serve up historically illiterate women who do not have the opportunity to talk back as the readily graspable, homogeneous subject of academic or policy debates. I prefer them as ghosts, wish to afford them that privacy and dignity. Journalist Philip Gourevitch writes about how the Tutsi survivors of the Rwandan genocide refused to answer certain questions, would not tell him the stories of their "normal" lives—household stories, funny stories, stories of annoyance, of work or school—but would only tell him of events relevant to the genocide. Gourevitch noticed a similarity in their silence to that of his Holocaust-survivor parents and grandparents, whose written memoirs end right in the middle of their lives, after their escape from the Nazis. "It occurred to me," he wrote, "that if others have so often made your life their business—made your life into a question, really, and made that question their business—then perhaps you will want to guard the memory of those times when you were freer to imagine yourself as the only times that are truly and inviolably your own." This is a book about the times when working class women's lives were made into a question. The rest is their own.

This, finally, is what this book tries to say to scholars and critics of colonialism in general. We have paged through the annals of modernism in our search for the position of innocence, and found our sources of optimism—Marxism, feminism, nationalism, and science—all wanting. As we find ourselves at the threshold of a new era, one that seems to have begun with a redoubling of the intensity and disingenuousness of colonialism, we have to find ways to make this chapter of the story turn out differently, to win, this time, a means of introducing differences, of producing new narratives within neocolonial knowledge that will alter its practice. Refusing the terms of the trope of women's dangerous sexuality and reproduction would be a good place to start.

Notes

INTRODUCTION

1. Johnson, *Latin America in Caricature;* Eileen Findlay also makes this argument in "Love in the Tropics."

2. Lapp, "Puerto Rico as Social Laboratory"; and Grosfoguel, "The Divorce of Nationalist Discourses from the Puerto Rican People."

3. A story makes the point. In researching this book, I worked with many wonderful archivists at the National Archives. However, while doing research there, I had the strange experience of encountering an archivist who would not look for material for me, because, he said, Puerto Rico was not part of the United States.

4. Ong, *Flexible Citizenship.*

5. See Ong's article on the various social (dis)locations of women factory workers, "The Gender and Labor Politics of Postmodernity."

6. Fadiman, *The Spirit Catches You and You Fall Down;* Tannette Johnson-Elie, "Hmong Workers Find Help in Job Market," *Milwaukee Journal Sentinel,* 10 August 1999, p. 1.

7. Chavez, *Out of the Barrio,* 142–43.

8. This argument is made particularly well by Richard Weisskoff in *Factories and Food Stamps.*

9. Bourgeois, *In Search of Respect.*

10. Don Feder, "No Statehood for Caribbean Dogpatch," *Boston Herald,* 30 November 1998.

11. See comics critic Raeburn, "The Brand Called Schmoo."

12. For the case of promiscuous sexuality, think of the line in the Rolling Stones' song "Miss You": "We're gonna come around at twelve / With some Puerto Rican girls that are just dyin' to meet you. / We're gonna bring a case of

wine / Hey, let's go mess and fool around," in which showing up with "Puerto Rican girls" is as reliable an assurance of bad-boy sex as the case of wine ("Miss You," *Some Girls* [Glimmer Twins, 1978]).

13. Cripps, *Human Rights in a United States Colony.* On the Justice Department coverup (and hence suspicion of FBI involvement), see Jim McGee, "Ex-Justice Official Cites 'Coverup' by FBI in '78 Puerto Rico Shootings," *Washington Post,* 9 May 1992, p. A3; and Mireya Navarro, "Puerto Rico Gripped by Its Watergate," *Washington Post,* 30 January 1992, p. A18.

14. "Puerto Rico Says No," *San Francisco Chronicle,* 16 December 1998, A26.

15. Grosfoguel, "The Divorce of Nationalist Discourses from the Puerto Rican People," 68.

16. Organization for Economic Cooperation and Development, *External Debt Statistics,* 21.

17. Bhabha, "Of Mimicry and Man," 158.

18. Stanton, *The Leopard's Spots;* Gould, *The Mismeasure of Man.*

19. The body of work here is quite large. Some indicative examples would be Smith-Rosenberg, *Disorderly Conduct;* Leavitt, *Typhoid Mary;* Martin, *The Woman in the Body;* Fausto-Sterling, *Myths of Gender;* Poovey, *Uneven Developments;* and Clarke, *Disciplining Reproduction.*

20. Findlay, "Domination, Decency, and Desire," 14, cited in Matos Rodríguez, "Women's History in Puerto Rican Historiography," 24.

21. Spivak, "Can the Subaltern Speak?"

CHAPTER 1

1. Walkowicz, *Prostitution and Victorian Society.*

2. Ballhatchet, *Race, Sex, and Class under the Raj.* See also Arnold, *Colonizing the Body;* Ware, *Beyond the Pale;* and Levine, "Venereal Disease, Prostitution, and the Politics of Empire."

3. Whiting, "The Social Hygiene Movement," RG 2, Series O: Rockefeller Boards, Subseries 2: Bureau of Social Hygiene, box 6, folder 40, Rockefeller Family Archives, Rockefeller Archive Center, Sleepy Hollow, N.Y. [hereafter cited as RFam-RAC].

4. Arnold, *Colonizing the Body,* 84.

5. Cited in Ballhatchet, *Race, Sex, and Class under the Raj,* 14.

6. Levine, "Venereal Disease, Prostitution, and the Politics of Empire," 586–87.

7. Ballhatchet, *Race, Sex, and Class under the Raj,* 40–67, 144–59; Arnold, *Colonizing the Body,* 83–87.

8. See, e.g., Armstrong, *Desire and Domestic Fiction.*

9. Hershatter, *Dangerous Pleasures,* 6–7.

10. Rosen, *The Lost Sisterhood,* 12.

11. Enloe, *Bananas, Beaches, and Bases.*

12. Ibid.

13. See Foucault, *Discipline and Punish;* and Foucault, "Govermentalities." While historians of earlier empires might contest the degree to which these tech-

nologies of rule were uniquely modern, they were nevertheless reliably characteristic of the state forms of Europe and the United States and their colonies in the nineteenth and twentieth centuries.

14. On statistics, see MacKenzie, *Statistics in Britain, 1865–1930*. On the question of the legitimating authority in U.S. public health, see Hammonds, *Childhood's Deadly Scourge*, and on its unpersuasiveness to immigrants and the working classes, see Leavitt, *Typhoid Mary*.

15. See, e.g. Bashford, " 'Is White Australia Possible?' "; Arnold, *Colonizing the Body;* and Anderson, "Where Every Prospect Pleases and Only Man Is Vile."

16. Levine, "Venereal Disease, Prostitution, and the Politics of Empire," 586–87; Van Heyningen, "The Social Evil in the Cape Colony, 1868–1902."

17. Warren, "Prostitution and the Politics of Venereal Disease"; Manderson, "Colonial Desires"; and Beswick and Spaulding, "Sex, Bondage, and the Market."

18. Murnane and Daniels, "Prostitutes as 'Purveyors of Disease'."

19. See Summers, "Intimate Colonialism"; Vaughan, *Curing Their Ills,* 132–37; and Jeater, *Marriage, Perversion, and Power.*

20. Van Heyningen, "The Social Evil in the Cape Colony 1868–1902," 173.

21. Hunt, *A Colonial Lexicon of Birth Ritual, Medicalization, and Mobility in the Congo.*

22. Enloe, *Bananas, Beaches, and Bases,* 83; Stoler, *Capitalism and Confrontation in Sumatra's Plantation Belt, 1870–1979;* Guy, *Sex and Danger in Buenos Aires;* and Caulfield, "The Birth of Mangue." Regulation was introduced in Cuba in 1873 (see Vigo, "Gendered and Racialized Discourses on Prostitution in Havana (1873–1926)." See also McCreery, " 'This Life of Misery and Shame' "; Garon, "The World's Oldest Debate"; Bernstein, *Sonia's Daughters;* and Gilman, "Plague in Germany, 1939/1989."

23. Van Heyningen, "The Social Evil in the Cape Colony 1868–1902," 177.

24. Manderson, "Colonial Desires," 378; she makes this point more broadly in her *Sickness and the State*. Similary, in "Le bebé en brousse," Nancy Hunt looks at questions of maternal health in relation to the reproduction of a colonial labor force in the Belgian Congo.

25. Chatterjee, "The Indian Prostitute as a Colonial Subject"; Guy, *Sex and Danger in Buenos Aires;* Feldman, "Prostitution, the Alien Woman, and the Progressive Imagination, 1910–1915," 195.

26. Warren, "Prostitution and the Politics of Venereal Disease."

27. See, e.g., Brandt, *No Magic Bullet,* 35. This is actually only partially true even of the mainland U.S.; there were quite a number of short-lived municipal ordinances between 1870 and 1910, including in St. Louis, Detroit, Minneapolis, Buffalo, Philadelphia, Cincinnati, San Francisco, and Douglas, Ariz. (see Pivar, *Purity Crusade,* 50–77; Burnham, "The Progressive Era Revolution in American Attitudes toward Sex"; Burnham, "Medical Inspection of Prostitutes in America in the Nineteenth Century"; and Weiss, "The Prostitution Problem in Its Relation to Law and Medicine," 2074).

28. Goodman, "The Antivenereal Disease Campaign In Panama"; Pivar, "The Military, Prostitution, and Colonial Peoples"; Orenstein, "Sanitary Inspection of the Canal Zone"; Health Department of the Panama Canal Zone, "Report."

29. Jenkinson, "Vera Cruz."

30. Senate Committee on Inter-Oceanic Canals, *Investigation of Panama Canal Matters,* 59th Cong., 2d sess. 11 January–12 February, 1907, vol. 1, 928–81. Thanks to Julie Greene, University of Colorado, for pointing me to this.

31. Goodman, "The Antivenereal Disease Campaign in Panama," 162.

32. Exner, "Prostitution in its Relation to the Army on the Mexican Border."

33. Young, *Hugh Young,* 301.

34. "A Warning Cry for Our Troops on the Border," *Literary Digest,* 29 July 1916, 254.

35. Jenkinson, "Vera Cruz."

36. "Military Government of Santo Domingo, Executive Order No. 96," *Gaceta Oficial* 33: 2859, RG 350, National Archives II, College Park, Md. [hereafter cited as NWCT2].

37. Dery, "Prostitution in Colonial Manila."

38. Tyrrell, *Woman's World / Woman's Empire,* 191–217.

39. See Kaplan's analysis in "Left Alone with America."

40. The phrase is William Appleman Williams's.

41. See Campomanes, "1898 and the Nature of the New Empire."

42. See Curtin, *Death by Migration;* and Curtin "The White Man's Grave."

43. See Arnold, *Imperial Medicine and Indigenous Societies,* 1–26.

44. Tropical medicine did not begin with Ross or his counterpart Patrick Manson (who studied the role of *Aedes* mosquitoes in malaria), but it clearly had a long history in the "diseases of warm climates" dating to the sixteenth century (see Arnold, *Warm Climates and Western Medicine*). It is with Ross, however, that it begins to take the distinctive shape I am interested in here.

45. See Arnold, *Imperial Medicine and Indigenous Societies,* 1–26; Latour, *The Pasteurization of France;* Thomas, "Sanitation and Seeing"; Packard, "The 'Healthy Reserve' and the 'Dressed Native' "; Anderson, "Colonial Pathologies"; and Anderson, "Excremental Colonialism." How these preeminently female activities became the responsibility of the Army under the new sanitary regime is a fascinating question.

46. Anderson, "Where Every Prospect Pleases and Only Man Is Vile," 508.

47. See, e.g., Brandt, *No Magic Bullet;* and Connelly, *The Response to Prostitution in the Progressive Era.*

48. The notion that the black community was extensively infected with syphilis laid the groundwork for the Tuskegee syphilis experiment, where from 1932 to 1972 four hundred black men in rural Alabama were denied medical treatment for syphilis in a study designed to determine the natural history of the disease in African Americans, among whom the disease was considered both different and endemic (see Jones, *Bad Blood;* and Brandt, "Racism and Research").

49. Quétel, *History of Syphilis,* 140–41; s.v. "Schaudinn," *Biographical Encyclopedia of Scientists,* 793; quote is from Dennie, *A History of Syphilis,* 94–95.

50. In 1913 the Rockefeller Foundation's researcher, Hideyo Noguchi, was able to infect rabbits with it (see Plesset, *Noguchi and His Patrons*).

51. Latour, *The Pasteurization of France;* Hacking, *Representing and Intervening.*

52. Dible, *Recent Advances in Bacteriology and the Study of the Infections,* 372–74; Quétel, *History of Syphilis,* 140–41.

53. Ehrlich, "Closing Notes to the Experimental Chemotherapy of Spiril-loses," 282, 294; Bäumler, *Paul Ehrlich;* and Marquardt, *Paul Ehrlich.*

54. Quétel, *History of Syphilis,* 141; Brandt, *No Magic Bullet,* 110–12.

55. Brandt, *No Magic Bullet,* 23.

56. George Kibbe Turner, "The Daughters of the Poor," *McClure's Magazine,* November 1909, 57–58, cited in Feldman, "Prostitution, the Alien Woman, and the Progressive Imagination, 1910–1915," 195.

57. "Ehrlich's Remedy a Medical Wonder," *New York Times,* 11 September 1910, p. 5.

58. *Program of Protective Social Measures,* U.S. Interdepartmental Social Hygiene Board pamphlet, cited in Brandt, *No Magic Bullet,* 72.

59. John H. Stokes, *Today's World Problem in Disease Prevention* (Washington, 1919), cited in Brandt, *No Magic Bullet,* 72; Lavinia Dock quote is from *Hygiene and Morality* (1910), 35, cited in Connolly, *The Response to Prostitution in the Progressive Era,* 68.

60. Ballenger, "The Social Evil," 21.

61. Wolbarst, "The Treatment of Syphilis with Ehrlich-Hata '606'-Salvarsan," 49.

62. Stamp affixed to correspondence of W. H. Zinsser, CTCA, to James H. Foster, SGO, 25 November 1918, RG 112, Entry 726.1, box 422, National Archives, Regional Archives, Northeast Region, New York City [hereafter cited as NRAN].

63. Hill, *The World Their Household,* 3.

64. Tyrrell, *Woman's World/Woman's Empire,* 197–212, Whiting, "The Social Hygiene Movement," p. 1, RG 2, Series O: Rockefeller Boards, Subseries 2: Bureau of Social Hygiene, box 6, folder 40, RFam-RAC.

65. Quote is from the NWCTU *Annual Report* for 1897, p. 107, cited in Tyrrell, *Woman's World/Woman's Empire,* 206. The question of Somerset's support for regulation was the major issue of the WWCTU convention of October 1897, resulting in protest and resignations of WCTU leaders in the British colonies and elsewhere, including Australia, India, New Zealand, South Africa, Canada, France, Denmark, and Sweden. In January 1989, as Willard's impending death threatened to exacerbate this fracture in the ranks of the WCTU, Lady Somerset recanted. Tyrrell tells this story (*Woman's World/Woman's Empire,* 202–9).

66. Tyrrell, *Woman's World/Woman's Empire,* 195.

67. Quoted in Enloe, *Bananas, Beaches, and Bases,* 83.

68. Walkowitz, *Prostitution and Victorian Society.*

69. Burton, "The White Woman's Burden," 137–57 (quote is on p. 145); see also Brumberg, "Zenanas and Girlless Villages"; di Leonardo, *Exotics at Home;* and Mohanty, "Under Western Eyes."

70. Warren, "Prostitution and the Politics of Venereal Disease"; Garon, "The World's Oldest Debate."

71. Manderson, "Colonial Desires"; see also her *Sickness and the State.*

72. Ballhatchet, *Race, Sex, and Class under the Raj;* Chaterjee, "The Indian Prostitute as a Colonial Subject."

73. Van Heyningen, "The Social Evil in the Cape Colony, 1868–1902," 187–93.

74. Smith, "The Contagious Diseases Acts Reconsidered," 215.

75. Garon, "The World's Oldest Debate"; Walkowitz, *Prostitution and Victorian Society*, 1–9.

CHAPTER 2

1. Puerto Rico, Office of the Attorney General, *Special Report of the Attorney General of Porto Rico to the Governor of Porto Rico;* and in Goodman, "Prostitution and Community Syphilis."

2. Hildreth, "The Awakening in PR: Vice Being Repulsed with Vigor," *Union Signal*, 3 October 1918, p. 4.

3. "WCTU Joins Hands with Police Department in Fight Against Vice," *Union Signal*, 29 August 1918, p. 7; "A Las Damas de Puerto Rico," *La Correspondencia* (San Juan), 14 August 1918, p. 3; Edith Hildreth, "El Próximo Paso," *La Democracia* (San Juan), 4 November 1918, p. 11; "Policia Femenina," *La Democracia* (San Juan), 29 July 1918, p. 4; Edith Hildreth, "Propósitos de la Asociación de Damas de la Temperancia y de la Policia Femenina," *La Democracia* (San Juan), 22 August 1918, p. 2; "Opportunity for Co-Operation," *The Times* (San Juan), 30 July 1918, p. 7.

4. Pivar, "The Military, Prostitution, and Colonial Peoples," 265.

5. Pasarell, "Medical Report of the District Jail at Ponce," in Puerto Rico, Office of the Attorney General, *Special Report of the Attorney General of Porto Rico to the Governor of Porto Rico*, 35.

6. Unsigned, "Una Cárcel para Mujeres," *La Correspondencia* (San Juan), 15 August 1918, p. 1. Translations here, and throughout, are mine.

7. Puerto Rico, Office of the Attorney General, *Special Report of the Attorney General of Porto Rico to the Governor of Porto Rico*, 618–19; "Por El Campamento Las Casas / Alocución dirigida por los Padres de Redententoristas a los Soldados," *La Democracia* (San Juan), 7 August 1918, p. 4.

8. Unsigned, "Lo que opina el fiscal Campillo," *La Correspondencia* (San Juan), 21 September 1918, p. 1.

9. Findlay, *Imposing Decency: The Politics of Sexuality and Race in Puerto Rico, 1870–1920* (Durham: Duke, 1999), 184.

10. "¡¡Basta Ya!! El Attorney General está violando las leyes del País," *La Correspondencia* (San Juan), 20 August 1918, p. 1; "Através de la Isla—Ponce," *La Correspondencia* (San Juan), 24 August 1918, p. 4; Puerto Rico, Office of the Attorney General, *Special Report of the Attorney General of Porto Rico to the Governor of Porto Rico*, 24; "Por Dios, Sr. Fiscal," *El Tiempo* (San Juan), 21 August, 1918, p. 1; "El pueblo esta con nosotros," *La Correspondencia* (San Juan), 23 August 1918, p. 3.

11. L. Yordan Pasarell, "Medical Report of the District Jail at Ponce," in Puerto Rico, Office of the Attorney General, *Special Report of the Attorney General of Porto Rico to the Governor of Porto Rico*, 35; "Notas de Ponce," *La Democracia* (San Juan), 30 August 1918, p. 7. The riots received only brief mention in a news column (see "Ponce," *La Correspondencia* [San Juan], 30 August 1918, p. 4). Advertisements for patent medicines were ubiquitous: KNOXIT for gonorrhea; EL COMPUESTO VEGETAL DE LYDIA E. PINKHAM (Lydia Pinkham's Veg-

etable Compound) for "sick women"; ELIXER DE LEONARDI PARA LA SANGRE (Leonardi's blood elixer) for syphilis, impure blood, and nervous debility (*La Democracia* [San Juan], 9 August 1918, p. 6; 13 September 1918, p. 5; 9 October 1918, p. 7, respectively).

12. "Earthquake," in Puerto Rico, Office of the Attorney General, *Special Report of the Attorney General of Porto Rico to the Governor of Porto Rico*, 10.

13. "El puritanismo del puritano Sr. Kern esta a prueba," and "Contra la vuelta de Mr. Kern como jefe, al Departamento de Justicia," *El Tiempo* (San Juan), 3 December 1918, p. 1.

14. "Levantamiento de mujeres," *El Tiempo* (San Juan), 27 March 1918, p. 1.

15. Puerto Rico, Office of the Attorney General, *Special Report of the Attorney General of Porto Rico to the Governor of Porto Rico*, 13.

16. The spelling of the name of the island and its inhabitants was Anglicized with the transfer of power from the Spanish, a change that was kept in place until 1932.

17. Ashford, *A Soldier in Science*, 80.

18. Lewis, *Puerto Rico.*

19. Flores Ramos, "Virgins, Whores, and Martyrs."

20. Dietz, *Economic History of Puerto Rico*, 21–25; González, *Puerto Rico*, 35–37; López, *The Puerto Ricans*, 475–90.

21. Muñoz Marín, *La Democracia* (San Juan), 1893, quoted in Findlay, "Domination, Decency, and Desire," 476.

22. Findlay, *Imposing Decency.*

23. Picó, *Historia general de Puerto Rico*, 193.

24. Verrill, *Porto Rico*, 139–40.

25. Baxter, "Porto Rico under the Stars and Stripes," 504. Indeed they did, though not exactly in the impersonal sense that Baxter imagined; rather, in subsequent years the diagnosis and treatment of hookworm became the basis for the involvement of Rockefeller philanthropies in setting up public health bureaucracies around the globe, training "native" elites as scientists and physicians, and setting agendas for both forms of colonialism and scientific research worldwide. But that is getting ahead of our story.

26. Arthur Warner, "Progress (and Poverty) in Porto Rico," *The Nation*, 15 August 1923, 159.

27. Clark et al., *Puerto Rico and Its Problems*, summarizes the death-rate figures from the annual governor's reports; from 1900 to 1930 the death rate remained relatively constant, between 22 and 25 per thousand.

28. Flores Ramos, "Virgins, Whores, and Martyrs."

29. Puerto Rico, Office of the Attorney General, *Special Report of the Attorney General of Porto Rico to the Governor of Porto Rico.*

30. Findlay, *Imposing Decency*, 88–94.

31. Findlay, "Love in the Tropics."

32. *Union Signal*, 3 May 1917, p. 3.

33. Hall, *Policing the Crisis.*

34. Payne wrote and distributed at least three versions of this article: one for the Attorney General (see Puerto Rico, Office of the Attorney General, *Special Report of the Attorney General of Porto Rico to the Governor of Porto Rico,*

48–49, 51); one for the military (see "Vice Problem in Porto Rico," RG 393, box 1, folder 80, 1–4, 9, National Archives I, Washington, D.C. [hereafter cited as NWCT1]); and one that was published in *Social Hygiene,* the journal of the American Social Hygiene Association (see Payne, "The Vice Problem in Porto Rico").

35. Thompson and Kingery, "Syphilis in the Negro"; Murrell, "Syphilis and the American Negro"; Fox, "A Case of Annular Papular Syphilis in a Negress"; Upshur, "The Future of the Negro from the Standpoint of the Doctor," 15; Quillian, "Racial Peculiarities as a Cause of the Prevalence of Syphilis in Negroes."

36. Hazen, "Syphilis in the American Negro," 463; McNeil, "Syphilis in the Southern Negro."

37. Capt. Stanley P. Davies, U.S. Army Sanitary Corps, to William A. Sawyer, 16 December 1918, RG 112, Entry 726.1 (Venereal Disease), NWCT1.

38. Correspondence of Capt. Springarn, in charge of venereal disease control for "colored" troops, RG 112, Entry 726.1 (Venereal Disease), boxes 421–23, NWCT1; Springarn uses "colored" and "negro" interchangeably in his discussions of VD control. Goodman, "The Intensive Treatment of Women with Neodiarsenol," lists his patients by case number, age, and race: mulatto, white, or Negress. Two other articles by Goodman emphasize "racial mixture" in characterizing the population of Puerto Rico in general terms: "Genital Defects and Venereal Diseases among the Porto Rican Draft Troops," and "The Porto Rican Experiment." A report published by the War Department, *Defects Found in Drafted Men,* relies on the 1914 census for demographic data and uses its racial categories (see p. 30).

39. "Objections to Negro Camp / South Carolina Delegation Particularly Opposed to Porto Ricans," *New York Times,* 21 August 1917; and "Have to Train in U.S. / Porto Ricans Defeated in Fight for Cantonment in Island," *Washington Post,* 9 November 1917; both cited in Estades Font, *La presencia militar de Estados Unidos en Puerto Rico, 1898–1918,* 192–99. See also "Doce muertos en un motín de raza en el estado de Georgia," *La Democracia* (San Juan), 5 November 1918, p. 7.

40. Eduardo Jiménez, "Declaración Jurada," Affidavit no. 2290, Proceedings of a Board of Officers convened at Camp Las Casas, P.R., pursuant to Special Order No. 9, considering the question of race, 20 January 1919, RG 395, box 5, folder 334, NWCT1.

41. Goodman, "The Prostitute in Jail," 485.

42. Puerto Rico, Office of the Attorney General, *Special Report of the Attorney General of Porto Rico to the Governor of Porto Rico,* 15; Goodman, "The Intensive Treatment of Women with Neodiarsenol," 646.

43. Ettling, *The Germ of Laziness.* The descriptor was the same in Puerto Rico; in fact, the earliest research on hookworm was in Puerto Rico, where Bailey K. Ashford discovered it (and, ironically, for those of us curious about the links between venereal disease and tropical medicine, Fritz Schaudinn confirmed it) at the beginning of the century.

44. Bhabha, "Of Mimicry and Man," 126.

45. Goodman, "Prostitution and Community Syphilis"; the quote also appears in Goodman, "The Prostitute in Jail," 485.

46. Goodman, "Prostitution and Community Syphilis," 519.

47. Goodman, "Ulcerating Granuloma of the Pudenda," 152; Goodman, "Genital Defects and Venereal Diseases among the Porto Rican Draft Troops," 909.

48. Quote is from Goodman, "Genital Defects and Venereal Diseases among the Porto Rican Draft Troops," 907. For the disease's "early start," see Goodman, "The Porto Rican Experiment," 185; for yaws, see Goodman, "Skin Diseases among the Porto Rican Troops," and Goodman, "Ulcerating Granuloma of the Pudenda"; for race, see Goodman, "Prostitution and Community Syphilis."

49. Ashis Nandy, *The Intimate Enemy: Loss and Recovery of Self under Colonialism* (Delhi: Oxford University Press, 1989), 11, cited in Santiago-Valles, *"Subject People" and Colonial Discourses,* 241.

50. Santiago-Valles, *"Subject People" and Colonial Discourses,* 240.

51. Jiménez-Muñoz, "Literacy, Class, and Sexuality in the Debate on Women's Suffrage in Puerto Rico during the 1920s," 144.

52. Women of different classes won suffrage at different moments; the first successful bill had a literacy requirement.

53. "Policía feminena, para eso?" *El Tiempo* (San Juan), 5 October 1918, p. 1.

54. Cited in Rivera, "Incorporation of Women into the Labor Force," 37.

55. See Azize-Vargas, "The Roots of Puerto Rican Feminism," 73–74; Picó, "The History of Women's Struggle for Equality in Puerto Rico," 48; and Buhle, *Women and American Socialism.* On Capetilla, see Azize-Vargas, ibid., 74; for price riots, see, e.g., "Motín en Caguas anoche," *La Correspondencia* (San Juan), 17 July 1918, p. 1; for tobacco strikes, see, e.g., "Continua la huelga" and "Para ayudar la huelga," both in *La Correspondencia* (San Juan), 14 September 1918, p. 4.

56. *El Tiempo* (San Juan), 4 January 1919.

57. "WCTU Joins Hands with Police Department in Fight Against Vice," *Union Signal,* 29 August 1918, p. 7; for representations as "girls," see, e.g., "Report on Arecibo Hospital," *The Times* (San Juan), 24 August 1918, p. 7, and "Awakening in Porto Rico," *Union Signal,* 3 October 1918, p. 4.

58. "Moral Uplift Given Vigorous Offensive / W.C.T.U. Joins Hands With Col. Shanton in Policing Up San Juan," *The Times* (San Juan), 26 July 1918, p. 7. Though unsigned, the article was evidently Hildreth's. Portions of it were reprinted in the *Union Signal* under Hildreth's signature, and some articles in *The Times* and other insular papers are signed by her.

59. For industrial labor, see "The Awakening in Porto Rico," *Union Signal,* 3 October 1918, p. 4.

60. Irvine-Rivera, *Adventures for a Better World,* 32; "Explaining Porto Rico's Election Victory," *Union Signal,* 16 August 1917, p. 7; "The Awakening in Puerto Rico," *Union Signal,* 3 October 1918, p. 4; Edith Hildreth, "Report on Arecibo Hospital," *The Times* (San Juan), 24 August 1918, p. 7; Edith Hildreth to the Surgeon General of the United States Army, 25 May 1920, RG 112, Entry 726.1, box 421, NRAN.

61. Hildreth, *Between Bay and Ocean.*

62. "Motín en Caguas anoche," *La Correspondencia* (San Juan), 17 July 1918, p. 1.

63. "¡¡Basta Ya!! El Attorney General está violando las leyes del País," *La Correspondencia* (San Juan), 20 August 1918, p. 1.

64. González, *Puerto Rico, 1–72*; Quintero Rivera, *La lucha obrera en Puerto Rico.* See also Acosta Belen, *La mujer puertorriqueña*; Dietz, *Economic History of Puerto Rico*; Carr, *Puerto Rico.*

65. "Keen for Evidence to Implicate Kern," *The Times* (San Juan), 14 January 1919, p. 7.

66. "The Investigation of the Attorney General" (editorial), *The Times* (San Juan), 22 January 1919, p. 8.

CHAPTER 3

1. The police force in that town, probably with the encouragement of the North American police chief and even the governor, opened fire on a Palm Sunday Nationalist march, killing seventeen and wounding more than two hundred. Two policemen also were killed (Extension of Remarks of Hon. John T. Bernard of Minnesota, *Congressional Record,* 75th Cong., 1st sess., 14 April 1937, vol. 81: 934–36; Harwood Hull, "Clash Rekindles Puerto Rico Feud," *New York Times,* 28 March 1937, p. 11; "7 Die in Puerto Rico Riot, 50 Injured as Police Fire on Fighting Nationalists," *New York Times,* 22 March 1937, p. 1).

2. Quoted in Vilar, *A Message from God in the Atomic Age,* 47–48. Irene Vilar, granddaughter of nationalist heroine Lolita Lebrón, complained that for Albizu, "Lolita represented a world where women and nation were synonymous . . . a syllogism written as an elegy. And always the same corollary: mother is nation" (see ibid., 48).

3. Robert Bazell, "Growth Industry," *New Republic,* 15 March 1993, 13–15.

4. "El sensacional caso de un médico norteamericano que dice haber asesinado a ocho puertorriqueños e ingertado gérmenes del cáncer a muchos más," *El Imparcial* (San Juan), 26 January 1932; "Charge Race Extermination Plot," *Porto Rico Progress,* 4 February 1932, pp. 8, 9, 12; "Notas Editoriales," *La Democracia* (San Juan), 3 February 1932; "Porto Ricochet, *Time,* 15 February 1932; "Medical Report of Doctors E. Garrido Morales and P. Morales Otero to the Attorney General Ramon Quiñones in Connection with the Case of Dr. Cornelius P. Rhoads," February 1932, RG 1.1, Series 243: International Health Division, Subseries: Anemia, box 1, folder 6, Rockefeller Foundation Archives, Rockefeller Archive Center, Sleepy Hollow, N.Y. [hereafter cited as RF-RAC]. Another, similar letter, perhaps more damning, was successfully suppressed by the Governor and Attorney General (see George Payne to Dr. H. H. Howard, 22 February 1932, and W. A. Sawyer to James Beverley, 9 February 1932, RG 1.1, Series 243: International Health Division, Subseries: Anemia, box 1, folder 6, RF-RAC). The Rockefeller Foundation also succeeded in quashing an article that was to be published in the *Journal of the American Medical Association* and attempted the same in other cases (see JAF to W. A. Sawyer and H. H. Howard, 19 February 1932, RG 1.1, Series 243: International Health Division, Subseries: Anemia, box 1, folder 6, RF-RAC; see also Clark, *Puerto Rico and the United States, 1917–33,* 152–54; Ramírez de Arellano and Seipp, *Colonialism, Catholicism, and Contraception,* 27).

5. José Lameiro, Secretary to the President, Nationalist Party of Puerto Rico, to Dr. Rafael Bernabe, President, Medical Association of Puerto Rico, 24 January 1932, translated and published in *Porto Rico Progress*, 4 February 1932, p. 9.

6. Theodore Schroeder, "Porto Rico's Population Problem," *Birth Control Review*, March 1932, 71–72.

7. José Enamorado Cuesta, "Porto Rico's Real Problem," *Birth Control Review*, May 1932, 157.

8. Cited in Ramírez de Arellano and Seipp, *Colonialism, Catholicism, and Contraception*, 17–18.

9. Huigens, Berntsen, and Lanauze Rolón, *El mal de los muchos hijos*, 27.

10. Cited in Ramírez de Arellano and Seipp, *Colonialism, Catholicism, and Contraception*, 18.

11. Huigens, Berntsen, and Lanauze Rolón, *El mal de los muchos hijos*, 34.

12. Cited in Ramírez de Arellano and Seipp, *Colonialism, Catholicism, and Contraception*, 39.

13. Edwin Byrne to Carlos Chardón, 4 August 1936, RG 323, Entry 36, box 4, NRAN.

14. M. J. Conley, "U.S. Government Finances 'Birth Control' Clinics / Bishop Byrne Indignantly Protests Federal Outlay in Puerto Rico," *Brooklyn Tablet*, 12 September 1936.

15. "Delegación de Damas Católicas y la Srta. Arcelay," *El Mundo* (San Juan), 10 April 1937, p. 4.

16. Cited in Ramírez de Arellano and Seipp, *Colonialism, Catholicism, and Contraception*, 49–50.

17. Gordon, *Woman's Body, Woman's Right;* McCann, *Birth Control in the United States, 1917–1945.*

18. Ledbetter, *A History of the Malthusian League, 1877–1927.*

19. For the decline of eugenics, see Kevles, *In the Name of Eugenics.* For feminist rebuttals, see Bandarage, *Women, Population, and Global Crisis;* Silliman and King, *Dangerous Intersections;* Hartmann, *Reproductive Rights and Wrongs;* McCann, *Birth Control in the United States, 1917–1945;* Gordon, *Woman's Body, Woman's Right.* See also the various position statements of feminist NGOs like the Committee on Women, Population, and the Environment.

20. Notestein, "Some Implications of Current Demographic Trends for Birth Control and Eugenics," 121; "The Infinitely Small," 219–20; Burch, "Headed for the Last Census?"; and Spengler, "The New England Puritans."

21. Boas, "Studies in Growth"; Pearl, "Contraception and Fertility in 2000 Women"; Pearl, "Sidelights on the Population Problem in Japan"; Gafafer, "Diseases of the Upper Respiratory Tract (Common Cold) in Jews and Non-Jews"; Mitchell, "A Study of Factors Associated with the Growth and Nutrition of Porto Rican Children."

22. See Reed, *The Birth Control Movement and American Society.*

23. See, e.g., Chester T. Crowell, "Babies, Just Babies," *The New Republic,* 29 May 1935, 71.

24. The earliest such usage I have found was in a 1919 article in the pro-American *Times* of San Juan, referring to recruiting for a labor migration to Georgia. Ricardo Campos and Juan Flores, in "National Culture and Migra-

tion," however, write that "in 1914, the Governor of Puerto Rico, Arthur F. Yager, submitted to the President and War Department of the United States a proposal advocating the planned emigration of Puerto Ricans as a solution to the pressing social problems on the island, problems that stemmed—in the Governor's view—from rampant unemployment and acute 'overpopulation'" (121).

25. M. Melendez Muñoz, "El problema de la población," *El Mundo* (San Juan), 23 August 1919, p. 10.

26. See, e.g., "Delinquency Blamed on Squalid Housing / Overpopulation Also Major Cause of Prostitution," *Porto Rico World Journal*, 1 December 1944, p. 1.

27. Valle Atiles, "Limitación de la Prole."

28. "Report of the Bureau of Vital Statistics, 1925–1926."

29. Theodore Schroeder, "Porto Rico's Population Problem," *Birth Control Review*, March 1932, 71–72; *Annual Report of the Governor of Puerto Rico* (1932), 1; Clark et al., *Porto Rico and Its Problems;* Huigens, Berntsen, and Lanauze Rolón, *El mal de los muchos hijos,* 6.

30. See Diffie and Diffie, *Porto Rico;* and Clark et al., *Porto Rico and Its Problems.*

31. Sugar production more than doubled, from 346,000 tons in 1913–14 to 749,000 in 1927–28, and the value of exports likewise increased more than twofold, from $43 million to $104 million (see *Annual Reports of the Governor of Puerto Rico* [1914 and 1928]). These numbers are conveniently summarized in Perloff, *Puerto Rico's Economic Future,* 159.

32. Asemblea Legislativa de Puerto Rico, *Primer informe de la Comisión Legislativa,* 61; *Annual Report of the Governor of Porto Rico* (1930), 2.

33. Flores, *Divided Borders,* esp. pt. 3; Santiago-Valles, *"Subject People" and Colonial Discourses,* ch. 3; also Dietz, *Economic History of Puerto Rico;* Picó, *Amargo café;* Quintero Rivera, *Patricios y Plebeyos.*

34. Furthermore, the numbers themselves were bad; even public health policymakers believed the birth rate figures to be wrong. There was no widespread nor reliable census; the local registrars of births and deaths did not even work for the Health Department, and the Bureau of Vital Statistics complained that far too many births and deaths were not registered at all, though they were at a loss to say how many. Yet this is the data on which the overpopulationist argument relied.

35. Based on per capita net income, according to the *Annual Reports of the Governor of Puerto Rico* (1928–51). See also Perloff, *Puerto Rico's Economic Future,* 160; and Baer, *The Puerto Rican Economy and United States Economic Fluctuations,* 16.

36. E.g., Ernest Gruening, "America's Dominion Over Palm and Pine: A Sweeping Survey of Our Territories and Overseas Possessions," *New York Times Magazine,* 20 September 1936, pp. 6–15; Roosevelt, "Do Our Colonies Pay?"; E. K. James, "Puerto Rico's Troubles," *Commonweal,* 9 June 1939, 171; H. Herring, "Forgotten Puerto Rico," *Christian Century,* 6 December 1933, 1533–34; J. Aronson, "Puerto Rico, Orphan of Imperialism," *Scholastic,* 11 May 1935, 20; C. S. Detweiler, "Studying Problems in Puerto Rico," *Missionary Review,* May 1935, 224–25; "Governor Gore Threatened and Applauded," *Newsweek,*

4 November 1933, 7; H. Herring, "Rebellion in Puerto Rico," *The Nation,* 29 November 1933, 618–19; Arthur Warner, "Progress (and Poverty) in Porto Rico," *The Nation,* 15 August 1923, 159; "Unhappy Island," *Literary Digest,* 23 May 1936, 8; "Puerto Rican Problem," *The New Republic,* 14 April 1937, 282; "Sedition and Students," *Time,* 23 March 1936, 22; "Troublous Isle: Too Many People and Not Enough Jobs," *Literary Digest,* 29 May 1937, 13–14.

37. Ernest Gruening, "America's Dominion Over Palm and Pine: A Sweeping Survey of Our Territories and Overseas Possessions," *New York Times Magazine,* 20 September 1936, p. 8.

38. Sherman, "A Glimpse of Social Economics in Porto Rico," 222. Raymond Crist, in "Sugar Cane and Coffee in Puerto Rico," compared the pauperization of peasants in Puerto Rico to the English Enclosure Acts.

39. "To Give Puerto Rico's Stork a Rest," *Literary Digest,* 8 October 1932, 11.

40. James Beverley to Margaret Sanger, 25 May 1933, Papers of Margaret Sanger, Library of Congress (hereafter cited as MS-LC).

41. See Tugwell, *The Stricken Land.* Tugwell, as a "brain-truster" economist for the New Deal administration and later as governor of Puerto Rico, had occasion to know firsthand of Roosevelt's views.

42. Clark et al., *Porto Rico and Its Problems,* 576.

43. Diffie and Diffie, *Porto Rico,* 7–8.

44. Brown, *Dynamite on Our Doorstep,* 195.

45. Phillips, *White Elephants in the Caribbean,* 150–54.

46. E.g., Huigens, Berntsen, and Lanauze Rolón, in *El mal de los muchos hijos,* quoted European authorities as often as U.S. ones.

47. Guzmán Rodríguez, "El control de la natalidad y su desarrollo en Puerto Rico"; "Se trate de enmendar el Código para legalizar la divulgación de los medios, por los cuales se consigne la limitación de la prole," *El Mundo* (San Juan), 28 June 1923, p. 1.

48. Ramírez de Arellano and Seipp, *Colonialism, Catholicism, and Contraception,* 16–56. For the 1925 organization, see Huigens, Berntsen, and Lanauze Rolón, *El mal de los muchos hijos;* and José Lanauze Rolón to Margaret Sanger, 23 February 1926 and 4 August 1926, MS-LC.

49. "Maltusianismo Práctico" (in column, "Desde Nueva York"), *La Democracia* (San Juan), 21 August 1922, p. 1.

50. Cited in Ramírez de Arellano and Seipp, *Colonialism, Catholicism, and Contraception,* 17.

51. *El Mundo* (San Juan), 28 November 1925, cited in Huigens, Berntsen, and Lanauze Rolón, *El mal de los muchos hijos,* 7–8.

52. Huigens, Berntsen, and Lanauze Rolón, *El mal de los muchos hijos,* 5.

53. Ibid.

54. The newspaper debates of 1925–26 are reproduced in Huigens, Berntsen, and Lanauze Rolón, *El mal de los muchos hijos,* 5–7.

55. *The Times* (San Juan), 30 November 1925, p. 9; Adolfo Bernabe to Sanger, 23 November 1925, MS-LC.

56. Quote is from *El Dia,* reprinted in Huigens, Berntsen, and Lanauze Rolón, *El mal de los muchos hijos,* 9; see also pp. 3, 5–9.

57. El representante Martínez Reyes presentará otra vez / El próxima legis-latura el proyecto sobre neomaltusianismo," *El Mundo* (San Juan), 11 January 1931, p. 1.

58. José Padín, speech entitled "La Maestra y las Actividades Cívico Social," from "Nuestro Escuela Portorriqueña es pobre por su débil ramificación," *El Mundo* (San Juan), 21 January 1931, p. 9.

59. Luis Muñoz Marín, "El partido socialista," *El Mundo* (San Juan), 27 June 1923, p. 3.

60. A number of women lobbied Francis Perkins's Labor Department for the extension of the minimum wage (wages on the island were extremely low, and for women, concentrated in the needlework and tobacco stripping trades, they were extremely so). This effort was finally defeated by the lobbying of industri-alists who employed Puerto Rican workers (see Orleck, *Common Sense and a Little Fire*). Dorothy Bourne was responsible for the professionalization of so-cial work on the island (see Rivera de Alvarado, "Quien es quien en el trabajo social en Puerto Rico," among others). Rosa González, a nurse who opened a clinic in Lares, was the person largely responsible for the consolidation of nurs-ing as an autonomous profession (see González, *Los hechos desconocidos*). My thanks to Yamila Azize-Vargas, who alerted me to the existence of the latter. Ac-cording to Azize, the network of professional women on the island (including North Americans) was largely responsible for the extension of suffrage to liter-ate women, through their involvement with the Liga, etc. (see Azize-Vargas and Aviles, "La mujer en las profesiones de salud").

61. Azize-Vargas, *La mujer en la lucha;* Picó, *La mujer y la política puertor-riqueña;* Barceló-Miller, "Halfhearted Solidarity"; Silvestrini, "Women as Workers"; and Valle Ferrer, "Feminism and Its Influence on Women's Organi-zations in Puerto Rico," 38.

62. There is one document that identifies Violet Callendar as North Ameri-can, but I believe it to be in error. Margaret Sanger referred to Callendar's "na-tive Puerto Rico," and Callendar worked at the Harlem clinic—rather than the Brooklyn one—which suggests she lived in Harlem and/or was not white. The Puerto Rican community in New York lived mostly in Harlem. Callendar's name is French, which could make her either Puerto Rican or North American. The document that identifies her as North American is Guzmán Rodríguez, "El con-trol de la natalidad y su desarrollo en Puerto Rico." While normally I would trust a Puerto Rican assessment of gradations of nationality and origin over a North American one, this document is full of errors of fact—identifying 1928, rather than 1932, as the year Governor Beverley wrote about overpopulation in his governor's report, for example, or identifying the senator who introduced pro–birth control legislation in 1931 as "Reyes Martínez" rather than Martínez Reyes, and saying that "Callander," as he spelled it, opened her clinic in 1933, rather than 1932. The one historical monograph that deals with Callendar, Ramírez de Arrellano and Seipp's *Colonialism, Catholicism, and Contraception,* declines to pronounce on her ancestry.

63. In early 1932, when Callendar was living in New York, Sanger blocked Callendar's efforts to apply for a job at the Harlem Birth Control Clinical Re-search Bureau Clinic (Violet Callendar to Margaret Sanger, 9 February 1932,

MS-NA; see also Sanger to Prevost, 16 February 1932; and Sanger to Callendar, 1 March 1932). A subsequent fundraising letter from Callendar to Puerto Rican birth control supporters and donors, and forwarded to Sanger, received this annotation from Sanger's staff: "Who is this person and what should I do about this?" (Callendar to "Dear Friend," 6 May 1932, MS-NA). Subsequent efforts to obtain support, and a letter from Holland Rantos offering to supply diaphragms to the financially bankrupt clinic if it had Sanger's support, were also rejected (see Murray to Sanger, 7 May 1932; and Kennedy to Zborowski, 15 February 1933, MS-NA).

64. Azize-Vargas and Aviles, "La mujer en las profesiones de salud," 11–12; Phyllis Page, Annotated card file of Puerto Rico contacts, 1937–38, box 46, folder 749, Clarence J. Gamble Papers, Countway Library of Medicine (hereafter cited as CJG-CLM).

65. Guzmán Rodríguez, "El control de la natalidad y su desarrollo en Puerto Rico," 346.

66. Callendar, "Dear Friend" fundraising letter, 6 May 1932, MS-LC.

67. Cited in the ruling on the group's legality, Arturo Ortiz Toro, Acting Attorney General, Department of Justice of Puerto Rico, to The Honorable Executive Secretary, San Juan, Puerto Rico, 26 September 1932, MS-LC.

68. Bermudez to Sanger, 22 June 1933, MS-LC.

69. Callendar to Sanger, 9 February 1932, MS-LC.

70. Morales Otero et al., "Health and Socioeconomic Conditions on a Sugar Cane Plantation."

71. For the governor, see Report of the Governor of Puerto Rico (1932), 1. Beverley's statement, which the Birth Control Review claimed was the first time "a government official of rank [saw] the relation between overpopulation and economic distress," provoked an outcry from the mainland Catholic press, a call by the Catholic Alumni Federation for Beverly's removal from office, more muted condemnation from the mainstream press, and celebration in the Birth Control Review (see Editorial, Birth Control Review, November 1932, 259–60; see also "To Give Porto Rico's Stork a Rest," Literary Digest, 8 October 1932, 11).

72. Phyllis Page, "Interview with Mrs. Bourne on November 5th in New York," [1936], box 45, folder 734, CJG-CLM; Carmen Rivera de Alvarado, "Informe del Programa de Salud Maternal," [1935?], RG 323, Entry 36, box 4, folder: RRD—Health Section, NRAN.

73. Guzmán Rodríguez, "El control de la natalidad y su desarrollo en Puerto Rico," 346.

74. Dorothy Bourne, "Professional Training for Social Work in Puerto Rico" (1936 pamphlet), Biblioteca Monserrate Santana de Palés de Trabajo Social.

75. Bourne, "Puerto Rico's Predicament."

76. Carmen Alvarado to Christopher Tietze, 6 November 1948, box 47, folder 764, CJG-CLM.

77. Bourne, "Puerto Rico's Predicament." See also Bourne and Bourne, Thirty Years of Change in Puerto Rico; and Rivera de Alvarado, "Quien es quien en el trabajo social en Puerto Rico."

78. Callendar to Sanger, 9 February 1932, MS-LC.

79. Cited in Ramírez de Arellano and Seipp, *Colonialism, Catholicism, and Contraception,* 41.

80. See, e.g., Mass, *Population Target.*

81. Kevles, *In the Name of Eugenics,* 58.

82. Ibid. See also Allen, "The Eugenics Record Office at Cold Spring Harbor, 1910–1940"; Allen, "Eugenics and American Social History, 1880–1950"; and Barkan, *The Retreat of Scientific Racism.*

83. Proctor, *Racial Hygiene;* Pernick, *The Black Stork.*

84. Lunbeck, *The Psychiatric Persuasion.*

85. McCann, *Birth Control in the United States, 1917–1945;* Larson, *Sex, Race, and Science.*

86. Meckel, *Save the Babies.*

87. Ortiz, "The Tropics from the Public Health Standpoint."

88. Fernós Isern, "The White—and the Tropics," 6.

89. Rather than referring to this entity by its many names—Commission, Board, Division—within the space of two paragraphs, I am referring to it somewhat anachronistically by the name it came ultimately to bear, the IHD.

90. H. H. Howard, "Special Report," p. 3, RG 1.1, Series 243: International Health Division, box 2, folder 21, RF-RAC.

91. Howard to Payne, 3 January 1934, p. 1, RG 1.1, Series 243: International Health Division, box 2, folder 21, RF-RAC.

92. "Report of Bureau of Social Medicine and Puericulture, 1925–26"; Fernós Isern, "The Development of the Public Health Organization of Porto Rico"; and Sherman, "A Glimpse of Social Economics in Porto Rico."

93. W. B. Castle to Wilbur A. Sawyer, 26 February 1932, RG 1.1, Series 243: International Health Division, box 1, folder 6, RF-RAC.

94. Gamble to Page, 21 November 1936, box 45, folder 733, CJG-CLM.

95. Gamble, "The Deficit in the Birthrate of College Graduates."

96. Gamble, "The College Birthrate."

97. Gamble had programs in Kentucky, West Virginia, Virginia, Florida, Tennessee, and North Carolina in the 1930s (see Reed, *The Birth Control Movement and American Society,* 225–80; and Williams and Williams, *Every Child a Wanted Child,* 119–29).

98. Williams and Williams, *Every Child a Wanted Child,* 149.

99. Gladys Gaylord to Clarence Gamble, 26 October 1936, box 45, folder 733, CJG-CLM.

100. Williams and Williams, *Every Child a Wanted Child,* 119; Reed, *The Birth Control Movement and American Society,* 257–80.

101. Gamble to Page, 21 November 1936, box 45, folder 733, CJG-CLM.

102. Beebe and Gamble, "Clinical Contraceptive Results in a Small Series of Patients."

103. Robert L. Dickinson to Hon. Mrs. Marjorie Farrer, 29 July 1927, Series 3.2: Projects, box 7, folder 173, Bureau of Social Hygiene Archives, Rockefeller Archive Center, Sleepy Hollow, New York [hereafter cited as BSH-RAC].

104. R. L. Dickinson to Katherine B. Davis, 11 November 1926, Series 3.2: Projects, box 7, folder 172, BSH-RAC.

105. That this reasoning was directly causal in the Bureau of Social Hygiene's decision to fund contraceptive research is made unusually explicit in a summary memo written by Ruth Topping of the BSH in 1931, in which she reviewed the reasons and progress to date. In the memo, Topping quotes the same passages on "foreign lands" and "dull-minded natives in India" as appear in the above-mentioned letters by Dickinson, as well as the section of the 1927 grant proposal which used virtually identical language to describe the need for birth control research (see Topping, "File Memorandum, Subject: Crew Spermaticide Study," 22 September 1931, Series 3.2: Projects, box 7, folder 174, BSH-RAC).

106. Borell, "Biologists and the Promotion of Birth Control Research, 1918–1938"; and Clarke, *Disciplining Reproduction.*

107. See Matsner to Phyllis Page, 12 November 1936, box 45, folder 733, CJG-CLM; Belaval to Matsner, 31 October 1936, box 45, folder 733; and Page to Matsner, 11 November 1936, box 45, folder 733, all in CJG-CLM.

108. González, *Los hechos desconocidos.*

109. Haraway, *Primate Visions,* 58, 71–73. It was Warren Weaver's program in vital processes and experimental biology that so influenced the future directions of biology (see Weaver, "Program in Experimental Biology," 17 April 1935, RG 1.1, Series 216, box 8, folder 103, RF-RAC).

110. The two groups would later merge to become the Birth Control Federation of America. For Rockefeller support of the Sangerists, see Series 3.2: Projects, box 7, folders 162–63, BSH-RAC. While there are important distinctions in terms of organizational history and program emphasis between contributions of Rockefeller money—in this case, between the personal (often anonymous) contributions of John D. Rockefeller Jr. to the Bureau of Social Hygiene and those of the Rockefeller Foundation—in the broad sense I am describing, they worked together. The Crew study, for example, was transferred from the Bureau to the Foundation with the reorganization of the late 1920s, and JDR Jr. and the Bureau both funded the Sangerists.

111. Gordon, *Woman's Body, Woman's Right.*

112. Ruth Topping, "File Memorandum: Interview with Mrs. Sanger," 16 April 1931, Series 3: Projects, box 7, folder 167, BSH-RAC.

113. Boxes 45–46, CJG-CLM.

114. See, e.g. Gamble, "A Note on the Clinical Significance of Paraformaldehyde in Contraceptive Foam Powders"; Belaval, Gould, and Gamble, "The Effectiveness of Contraceptive Advice among the Underprivileged of Puerto Rico"; Beebe and Gamble, "Clinical Contraceptive Results in a Small Series of Patients"; Brown, "The Comparative Spermicidal Powers of Fifteen Commercial Contraceptives"; Beebe and Gamble, "Fertility and Contraception in Puerto Rico"; and Brown and Becker, "The Spermicidal Times of Samples of Commercial Contraceptives Secured in 1943." That these are mostly in obscure journals underscores the mutual antagonism between Gamble and the mainstream medical research establishment, which predated his forays into contraceptive work (see Williams and Williams, *Every Child a Wanted Child,* ch. 4).

115. Dr. Karlis Adamsons, Chair, Department of Obstetrics and Gynecology, University of Puerto Rico, Medical Sciences Campus, made this point in a personal interview with me on 23 April 1996. Dr. Adamsons was a member of

the NIH advisory committee that made the decision to authorize the safety of the pill.

CHAPTER 4

1. Escobar, *Encountering Development*; Fergusen, *The Anti-Politics Machine*.
2. Galbraith and Solo, "Puerto Rican Lessons in Economic Development," 55.
3. There are many accounts of this process. See, e.g., Lewis, *Puerto Rico;* Carr, *Puerto Rico;* Muñoz Marín, *Memorias;* Goodsell, *Administration of a Revolution;* Tugwell, *The Stricken Land;* and Hanson, *Transformation.*
4. The major monographs are Hatt, *Backgrounds of Human Fertility in Puerto Rico;* Stycos, *Family and Fertility in Puerto Rico;* Hill, Stycos, and Back, *The Family and Population Control.*
5. Stycos, "Experiments in Social Change."
6. Tietze, "Revised Outline for an Experiment in Population Control," 13 December 1948, box 47, folder 764, CJG-CLM.
7. *El Mundo* (San Juan), 28 June 1946, quoted in Ramírez de Arellano and Seipp, *Colonialism, Catholicism, and Contraception,* 73. See also ibid., 57–81; Goodsell, *Administration of a Revolution;* and Tugwell, *The Stricken Land.*
8. Carr, *Puerto Rico.*
9. Safa, "Female Employment in the Puerto Rican Working Class," 85–87.
10. For disproportionate male rates, see Monk, "Social Change and Sexual Differences in Puerto Rican Rural Migration."
11. Ramírez de Arellano and Seipp, *Colonialism, Catholicism, and Contraception,* 73 n. 11, 193; Tugwell, *The Stricken Land.* See esp. Whalen, *From Puerto Rico to Philadelphia,* for an excellent account of this process.
12. Vázquez Calzada, *La población de Puerto Rico y su trayectoria histórica,* 231.
13. Ibid., 104.
14. Ibid., 15.
15. Muñoz Marín, in response to a question from Roberto Márquez about why Puerto Rico cannot be independent, first argues that Puerto Ricans don't want independence, then adds, "¿Qué es Puerto Rico? Una isla caribeña sobrepoblada" (Rodríguez Juliá, *Las tribulaciones de Jonás,* 34).
16. Quoted in Ramírez de Arellano and Seipp, *Colonialism, Catholicism, and Contraception,* 74.
17. Davin, "Imperialism and Motherhood"; Reed, *The Birth Control Movement and American Society,* 197–210.
18. Riesman, Glazer, and Denney, *The Lonely Crowd,* 22–25.
19. In the 1930s two journals were publishing on population: the *Milbank Memorial Fund Quarterly* and the Office of Population Research's *Population Index.* Then, in 1945, the Rockefeller Foundation's Population Reference Bureau began publishing *Population Bulletin,* and the Population Investigation Committee began *Population Studies* in 1947. The United Nations Population Division began *Population Bulletin* in 1951, and in April 1955 the International Union for the Scientific Study of Population put out the first issue of *Le Démographe.*
20. Black, "Population Increase and Economic Development," 83, 87.
21. Huxley, "Too Many People," 226–27.

22. Guttmacher, "The Place of Sterilization," 206.

23. Stycos, "Fertility Control in Underdeveloped Areas."

24. Lewis, *Puerto Rico,* 19–22.

25. Marston Bates and Marshall Balfour, "Special Report to the Board of Scientific Directors of the International Health Division of the Rockefeller Foundation: Human Ecology (Population)," RG 3.2, Series 900, Subseries: Population, box 57, folder 310, RF-RAC.

26. *Time,* 2 May 1949, 33 (cover article).

27. Lapp, "Puerto Rico as a Social Laboratory."

28. Hansen, "Training and Research in Puerto Rico," 111.

29. *Annals of the American Academy of Political and Social Science* 285 (January 1953).

30. Cited in Hill, Stycos, and Back, *The Family and Population Control,* 13.

31. Stycos and Hill, "The Prospects for Birth Control in Puerto Rico," 140.

32. Perloff, *Puerto Rico's Economic Future.*

33. Davis, "Puerto Rico," 20.

34. Hill, Stycos, and Back, *The Family and Population Control,* 21.

35. Muñoz Marín, "Development Through Democracy."

36. Hill, Stycos, and Back, *The Family and Population Control,* 24.

37. Wolf, "San José"; and Mintz, "Cañamelar."

38. See Vázquez Calzada, *La población de Puerto Rico y su trayectoria histórica,* 157.

39. Thimmesch, "Puerto Rico and Birth Control."

40. For an account of the considerable wartime hardship endured by Puerto Rico, see Tugwell, *The Stricken Land;* and Rivera de Alvarado and Tietze, "Birth Control in Puerto Rico," 17. See also typescript, p. 6, box 46, folder 760, CJG-CLM.

41. Ramírez de Arellano and Seipp, *Colonialism, Catholicism, and Contraception,* 93–104; 124–33.

42. CJG to Funders, June 1950, box 47, folder 771, CJG-CLM.

43. Alfred L. Severson, Sunnen Foundation, to The Family Planning Association, 8 August 1956, copy in box 48, folder 782, CJG-CLM.

44. Clarke, "Controversy and the Development of Reproductive Sciences."

45. Mathew Tayback to Gamble, 2 August 1956, box 48, folder 784, CJG-CLM. See also Rice-Wray to Gamble, 20 January 1956, box 48, folder 785, CJG-CLM; her title at the Health Department was Director of Public Health, District of Río Piedras.

46. Gamble to Youngs Rubber Corporation, 24 March 1947, box 46, folder 759, CJG-CLM.

47. Gamble to Wilson Wing, 23 May 1955, box 47, folder 779, CJG-CLM.

48. E.g., see Gamble, "State Sterilization Programs for the Prophylactic Control of Mental Disease and Mental Deficiency"; Gamble, "Sterilization of the Mentally Deficient Under State Laws"; Gamble, "Preventive Sterilization in 1948"; and Gamble, "College Study Reports."

49. Diane Paul dates the end of eugenics to the postwar period (*Controlling Heredity*); others place its decline even earlier, in the 1930s (see Barkan, *The Retreat of Scientific Racism;* and Degler, *In Search of Human Nature*).

50. Editorial, *Journal of the American Medical Association.*

51. Milbank Memorial Fund, *International Approaches to Problem of Underdeveloped Areas.*

52. Jones, *Bad Blood.*

53. Celestina Zalduondo to Gamble, 9 May 1957, box 48, folder 789, CJG-CLM.

54. Celestina Zalduondo to Sr. Bosco Nedelcovic, Argentina, 7 December 1961, copy in box 52, folder 835, CJG-CLM.

55. Zalduondo wrote Gamble that though the Catholic Church continued to attack them, "the little people continue wanting our services" (Zalduondo to Gamble, 26 February 1958, box 49, folder 801, CJG-CLM).

56. Tietze et al.'s report of the Trujillo Alto project, "A Family Planning Service in Rural Puerto Rico," described it as a failure because the jelly method it promoted had such a low success rate and underscored the notably higher success rates and the good acceptance of the handful of diaphragms that were distributed. In fact, the evidence suggested that simple methods hardly worked better than random chance in preventing pregnancy. The jelly-and-syringe method had a 40 percent failure rate. Although this didn't look terrible in the published reports next to an 80 percent pregnancy rate with no contraception (80 pregnancies per 100 woman-years of exposure), this was a drastic overstatement of pregnancy rates. As the *Milbank Memorial Fund Quarterly* noted when they rejected a Gamble article on the study (an article subsequently published in *Eugenics Quarterly,* whose editors apparently were not similarly troubled by his methodology), these were retrospective fertility rates—based on the same women's past experience when not using contraception—and ignored that the women studied were not as fertile at the age of 40, say, than at 20. Fertility should have been compared based on an age-matched cohort, not retrospectively. However, what Gamble didn't publish was that he (inadvertently) had a control group, of sorts: individuals who came and registered at the clinic but elected not to use birth control. Wilson Wing, a Johns Hopkins demographer who worked with Gamble on this study, computed a pregnancy rate for them: 49.6 percent (Wing to Gamble, 24 March 1956, p. 4, box 48, folder 783, CJG-CLM). While Wing didn't record other characteristics, like sample size or the women's ages (except that there were more than twenty women in his group) that would enable assessment of whether it was a representative control group, his figure does suggest that the true fertility rates with and without "simple" contraception were awfully close together, perhaps as close as 50 and 40 percent.

57. Guillermo Arbona to Wilson Wing, 10 January 195[1] (misdated 1950), box 47, folder 775, CJG-CLM.

58. See Arbona to Wing, ibid.; see also Wing to Arbona, 22 December 1950, box 47, folder 771; Gamble to Wing, 19 July 1950; box 47, folder 771; Leo Coel, Sales Manager, Youngs Rubber to CJG, 21 February 1950, box 47, folder 772, all in CJG-CLM.

59. Gamble to Coel, 20 June 1950, box 47, folder 772, CJG-CLM.

60. Gamble, "Improved Test of Spermicidal Activity Without Dilution or Mixing."

61. Paniagua, Vaillant, and Gamble, "Field Trial of a Contraceptive Foam in Puerto Rico."

62. Thimmesch, "Puerto Rico and Birth Control"; Population Council, "Puerto Rico"; Marchand, "Su obra pro bienestar de la familia"; and Zalduondo, "Planificación de la familia en Puerto Rico."

63. Satterthwaite, "Experience with Oral and Intrauterine Contraception in Rural Puerto Rico."

64. Population Council, "Puerto Rico."

65. Cited in Djerassi, *The Pill, Pygmy Chimps, and Degas' Horse,* 118–19.

66. Clarke, "Emergence of the Reproductive Research Enterprise."

67. Perone, "The Progestins."

68. Allen and Weintersteiner, "Crystalline Progestin," 190.

69. Makepeace, Weinstein, and Friedman, "The Effect of Progestin and Progesterone on Ovulation in the Rabbit."

70. Kuzrok, "The Prospects for Hormonal Sterilization."

71. Oudshoorn, *Beyond the Natural Body,* 73–108.

72. Marker et al., "Diosgenin"; and Marker and Rohrman, "Conversion of Sarsapogenin to Pregnanediol-3(α),20(α)."

73. Sturgis and Albright, "Estrin Therapy in Dysmenorrhea."

74. Cited in Reed, *The Birth Control Movement and American Society,* 316.

75. Cited in Marks, " 'A Cage of Ovulating Females.' "

76. Vaughan, *The Pill on Trial,* 35.

77. Cited in Gunn, *Oral Contraception in Perspective,* 36.

78. Reed, *The Birth Control Movement and American Society,* 340–41.

79. Pincus, *The Control of Fertility,* 6.

80. Perone, "The Progestins," 13.

81. Reed, *The Birth Control Movement and American Society,* 343–54; Vaughan, *The Pill on Trial,* 26–28.

82. Gregory Pincus, "Paradoxical Hormone is Basis of Birth Control Pill," *Washington Post,* 2 August 1959, p. E8.

83. Pincus, *The Control of Fertility,* 6–8.

84. Pincus and Chang, "The Effects of Progesterone and Related Compounds on Ovulation and Early Development in the Rabbit"; Slechta, Chang, and Pincus, "Effects of Progesterone and Related Compounds on Mating and Pregnancy in the Rat," 282; Maisel, *The Hormone Quest,* 12; Oudshoorn, *Beyond the Natural Body,* 119.

85. Reed, *The Birth Control Movement and American Society,* 351–52. Beginning in 1955, they were also working out of Rock's clinic across the street, the Rock Reproductive Study Center (McLaughlin, *The Pill, John Rock, and the Church,* 115).

86. Rock, *The Time Has Come.*

87. McLaughlin, *The Pill, John Rock, and the Church,* 124–27.

88. Rock, Ramon Garcia, and Pincus, "Synthetic Progestins in the Normal Human Menstrual Cycle"; Asbell, *The Pill,* 127–29.

89. Pincus, "Some Effects of Progesterone and Related Compounds Upon Reproduction and Early Development in Mammals"; McLaughlin, *The Pill, John Rock, and the Church,* 117; Oudshoorn, *Beyond the Natural Body,* 118–20; Maisel, *The Hormone Quest,* 119; Reed, *The Birth Control Movement and American Society,* 356, Asbell, *The Pill;* Vaughan, *The Pill on Trial,* 30–31;

Ramírez de Arellano and Seipp, *Colonialism, Catholicism, and Contraception,* 105–8.

90. For examples of this narrative, see esp. the popular accounts, Maisel, *The Hormone Quest,* and Vaughan, *The Pill on Trial.* Pincus and Rock were also constructing a progesterone story; the name of the 1954 project at Rock's clinic was the Pincus Progesterone Project (the PPP, or "pee, pee, pee," as it came to be called, for the endless urine collections).

91. Rock, *The Time Has Come,* 167.

92. Pincus, "Some Effects of Progesterone and Related Compounds."

93. Oudshoorn, *Beyond the Natural Body,* 1–41; Fausto-Sterling, *Myths of Gender,* 90–155; and Fausto-Sterling, *Sexing the Body,* 170–94.

94. This dates back to the earliest studies of "organotherapy" by Charles Edouard Brown-Séquard in the late nineteenth century.

95. Letter from anonymous reviewer for *Medical Letter* article, "Enovid, Ortho-Novum, and Thromboembolic Effects," 13 March 1963, RG 891, box 45, folder 1, Rockefeller University Archives, Rockefeller Archive Center, Sleepy Hollow, N.Y. [hereafter cited as RU-RAC].

96. Marks, " 'A Cage of Ovulating Females'."

97. McLaughlin, *The Pill, John Rock, and the Church,* 118–20; Marks, " 'A Cage of Ovulating Females' "; Oudshoorn, *Beyond the Natural Body,* 122–24; Ramírez de Arellano and Seipp, *Colonialism, Catholicism, and Contraception,* 110, Vaughan, *The Pill on Trial,* 37–38; Pincus, "Long Term Administration of Enovid to Human Subjects."

98. Pincus, "Long Term Administration of Enovid to Human Subjects," and subsequent discussion.

99. Satterthwaite and Gamble, "Conception Control with Norethynodrel."

100. Oudshoorn, *Beyond the Natural Body,* 122–32; Ramírez de Arellano and Seipp, *Colonialism, Catholicism, and Contraception,* 105–23; Marks, " 'A Cage of Ovulating Females' "; Gordon, *Woman's Body, Woman's Right,* 416.

101. The dropout rate on the Río Piedras series was 109 women out of 221 participants, 22 percent of whom dropped out because of side effects (Ramírez de Arellano and Seipp, *Colonialism, Catholicism, and Contraception,* 107–23). For the Ryder series, 32.4 percent of participants dropped out because of side effects, and a total of 57 percent had discontinued after two years (Satterthwaite, "Experience with Oral and Intrauterine Contraception in Rural Puerto Rico," 476).

102. Christopher Tietze to Margaret Snyder, 15 August 1957, box 48, folder 788, CJG-CLM; Pincus et al., "Fertility Control with Oral Medication." Oudshoorn criticizes the use of the kind of "woman-years" statistic used in the pill trials in Puerto Rico. However, this statistical device was not unique to these trials, but dated back to the 1930s. Its strength was that it enabled researchers to compare divergent experiences in length of use of a method and made it a simple matter to deduct, for example, 10 months for a pregnancy or 3 months of a sexual partner's absence. Its shortcomings—in overstating researchers' knowledge of a method by making twelve women's experiences for one month comparable to one woman's experience for a year—were well known to researchers, and had spawned a literature of their own, establishing guidelines such as one

requiring that at least half of any cases reported in this way involve long-term administration (see Pearl, "Contraception and Fertility in 2,000 Women"). Researchers were aware that there was something wrong with the way it was used in the pill study. Wrote Christopher Tietze, "The aggregate number of person years of exposure to the risk of pregnancy through June 1957 was 139. Of this total, only 50 years were contributed by women observed 12 months or more, the maximum being 16 months. The proportion of the total exposure contributed by these "long" cases was only 36%, about half of what is normally considered desirable" (Christopher Tietze to Margaret Snyder, 15 August 1957, box 48, folder 788, CJG-CLM).

103. Pincus et al., "Fertility Control with Oral Medication."

104. Cook, Gamble, and Satterthwaite, "Oral Contraception with Norethynodrel."

105. Satterthwaite to Gamble, 21 June 1957, box 49, folder 797, CJG-CLM.

106. See, e.g. Seaman, *The Doctor's Case Against the Pill.*

107. The article is Albert Q. Maisel's misleadingly titled, "New Hope for Childless Women," *Ladies Home Journal,* August 1957, 46, 47, 85.

108. James Reed, interview by Adeline Pendleton Satterthwaite, M.D., 7 September 1974, Women's Studies Manuscript Collection of the Schlesinger Library, Radcliffe College, Series 3: Sexuality, Sex Education, and Reproductive Rights, Part A: Family Planning Oral History Project; Rice-Wray et al., "Long-Term Administration of Norethindrone in Fertility Control."

109. Reed, interview.

110. Edris Rice-Wray, "Study Project of SC-4642, January 1957," p. 78, box 49, folder 797, CJG-CLM.

111. Rice-Wray et al., "Long-Term Administration of Norethindrone in Fertility Control," 355.

112. Edris Rice-Wray, "Study Project of SC-4642, January 1957," p. 78, box 49, folder 797, CJG-CLM.

113. Penny Satterthwaite to Gamble, 12 December 1957, box 49, folder 797, CJG-CLM.

114. Satterthwaite correspondence with Gamble, 1959, box 50, folder 819, CJG-CLM.

115. Reed, interview.

116. Satterthwaite correspondence with Gamble, 1957–58, box 49, folders 797–98, CJG-CLM.

117. Ramírez de Arellano and Seipp, *Colonialism, Catholicism, and Contraception,* 107–23.

118. Satterthwaite, "Experience with Oral and Intrauterine Contraception in Rural Puerto Rico."

119. Thomas Parran to Raymond Fosdick, 28 October 1946, RG 3.2; Series 900, Subseries: Population, box 57, folder 310, RF-RAC.

120. José Belaval to Margaret Sanger, 21 January 1941, and Sanger to Belaval, 8 February 1941, MS-LC; Gamble to Belaval, 4 April 1941, and Gamble to Charis Gould, 25 January 1941, box 46, folder 752, CJG-CLM.

121. Dr. Charis Gould, Presbyterian Hospital, San Juan, 17 July 1941, box 46, folder 752, CJG-CLM.

122. Gamble to Charis Gould, 12 August 1941, box 46, folder 752, CJG-CLM.

123. Cook, Gamble, and Satterthwaite, "Oral Contraception with Norethynodrel."

CHAPTER 5

1. Presser, *Sterilization and Fertility Decline in Puerto Rico;* Davila, "Esterilización y práctica anticonceptiva en Puerto Rico, 1982."

2. Mass, *Population Target,* 87–108.

3. Gordon, *Woman's Body, Woman's Right,* 160–69.

4. Davis, *Women, Race, and Class,* 219–21.

5. García, *La operación.*

6. Donna Haraway has suggested that the women's health movement has always been multiracial (see *Modest_Witness@Second_Millenium*). Such an assertion runs the risk of eliding the very real conflicts and tensions within the movement; however, I think it can be said to be true if one includes the organizations of women of color that worked in tandem and sometimes at odds with mostly white women's health groups. To the extent that the movement was multiracial, it was in part because of this willingness to consider colonialism and racism as integral to the analysis of reproductive freedom and women's health more generally.

7. Azize-Vargas, *La mujer en la lucha;* Orleck, *Common Sense and a Little Fire,* 153.

8. Mass, *Population Target,* 94.

9. Carmen Rivera de Alvarado, "Informe del Programa de Salud Maternal," [1935], RG 323, Entry 36, box 4, folder: RRD—Health Section, NRAN; Carmen Rivera de Alvarado to Christopher Tietze, 6 November 1948, box 47, folder 764, CJG-CLM.

10. Spivak, "Can the Subaltern Speak?"

11. Rodriguez-Trias, "Sterilization Abuse," 11; Jack Slater, "Sterilization: Newest Threat to the Poor," *Ebony,* October 1973, 152.

12. Aptheker, "Sterilization, Experimentation, and Imperialism," 38–39; Jack Slater, "Sterilization: Newest Threat to the Poor," *Ebony,* October 1973, 150–56; Krauss, *Hospital Survey on Sterilization Policies;* Les Payne, "Forced Sterilization for the Poor?," *San Francisco Chronicle,* 26 February 1974. See also Reilly, *The Surgical Solution.*

13. Jones, *Bad Blood.*

14. Aptheker, "Sterilization, Experimentation, and Imperialism," 40.

15. Rodríguez-Trias, "Sterilization Abuse," 12.

16. Sheehan, *A Bright Shining Lie.*

17. Mass, *Population Target,* 158–59.

18. Weisbord, *Genocide?,* 3–10; Littlewood, *The Politics of Population Control,* 69–87; Stycos, "Some Minority Opinions on Birth Control"; Murray, "The Ethical and Moral Values of Black Americans and Population Policy."

19. Peter Khiss, "A Puerto Rican Sees 'Genocide,'" *New York Times,* 31 October 1974, p. 8.

20. Claudia Dreifus, "Sterilizing the Poor," *The Progressive,* December 1975, 13–19; Arlene Eisen, "They're Trying to Take Our Future—Native American Women and Sterilization," *The Guardian,* 23 March 1972, 13–19.

21. Ironically, though Rodríguez-Trias is often taken to endorse the argument against "sterilization abuse" in Puerto Rico (see, e.g., García, *La operación*), she in fact makes my argument: coercion was probably exercised on the mainland, but in Puerto Rico, high rates of sterilization can be understood as the legacy of the combination of large numbers of women entering the labor force at a time when the government made the operation available for free (see Rodríguez-Trias, "Sterilization Abuse").

22. García, *La operación.*

23. Rodríguez-Trias, "The Women's Health Movement," 120; Shapiro, *Population Control Politics,* 137–39.

24. Reed, *The Birth Control Movement and American Society,* 210–61; Williams and Williams, *Every Child a Wanted Child,* 159–70.

25. Shorter, review of *Woman's Body, Woman's Right;* Kennedy, review of *Woman's Body, Woman's Right;* Lemons, review of *Woman's Body, Woman's Right.*

26. Genovese, "Comment on the Reviews of *Woman's Body, Woman's Right*"; Elbert and Kelman, "Reply to Shorter on *Woman's Body, Woman's Right*"; Fee and Wallace, "The History and Politics of Birth Control"; Lane, "The Politics of Birth Control."

27. Reed, *The Birth Control Movement and American Society,* xv–xxii; Gordon, *Woman's Body, Woman's Right,* vii–xii.

28. Marqués, "El puertorriqueño dócil," 175.

29. Quoted in Thimmesch, "Puerto Rico and Birth Control," 256.

30. Ramírez de Arellano and Seipp, *Colonialism, Catholicism, and Contraception,* 204.

31. See Senior, "An Approach to Research in Overcoming Cultural Barriers to Family Limitation," 150; Stycos, "Female Sterilization in Puerto Rico," 7; Christopher Tietze to Clarence Gamble, Report #9, 26 September 1946, box 46, folder 756, CJG-CLM; and Presser, *Sterilization and Fertility Decline in Puerto Rico,* 33.

32. Luis Hernandez Aquino, "Son ya 3,373 las mujeres esterilizadas," *El Mundo* (San Juan), 21 October 1947, p. 1; Ramírez de Arellano and Seipp, *Colonialism, Catholicism, and Contraception,* 137.

33. "Obispado de San Juan dice falta moral," *El Mundo* (San Juan), 27 October 1947, p. 1.

34. "Dr. Pons a Favor Intenso Control de la Natalidad," *El Mundo* (San Juan), 14 February 1949, pp. 1, 14.

35. "Pons Explica no Existen Planes Oficiales Para la Esterización," *El Mundo* (San Juan), 18 February 1949, pp. 1, 14.

36. "Los Obispos Católicos Piden Muñoz Se Defina Sobre la Esterilización," *El Mundo* (San Juan), 5 March 1949, pp. 1, 16.

37. Cofresí, *Realidad poblacional de Puerto Rico;* "Líderes Católicos Sostienen Que Gobierno Apoya Esterilización," *El Mundo* (San Juan), 29 August 1951, p. 7.

38. "Nuevo Grupo Declara Combatirá Violación Derechos Naturales," *El Mundo* (San Juan), 17 September 1951, p. 11.

39. "Católica Ataca Las Prácticas Esterilización," *El Mundo* (San Juan), 11 September 1951, p. 1.

40. See, e.g., "Pons Declara No Hay Programa de Esterilización de la Isla," *El Mundo* (San Juan), 15 September 1951, pp. 1, 16; "Unión Pro Moral Natural Alega Pons Confirma Sus Denuncias," *El Mundo* (San Juan), 17 September 1951, pp. 1, 14; "Obispo de Ponce Dice Problema de Isla es Falta de Recursos," *El Mundo* (San Juan), 19 September 1951, p. 11; "Pons Niega Hospitales Gobierno Esterilizaran 14,000 Mujeres," *El Mundo* (San Juan), 22 September 1951, pp. 1, 16; "Los Católicos Piden Constitución Prohiba las Esterilizaciones," *El Mundo* (San Juan), 25 September 1951, p. 11.

41. "Asamblea Santo Nombre en E.U. Condena Esterilización Aquí," *El Mundo* (San Juan), 18 October 1951, p. 5.

42. "El Dr. Asencio Combate Práctica de la Esterilización en Masa," *El Mundo* (San Juan), 29 May 1953, p. 5.

43. Ramírez de Arellano and Seipp, *Colonialism, Catholicism, and Contraception,* 100.

44. These events drew considerable interest up north, where John F. Kennedy was trying to persuade Americans that his political conscience would not be kept by the Pope in Rome. As *Life* magazine captured Muñoz Marín's wife walking out of a church service for its cover photo, Cardinal Spellman of New York and even the Pope's legate to North America made disapproving noises about the actions of the Puerto Rican bishops, no doubt to Kennedy's great relief (see Ramírez de Arellano and Seipp, *Colonialism, Catholicism, and Contraception,* 149–58).

45. Ibid.

46. *Pa'lante, siempre pa'lante!"* produced and directed by Iris Morales; Torres and Velázquez, *The Puerto Rican Movement.*

47. Warwick and Williamson, "Population Policy and Spanish-Surnamed Americans," 223.

48. Nelson, "Abortions Under Community Control."

49. George Payne, "Chronological Summary of Birth Control Movement in Puerto Rico in its Relation to the Development of Public Health Units," 1 May 1936, RG 1.1, Series 243: International Health Division, box 1, folder 15, RF-RAC; George Payne to William Sawyer, 1 May 1936, RG 1.1, Series 243: International Health Division, box 1, folder 15, RF-RAC.

50. Ramírez de Arellano and Seipp, *Colonialism, Catholicism, and Contraception,* 45–49.

51. Ibid., 60–92; Rivera de Alvarado and Tietze, "Birth Control in Puerto Rico," 17.

52. Christoper Tietze, typescript of "Birth Control in Puerto Rico," box 46, folder 760, CJG-CLM.

53. Azize-Vargas and Aviles, "La mujer en las profesiones de salud."

54. Presser, *Sterilization and Fertility Decline in Puerto Rico,* 50. As late as 1945 one of the most prominent obstetricians in San Juan, José Belaval, wrote that 80 percent of women were delivered by a midwife (see Belaval, "Declinación de la mortalidad puerperal en Puerto Rico de 1943–1943").

55. King, "Cultural Aspects of Birth Control in Puerto Rico."

56. Wilson Wing to Clarence Gamble, Confidential Report, 18 May 1951, box 47, folder 774, CJG-CLM.

57. Christopher Tietze to Clarence Gamble, Report #3, 19 September 1946, box 46, folder 756, CJG-CLM.

58. José Belaval to Clarence J. Gamble, 21 August 1946, box 46, folder 754, CJG-CLM.

59. Wing to Gamble, 18 May 1951, box 47, folder 775, CJG-CLM. The "attached confidential report" records a nameless official's drive through the towns of the island, interviewing mayors about their (considerable) support for sterilization, discussed below. The memo records that they said they were inundated by requests and that they paid for some women's sterilizations.

60. Boring et al., "Sterilization Regret among Puerto Rican Women."

61. Panaigua et al., "Medical and Psychological Sequelae of Surgical Sterilization," 428.

62. Henderson, "Population Policy, Social Structure, and the Health System of Puerto Rico," 213.

63. Vázquez Calzada, "La esterilización feminina en Puerto Rico."

64. Hatt, *Backgrounds of Human Fertility in Puerto Rico,* 444. Percentages have been recomputed to eliminate the distinction between those who were legally married and those who were not.

65. Stycos, "Female Sterilization in Puerto Rico," 5.

66. Hill, Stycos, and Back, *The Family and Population Control,* 181.

67. Panaigua et al., "Medical and Psychological Sequelae of Surgical Sterilization."

68. Christopher Tietze to Clarence Gamble, Report #2, 18 September 1946, box 46, folder 756, CJG-CLM.

69. Stokes, "Tubal Ligations." The paper was read before the staff of St. Luke's Memorial Hospital in January 1948.

70. Belaval, Cofresí, and Janer, "Opinión de la clase médica de Puerto Rico sobre el uso de esterilización y los contraceptivos."

71. Henderson, "Population Policy, Social Structure, and the Health System of Puerto Rico," 119–45.

72. Christopher Tietze to Clarence Gamble, Report #2, 18 September 1946, box 46, folder 756, CJG-CLM.

73. James Reed, interview by Adeline Pendleton Satterthwaite, M.D., 7 September 1974, Women's Studies Manuscript Collection of the Schlesinger Library, Radcliffe College, Series 3: Sexuality, Sex Education, and Reproductive Rights, Part A: Family Planning Oral History Project.

74. Wilson Wing to Clarence Gamble, Confidential Report, 18 May 1951, box 47, folder 774, CJG-CLM.

75. Presser, *Sterilization and Fertility Decline in Puerto Rico,* 38; Reed, interview; Mass, *Population Target,* 95.

76. Ostolaza Bey, *Política sexual en Puerto Rico,* 78–82.

77. Ibid., 78–88.

78. Azize-Vargas, *La mujer en la lucha;* Azize-Vargas, "The Emergence of Feminist Consciousness in Puerto Rico, 1870–1930."

79. Gordon, *Woman's Body, Woman's Right,* 233–36.

80. López, "Agency and Constraint," 299–324.

81. Chow, "Where Have All the Natives Gone."

CHAPTER 6

1. Colón, *The Puerto Rican in New York and Other Sketches*, 9–10.

2. See Sánchez Korrol's brilliant study of that early community, *From Colonia to Community*; and James's monograph on the larger Caribbean community, *Holding Aloft the Banner of Ethiopia*.

3. Lewis, *La Vida*; Dugdale, *The Jukes*; Goddard, *The Kallikak Family*.

4. Cited in Monserrat, "Puerto Rican Migration," 78.

5. For indirect but extensive documentation of employers' reliance on the "culture of poverty" as a proxy for older, science-based racial categories, see Wilson, *When Work Disappears*. Wilson is among those who believes that there is a homogeneous culture of the underclass (though his effort to mark it geographically unintentionally points up the incredible diversity of labor experiences even within a neighborhood). Nevertheless, he is also increasingly clear that "culture" is an alibi for "race" for discriminatory employers.

6. Espada, "City of Coughing and Dead Radiators."

7. Torres, Rodríguez Vecchini, and Burgos, *The Commuter Nation*; Sánchez, *Guagua aérea*; Sandoval Sánchez, "Puerto Rican Migration Up in the Air."

8. Bureau of the Census, *U.S. Census of Population: 1950*, Vol. 4, *Special Reports: Puerto Ricans in the Continental U.S.*, pt. 3, ch. D, p. 4.

9. Cordasco, Foreword to *Puerto Ricans on the United States Mainland*, ix. This volume is based on the Census Bureau's sample-survey data for November 1969, as well as data from the Commonwealth of Puerto Rico, Department of Labor, Migration Division.

10. "Aid Planned Here for Puerto Ricans," *New York Times*, 12 January 1947, p. 25.

11. "Columbia is Ready for Migrant Study," *New York Times*, 14 October 1947, p. 31. The 1950 Census found 226,110 Puerto Ricans living on the mainland, and an additional 75,265 children born on the mainland to Puerto Rican parents. Even if the census had undercounted Puerto Ricans by 100 percent, the *Times*'s numbers would still have to be significantly inflated (see Bureau of the Census, *U.S. Census of Population: 1950*, vol. 4, *Special Reports: Puerto Ricans in the Continental United States*, pt. 3, ch. D, p. 4).

12. Commonwealth of Puerto Rico, Department of Labor, Migration Division, *A Summary of Facts and Figures*, 15.

13. Wakefield, *Island in the City*, 213.

14. "Puerto Rico Seeks to Curb Migration," *New York Times*, 23 February 1947, p. 20; "Why Puerto Ricans Flock to the U.S.," *New York Times*, 1 June 1947, p. E5; "Puerto Ricans Drift to Mainland Gains," *New York Times*, 31 July 1947, p. 18.

15. "Rhatigan Reports on Relief Spending," *New York Times*, 25 May 1947, pp. 1, 3; Edward Ranzal, "Puerto Rico Seeks to Curb Migration," *New York Times*, 23 February 1947, p. 20.

16. "$2,000,000 Rise in Relief is Seen," *New York Times*, 17 October 1947, pp. 1, 14.

17. "New York Relief Cases Increase," *New York World Telegram*, 20 October 1947, p. 10.

18. "Migration Spontaneous: Puerto Rico Officials Say Flow to New York is Not Forced," *New York Times*, 1 August 1947, p. 3; "Officials Worried by Influx of Migrant Puerto Ricans," *New York Times*, 2 August 1947, pp. 1, 15; Albert Gordon, "Crime Increasing in 'Little Spain'—Puerto Rican Migrants Jammed Into East Harlem District Keep the Police Busy—Boy Gangs Roam Streets—Robberies, Gambling and Vice are Common—Authorities Urge More Play Areas," and "117 Arrive at Newark," *New York Times*, 3 August 1947, p. 12; "The Tragedy of Puerto Rico," *New York Times*, 3 August 1947, p. IV-6; Albert Gordon, "Solution is Sought to Migrant Influx—Puerto Rico Plans to Develop Island Resources to Reduce Number Leaving Home—Relief Costs Here Soar—Surveys Show Many Diseases Prevalent in 'Little Spain' and Other Settlements," *New York Times*, 4 August 1947, pp. 19, 35; Letter to the editor, *New York Times*, 5 August 1947, p. 4; Letter to the editor, *New York Times*, 7 August 1947, p. 20.

19. "Governor of Puerto Rico Planning Study by Columbia of Migration," *New York Times*, 8 August 1947, pp. 1, 4; "Columbia Accepts Puerto Rico Study," *New York Times*, 10 August 1947, p. 54.

20. "Puerto Rican Migrants Jam New York," *Life*, 25 August 1947, 25–29.

21. Kelley, *Yo' Mama's Disfunktional!*, 2.

22. Rainwater and Yancy, *The Moynihan Report and the Politics of Controversy*, 7.

23. *News Letter of the Institute of Ethnic Affairs*, vol. 3, no. 2 (March 1948); New York University, Graduate School of Public Administration and Social Service, *The Impact of Puerto Rican Migration on Governmental Services in New York City*; Handlin, *The Newcomers*; Glazer and Moynihan, *Beyond the Melting Pot*.

24. "Columbia is Ready for Migrant Study," *New York Times*, 14 October 1947, p. 31; Mills, Senior, and Goldsen, *The Puerto Rican Journey*.

25. New York (N.Y.) Board of Education, Puerto Rican Study, *Teaching Children of Puerto Rican Background in New York City Schools*; Welfare Council of New York City, Committee on Puerto Ricans in New York City, *Puerto Ricans in New York City*; Community Council of Greater New York, Research Bureau, *Population of Puerto Rican Birth or Parentage, New York City, 1950*; Brooklyn Council for Social Planning, *Report on Survey of Brooklyn Agencies Rendering Services to Puerto Ricans*.

26. Mills, Senior, and Goldsen, *The Puerto Rican Journey*, 60, 61, 63, 88–89, 95–98.

27. Wakefield, *Island in the City*; Padilla, *Up from Puerto Rico*; Welfare Council of New York City, Committee on Puerto Ricans in New York City, *Puerto Ricans in New York City*; Community Council of Greater New York, Research Bureau, *Population of Puerto Rican Birth or Parentage, New York City, 1950*.

28. James, *Holding Aloft the Banner of Ethiopia*.

29. Rodríguez-Morazzani, "Political Cultures of the Puerto Rican Left in the United States."

30. Clooney worked with Lloyd Rogler on *Puerto Rican Families in New York City*. Another important Puerto Rican intellectual who participated in the

creation of the social science of Puerto Ricans was Francisca Muriente, a social worker who worked extensively with Oscar Lewis to develop the ethnographic materials for *La Vida*. There is a story to tell here about the participation of Puerto Rican researchers in the development of the social science of working-class Puerto Ricans. It would be a fascinating one. The other story I do not tell here is the one that examines who the North American researchers were and what were their motivations. It, too, is well worth attention. Those who did poverty research in the 1960s and later made the turn to neoconservatism were not traditional academic insiders, and many of them grew up working class, just as their subjects had. Oscar Lewis, Oscar Handlin, Nathan Glazer, and Daniel Patrick Moynihan were among the first generation of Jewish and Catholic scholars to become respected social scientists at places like Chicago and Harvard. Their research agendas, on the one hand, stressed the dignity of working people precisely by making them the subjects of academic study—and many of these scholars also had socialist and communist leanings before coming to academe. On the other hand, their radicalism did not survive the turn from "white ethnics," to Puerto Ricans and "Negroes," nor, perhaps, simply the political sea change from the legal reform embraced by the civil rights movements to nationalism and calls for substantive economic restructuring (see Glazer, "From Socialism to Sociology").

31. Rodríguez-Fratricelli and Tirado, "Notes toward a History of Puerto Rican Community Organization in New York City."

32. Commonwealth of Puerto Rico, Department of Labor, Migration Division, *A Summary in Facts and Figures*.

33. Letter, Martha Gellhorn to Leonard Bernstein, undated [1957], reproduced at www.leonardbernstein.com.

34. The classic statements of this model are, first, Thomas, *The Polish Peasant in Europe and America;* and, paradigmatically, Park, *Introduction to the Science of Sociology.*

35. William Shakespeare, *Romeo and Juliet* / Arthur Laurents, *West Side Story,* introduction by Norris Houghton, notes by John Bettenbender (New York: Dell, 1965).

36. Garebian, *The Making of West Side Story,* 30.

37. See Duggan, *Sapphic Slashers,* for a brilliant take on how this discourse worked in an earlier moment.

38. Garebian, *The Making of West Side Story.*

39. See, e.g. Sandoval Sánchez, "Una lectura puertorriqueña de la América de West Side Story"; a slightly different version is to be found in his *José Can You See?,* 62–82.

40. Bernstein is cited in Sandoval Sánchez, *José Can You See?,* which is also the source for the original lyrics from the Broadway version.

41. "The Facts Don't Rhyme," *New York Times,* 29 September 1947, p. 83.

42. Handlin, *The Newcomers,* 102.

43. Ibid.

44. Ibid., 161–62 n. 93.

45. In an interview with Oscar Handlin in December 1999, I asked him if he still thought this was a good choice of sources. He replied, "You always wish you had better sources, but given what there was, yes, it made sense."

46. Handlin, *The Newcomers,* 117.

47. Ibid., 115.

48. Ibid., 103, 110, 111.

49. Herzog, "The Culture of Poverty."

50. Lewis, *Children of Sanchez,* xxiv, cited in Herzog, "The Culture of Poverty."

51. Herzog, "The Culture of Poverty," 391.

52. Mayhew, *London Labour and the London Poor.*

53. Herzog, "The Culture of Poverty," 390.

54. See, e.g., West, *The National Welfare Rights Movement;* and Harrington's own account of these events (p. ix) in his Introduction to *A Welfare Mother,* by Susan Sheehan.

55. José Sánchez, "Housing Puerto Ricans in New York, 1945 to 1984: A Study in Class Powerlessness (Ph.D. diss., New York University, 1990), cited in Aponte-Parés, "Lessons from *El Barrio,*" 46.

56. Moynihan, *Politics of the Guaranteed Income.*

57. Department of Labor, Office of Policy Planning and Research, *The Negro Family.*

58. Rainwater and Yancey, *The Moynihan Report and the Politics of Controversy.*

59. The person who is best on this point is Wahneema Lubiano; see her "Black Nationalism and Black Common Sense," and "Black Ladies, Welfare Queens, and State Minstrels."

60. Glazer, Foreword to *The Negro Family in the United States.*

61. Lewis, *La Vida,* 4–5.

62. Ibid., 5.

63. Ibid. 92.

64. Elmer Bendiner, "Outside the Kingdom of the Middle Class," *The Nation,* 2 January 1967, 22–23.

65. Lewis, *La Vida,* 27.

66. Ibid., 535.

67. Ibid.

68. Ibid., 538.

69. Ibid., 662.

70. Nathan Glazer, "One Kind of Life," *Commentary,* February 1967, 83–85.

71. Horowitz, "Meurte en Vida."

72. Lewis, *A Study of Slum Culture,* 116.

73. Rigdon, *The Culture Facade,* 76.

74. Ibid., 90.

75. Ibid., 94.

76. Michael Harrington, "Everyday Hell," *New York Times Book Review,* 20 November 1966, pp. 1, 92.

77. Maldonado-Denis, "Oscar Lewis: *La vida* y la enajenación."

78. "*La Vida:* Whose Life?"; Cordasco, "Another Face of Poverty."

79. Oscar Handlin, "Reader's Choice," *Atlantic Monthly,* December 1966, 142.

80. Saul Maloff, "Man's Fate?" *Newsweek,* 21 November 1966, 131–32.

81. Glazer, "One Kind of Life," 82.

82. Elmer Bendiner, "Outside the Kingdom of the Middle Class," *The Nation,* 2 January 1967, 22–23.

83. Ibid., 22.

84. The evidence for this in Lewis's case is the introduction; for Moynihan, it is his other published writing (see, e.g., Moynihan, "The President and the Negro: The Moment Lost," *Commentary,* February 1967, 31–45).

85. Puerto Rican Forum, *The Puerto Rican Community Development Project,* 4–5.

86. Ibid., 9.

87. Abrahmson and the Young Lords Party, *Palante,* 150.

88. *Pa'lante, siempre pa'lante!,* produced and directed by Iris Morales.

89. Torres, "Political Radicalism in the Diaspora—The Puerto Rican Experience."

90. See the various neoconservative declarations on race, poverty, and family, e.g., Rainwater, Rein, and Esping-Andersen, *Stagnation and Renewal in Social Policy;* Kaus, *The End of Equality;* Williams, *America, A Minority Viewpoint;* and Murray, *Losing Ground.* Murray's subsequent book, with Richard Herrnstein, *The Bell Curve,* also argues, but in a biological register, that reproduction of the "wrong sort"—that is, of passing along heritable low IQ—causes poverty. These scholars tie their own genealogy directly to the Moynihan Report: see Williams et al., "Sex, Families, Race, Poverty, Welfare."

91. See Katha Pollit, "Subject to Debate," *The Nation,* 13 February 1995, 192.

92. Frazier, *The Negro Family in the United States;* and Genovese, *Roll, Jordan, Roll.*

EPILOGUE

1. The early one; another "PSP" was organized in the 1980s.

2. Faulkner, *Requiem for a Nun,* 80.

3. On this point, see also Poovey, *A History of the Modern Fact.*

4. Lienhard, *La voz y su huella.*

5. Mahmood Mamdani, cited in Gourevitch, *We Wish to Inform You that Tomorrow We Will Be Killed with Our Families.*

6. Trouillot, *Silencing the Past.*

7. Nader, "Up the Anthropologist—Perspectives Gained from Studying Up."

8. Gordon, *Ghostly Matters.*

9. Lewis, *La Vida,* 177.

Bibliography

ARCHIVAL AND MANUSCRIPT COLLECTIONS

Biblioteca Monserrate Santana de Palés de Trabajo Social, Universidad de Puerto Rico, Río Piedras, P.R. Pamphlet collection

Bureau of Social Hygiene Archives, Rockefeller Archive Center, Sleepy Hollow, New York [BSH-RAC]

Countway Library of Medicine, Harvard University, Cambridge, Mass.
Clarence J. Gamble Papers (H MS c23), Puerto Rico Files. Used with permission of the Francis A. Countway Library of Medicine. [CJG-CLM]

Library of Congress, Manuscript Division, Washington, D.C.
Papers of Margaret Sanger (microform). Professional correspondence, 1914–65, Foreign File, Peurto Rico Folder. [MS-LC]

National Archives I, Washington, D.C. [NWCT1]
Record Group 112: Records of the Office of the Surgeon General (Army) [RG 112]
Record Group 393: Records of U.S. Army Continental Commands, 1821–1920 [RG 393]
Record Group 395: Records of U.S. Army Overseas Operations and Commands, 1898–1942 [RG 395]

National Archives II, College Park, Md. [NWCT2]
Record Group 350: Records of the Bureau of Insular Affairs [RG 350]
Record Group 323: Records of the Puerto Rico Reconstruction Administration (PRRA) [RG 323]

National Archives, Regional Archives, Northeast Region, New York City [NRAN]

Rockefeller Family Archives, Rockefeller Archive Center, Sleepy Hollow, New York [RFam-RAC]

Record Group 2: Office of the Messrs. Rockefeller General Files, 1891–1961 [RG 2]
Rockefeller Foundation Archives, Rockefeller Archive Center, Sleepy Hollow, New York [RF-RAC]
Record Group 1: Projects, 1912–1989 [RG 1]
Record Group 3: Administration, Program, and Policy, 1910 (1913–1989) [RG 3]
Rockefeller University Archives, Rockefeller Archive Center, Sleepy Hollow, New York [RU-RAC]
Record Group 891: *The Medical Letter on Drugs and Therapeutics* Editorial Files, 1959–1969 [RG 891]
Schlesinger Library, Radcliffe College, Cambridge, Mass.
Women's Studies Manuscript Collection, Series 3: Sexuality, Sex Education, and Reproductive Rights, Part A: Family Planning Oral History Project
Universidad de Puerto Rico, Río Piedras
Colección Puertorriqueña

GOVERNMENT DOCUMENTS

Annual Reports of the Governor of Puerto Rico. 49 vols. Washington, D.C.: Government Printing Office, 1901–1951.
Asamblea Legislativa de Puerto Rico. *Primer informe de la Comisión Legislativa para investigar el malestar y desasosiego industrial y agrícola y que origina el desempleo en Puerto Rico.* San Juan, 3 February 1930.
Commonwealth of Puerto Rico. Department of Labor, Migration Division. *Puerto Rican Migration, 1940–1955.* New York: The Department, 1956.
———. *A Summary of Facts and Figures.* New York: The Department, April 1957.
[Commonwealth of] Puerto Rico. Office of the Attorney General. *Special Report of the Attorney General of Porto Rico to the Governor of Porto Rico Concerning the Suppression of Vice and Prostitution in Connection with the Mobilization of the National Army at Camp Las Casas, February 1, 1919.* San Juan, P.R.: Bureau of Supplies, Printing, and Transportation, 1919.
Congressional Record. 1937. Washington, D.C.
U.S. Bureau of the Census. *U.S. Census of Population: 1950.* Vol. 4: *Special Reports: Puerto Ricans in the Continental U.S.* Washington, D.C.: Government Printing Office, 1953.
U.S. Department of Labor. Office of Policy Planning and Research. *The Negro Family: The Case for National Action,* by Daniel P. Moynihan. Washington, D.C.: Government Printing Office, 1965.
U.S. Senate. Committee on Inter-Oceanic Canals. *Investigation of Panama Canal Matters.* Vol. 1. 59th Cong., 2d sess. 11 January–12 February, 1907.
U.S. War Department. *Defects Found in Drafted Men.* Washington, D.C.: Government Printing Office, 1920.

NEWSPAPERS AND PERIODICALS

Birth Control Review
La Correspondencia (San Juan)
La Democracia (San Juan)
El Imparcial (San Juan)
El Mundo (San Juan)
New York Times
El Tiempo (San Juan)
The Times (San Juan)
Union Signal (official newspaper of the WCTU)

OTHER SOURCES

Abrahmson, Michael, and the Young Lords Party. *Palante: The Young Lords Party.* New York: McGraw-Hill, 1971.

Acosta Belen, Edna, ed. *La mujer en la sociedad puertorriqueña.* Río Piedras, P.R.: Ediciones Huracán, 1980.

Allen, Garland. "Eugenics and American Social History, 1881–1950." *Genome* 31, no. 2 (1989): 885–89.

———. "The Eugenics Record Office at Cold Spring Harbor, 1910–1940." *Osiris,* 2d series (1986): 225–64.

Allen, W. M., and O. Weintersteiner. "Crystalline Progestin." *Science* 80, no. 2069 (1934): 190–91.

Anderson, Warwick. "Colonial Pathologies: American Medicine in the Philippines, 1898–1921." Ph.D. diss., University of Pennsylvania, 1992.

———. "Excremental Colonialism: Public Health and the Poetics of Pollution." *Critical Inquiry* 21 (spring 1995): 460–69.

———. "Where Every Prospect Pleases and Only Man Is Vile: Laboratory Medicine as Colonial Discourse." *Critical Inquiry* 18, no. 3 (spring 1992): 506–29.

Aponte-Parés, Luis. "Lessons from *El Barrio.*" In *Latino Social Movements: Historical and Theoretical Perspectives,* edited by Rodolfo Torres and George Katsiaficas, 43–77. New York: Routledge, 1999.

Aptheker, Herbert. "Sterilization, Experimentation, and Imperialism." *Political Affairs* 53, no. 1 (January 1974): 37–48.

Armstrong, Nancy. *Desire and Domestic Fiction: A Political History of the Novel.* New York: Oxford, 1987.

Arnold, David. *Colonizing the Body: State Medicine and Epidemic Disease in Nineteenth Century India.* Berkeley: University of California Press, 1993.

———. *Warm Climates and Western Medicine.* Atlanta: Rodopi, 1996.

———, ed. *Imperial Medicine and Indigenous Societies.* New York: Manchester University Press, 1988.

Asbell, Bernard. *The Pill: A Biography of the Drug that Changed the World.* New York: Random House, 1995.

Ashford, Bailey K. *A Soldier in Science: The Autobiography of Bailey K. Ashford.* 1934; reprint, San Juan: Editorial de la Universidad de Puerto Rico, 1998.

Atiles, F. del Valle. "Limitación de la prole." *Boletín de la Asociación Médica de Puerto Rico* 12, no. 114 (March 1917): 1–7.

Azize-Vargas, Yamila. "The Emergence of Feminist Consciousness in Puerto Rico, 1870–1930." In *Unequal Sisters: A Multicultural Reader in U.S. Women's History,* edited by Vicki Ruiz and Ellen DuBois. 2d ed. New York: Routledge, 1994.

———. *La mujer en la lucha: Historia del feminismo en Puerto Rico, 1898–1930.* Rio Piedras, P.R.: Ediciones Cultural, 1985.

———. "The Roots of Puerto Rican Feminism: The Struggle for Universal Suffrage." *Radical America* 23, no. 1 (14 June 1990): 73–74.

Azize-Vargas, Yamila, and Luis Alberto Aviles. "La mujer en las profesiones de salud: Los hechos desconocidos: Participación de la mujer en las profesiones de salud en Puerto Rico (1898–1930)." *Puerto Rico Health Sciences Journal* 9, no. 1 (April 1990): 9–16.

Baer, Werner. *The Puerto Rican Economy and United States Economic Fluctuations.* Río Piedras, P.R.: Social Science Research Center, University of Puerto Rico; Barcelona, Spain: Ediciones Rumbos, 1960.

Ballenger, Edgar. "The Social Evil." *Charlotte Medical Journal* 30, no. 1 (January 1907): 21–24.

Ballhatchet, Kenneth. *Race, Sex, and Class under the Raj: Imperial Attitudes and Policies and Their Critics, 1793–1905.* London: Weidenfeld and Nicolson, 1980.

Bandarage, Asoka. *Women, Population, and Global Crisis.* London: Zed Books, 1997.

Barceló-Miller, María de Fátima. "Halfhearted Solidarity: Women Workers and the Women's Suffrage Movement in Puerto Rico During the 1920s." In *Puerto Rican Women's History: New Perspectives,* edited by Félix Matos Rodríguez and Linda Delgado, 143–70. Armonk, N.Y.: M. E. Sharpe, 1998.

Barkan, Elazar. *The Retreat of Scientific Racism: Changing Concepts of Race in Britain and the United States between the World Wars.* Cambridge: Cambridge University Press, 1992.

Bashford, Alison. " 'Is White Australia Possible?': Race, Colonialism, and Tropical Medicine." *Ethnic and Racial Studies* 23, no. 2 (1 March 2000): 248–71.

Bäumler, Ernst. *Paul Ehrlich: Scientist for Life.* Translated by Grant Edwards. New York: Holmes and Meier, 1984.

Baxter, Sylvester. "Porto Rico under the Stars and Stripes: A Quarter Century of Progress." *The American Review of Reviews* 67 (May 1923): 504.

Beebe, Gilbert, and Clarence J. Gamble. "Clinical Contraceptive Results in a Small Series of Patients." *Journal of the American Medical Association* 115, no. 17 (26 October 1940): 1451–54.

———. "Fertility and Contraception in Puerto Rico." *Puerto Rico Journal of Public Health and Tropical Medicine* 18, no. 1 (1942): 3–52.

Belaval, José. "Declinación de la mortalidad puerperal en Puerto Rico de 1923–1943." *Puerto Rico Public Health Journal of Tropical Medicine* 20, no. 4 (1945): 524–28.

Belaval, José, Emilio Cofresí, and José Janer. "Opinión de la clase médica de Puerto Rico sobre el uso de esterilización y los contraceptivos" (mimeographed private release, 1953). Reproduced in J. Mayone Stycos, "Female Sterilization in Puerto Rico," *Eugenics Quarterly* 1, no. 2 (June 1954): 3–9.

Belaval, José, Charis Gould, and Clarence Gamble. "The Effectiveness of Contraceptive Advice among the Underprivileged of Puerto Rico." *Journal of Contraception* 3, no. 12 (December 1938): 224–27.

Bernstein, Laurie. *Sonia's Daughters: Prostitutes and Their Regulation in Imperial Russia.* Berkeley: University of California Press, 1995.

Best, Joel. *Controlling Vice: Regulating Brothel Prostitution in St. Paul, 1865–1883.* Columbus: Ohio State University Press, 1998.

Beswick, Stephanie, and Jay Spaulding. "Sex, Bondage, and the Market: The Emergence of Prostitution in Northern Sudan, 1750–1950." *Journal of the History of Sexuality* 5, no. 4 (1995): 512–34.

Bhabha, Homi. "Of Mimicry and Man: The Ambivalence of Colonial Discourse." In *Tensions of Empire: Colonial Cultures in a Bourgeois World,* edited by Ann Laura Stoler and Frederick Cooper. Berkeley: University of California Press, 1997.

Black, Eugene. "Population Increase and Economic Development." In *Our Crowded Planet,* edited by Osborn Fairfield. Garden City, N.Y.: Doubleday, 1962.

Boas, Franz. "Studies in Growth." *Human Biology* 3, no. 3 (September 1931): 307–50.

Borell, Merriley. "Biologists and the Promotion of Birth Control Research, 1918–1938." *Journal of the History of Biology* 20, no. 1 (spring 1987): 51–87.

Boring, Catherine, R. W. Rochat, and J. Becerra. "Sterilization Regret among Puerto Rican Women." *Fertility and Sterility* 49, no. 6 (June 1988): 973–81.

Bourgeois, Philippe. *In Search of Respect: Selling Crack in El Barrio.* New York: Cambridge University Press, 1996.

Bourne, Dorothy Dulles. "Puerto Rico's Predicament." *The Survey* 25, no. 7 (July 1936): 201–2.

Bourne, Dorothy Dulles, and James R. Bourne. *Thirty Years of Change in Puerto Rico.* New York: Praeger, 1966.

Brandt, Alan. *No Magic Bullet: A Social History of Venereal Disease in the United States Since 1880.* Expanded ed. New York: Oxford, 1987.

———. "Racism and Research: The Case of the Tuskegee Syphilis Study." *Hastings Center Report* 8 (December 1978): 21–28.

Brooklyn Council for Social Planning. *Report on Survey of Brooklyn Agencies Rendering Services to Puerto Ricans,* edited by Jeannette Taylor. New York: Welfare Council of New York City, 1953.

Brown, Wenzell. *Dynamite on Our Doorstep: Puerto Rican Paradox.* New York: Greenberg, 1945.

Browning, Frank. "From Rumble to Revolution: The Young Lords and Young Lords Party, 'Pa'lante.'" In *The Puerto Rican Experience: A Sociological Sourcebook,* edited by Francesco Cordasco and Eugene Bucchioni. Totowa, N.Y.: Rowman and Littlefield, 1973.

Brumberg, Joan Jacobs. "Zenanas and Girlless Villages: The Ethnology of American Evangelical Women, 1870–1910." *Journal of American History* 69, no. 2 (September 1982): 347–71.

Buhle, Mary Jo. *Women and American Socialism.* Urbana: University of Illinois Press, 1981.

Burch, Guy. "Headed for the Last Census?," pts. 1 and 2. *Journal of Heredity*
vol. 28, no. 6 (June 1937): 203–12; no. 7 (July 1937): 241–54.
Burnham, John. "Medical Inspection of Prostitutes in America in the Nineteenth
Century." *Bulletin of the History of Medicine* 45, no. 3 (1971): 203–18.
———. "The Progressive Era Revolution in American Attitudes toward Sex."
Journal of American History 59, no. 4 (1973): 885–908.
Burton, Antoinette. "The White Woman's Burden: British Feminists and 'The In-
dian Woman,' 1865–1915." In *Western Women and Imperialism: Complic-
ity and Resistance*, edited by Nupur Chaudhuri and Margaret Strobel. Bloom-
ington: Indiana University Press, 1992.
Butler, Anne M. *Daughters of Joy, Sisters of Misery: Prostitutes in the American
West, 1865–1890*. Urbana: University of Illinois Press, 1985.
Butler, Fred O., and Clarence J. Gamble. "Sterilization in a California School for
the Mentally Deficient." *American Journal of Mental Deficiency* 51, no. 4
(1947): 745–47.
Campomanes, Oscar. "1898 and the Nature of the New Empire." *Radical His-
tory Review* 73, no. 1 (1998): 1–14.
Campos, Ricardo, and Juan Flores. "National Culture and Migration: Perspectives
from the Puerto Rican Working Class." In *Divided Borders: Essays on Puerto
Rican Identity*, edited by Juan Flores. Houston: Arte Público Press, 1993.
Carr, Raymond. *Puerto Rico: A Colonial Experiment*. New York: Vintage, 1984.
Caulfield, Sueann. "The Birth of Mangue: Race, Nation, and the Politics of Prostitution in Rio de Janeiro, 1850–1942." In *Sex and Sexuality in Latin America*, edited by Daniel Balderston and Donna Guy. New York: New York University Press, 1997.
Chatterjee, Ratnabali. "The Indian Prostitute as a Colonial Subject: Bengal,
1864–1883." *Canadian Women's Studies / Les Cahiers de la Femme* 13, no. 1
(1992): 51–55.
Chavez, Linda. *Out of the Barrio: Toward a New Politics of Hispanic Assimilation*. New York: Basic Books, 1991.
Cheng Hirata, Lucie. "Free, Endentured, Enslaved: Chinese Prostitutes in Nineteenth Century America." *Signs* 5 (autumn 1979): 3–29.
Chow, Rey. "Where Have All the Natives Gone?" In *Writing Diaspora: Tactics
of Intervention in Contemporary Cultural Studies*. Bloomington: Indiana Uni-
versity Press, 1993.
Clark, Truman. *Puerto Rico and the United States, 1917–33*. Pittsburgh: Uni-
versity of Pittsburgh Press, 1975.
Clark, Victor. *Porto Rico and Its Problems*. New York: Brookings Institute,
1930.
Clarke, Adele. "Controversy and the Development of Reproductive Sciences."
Social Problems 37, no. 1 (1990): 18–37.
———. *Disciplining Reproduction: Modernity, American Life Sciences, and
"The Problems of Sex."* Berkeley: University of California Press, 1998.
———. "Emergence of the Reproductive Research Enterprise: A Sociology of
Biological, Medical, and Agricultural Science in the United States." Ph.D.
diss., University of California, San Francisco, 1985.
Cofresí, Emilio. *Realidad poblacional de Puerto Rico*. San Juan: Universidad de
Puerto Rico, 1951.

Colón, Jesus. *The Puerto Rican in New York and Other Sketches.* New York: Arno, 1975.

Commission of Inquiry on Civil Rights in Puerto Rico. *Report of the Commission of Inquiry on Civil Rights in Puerto Rico, May 22, 1937.* New York: American Civil Liberties Union, 1937.

Community Council of Greater New York. Research Bureau. *Population of Puerto Rican Birth or Parentage, New York City, 1950: Data for Boroughs, Health Areas, and Census Tracts.* New York: Health and Welfare Council of New York City, 1950.

Connelly, Mark. *The Response to Prostitution in the Progressive Era.* Chapel Hill: University of North Carolina Press, 1980.

Cook, Hale, Clarence Gamble, and Adaline P. Satterthwaite. "Oral Contraception with Norethynodrel." *American Journal of Obstetrics and Gynecology* 82, no. 2 (August 1961): 437–45.

Cordasco, Francesco. "Another Face of Poverty." *Phylon* 29, no. 1 (spring 1968): 88–92.

———. Foreword to *Puerto Ricans on the United States Mainland: A Bibliography of Reports, Texts, Critical Studies, and Related Materials,* by Francesco Cordasco, with Eugene Bucchioni and Diego Castellanos. Totowa, N.Y.: Rowman and Littlefield, 1972.

Cripps, L. L. *Human Rights in a United States Colony.* Cambridge, Mass.: Schenkman, 1982.

Crist, Raymond. "Sugar Cane and Coffee in Puerto Rico: The Pauperization of the Jíbaro, Land Monopoly, and Monoculture." *American Journal of Sociology and Economics* 7 (January–July 1948): 181–82.

Curtin, Philip. *Death by Migration: Europe's Encounter with the Tropical World in the Nineteenth Century.* Cambridge: Cambridge University Press, 1989.

———. "The White Man's Grave: Image and Reality, 1780–1850." *Journal of British Studies* 1, no. 1 (1961): 94–110.

Dávila, Ana Luisa. "Esterilización y práctica anticonceptiva en Puerto Rico, 1982." *Puerto Rico Health Sciences Journal* 9, no. 1 (April 1990): 61–67.

Davin, Anna. "Imperialism and Motherhood." In *Tensions of Empire: Colonial Cultures in a Bourgeois World,* edited by Ann Stoler and Frederick Cooper. Berkeley: University of California Press, 1997.

Davis, Angela. *Women, Race, and Class.* New York: Random House, 1983.

Davis, Kingsley. "Puerto Rico: A Crowded Island." *Annals of the American Academy of Political and Social Science* 285 (January 1953): 116–22.

Degler, Carl. *In Search of Human Nature: The Decline and Revival of Darwinism in American Social Thought.* New York: Oxford University Press, 1991.

Dennie, Charles Clayton. *A History of Syphilis.* Springfield (Illinois), 1962.

Dery, Luis. "Prostitution in Colonial Manila." *Philippine Studies* 39, no. 4 (1991): 475–89.

di Leonardo, Michaela. *Exotics at Home: Anthropologies, Others, American Modernity.* Chicago: University of Illinois Press, 1998.

Dible, J. Henry. *Recent Advances in Bacteriology and the Study of the Infections.* 2d ed. Philadelphia: P. Blakiston's Son & Co., 1932.

Dietz, James. *Economic History of Puerto Rico: Institutional Change and Capitalist Development.* Princeton, N.J.: Princeton University Press, 1986.

Diffie, Justine, and Bailey Diffie. *Porto Rico: A Broken Pledge.* New York: Vanguard Press, 1931.

Djerassi, Carl. *The Pill, Pygmy Chimps, and Degas' Horse.* New York: Basic Books, 1992.

Duggan, Lisa. *Sapphic Slashers: Sex, Violence, and American Modernity.* Durham, N.C.: Duke University Press, 2000.

Editorial. *Journal of the American Medical Association* 177, no. 2 (July 1961): 129.

Ehrlich, Paul. "Closing Notes to the Experimental Chemotherapy of Spirilloses." In *The Collected Papers of Paul Ehrlich,* vol. 2, *Chemotherapy,* translated by F. Himmelweit, Martha Marquardt, and Sir Henry Dale. London: Pergamon Press, 1960.

Elbert, Sarah, and Sander Kelman. "Reply to Shorter on *Woman's Body, Woman's Right.*" *Journal of Social History* 12, no. 1 (fall 1978): 173–77.

Enloe, Cynthia. *Bananas, Beaches, and Bases: Making Feminist Sense of International Politics.* Berkeley: University of California Press, 1990.

Escobar, Arturo. *Encountering Development: The Making and Unmaking of the Third World.* Princeton, N.J.: Princeton University Press, 1995.

Espada, Martín. "City of Coughing and Dead Radiators." In *City of Coughing and Dead Radiators: Poems.* New York: Norton, 1993.

Ettling, John. *The Germ of Laziness: Rockefeller Philanthropy and Public Health in the New South.* Cambridge, Mass.: Harvard University Press, 1981.

Exner, M. J. "Prostitution in its Relation to the Army on the Mexican Border." *Social Hygiene* 3, no. 2 (April 1917): 220.

Fadiman, Ann. *The Spirit Catches You and You Fall Down: A Hmong Child, Her American Doctors, and the Collision of Two Cultures.* New York: Farrar, Strauss, and Giroux, 1997.

Faulkner, William. *Requiem for a Nun.* New York: Vintage, 1975.

Fausto-Sterling, Anne. *Myths of Gender: Biological Theories of Women and Men.* New York: Basic Books, 1992.

———. *Sexing the Body: Gender Politics and the Construction of Sexuality.* New York: Basic Books, 2000.

Fee, Elizabeth, and Michael Wallace. "The History and Politics of Birth Control." *Feminist Studies* 5, no. 1 (spring 1979): 201–15.

Feldman, Egal. "Prostitution, the Alien Woman, and the Progressive Imagination, 1910–1915." *American Quarterly* 19 (June 1967): 192–206.

Fergusen, James. *The Anti-Politics Machine: "Development," Depoliticization, and Bureaucratic Power in Lesotho.* Minneapolis: University of Minnesota Press, 1994.

Fernós Isern, Antonio. "The Development of the Public Health Organization of Porto Rico." *Porto Rico Health Review* 2, no. 6 (February 1926): 3–10.

———. "The White—and the Tropics." *Porto Rico Health Review* 2, no. 1 (July, 1926): 6–7.

Findlay, Eileen. "Domination, Decency, and Desire: The Politics of Sexuality in Ponce, Puerto Rico, 1870–1920." Ph.D. diss., University of Wisconsin at Madison, 1995.

———. *Imposing Decency: The Politics of Sexuality and Race in Puerto Rico, 1870–1920.* Durham, N.C.: Duke University Press, 1999.

———. "Love in the Tropics: Marriage, Divorce, and the Construction of

Benevolent Colonialism in Puerto Rico." In *Close Encounters of Empire: Writing the Cultural History of U.S.–Latin American Relations,* edited by G. M. Joseph, Catherine LeGrand, and Ricardo Donato Salvatore. London: Duke University Press, 1998.

Flores, Juan. *Divided Borders: Essays on Puerto Rican Identity.* Houston: Arte Público Press, 1993.

Flores Ramos, José. "Virgins, Whores, and Martyrs: Prostitution in the Colony, 1898–1917." In *Puerto Rican Women's History: New Perspectives,* edited by Félix Matos Rodríguez and Linda Delgado, 83–104. Armonk, N.Y.: M. E. Sharpe, 1998.

Foucault, Michel. *Discipline and Punish: The Birth of the Prison.* Translated by Alan Sheridan. New York: Pantheon, 1977.

———. "Govermentalities." In *The Foucault Effect: Studies in Governmentality,* edited by Graham Burchell, Colin Gordon, and Peter Miller. London: Harvester Wheatsheaf, 1991.

Fox, Howard. "A Case of Annular Popular Syphilis in a Negress." *Journal of the American Medical Association* 60, no. 14 (10 May 1913): 1420–21.

Frazier, E. Franklin. *The Negro Family in the United States.* Chicago: University of Chicago Press, 1939.

Gafafer, William. "Diseases of the Upper Respiratory Tract (Common Cold) in Jews and Non-Jews." *Human Biology* 3, no. 3 (September 1931): 429–33.

Galbraith, J. K., and Carolyn Shaw Solo. "Puerto Rican Lessons in Economic Development." *Annals of the American Academy of Political Science* 285 (January 1953): 55–59.

Gamble, Clarence. "The College Birthrate." *Journal of Heredity* 38, no. 11 (November 1947): 355.

———. "The Deficit in the Birthrate of College Graduates." *Human Fertility* 11, no. 4 (June 1946): 41–47.

———. "Improved Test of Spermicidal Activity Without Dilution or Mixing": Report to Council on Pharmacy and Chemistry. *Journal of the American Medical Association* 152, no. 11 (July 1953): 1037–41.

———. "A Note on the Clinical Significance of Paraformaldehyde in Contraceptive Foam Powders." *Journal of Contraception* 3, no. 13 (1938): 15–25.

———. "Preventive Sterilization in 1948." *Journal of the American Medical Association* 141, no. 11 (12 November 1949): 773.

———. "State Sterilization Programs for the Prophylactic Control of Mental Disease and Mental Deficiency." *American Journal of Psychiatry* 102, no. 3 (1945): 289–93.

———. "Sterilization of the Mentally Deficient under State Laws." *American Journal of Mental Deficiency* 51, no. 2 (1946): 164–69.

Gamble, Clarence, and G. W. Beebe. "The Clinical Effectiveness of Lactic Acid Jelly as a Contraceptive." *American Journal of the Medical Sciences* 194, no. 1 (July 1937): 79–84.

Gamble, Clarence, and Betty U. Kibbe. "College Study Reports." *Population Bulletin* 10, no. 4 (1954): 41–56.

Gamble, Clarence, Leo Shedlovsky, and G. W. Beebe. "Desirable Properties and Important Ingredients of Contraceptive Jellies." *Journal of Contraception* 1, no. 1 (1936): 203–8.

García, Ana María. *La operación*. Produced and directed by Latin American Film Project. Skylight Pictures, 1982.

Garebian, Keith. *The Making of West Side Story*. Buffalo, N.Y.: Mosaic Press, 1995.

Garon, Sheldon. "The World's Oldest Debate: Prostitution and the State in Imperial Japan." *American Historical Review* 98, no. 3 (1993): 710–32.

Genovese, Elizabeth Fox. "Comment on the Reviews of *Woman's Body, Woman's Right*." *Signs* 4, no. 4 (summer 1979): 804–8.

Genovese, Eugene. *Roll, Jordan, Roll: The World the Slaves Made*. New York: Pantheon, 1974.

Gilman, Sander. "Plague in Germany, 1939/1989: Cultural Images of Race, Space, and Disease." In *Nationalisms and Sexualities*, edited by Andrew Parker, Mary Russo, Doris Summer, and Patricia Yeager, 175–200. New York: Routledge, 1992.

Glazer, Nathan. Foreword to *The Negro Family in the United States*, revised and abridged by E. Franklin Frazier, vii–xvii. Chicago: University of Chicago Press, 1966.

———. "From Socialism to Sociology." In *Authors of Their Own Lives: Intellectual Autobiographies by Twenty American Sociologists*, edited by Bennet Berger, 190–209. Berkeley: University of California Press, 1990.

Glazer, Nathan, and Daniel Patrick Moynihan. *Beyond the Melting Pot: The Negroes, Puerto Ricans, Jews, Italians, and Irish of New York City*. Cambridge, Mass.: MIT Press, 1963.

González, José Luis. *Puerto Rico: The Four-Storeyed Country*. Translated by Gerald Guinness. New York: Markus Wiener Publishing, 1993. Originally published as *El país de cuatro pisos*, 4th ed. (Río Piedras, P.R.: Ediciones Huracán, 1984).

González, Rosa. *Los hechos desconocidos*. San Juan: Venezuela, 1929.

Goodman, Herman. "The Antivenereal Disease Campaign in Panama." *Journal of Social Hygiene* 9 (March 1923): 160–67.

———. "Genital Defects and Venereal Diseases among the Porto Rican Draft Troops." *Journal of the American Medical Association* 72, no. 13 (29 March 1919): 907–13.

———. "The Intensive Treatment of Women with Neodiarsenol: Procedure and Result at the Hospital Jail of San Juan, Porto Rico." *American Journal of Syphilis* 3, no. 4 (1919): 661–64.

———. "The Porto Rican Experiment." *Social Hygiene* 5, no. 2 (April 1919): 185–92.

———. "The Prostitute in Jail: An Opportunity for Public Health Work that Gives Results." *Medical Record* 97 (20 March 1920): 483–86.

———. "Prostitution and Community Syphilis." *American Journal of Public Health* 9, no. 9 (1919): 515–20.

———. "Skin Diseases among the Porto Rican Troops." *New Orleans Medical and Surgical Journal* 72 (December 1919): 343–46.

———."Ulcerating Granuloma of the Pudenda: A Review of the Literature with a Bibliography and Some Observation of the Disease as Seen in Porto Rico." *Archives of Dermatology and Syphilis* 1, n.s., 1 (1920): 151–69.

Goodsell, Charles. *Administration of a Revolution: Executive Reform in Puerto Rico under Governor Tugwell, 1941–1946.* Cambridge, Mass.: Harvard University Press, 1965.

Gordon, Avery. *Ghostly Matters: Haunting and the Sociological Imagination.* Minneapolis: University of Minnesota Press, 1996.

Gordon, Linda. *Woman's Body, Woman's Right.* 1976. Reprint, New York: Penguin, 1990.

Gould, Stephen J. *The Mismeasure of Man.* 1981. Reprint, New York: Norton, 1996.

Gourevitch, Philip. *We Wish to Inform You That Tomorrow We Will Be Killed with Our Families: Stories From Rwanda.* New York: Farrar, Straus and Giroux, 1998.

Grosfoguel, Ramón. "The Divorce of Nationalist Discourses from the Puerto Rican People." In *Puerto Rico Jam: Rethinking Colonialism and Nationalism,* edited by Frances Negrón-Muntaner and Ramón Grosfoguel. Minneapolis: University of Minnesota Press, 1997.

Gunn, A. D. G. *Oral Contraception in Perspective: Thirty Years of Clinical Experience with the Pill.* Carnforth, U.K.: Parthenon, 1987.

Guttmacher, Alan. "The Place of Sterilization." In *Population Crisis: Implications and Plans for Action,* edited by Larry Ng. Bloomington: Indiana University Press, 1965.

Guy, Donna. *Sex and Danger in Buenos Aires: Prostitution, Family, and Nation in Argentina.* Lincoln: University of Nebraska Press, 1991.

Guzmán Rodríguez, Manuel. "El control de la natalidad y su desarrollo en Puerto Rico." *Boletín de la Asociación Médica de Puerto Rico* 29, no. 7 (July 1937): 345–48.

Hacking, Ian. *Representing and Intervening: Introductory Topics in the Philosophy of Natural Science.* New York: Cambridge University Press, 1983.

Hall, Stuart. *Policing the Crisis: Mugging, the State, and Law and Order.* London: Macmillan, 1978.

Hammonds, Evelynn Maxine. *Childhood's Deadly Scourge.* Baltimore: Johns Hopkins University Press, 1999.

Handlin, Oscar. *The Newcomers: Negroes and Puerto Ricans in a Changing Metropolis.* Cambridge, Mass.: Harvard University Press, 1959.

Hansen, Millard. "Training and Research in Puerto Rico." *Annals of the American Academy of Political and Social Science* 285 (January 1953): 110–15.

Hanson, Earl Parker. *Transformation: The Story of Modern Puerto Rico.* New York: Simon and Schuster, 1955.

Haraway, Donna. "A Manifesto for Cyborgs: Science, Technology, and Socialist-Feminism in the 1980s." *Socialist Review* 15, no. 80 (1985): 65–108.

———. *Modest_Witness@Second_Millenium. FemaleMan©_Meets_OncoMouse™: Feminism and Technoscience.* New York: Routledge, 1997.

———. *Primate Vision: Gender, Race, and Nature in the World of Modern Science.* New York: Routledge, 1989.

Harrington, Michael. Introduction to *A Welfare Mother,* by Susan Sheehan. Boston: Houghton Mifflin, 1976.

Hartmann, Betsy. *Reproductive Rights and Wrongs: The Global Politics of Population Control.* Rev. ed. Boston : South End Press, 1995.

Hatt, Paul. *Backgrounds of Human Fertility in Puerto Rico.* Princeton, N.J.: Princeton University Press, 1952.

Hazen, H. H. "Syphilis in the American Negro." *Journal of the American Medical Association* 63, no. 6 (8 August 1914): 463–66.

Health Department of the Panama Canal Zone. "Report." *Social Hygiene* 5, no. 2 (April 1919): 259–64.

Henderson, Peta Murray. "Population Policy, Social Structure, and the Health System of Puerto Rico: The Case of Female Sterilization." Ph.D. diss., University of Connecticut, 1976.

Hershatter, Gail. *Dangerous Pleasures: Prostitution and Modernity in Twentieth-Century Shanghai.* Berkeley: University of California Press, 1997.

Herzog, Elizabeth. "The Culture of Poverty." *Social Science Review* 37, no. 4 (December 1963): 389–402.

Hildreth, Edith Wardell. *Between Bay and Ocean.* New York: Vantage Press, 1960.

Hill, Patricia. *The World Their Household: The American Women's Foreign Mission Movement and Cultural Transformation.* Ann Arbor: University of Michigan Press, 1984.

Hill, Reuben, J. Mayone Stycos, and Kurt W. Back. *The Family and Population Control.* Chapel Hill: University of North Carolina Press, 1959.

Horowitz, Irving Louis. "Meurte en Vida." *Transaction* 4 (March 1967): 50–52.

Huigens, Marcos, Martin Berntsen, and José Lanauze Rolón. *El mal de los muchos hijos: Polémica sobre el neo-Maltusianismo.* Ponce (P.R.), 1926.

Hunt, Nancy Rose. *A Colonial Lexicon of Birth Ritual, Medicalization, and Mobility in the Congo.* Durham, N.C.: Duke University Press, 1999.

——— "Le bebé en brousse: European Women, African Birth Spacing, and Colonial Intervention in Breast Feeding in the Belgian Congo." In *Tensions of Empire: Colonial Cultures in a Bourgeois World,* edited by Ann Stoler and Frederick Cooper. Berkeley: University of California Press, 1997.

Huxley, Julian. "Too Many People." In *Our Crowded Planet,* edited by Osborn Fairfield. Garden City, N.Y.: Doubleday, 1962.

Iglesias, César Andreu. *Los derrotados.* Mexico City: Los Presentes, 1956.

"The Infinitely Small." *Journal of Heredity* 28, no. 6 (June 1937): 219–20.

Irvine-Rivera, Edith Mary. *Adventures for a Better World.* Philadelphia: Dorrance, 1968.

James, Winton. *Holding Aloft the Banner of Ethiopia: Caribbean Radicalism in Early Twentieth-Century America.* New York: Verso, 1998.

Jeater, Diana. *Marriage, Perversion, and Power: The Construction of Moral Discourse in Southern Rhodesia, 1894–1930.* Oxford: Clarendon Press, 1993.

Jenkinson, Charles. "Vera Cruz: What American Occupation Has Meant to a Mexican Community." *The Survey* 33 (7 November 1914): 138.

Jiménez-Muñoz, Gladys. "Literacy, Class, and Sexuality in the Debate on Women's Suffrage in Puerto Rico during the 1920s." In *Puerto Rican Women's History: New Perspectives,* edited by Félix Matos Rodríguez and Linda Delgado. Armonk, N.Y.: M. E. Sharpe, 1998.

Johnson, John. J. *Latin America in Caricature.* Austin: University of Texas Press, 1980.

Jones, James. *Bad Blood: The Tuskegee Syphilis Experiment*. New York: Macmillan, 1993.

Kaplan, Amy. "Left Alone with America." In *Cultures of United States Imperialism*, edited by Amy Kaplan and Donald E. Pease. Durham, N.C.: Duke University Press, 1993.

Katz, Michael. *The "Underclass" Debate: Views from History*. Princeton, N.J.: Princeton University Press, 1993.

Kaus, Mickey. *The End of Equality*. New York: Basic Books, 1992.

Kelley, Robin D. G. *Yo' Mama's Disfunktional!* Boston: Beacon Press, 1997.

Kennan, George F. *American Diplomacy, 1900–1950*. Chicago: University of Chicago Press, 1984.

Kennedy, David. Review of *Woman's Bodies, Woman's Right*, by Linda Gordon. *Journal of American History* 64, no. 3 (December 1977): 823–24.

Kevles, Daniel. *In the Name of Eugenics*. Berkeley: University of California Press, 1985.

King, Marguerite. "Cultural Aspects of Birth Control in Puerto Rico." *Human Biology* 20, no. 1 (February 1948): 520–28.

Krauss, Elissa. *Hospital Survey on Sterilization Policies*. ACLU Report, March 1975. New York: American Civil Liberties Union, 1975.

Kuzrok, Rafael. "The Prospects for Hormonal Sterilization." *Journal of Contraception* 2, no. 2 (February 1937): 27–29.

Lane, Ann J. "The Politics of Birth Control." *Marxist Perspectives* 7 (fall 1979): 160–69.

Lapp, Michael. "Puerto Rico as Social Laboratory." *Social Science History* 19 (summer 1995): 169–99.

Larson, Edward. *Sex, Race, and Science: Eugenics in the Deep South*. Baltimore: Johns Hopkins University Press, 1995.

Latour, Bruno. *The Pasteurization of France*. Cambridge, Mass.: Harvard University Press, 1988.

Leavitt, Judith Walzer. *Typhoid Mary: Captive to the Public's Health*. Boston: Beacon Press, 1996.

Ledbetter, Rosanna. *A History of the Malthusian League, 1977–1927*. Columbus: Ohio State University Press, 1976.

Lemons, J. Stanley. Review of *Woman's Bodies, Woman's Right*, by Linda Gordon. *American Historical Review* 82, no. 4 (October 1977): 1095.

Levine, Philippa. "Venereal Disease, Prostitution, and the Politics of Empire: The Case of British India." *Journal of the History of Sexuality* 4, no. 4 (April 1994): 579–602.

Lewis, Gordon. *Puerto Rico: Freedom and Power in the Caribbean*. New York: Monthly Review Press, 1963.

Lewis, Oscar. *Children of Sanchez: Autobiography of a Mexican Family*. New York: Random House, 1961.

———. *La Vida: A Puerto Rican Family in the Culture of Poverty—San Juan and New York*. New York: Random House, 1965.

———. *A Study of Slum Culture: Backgrounds for* La Vida. New York: Random House, 1968.

Lienhard, Martin. *La voz y su huella: Escritura y conflicto étnico-social en América Latina, 1492–1988*. Hanover, N.H.: Ediciones del Norte, 1991.

Littlewood, Thomas. *The Politics of Population Control.* Notre Dame, Ind.: University of Notre Dame Press, 1977.

López, Adalberto, ed. *The Puerto Ricans: Their History, Culture, and Society.* Cambridge Mass.: Schenkman Publishing Co., 1980.

López, Iris. "Agency and Constraint: Sterilization and Reproductive Freedom among Puerto Rican Women in New York City." *Urban Anthropology* 22, no. 3–4 (fall 1993): 299–323.

Lubiano, Wahneema. "Black Ladies, Welfare Queens, and State Minstrels: Ideological War by Narrative Means." In *Race-ing Justice, En-gendering Power,* edited by Toni Morrison, 323–63. New York: Pantheon, 1992.

———. "Black Nationalism and Black Common Sense: Policing Ourselves and Others." In *The House that Race Built: Black Americans, U.S. Terrain,* edited by Wahneema Lubiana. New York: Pantheon, 1997.

Lunbeck, Elizabeth. *The Psychiatric Persuasion.* Princeton, N.J.: Princeton University Press, 1994.

MacKenzie, Donald. *Statistics in Britain, 1865–1930: The Social Construction of Scientific Knowledge.* Edinburgh: Edinburgh University Press, 1981.

Maisel, Albert Q. *The Hormone Quest.* New York: Random House, 1965.

Makepeace, A. W., George L. Weinstein, and Maurice H. Friedman. "The Effect of Progestin and Progesterone on Ovulation in the Rabbit." *American Journal of Physiology* 119, no. 3 (July 1937): 512–16.

Maldonado-Denis, Manuel. "Oscar Lewis: *La vida* y la enajenación." *Revista de Ciencias Sociales* 11, no. 2 (1967): 253–59.

Mamdani, Mahmood. *The Myth of Population Control: Family, Caste, and Class in an Indian Village.* New York: Monthly Review Press, 1973.

Manderson, Lenore. "Colonial Desires: Sexuality, Race, and Gender in British Malaya." *Journal of the History of Sexuality* 7, no. 3 (1997): 372–88.

———. *Sickness and the State: Health and Illness in Colonial Malaya, 1870–1940.* New York: Cambridge University Press, 1996.

Marchand, Julia Carmen. "Celestina Zalduondo: Su obra pro bienestar de la familia." Paper presented at the Segundo Seminario de Planificación de la Familia para Líderes Latinoamericanos, New York, October 1963.

Marker, Russell, and E. Wald Rohrman. "Conversion of Sarsapogenin to Pregnanediol-3(α),20(α)." *Journal of the American Chemical Society* 61, no. 12 (December 1939): 3592.

Marker, Russell, E. Wald Rohrman, Takeo Tsukamoto, and D. L. Turner. "Diosgenin." *Journal of the American Chemical Society* 62, no. 9 (September 1940): 2525.

Marks, Lara. "'A Cage of Ovulating Females': The History of the Early Oral Contraceptive Pill Clinical Trials, 1950–59." In *Molecularizing Biology and Medicine: New Practices and Alliances, 1910s–1970s,* edited by Soraya de Chadarevian and Harmke Kamminga. Amsterdam: Harwood Academic Publishers, 1998.

Marquardt, Martha. *Paul Ehrlich.* New York: Henry Schuman, 1951.

Marqués, René. "El puertorriqueño dócil: Literatura y realidad psicológica." In *Ensayos.* 1960. Reprint, Spain: Editorial Antillana, 1972.

Martin, Emily. *The Women in the Body: A Cultural Analysis of Reproduction.* Boston: Beacon Press, 1987.

Mass, Bonnie. *Population Target: The Political Economy of Population Control in Latin America.* Toronto: Women's Educational Press, 1977.

Matos Rodríguez, Félix. "Women's History in Puerto Rican Historiography: The Last Thirty Years." In *Puerto Rican Women's History,* edited by Félix Matos Rodríguez and Linda C. Delgado. Armonk, N.Y.: M. E. Sharpe, 1998.

McCann, Carole. *Birth Control in the United States, 1917–1945.* Ithaca, N.Y.: Cornell University Press, 1994.

McCreery, David J. "'This Life of Misery and Shame': Female Prostitution in Guatemala City, 1880–1920." *Journal of Latin American Studies* 18, no. 2 (November 1986): 333–53.

McLaughlin, Loretta. *The Pill, John Rock, and the Church.* New York: Little, Brown, 1982.

McNeil, H. L. "Syphilis in the Southern Negro." *Journal of the American Medical Association* 67, no. 14 (30 September 1916): 1001–1004.

Meckel, Richard. *Save the Babies: American Public Health Reform and the Prevention of Infant Mortality, 1850–1929.* Baltimore: Johns Hopkins University Press, 1990.

Milbank Memorial Fund. *International Approaches to Problems of Underdeveloped Areas.* New York: Milbank, 1948.

Mills, Wright, Clarence Senior, and Ruth Kohn Goldsen. *The Puerto Rican Journey: New York's Newest Migrants.* New York: Russell and Russell, 1950.

Mintz, Morton. *"The Pill": An Alarming Report.* Boston: Beacon Press, 1970.

Mintz, Sidney. "Cañamelar: The Subculture of a Rural Sugar Plantation Proletariat." In *The People of Puerto Rico: A Study in Social Anthropology,* edited by Julian H. Steward et al. Chicago: University of Illinois Press, 1956.

Mitchell, Harold. "A Study of Factors Associated with the Growth and Nutrition of Porto Rican Children." *Human Biology* 3, no. 4 (December 1931): 469–508.

Mohanty, Chandra. "Under Western Eyes." In *Third World Women and the Politics of Feminism,* edited by Chandra Mohanty, Ann Russo, and Lourdes Torres, 51–80. Bloomington: Indiana University Press, 1991.

Monk, Jan. "Social Change and Sexual Differences in Puerto Rican Rural Migration." In *Papers in Latin American Geography in Honor of Lucia G. Harrison,* vol. 1. Muncie, Ind.: Conference of Latin Americanist Geographers, 1981.

Monserrat, Joseph. "Puerto Rican Migration: The Impact on Future Relations." In *The Puerto Ricans, 1493–1973: A Chronology and Fact Book,* edited by Francesco Cordasco. Dobbs Ferry, N.Y.: Oceana Publications, 1973.

Morales Otero, P., et al. "Health and Socioeconomic Conditions on a Sugar Cane Plantation." *Puerto Rico Journal of Public Health and Tropical Medicine* 12, no. 4 (June 1937): 405–80.

Moynihan, Daniel Patrick. *Politics of the Guaranteed Income.* New York: Vintage, 1973.

———. "The President and the Negro: The Moment Lost." *Commentary* 43, no. 2 (February 1967): 31–45.

Muñoz Marín, Luis. "Development Through Democracy." *Annals of the American Academy of Political and Social Science* 285 (January 1953): 1–8.

————. *Memorias.* San Juan: Universidad Interamericana de Puerto Rico, 1982.

Murnane, Mary, and Kay Daniels. "Prostitutes as 'Purveyors of Disease': Venereal Disease Legislation in Tasmania, 1868–1945." *Hecate* 5 (1979): 5–21.

Murray, Charles A. *Losing Ground: American Social Policy, 1950–1980.* New York: Basic Books, 1984.

Murray, Charles A., and Richard Herrnstein. *The Bell Curve.* New York: Basic Books, 1992.

Murray, Robert. "The Ethical and Moral Values of Black Americans and Population Policy." In *Population Policy and Ethics,* edited by Robert Veatch, 197–210. New York: Irvington, 1977.

Murrell, Thomas. "Syphilis and the American Negro." *Journal of the American Medical Association* 54, no. 11 (12 March 1910): 846–47.

Nader, Laura. "Up the Anthropologist—Perspectives Gained from Studying Up." In *Reinventing Anthropology,* edited by Dell Hymes, 284–311. New York: Pantheon, 1972.

Nash, June, and Helen Safa. *Women and Change in Latin America.* New York: Bergin and Garvey, 1984.

Negrón-Muntaner, Frances, and Ramón Grosfoguel, eds. *Puerto Rico Jam: Rethinking Colonialism and Nationalism.* Minneapolis: University of Minnesota Press, 1997.

Nelson, Jennifer A. "Abortions under Community Control": Feminism, Nationalism, and the Politics of Reproduction among New York City's Young Lords." *Journal of Women's History* 13, no. 1 (2001): 157–80.

New York (N.Y.) Board of Education. Puerto Rican Study. *Teaching Children of Puerto Rican Background in New York City Schools,* by J. Cayce Morrison, director. New York: City Board of Education, 1953.

New York University. Graduate School of Public Administration and Social Service. *The Impact of Puerto Rican Migration on Governmental Services in New York City,* by Martin B. Dworkis, project director and editor. New York: New York University Press, 1957.

Notestein, Frank. "Reminiscences: The Role of Foundations, the Population Association America, Princeton University, and the United Nations in Fostering American Interest in Population Problems." *Milbank Memorial Fund Quarterly* 26, no. 3 (July 1948): 245–48.

————. "Some Implications of Current Demographic Trends For Birth Control and Eugenics." *Journal of Heredity* 30, no. 3 (March 1939): 121–26.

Ong, Aihwa. *Flexible Citizenship: The Cultural Logics of Transnationality.* London: Duke University Press, 1999.

————. "The Gender and Labor Politics of Postmodernity." In *The Politics of Culture in the Shadow of Capital,* edited by L. Lowe and D. Lloyd. Durham, N.C.: Duke University Press, 1997.

Orenstein, A. J. "Sanitary Inspection of the Canal Zone." *Public Health Papers and Reports* 28 (1913): 65–76.

Organization for Economic Cooperation and Development. *External Debt Statistics.* Paris: Organization for Economic Cooperation and Development, 1998.

Orleck, Annelise. *Common Sense and a Little Fire: Women and Working-Class Politics in the United States.* Chapel Hill: University of North Carolina Press, 1995.

Ortiz, Pedro. "The Tropics from the Public Health Standpoint." *Porto Rico Health Review* 11, no. 12 (June 1927): 3–13.

Osborn, Fairfield. *Our Crowded Planet.* Garden City, N.Y.: Doubleday, 1962.

Ostolaza Bey, Margarita. *Política sexual en Puerto Rico.* Río Piedras, P.R.: Ediciones Huracán, 1989.

Oudshoorn, Nelly. *Beyond the Natural Body: An Archaeology of Sex Hormones.* New York: Routledge, 1994.

Packard, Randall. "The 'Healthy Reserve' and the 'Dressed Native': Discourses on Black Health and the Language of Legitimation in South Africa." *American Ethnologist* 16, no. 4 (1989): 686–703.

Padilla, Elena. *Up from Puerto Rico.* New York: Columbia University Press, 1958.

Pa'lante, siempre pa'lante!: The Young Lords. Produced and directed by Iris Morales. Columbia University Station, New York. 1996.

Paniagua, Manuel, Mathew Tayback, José L. Janer, and José L. Vásquez. "Medical and Psychological Sequelae of Surgical Sterilization." *American Journal of Obstetrics and Gynecology* 90, no. 4 (15 October 1964): 421–30.

Paniagua, Manuel, Henry Vaillant, and Clarence Gamble. "Field Trial of a Contraceptive Foam in Puerto Rico." *Journal of the American Medical Association* 177, no. 2 (15 July 1961): 125–29.

Park, Robert. *Introduction to the Science of Sociology.* Chicago: University of Chicago Press, 1921.

Pascoe, Peggy. "Miscegenation Law, Court Cases, and Ideologies of 'Race' in Twentieth-Century America." *Journal of American History* 83, no. 1 (June 1996): 44–69.

———. *Relations of Rescue: The Search for Female Moral Authority in the American West, 1874–1939.* New York: Oxford University Press, 1990.

Paul, Diane. *Controlling Heredity: 1865 to the Present.* Atlantic Highlands, N.J.: Humanities Press, 1995.

Pearl, Raymond. "Contraception and Fertility in 2,000 Women." *Human Biology* 3, no. 3 (September 1931): 363–407.

———. "Sidelights on the Population Problem in Japan." *Human Biology* 3, no. 3 (September 1931): 408–20.

Pendell, Elmer. *Population on the Loose.* N.Y.: W. Funk, 1956.

Perez, Louis. "The Meaning of the *Maine:* Causation and the Historiography of the Spanish-American War." *Pacific Historical Review* 58, no. 3 (August 1989): 293–322.

Perloff, Harvey. *Puerto Rico's Economic Future: A Study in Planned Development.* Chicago: University of Chicago Press, 1950.

Pernick, Martin. *The Black Stork: Eugenics and the Death of Defective Babies in American Medicine and Motion Pictures since 1915.* New York: Oxford University Press, 1996.

Perone, Nicola. "The Progestins." In *Pharmacology of Contraceptive Steroids,* edited by Joseph Goldzieher. New York: Raven Press, 1994.

Petersen, William. *The Politics of Population*. Garden City, N.Y.: Doubleday, 1964.

Phillips, Henry Albert. *White Elephants in the Caribbean: A Magic Journey Through All the West Indies*. New York: Robert M. McBride, 1936.

Picó, Fernando. *Amargo café*. Río Piedras, P.R.: Ediciones Huracán, 1993.

———. *La guerra despues de la guerra 1898*. Río Piedras, P.R.: Ediciones Huracán, 1987.

———. *Historia general de Puerto Rico*. Río Piedras, P.R.: Ediciones Huracán, 1986.

Picó, Isabel. "The History of Women's Struggle for Equality in Puerto Rico." In *The Puerto Rican: Perspectives on Culture, History, and Society*, edited by Edna Acosta Belén. 2d ed. New York: Praeger, 1986.

———. *La mujer y la política puertorriqueña*. Rio Piedras, P.R.: Centro de Investigaciones Sociales, Universidad de Puerto Rico, 1983.

Piddington, R. A. *The Limits of Mankind*. Bristol, U.K.: J. Wright, 1956.

Pincus, Gregory. *The Control of Fertility*. New York: Academic Press, 1965.

———. "Long Term Administration of Enovid to Human Subjects." In *Proceedings of a Symposium on 19-Nor Progestational Steroids*, 105–19. Chicago: Searle Research Laboratories, 1957.

———. "Paradoxical Hormone is Basis of Birth Control Pill." *Washington Post*, 2 August 1959, p. E8.

———. "Some Effects of Progesterone and Related Compounds upon Reproduction and Early Development in Mammals." *Acta Endocrinológica Supplementum* 28 (1956): 18–36.

Pincus Gregory, et al. "Fertility Control with Oral Medication." *American Journal of Obstetrics and Gynecology* 75, no. 6 (June 1958): 1333–46.

Pincus, Gregory, and Min-Chueh Chang. "The Effects of Progesterone and Related Compounds on Ovulation and Early Development in the Rabbit." *Acta Physiológica Latinoamericana* 3 (1953): 177–83.

Pivar, David. "The Military, Prostitution, and Colonial Peoples: India and the Philippines, 1885–1917." *Journal of Sexuality Research* 17, no. 3 (1981): 256–69.

———. *Purity Crusade: Sexual Morality and Social Control, 1868–1900*. Westport, Conn.; Greenwood Press, 1973.

Plesset, Isabel. *Noguchi and His Patrons*. Teaneck, N.J.: Fairleigh Dickinson University Press, 1980.

Poovey, Mary. *A History of the Modern Fact: Problems of Knowledge in the Sciences of Wealth and Society*. Chicago: University of Chicago Press, 1998.

———. *Uneven Developments: The Ideological Work of Gender in Mid-Victorian Britain*. Chicago: University of Chicago Press, 1988.

Population Council. "Puerto Rico: El programo del Emko." *Estudios de Planificación* 1, no. 1 (1966): 273–78.

Presser, Harriet. *Sterilization and Fertility Decline in Puerto Rico*. Berkeley: University of California, Institute of International Studies, 1973.

Proctor, Robert. *Racial Hygiene: Medicine under the Nazis*. Cambridge, Mass.: Harvard University Press, 1988.

Puerto Rican Forum. *The Puerto Rican Community Development Project*. 1964. Reprint, New York: Arno, 1975.

Quétel, Claude. *History of Syphilis*. London: Polity Press in association with Basil Blackwell, 1990.

Quilliam, Daniel D. "Racial Peculiarities as a Cause of the Prevalence of Syphilis in Negroes." *American Journal of Dermatology and Genito-Urinary Diseases* 10 (1906): 277–79.

Quintero Rivera, Angel. *La lucha obrera en Puerto Rico*. Río Piedras, P.R.: Ediciones Huracán, 1970.

———. *Patricios y plebeyos: Burgueses, hacendados, artesanos y obreros*. Río Piedras, P.R.: Ediciones Huracán, 1988.

Raeburn, Dan. "The Brand Called Schmoo: *Li'l Abner* from Left to Right." *The Baffler* 13 (October 1999): 13–26.

Rainwater, Lee. *And the Poor Get Children: Sex, Contraception, and Family Planning in the Working Class*. Chicago: Quadrangle, 1960.

Rainwater, Lee, Martin Rein, and Gosta Esping-Andersen. *Stagnation and Renewal in Social Policy*. Armonk, N.Y.: M. E. Sharpe, 1987.

Rainwater, Lee, and William Yancy. *The Moynihan Report and the Politics of Controversy*. Cambridge, Mass.: MIT Press, 1967.

Ramírez de Arellano, Annette, and Conrad Seipp. *Colonialism, Catholicism, and Contraception: A History of Birth Control in Puerto Rico*. Chapel Hill: University of North Carolina Press, 1983.

Reed, James. *The Birth Control Movement and American Society: From Private Vice to Public Virtue*. 1978. Reprint, with a new preface on the relationship between historical scholarship and feminist issues, Princeton, N.J.: Princeton University Press, 1983.

Regional Plan Association. "People, Jobs, and Land, 1955–1975." *RPA Bulletin* 87 (June 1957): 18–20.

Reilly, Philip. *The Surgical Solution: A History of Involuntary Sterilization in the United States*. Baltimore: Johns Hopkins University Press, 1991.

"Report of the Bureau of Social Medicine and Puericulture, 1925–26." *Porto Rico Health Review* 2, no. 7 (December 1927): 21–26.

"Report of the Bureau of Vital Statistics, 1925–1926." *Porto Rico Health Review* 2, no. 4 (October 1926): 15–23.

Rice-Wray, Edris, Miguel Shultz-Contreras, Irma Guerrero, and Alberto Aranda-Rosell. "Long-Term Administration of Norethindrone in Fertility Control." *Journal of the American Medical Association* 180, no. 5 (5 May 1962): 355–61.

Riesman, David, Nathan Glazer, and Reuel Denney. *The Lonely Crowd: A Study of the Changing American Character*. Abridged ed. New York: Doubleday, 1953.

Rigdon, Susan. *The Culture Facade: Art, Science, and Politics in the Work of Oscar Lewis*. Urbana: University of Illinois Press, 1988.

Rivera, Marcia. "Incorporation of Women into the Labor Force." In *La mujer en la sociedad puertorriqueña*, edited by Edna Acosta Belen. Río Piedras, P.R.: Ediciones Huracán, 1980.

Rivera de Alvarado, Carmen. "Quién es quién en el trabajo social en Puerto Rico." *Revista de Trabajo Social* 1, no. 1 (February 1939): 13.

Rivera de Alvarado, Carmen, and Christopher Tietze. "Birth Control in Puerto Rico." *Human Fertility* 12, no. 1 (March 1947): 15–17, 24–25.

Rock, John. *The Time Has Come: A Catholic Doctor's Proposal to End the Battle over Birth Control.* New York: Knopf, 1963.

Rock, John, Celso Ramon Garcia, and Gregory Pincus. "Synthetic Progestins in the Normal Human Menstrual Cycle." *Recent Progress in Hormone Research* 13 (1957): 323–46.

Rodríguez Juliá, Edgardo. *Las tribulaciones de Jonás.* Río Piedras, P.R.: Ediciones Huracán, 1981.

Rodríguez-Fratricelli, Carlos, and Amílcar Tirado. "Notes toward a History of Puerto Rican Community Organization in New York City." *Centro de Estudios Puertorriqueños Bulletin* 3, no. 4 (summer 1989): 35–47.

Rodríguez-Morazzani, Roberto. "Political Cultures of the Puerto Rican Left in the United States." In *The Puerto Rican Movement: Voices from the Diaspora,* edited by Andrés Torres and José Velázquez, 25–47. Philadelphia: Temple University Press, 1999.

Rodríguez-Trias, Helen. "Sterilization Abuse." *Women and Health* 3, no. 1 (1977): 10–15.

———. "The Women's Health Movement: Women Take Power." In *Reforming Medicine: Lessons of the Last Quarter Century,* edited by Victor Sidel and Ruth Sidel, 107–26. New York: Pantheon, 1984.

Rogler, Lloyd. *Puerto Rican Families in New York City: Intergenerational Processes.* Maplewood, N.J.: Waterfront Press, 1984.

Roosevelt, Theodore, Jr. "Do Our Colonies Pay?" *Asia* 37 (August 1937): 536–40.

Rosen, Ruth. *The Lost Sisterhood: Prostitution in America, 1900–1918.* Baltimore: Johns Hopkins University Press, 1982.

Safa, Helen. "Female Employment in the Puerto Rican Working Class." In *Women and Change in Latin America,* edited by June Nash and Helen Safa. New York: Bergin and Garvey, 1984.

Samoiloff, Louise C. *Human Rights in a United States Colony.* Cambridge, Mass.: Schenkman, 1982.

Sánchez, Luis Rafael. *Guagua aérea.* San Juan: Editorial Cultural, 1994.

Sánchez Korrol, Virginia. *From Colonia to Community: The History of Puerto Ricans in New York City, 1917–1948.* Westport, Conn.: Greenwood, 1983.

Sandoval Sánchez, Alberto. *José Can You See? Latinos On and Off Broadway.* Madison: University of Wisconsin, 1999.

———. "Puerto Rican Migration Up in the Air: Air Migration, Its Cultural Representations, and Me 'Cruzando el Charco.'" In *Puerto Rican Jam: Essays on Culture and Politics,* edited by Frances Negrón-Muntaner and Ramón Grosfoguel, 189–208. Minneapolis: University of Minnesota Press, 1997.

———. "Una lectura puertorriqueña de la América de West Side Story." *Cupey* 7, no. 1–2 (December 1990): 30–45.

Santiago-Valles, Kelvin. *"Subject People" and Colonial Discourses: Economic Transformation and Social Disorder in Puerto Rico, 1898–1947.* Albany: State University of New York Press, 1994.

Satterthwaite, Adaline Pendleton. "Experience with Oral and Intrauterine Contraception in Rural Puerto Rico." In *Public Health and Population Change: Current Research Issues,* ed. Mindel Sheps and Jeanne Ridley, 474–80. Pittsburgh: University of Pittsburgh Press, 1965.

Satterthwaite, Adaline Pendleton, and Clarence Gamble. "Conception Control with Norethynodrel." *Journal of the American Medical Women's Association* 17, no. 10 (October 1962): 797–802.

Seaman, Barbara. *The Doctor's Case against the Pill.* New York: Random House, 1969.

Senior, Clarence. "An Approach to Research in Overcoming Cultural Barriers to Family Limitation." In *Studies in Population: Proceedings of the Annual Meeting of the Population Association,* edited by George Mair. Princeton, N.J.: Population Association, 1949.

Shapiro, Thomas M. *Population Control Politics: Women, Sterilization, and Reproductive Choice.* Philadelphia: Temple University Press, 1985.

Sheehan, Neil. *A Bright Shining Lie: John Paul Vann and America in Vietnam.* New York: Random House, 1988.

Sheehan, Susan. *A Welfare Mother.* Boston: Houghton Mifflin, 1976.

Sherman, H. C. "A Glimpse of Social Economics in Porto Rico." *Porto Rico Journal of Public Health and Tropical Medicine* 6, no.2 (December 1930): 221–28.

Shorter, Edward. Review of *Woman's Body, Woman's Right,* by Linda Gordon. *Journal of Social History* 11, no. 2 (winter 1977): 269–73.

Silliman, Jael, and Ynestra King. *Dangerous Intersections: Feminist Perspectives on Population, Environment, and Development.* Cambridge, Mass.: South End Press, 1999.

Silvestrini, Blanca. "Women as Workers: The Experience of the Puerto Rican Woman in the 1930's." In *The Puerto Rican Woman: Perspectives on Culture, History and Society,* edited by Edna Acosta-Belén, 59–74. 2d ed. New York: Praeger, 1986.

Slechta, R. F., M. C. Chang, and G. Pincus. "Effects of Progesterone and Related Compounds on Mating and Pregnancy in the Rat." *Fertility and Sterility* 5 (1954): 282–93.

Smith, F. B. "The Contagious Diseases Acts Reconsidered." *Bulletin of the History of Medicine* 3, no. 3 (1990): 197–215.

Smith-Rosenberg, Caroll. *Disorderly Conduct.* 1985. Reprint, New York: Oxford University Press, 1986.

Solinger, Rickie. *Wake Up Little Susie: Single Pregnancy and Race before Roe v. Wade.* New York: Routledge, 1992.

Spengler, J. J. "The New England Puritans: An Obituary." *Journal of Heredity* 23, no. 2 (February 1932): 71–76.

Spivak, Gayatri Chakravorty. "Can the Subaltern Speak?" In *Marxism and the Interpretation of Cultures,* edited by Cary Nelson and Lawrence Grossberg, 271–316. Urbana: University of Illinois Press, 1988.

Stanton, William R. *The Leopard's Spots: Scientific Attitudes toward Race in America, 1815–59.* Chicago: University of Chicago Press, 1972.

Stepan, Nancy Leys. *The Hour of Eugenics: Race, Gender, and Nation in Latin America.* Ithaca, N.Y.: Cornell University Press, 1991.

Steward, Julian, et al., eds. *The People of Puerto Rico: A Study in Social Anthropology.* Urbana: University of Illinois Press, 1956.

Stokes, Roy. "Tubal Ligations." *Boletín de la Asociación Médica de Puerto Rico* 40, no. 3 (March 1948): 104–8.

Stoler, Ann. *Capitalism and Confrontation in Sumatra's Plantation Belt, 1870–1979.* New Haven, Conn.: Yale University Press, 1985.

Stoler, Ann Laura, and Frederick Cooper, eds. *Tensions of Empire: Colonial Cultures in a Bourgeois World.* Berkeley: University of California Press, 1997.

Sturgis, S. H., and F. Albright. "Estrin Therapy in Dysmenorrhea." *Endocrinology* 26, no. 6 (1940): 68–72.

Stycos, J. Mayone. "Experiments in Social Change: The Caribbean Fertility Studies." In *Research in Family Planning,* edited by Clyde Kiser, 305–16. Princeton, N.J.: Princeton University Press, 1962.

———. *Family and Fertility in Puerto Rico: A Study of the Lower Income Group.* New York: Columbia University Press, 1955.

———. "Female Sterilization in Puerto Rico." *Eugenics Quarterly* 1, no. 2 (June 1954): 3–9.

———. "Fertility Control in Underdeveloped Areas." In *The Population Crisis: Implications and Plans for Action,* edited by Larry K. Y. Ng and Stuart Mudd, 55–56. Bloomington: Indiana University Press, 1965.

———. "Some Minority Opinions on Birth Control." In *Population Policy and Ethics,* edited by Robert Veatch, 169–96. New York: Irvington, 1977.

Stycos J. Mayone, and Reuben Hill. "The Prospects for Birth Control in Puerto Rico." *Annals of the American Academy of Political and Social Science* 285 (January 1953): 137–44.

Summers, Carol. "Intimate Colonialism: The Imperial Production of Reproduction in Uganda, 1907–1925." *Signs* 16, no. 4 (1991): 787–807.

Thimmesch, Nick. "Puerto Rico and Birth Control." *Journal of Marriage and the Family* 30, no. 2 (May 1968): 252–65.

Thomas, Nicholas. "Sanitation and Seeing: The Creation of State Power in Early Colonial Fiji." *Comparative Studies in Societies and Histories* 32, no. 1 (1990): 149–70.

Thomas, William. *The Polish Peasant in Europe and America.* Chicago: University of Chicago Press, 1918.

Thompson, Loyd, and Lyle Kingery. "Syphilis in the Negro." *American Journal of Syphilis* 3, no. 3 (July 1919): 385–86.

Tietze, Christopher, Dattatrana N. Pai, Carl E. Taylor, and Clarence Gamble. "A Family Planning Service in Rural Puerto Rico." *American Journal of Obstetrics and Gynecology* 81, no. 1 (January 1961): 174–82.

Torres, Andrés. "Political Radicalism in the Diaspora—The Puerto Rican Experience." In *The Puerto Rican Movement: Voices From the Diaspora,* edited by Andrés Torres and José E. Velázquez, 1–24. New York: Temple University Press, 1998.

Torres, Andrés, and José E. Velázquez, eds. *The Puerto Rican Movement: Voices From the Diaspora.* New York: Temple University Press, 1998.

Torres, Carlos Antonio, Hugo Rodríguez Vecchini, and William Burgos. *The Commuter Nation: Perspectives on Puerto Rican Migration.* Río Piedras, P.R.: Editorial de la Universidad de Puerto Rico, 1994.

Trouillot, Michel Rolph. *Silencing the Past: Power and the Production of History.* Boston: Beacon Press, 1995.

Tugwell, Rexford. *The Stricken Land: The Story of Puerto Rico.* Garden City, N.Y.: Doubleday, 1947.

Tyrrell, Ian R. *Woman's World / Woman's Empire: The Woman's Christian Temperance Union in International Perspective, 1880–1930.* Chapel Hill: University of North Carolina Press, 1991.

Upshur, John. "The Future of the Negro from the Standpoint of the Doctor." *The Charlotte Medical Journal* 30, no. 1 (January 1907): 14–16.

Valle Atiles, F. del. "Limitación de la Prole." *Boletín de la Asociación Médica de Porto Rico* 12, no. 114 (March 1917): 1–7.

Valle Ferrer, Norma. "Feminism and Its Influence on Women's Organization in Puerto Rico." In *The Puerto Rican Woman: Perspectives on Culture, History and Society,* edited by Edna Acosta-Belén. 2d ed.. New York: Praeger, 1986.

van Heyningen, Elizabeth. "The Social Evil in the Cape Colony, 1868–1902: Prostitution and the Contagious Diseases Acts." *Journal of Southern African Studies* 10, no. 2 (April 1984): 170–97.

Vaughan, Megan. *Curing Their Ills: Colonial Power and African Illness.* Stanford, Calif.: Stanford University Press, 1991.

Vaughan, Paul. *The Pill on Trial.* New York: Coward-McCann, 1970.

Vázquez Calzada, José. "La esterilización feminina en Puerto Rico." *Revista de Ciencias Sociales* 17, no. 3 (September 1973): 281–308.

———. *La población de Puerto Rico y su trayectoria histórica.* San Juan: Escuela Graduada de Salúd Publica, Recinto de Ciencias Médicas, Universidad de Puerto Rico, 1988.

Verrill, Hyatt A. *Porto Rico: Past and Present and San Domingo of Today.* New York: Dodd, Mead, 1926.

"*La Vida:* Whose Life?" *IRCD Bulletin* (January 1968): 1, 6–8.

Vigo, Ligia. "Gendered and Racialized Discourses on Prostitution in Havana (1873–1926): A Nation-Building Project." Unpublished paper, University of Arizona, Department of History.

Vilar, Irene. *A Message from God in the Atomic Age.* Translated by Gregory Rabassa. New York: Pantheon, 1996.

Vogt, William. *People! Challenge to Survival.* London: William Clowes and Sons, 1960.

Walkowitz, Judith. *Prostitution and Victorian Society: Women, Class, and the State.* New York: Cambridge University Press, 1980.

Ware, Vron. *Beyond the Pale: White Women, Racism, and History.* New York: Verso, 1992.

Warren, James Frances. "Prostitution and the Politics of Venereal Disease: Singapore, 1870–98." *Journal of Southeast Asian Studies* 21, no. 2 (September 1990): 360–83.

Warwick, Donald, and Nancy Williamson. "Population Policy and Spanish-Surnamed Americans." In *Population Policy and Ethics,* edited by Robert Veatch. New York: Irvington, 1977.

Weisbord, Robert. *Genocide? Birth Control and the Black American.* Westport, Conn.: Greenwood Press, 1975.

Weiss, Ludwig. "The Prostitution Problem in Its Relation to Law and Medicine." *Journal of the American Medical Association* 47, no. 25 (22 December 1906): 2071–75.

Weisskoff, Richard. *Factories and Food Stamps: The Puerto Rico Model of Development.* Baltimore: Johns Hopkins University Press, 1985.

Welfare Council of New York City. Committee on Puerto Ricans in New York City. *Puerto Ricans in New York City.* 1948. Reprint, New York: Arno, 1975.

West, Guida. *The National Welfare Rights Movement: The Social Protest of Poor Women.* New York: Praeger, 1981.

Whalen, Carmen Teresa. *From Puerto Rico to Philadelphia: Puerto Rican Workers and Postwar Economies.* Philadelphia: Temple University Press, 2001.

White, Trumbull. *In the Shadow of Death: Martinique and the World's Great Disasters.* [Chicago?]: The Publishers Association, 1902.

Williams, Doone, and Greer Williams. *Every Child a Wanted Child: Clarence James Gamble, M.D., and His Work in the Birth Control Movement.* Edited by Emily Flint. Boston: Harvard University Press for the Francis A. Countway Library of Medicine, 1978.

Williams, Walter E. *America, A Minority Viewpoint.* Stanford, Calif.: Hoover Institution Press, Stanford University, 1982.

Williams, Walter E., Barbara Dafoe Whitehead, Lee Rainwater, Charles Murray, Glenn C. Loury, Joe Lieberman, Mickey Kaus, George Gilder, Eugene D. Genovese, and Martin Anderson. "Sex, Families, Race, Poverty, Welfare: A Symposium Revisiting the Moynihan Report at Its Thirtieth Anniversary (Blueprints for a New World of Welfare)." *The American Enterprise* 6, no. 1 (January–February 1995): 33–38.

Williams, William Appleman. *The Tragedy of American Diplomacy.* New York: Dell, 1960.

Wilson, William Julius. *When Work Disappears: The World of the New Urban Poor.* New York: Knopf, 1996.

Wing, Wilson, Matthew Tayback, and Clarence Gamble. "Birth Control in a Rural Area of Puerto Rico." *Eugenics Quarterly* 5, no. 3 (September 1958): 154–61.

Wolbarst, Abraham. "The Treatment of Syphilis with Ehrlich-Hata '606'–Salvarsan." *Interstate Medical Journal* 18 (January 1911): 48–52.

Wolf, Eric. "San José: Subcultures of a 'Traditional' Coffee Municipality." In *The People of Puerto Rico: A Study in Social Anthropology,* edited by Julian Steward et al. Chicago: University of Illinois Press, 1956.

Young, Hugh Hampton. *Hugh Young: A Surgeon's Autobiography.* New York: Harcourt, 1940.

Yung, Judy. "The Social Awakening of Chinese American Women as Reported in *Chung Sai Yat Po,* 1900–1911." In *Unequal Sisters: A Multicultural Reader in U.S. Women's History,* edited by Vicky Ruiz and Ellen DuBois. 2d ed. New York: Routledge, 1994.

Zalduondo, Celestina. "Planificación de la familia en Puerto Rico." Paper presented at the Segundo Seminario de Planificación de la Familia para Líderes Latinoamericanos, New York, October 1963 (in the files of Idalia Colón Rodón, former director of the Asociación Puertorriqueña Pro Bienestar de la Familia).

Index

Compositor:	Binghamton Valley Composition
Text:	10/13 Sabon
Display:	Sabon
Printer and Binder:	Malloy Lithographing, Inc.